SOPHIA PARNOK

The Cutting Edge:
Lesbian Life and Literature

The Cutting Edge:
Lesbian Life and Literature

Series Editor: Karla Jay

Ladies Almanack
BY DJUNA BARNES
WITH AN INTRODUCTION BY SUSAN SNIADER LANSER

Adventures of the Mind:
The Memoirs of Natalie Clifford Barney
TRANSLATED BY JOHN SPALDING GATTON
WITH AN INTRODUCTION BY KARLA JAY

Paint It Today
BY H.D. (HILDA DOOLITTLE)
EDITED AND WITH AN INTRODUCTION BY
CASSANDRA LAITY

(Sem)Erotics: Theorizing Lesbian : Writing
BY ELIZABETH A. MEESE

The Search for a Woman-Centered Spirituality
BY ANNETTE J. VAN DYKE

I Know My Own Heart: The Diaries of Anne Lister, 1791–1840
EDITED BY HELENA WHITBREAD

No Priest But Love: The Diaries of Anne Lister, 1824–1826
EDITED BY HELENA WHITBREAD

Lover
BY BERTHA HARRIS

Changing Our Minds: Lesbian Feminism
and Psychology
BY CELIA KITZINGER AND RACHEL PERKINS

Elizabeth Bowen: A Reputation in Writing
BY RENÉE C. HOOGLAND

Sophia Parnok: The Life and Work of Russia's Sappho
BY DIANA LEWIS BURGIN

The Cutting Edge:
Lesbian Life and Literature

Series Editor: Karla Jay
PROFESSOR OF ENGLISH AND WOMEN'S STUDIES
PACE UNIVERSITY

EDITORIAL BOARD

Judith Butler
Humanities Center
The Johns Hopkins University

Blanche Wiesen Cook
History and Women's Studies
John Jay College and
City University of New York
Graduate Center

Diane Griffin Crowder
French and Women's Studies
Cornell College

Joanne Glasgow
English and Women's Studies
Bergen Community College

Marny Hall
Psychotherapist and Writer

Celia Kitzinger
Social Sciences
Loughborough University, U.K.

Jane Marcus
English and Women's Studies
City University of New York
Graduate Center

Biddy Martin
German and Women's Studies
Cornell University

Elizabeth Meese
English
University of Alabama

Esther Newton
Anthropology
State University of New York
Purchase

Terri de la Peña
Novelist/Short Story Writer

Ruthann Robson
Writer
Law School at Queens College
City University of New York

Ann Allen Shockley
Librarian
Fisk University

Elizabeth Wood
Lesbian and Gay Studies
Sarah Lawrence College

Bonnie Zimmerman
Women's Studies
San Diego State University

SOPHIA PARNOK

The Life and Work of Russia's Sappho

DIANA LEWIS BURGIN

New York University Press

New York and London

NEW YORK UNIVERSITY PRESS
New York and London

Copyright © 1994 by New York University
All rights reserved

Library of Congress Cataloging-in-Publication Data
Burgin, Diana Lewis.
Sophia Parnok : the life and work of Russia's Sappho / Diana Lewis Burgin.
p.   cm. — (Cutting edge : lesbian life and literature)
Includes bibliographical references and index.
ISBN 0-8147-1190-1 (cloth : alk. paper). — ISBN 0-8147-1221-5 (pbk.)
1. Parnok, Sofia—Criticism and interpretation. 2. Lesbians' writings, Russian—History and criticism. 3. Lesbianism in literature—History—20th century. 4. Women in literature—History—20th century. 5. Lesbians—Russia—Intellectual life.
I. Title. II. Series: Cutting edge (New York, N.Y.)
PG3476.P25915Z59   1994
891.71′42—dc20   94-1266
                        CIP

New York University Press books are printed on acid-free paper, and their binding materials are chosen for strength and durability.

Manufactured in the United States of America

10   9   8   7   6   5   4   3   2   1

To the memory of Sophia Parnok

Contents

Foreword — xiii

Acknowledgments — xix

Author's Note — xxiii

Introduction — 1

1. "That Marvelous Female Tenderness..." — 15
2. "Love Summons Me, and I Won't Contradict Her..." — 44
3. "Oh, Steal Me Away from My Death..." — 89
4. "There's No Way Back, for You, Me, or Us..." — 139
5. "While My Other Self Roams in the Wilds..." — 192
6. "Into the Darkness... the Secret Drawer!" — 241
7. "Hello, My Love! My Grey-Haired Eve!" — 270

Epilogue — 307

Appendix — 311

Notes — 313

Bibliography 341

Index Of First Lines of Poems by Parnok 345

Index 351

All illustrations appear as a group following page 134.

Foreword

Despite the efforts of lesbian and feminist publishing houses and a few university presses, the bulk of the most important lesbian works has traditionally been available only from rare book dealers, in a few university libraries, or in gay and lesbian archives. This series intends, in the first place, to make representative examples of this neglected and insufficiently known literature available to a broader audience by reissuing selected classics and by putting into print for the first time lesbian novels, diaries, letters, and memoirs that are of special interest and significance, but which have moldered in libraries and private collections for decades or even for centuries, known only to the few scholars who had the courage and financial wherewithal to track them down.

Their names have been known for a long time—Sappho, the Amazons of North Africa, the Beguines, Aphra Behn, Queen Christina, Emily Dickinson, the Ladies of Llangollen, Radclyffe Hall, Natalie Clifford Barney, H. D., and so many others from every nation, race, and era. But government and religious officials burned their writings, historians and literary scholars denied they were lesbians, powerful men kept their books out of print, and influential archivists locked up their ideas far from sympathetic eyes. Yet some dedicated scholars and readers still knew who they were, made pilgrimages to the cities and villages where they had lived and to the graveyards where they rested. They passed around tattered volumes of letters, diaries, and biographies, in which they had underlined what seemed to be telltale hints of a secret or different kind of life. Where no hard facts existed, legends were invented. The few precious and often available pre-Stonewall lesbian classics, such as *The Well of Loneliness* by Radclyffe Hall, *The Price of Salt* by Claire Morgan [Patricia Highsmith], and *Desert of the Heart* by Jan Rule, were cherished. Lesbian pulp was devoured. One of the primary goals of this series is to give the more neglected works, which constitute the vast majority of lesbian writing, the attention they deserve.

A second but no less important aim of this series is to present the "cutting edge" of contemporary lesbian scholarship and theory across a wide range of disciplines. Practitioners of lesbian studies have not adopted a uniform approach to literary theory, history, sociology, or any other discipline, nor should they. This series intends to present an array of voices that truly reflect the diversity of the lesbian community. To help me in this task, I am lucky enough to be assisted by a distinguished editorial board that reflects various professional, class, racial, ethnic, and religious backgrounds as well as a spectrum of interests and sexual preferences.

At present the field of lesbian studies occupies a small, precarious, and somewhat contested pied-à-terre between gay studies and women's studies. The former is still in its infancy, especially if one compares it to other disciplines that have been part of the core curriculum of every child and adolescent for several decades or even centuries. However, although it is one of the newest disciplines, gay studies may also be the fastest growing one—at least in North America. Lesbian, gay, and bisexual studies conferences are doubling and tripling their attendance. Although only a handful of degree-granting programs currently exist, that number is also apt to multiply quickly during the next decade.

In comparison, women's studies is a well-established and burgeoning discipline with hundreds of minors, majors, and graduate programs throughout the United States. Lesbian studies occupies a peripheral place in the discourse in such programs, characteristically restricted to one lesbian-centered course, usually literary or historical in nature. In the many women's studies series that are now offered by university presses, generally only one or two books on a lesbian subject or issue are included, and lesbian voices are restricted to writing on those topics considered of special interest to gay people. We are not called upon to offer opinions on motherhood, war, education, or on the lives of women not publicly identified as lesbians. As a result, lesbian experience is too often marginalized and restricted.

In contrast, this series will prioritize, centralize, and celebrate lesbian visions of literature, art, philosophy, love, religion, ethics, history, and a myriad of other topics. In "The Cutting Edge," readers can find authoritative versions of important lesbian texts that have been carefully prepared and introduced by scholars. Readers can also find the work of academics and independent scholars who write about other aspects of life from a distinctly lesbian viewpoint. These visions are not only various but intentionally contradictory, for lesbians speak from differing class, racial, ethnic, and religious perspectives. Each author also speaks from and about a certain moment of time, and few would argue that being a lesbian today is the same as it was for Sappho or Anne Lister. Thus no attempt has been made to homogenize that diversity, and no agenda exists to attempt to carve out a "politically correct" lesbian studies perspective at this juncture in history or to pinpoint the "real" lesbians in history. It seems more important for all the voices to be heard before those with the blessings of aftersight lay the mantle of authenticity on any one vision of the world, or on any particular set of women.

What each work in this series does share, however, is a common realization that gay women are the "Other" and that one's perception of culture and literature is filtered by sexual behaviors and preferences. Those perceptions are not the same as those of gay men or of nongay women, whether the writers speak of gay or feminist issues or whether the writers choose to look at nongay figures from a lesbian perspective. The role of this series is to create space and give a voice to those interested in lesbian studies. This series speaks to any person who is interested in gender studies, literary criticism, biography, or important literary works, whether she or he is a student, professor, or serious reader, for the series is neither for lesbians only nor even by lesbians only. Instead, "The Cutting Edge" attempts to share some of the best of lesbian literature and lesbian studies with anyone willing to look at the world through lesbians' eyes. The series is proactive in that it will help to formulate and foreground the very discipline on which it focuses. Finally, this series has answered the call to make lesbian theory, lesbian experience, lesbian lives, lesbian literature, and lesbian visions the heart and nucleus, the weighty planet around which for once other viewpoints will swirl as moons to our earth. We invite readers of all persuasions to join us by venturing into this and other books in the series.

Sophia Parnok is one of many "lost lesbians." Despite her ardent Sapphic poetry, which was admired by her contemporaries in the Soviet Union, and her equally passionate love life, she has been unknown to those of us who could not read her poems in Russian, and even those who would have a difficult time finding her work in most anthologies. However, a quarter of a century after Stonewall, we are fortunate enough to be able to expand our horizons beyond our foremothers in North America and western Europe, beyond Radclyffe Hall, Gertrude Stein, Virginia Woolf, Djuna Barnes, H. D., and Audre Lorde. Those of us whose native language is English or who read primarily in English have been greatly limited to translations of those the academies or the mainstream publishing establishments deem worthy of our consideration. And the farther we roam from the core of "Western Civilization," the fewer our links with our lesbian sisters become. It is as if we have been given the Pleiades instead of the Milky Way. Diana Burgin's diligent research has uncovered the life and work of Sophia Parnok, a brilliant Russian poet, whose voice will finally reverberate beyond her native land.

KARLA JAY
Pace University

Acknowledgments

Several people have given me help and support in realizing this book, the result of six years' research and writing. First of all, I am deeply and forever grateful to Karla Jay for encouraging me to send my prospectus to New York University Press and to Niko Pfund for taking a chance on Parnok and agreeing to publish my book. I also appreciated both Karla's and Niko's suggestions for revising the manuscript.

The University of Massachusetts at Boston, where I am on the faculty, supported my research in its initial stages with a faculty development grant for travel to the Soviet Union in August 1987. I would also like to thank Louis Esposito, Acting Dean of the College of Arts and Sciences, for granting me a course load reduction during the spring semester 1993, which enabled me to complete the writing and revisions of the book.

Part of the research for this book was done when I was an IREX/ACLS exchange scholar in Leningrad under the auspices of the Soviet Academy of Sciences (1988–89). I am especially grateful for the assistance given me by the archivists in the Leningrad Institute of Theater, Music, and Cinematography. While in Leningrad on numerous research trips over the years, I have enjoyed a home away from home in the boundless hospitality, stimulating conversation, and moral support of Sophia Polyakova, Elizaveta Appelbaum, and Nadezhda Rykova.

More recently, in Moscow, the Tsvetaeva specialist Lena Korkina generously shared information and materials from her archives with me and took me on a walking tour of several of the neighborhoods where Parnok lived. My work in Moscow was also helped by Tatyana Zhukovskaya, who allowed me to read and copy several letters in the archives of Eugenia Gertsyk. My two visits to Moscow would not have been nearly so pleasant and productive as they were without the hospitality and motherly ministrations of my recently discovered "aunt," Natasha Gribova.

Major changes have taken place in my life and scholarly interests as a result of my work on Parnok. Bringing this book into the world has not always been easy, and I would like to thank my mother, Ruth Posselt Burgin, for her love and support, and especially for believing in my courage.

Pamela Gore has my special and everlasting gratitude not only for her patient and careful word processing of my manuscript in all its seemingly endless and often impossible-to-read redactions, but for her steadfast moral support and loving interest in my book and in Parnok.

Katherine O'Connor has been with me through all the intensity and joy of the "Parnok years," a distinct period in our long friendship. I shall always be grateful for her love, good advice, and insights into Parnok's poems that have enriched this book, and especially for her unique habit of *listening,* no matter how crazed my rantings.

This book would hardly have been possible without the inspiring scholarship, personal encouragement and generosity of Sophia Polyakova, whom I did not know when I "discovered" Parnok, but whom I was fortunate soon to have as a colleague and a dear dear friend for several years. Sophia Viktorovna died after a long illness, on April 30, 1994, just as this book was going to press.

Finally, I owe special thanks to Utyeshka, who listened doggedly and devotedly to every page of this book in at least four different versions. She seems to like Parnok's poems; they dispose her to tranquility and inspire dreams.

Author's Note

There are various matters relating to the different forms of Parnok's last name as I use them in this book, the transliteration systems I employ, my translations of Parnok's poems, and the book's title, which require some clarification and/or explanation.

Upon the publication of her first poem in late 1906, Parnok changed her birth name, *Parnokh*. She replaced the final letter, *kh* (designated in the cyrillic alphabet by the letter *x*), with the letter *k*. I discuss the possible significances of the poet's name change in chapter 2. It represented a change of identity, a way of separating her published self from her prepublished self. In an effort to make readers aware of this important change in my subject's destiny, I refer to her generally by her birth name, Parnokh, in the life contexts of her prepseudonym period, i.e., in chapter 1 and the beginning of chapter 2. Even in these early chapters I occasionally call her Parnok, however, whenever the context concerns the poet in general, rather than the young, prepublished poet in particular. Perhaps it would also be helpful to readers to know that the name *Parnokh* is stressed on the first syllable. Russians would (and do) naturally stress the first syllable of the name Parnok, too; the poet, however, accented the last syllable of her chosen name, pronouncing it Par*nok*. Her idiosyncratic accentuation of her "own name" (as she considered it to be) gives it a French sound to a Russian ear. Finally, to add to this confusion of names, Parnok's brother changed his birth name also. He is referred to throughout the book by his pen name, *Par*nakh (stressed on the first syllable).

For the transliteration of Russian names (and occasional words) in this book, I use essentially the system approved by the U.S. Board on Geographic Names, which comes closest to popular usage. I have made several exceptions to this system, however, and would like to explain them here. In order not to burden Anglophone readers with the presence of apparently meaningless apostrophes ('), I have not transliterated the so-called soft sign that indicates palatalization of the consonant that comes before it. With regard to the spelling of iotized vowels and the *i kratkoe* in some place names and surnames, I have used the Library of Congress system wherever that transliteration is now the more common one in English language publications, card catalogs, dictionaries and the like. (I also use the Library of Congress system in the bibliography.) Thus, I use Dniepr (rather than Dnepr) for the river and place names derived from it; Bolshoi (rather than Bolshoy) for the Moscow theater. I have transliterated Russian surnames ending in the suffix "skiy"/"skii" with the commonly accepted and far less alienating "sky," e.g. Dostoevsky, Vazlinsky, Nikitinsky, etc. For similar reasons I transliterated the non-Russian surnames of Parnok's husband and two composer-colleagues as Volkenshtein, Shteinberg, and Veisberg (rather than Volkenshteyn, Shteynberg, and Veysberg). Since Parnok uses the surname of her last lover, Vedeneyeva in a poem, I have inserted a "y" between the last two "e's" in order to make the sound and syllabic structure of the name clearer from the way it is spelled. Finally, the cities of Moscow and St. Petersburg are given in their anglicized form as are some Russian first names, e.g., Sophia, Alexander, Eugenia, Eudoxia, and Nicholas II.

One of my cherished aims in writing this book is to acquaint Anglophone readers with Parnok's poems. The ninety-odd lyrics that appear here in their entirety represent the first English verse translations of roughly a quarter of Parnok's extant poetic "produce," as she called her lyrics in a late poem. My translations attempt to be as literal renderings of the originals as possible while still being English poems, rather than poetic prose. In almost all cases I have retained the metrical patterns of the original poems. Each translation also strives to convey something of the original poem's rhythm although the irreconcilable differences between the music of Russian and English have too often, I fear, made the goal impossible to achieve. To my great regret, I have been unable to provide much of a sense of Parnok's often brilliant use of sound and her frequently innovative and original rhymes. I sacrificed her rhymes mainly in the interests of accuracy, but also in an effort to avoid the singsong, doggerel effect that rhyming tends to have in modern English poetry where rhyme has long since gone out of fashion. Avoiding rhyme altogether seemed too great a sacrifice, however, especially in view of the prosaic, colloquial diction of Parnok's best poems. I have therefore made use of assonances, imperfect rhymes (characteristic of many of Parnok's late poems), and even some old-fashioned perfect ones, so long as they were unforced and did not interfere with accuracy and normal poetic syntax.

Readers who have read or will read the original of the poems I have translated in the 1979 Ardis edition of Parnok's *Collected Poems*, the only edition of her lyrics so far available, may notice words, phrases, and even whole lines in some of my translations that appear to belie my claims for their accuracy. Unfortunately, many of the texts in the Ardis edition contain errors. I have corrected any errors in the printed texts of the Russian poems I have translated. A list of these corrections is provided in the appendix.

Parnok's poems provide the best testimony to the evolution of her creativity, which constitutes the central focus of this literary life. The poet's long search for her native (lesbian) inspiration, for her muse, and her complex, often ambivalent relationship with her creative self suggest to me that for much of her life she was as if "musebound" (a word of my own coinage that I had originally suggested for the title of this book). The poet in Parnok was musebound in the same way as the orphaned stepdaughter in her could be said to be homeward bound. At the same time, in her relationship with her muse Parnok both desired, and chafed at, the bonds of love. Those bonds were similar to the "religious fetters of love" that she "did not endeavor to break" in her most intense and creatively significant love relationships. Parnok's unique "muse-bounded-ness," the simultaneous striving toward and fusion of life, love, and lyric in her creative journey, constitutes one important reason why she deserves the epithet, Russia's Sappho. In the pages to come, readers may, I hope, discover others.

Introduction

The biography of a poet is found in what happens to those who read [her].—Boris Pasternak

The first thought of many prospective readers of this biography will probably be: "Who is Sophia Parnok?" The simplest answer explains why the question arises and why this book exists.

Sophia Parnok is a Russian poet and the only openly lesbian voice in Russian poetry.

From the standpoint of her traditional Russian poetic family, Parnok was an outsider and a "fair stranger."[1] From her own perspective, however, she was an insider, the possessor of esoteric, elemental knowledge. She believed that communicating that knowledge through her lyrics, "from one soul straight into another soul," had the power to bind and unbind spells.

In her poems, Parnok often located her poetic speaker in the space by a window from which she looked out on a world that, natural or urban, unpeopled or crowded, happy or sad, good or evil, was always apart from her, and yet, a part of her.

During her lifetime Parnok published five volumes of poetry and a substantial body of literary criticism, and she authored the libretti of several operas, one of which had a major success in its first production at the Bolshoi Theater in Moscow in 1930.

Nevertheless, at the time of her death three years later, few Russian readers had heard of her.

We owe the rediscovery of Sophia Parnok to the labor, love, and courage of Sophia Polyakova, a Russian philologist and former professor of classics at Leningrad State University. Polyakova's edition of Parnok's *Collected Poems,* supplied with a monograph-length biographical and critical introduction, as well as extensive notes (all in Russian), appeared in the West from Ardis Publishers in 1979.

Thirteen years have passed since its appearance; yet the "invisible poet" status, which Parnok herself realized had devolved upon her by 1927, continues in effect. Many Russian poetry lovers, and even some Slavic specialists, are still only vaguely familiar with who Parnok is, or have not read her work. Despite her unique contribution to modern Russian lyricism, no specialists besides Polyakova (in Russian) and myself (in English) have studied Parnok's poetry in a systematic way.

Large portions of Parnok's life also remain sunk in obscurity. The reasons for her persistent invisibility as a poet and a person are varied and instructive.

First, there is the natural opacity of any human life, especially a female life, more especially, a lesbian life, and perhaps most especially, a Russian lesbian life.

Second, there is the way Parnok lived. Though brought up in relative affluence in a Victorian professional home, as an adult she rebelled against settled, "bourgeois" existence, which constrained her creativity and oppressed her spirit, as it has many Russian poets. An intense wanderlust periodically overcame her, and for most of her short life, she lived like a déclassé, Dostoevskian intellectual. From 1909 until 1932 she changed her address in Moscow alone seventeen times.

In her wandering, Parnok traveled light. She saved little in the way of letters and personal memorabilia. The life she wished to have remembered was the life she wrote into her largely autobiographical poems. But she was not particularly careful about her manuscripts either. All of her prose works, including a novella she worked on for more than a year, have been lost, and it is very likely that a number of her poems met the same fate.

Third, there is the scarcity of memoiristic sources for Parnok's biography, a gap that is explained, in view of her large number of devoted, creative friends, by her gender and status in her hierarchical and sexist poetic culture. Russia loves her poets, but she loves her poet sons more than her poet daughters. In the minds and hearts of most Russians, including memoirists of either sex, male genius outranks female genius in interest and importance; male excellence, strength, and even mediocrity consistently are preferred to female excellence and strength.

As in other poetic landscapes, so in the Russian: genius, innate or in close proximity, helps one's posthumous fame. It is therefore not surprising, but rather ironic, considering the homophobia rampant in Russian culture, that the best-known period of Parnok's life is the eighteen months of her love affair with Marina Tsvetaeva, who is justifiably considered one of the four greatest twentieth-century Russian poets. To the degree that Parnok is remembered in Russian poetry and criticism, she exists as Tsvetaeva's lover who also happened to be a poet.[2]

Now that publishing restrictions in Russia have disappeared, some selections of Parnok's poems have recently appeared in literary journals.[3] The brief introductions to her work that commonly accompany these publications focus on Parnok's literary relations with famous male poets. The poet's lesbian preference, not to mention its centrality to her creativity, is never mentioned (at most, there may be an allusion to her "complicated friendship" with Tsvetaeva), and the poems of hers that are chosen for republication are invariably "lesbian-free," at least when read out of the context of the life story that her opus tells in its entirety.

Thus, the fourth and, in my opinion, most profound reason for the semiobscurity that enveloped Parnok's life and continues to hamper the recognition and acceptance of her poetry is the universal disease of homophobia, more specifically, fear of lesbians. One example from the time of Parnok's girlhood should suffice.

On December 6, 1895, the great writer Anton Chekhov, whose stories have gained him a reputation the world over for humane attitudes, wrote to his friend, the publisher Suvorin: "The weather in Moscow is good, there's no cholera, there's also no lesbian love ... Brrr!! Remembering those persons of whom you write me makes me nauseous as if I'd eaten a rotten sardine. Moscow doesn't have them—and that's marvelous."[4]

How much acceptance is a poet going to have among readers who feel "nauseated" by the emotional and, I would argue, spiritual contents and perspective of her poems? More important, how is a lesbian poet in that culture going to find the courage and the words to express herself, knowing her readers' fastidious horror at the word "lesbian" and love called "lesbian love"?

It is not the gaps in Parnok's biography or the slimness of her extant oeuvre that should surprise us, but the fact that so much of her biography and so many of her poems exist at all. Parnok's opus in its extant entirety expresses the evolution of her thought about and her relationship with life. She wrote her real (inner) life in her lyrics and believed that their primary function was the communication of that life's spiritual existence. In this respect Parnok's creativity seemed to anticipate the autobiographical, truth-telling poems of American twentieth-century women poets like Adrienne Rich, Maxine Kumin, Anne Sexton, and others of that generation.[5]

In writing poetry about her real life, Parnok engaged in a struggle of becoming her self. It resembled the creative struggles of other women writers of her generation in western cultures, but it was also unique. Like all poets, she had to find her own voice, her own words, and like all women writers, she had to grapple with the reality that the culturally accepted and revered word more repressed than expressed her way of thinking and living. Parnok's awe of words was so great that for a time it actually impeded her realization of her verbal gift. She was painfully aware that as a female poet she had only one Russian foremother, the nineteenth-century poet Karolina Pavlova, whom she acknowledged in one of her poems as a "glorious great-grandmother."

When Parnok began to publish, during the Silver Age of Russian letters (1893–1917), women poets were emerging in large numbers. The alleged "femaleness" or "femininity" of their work was quickly noted by their male peers and critics and just as quickly turned against them. In 1909 the decadent poet, playwright, and classical scholar Innokenty Annensky hailed the advent of Russian female poets as one of the historic achievements of modernism and the triumph of musicality in poetry over intellectuality and irony. A mere seven years later, the poet and critic Vladislav Khodasevich paid Parnok a great compliment (in a review of her first volume of poems) by distinguishing her manly voice from what he denounced as the hysterical effusions of "ladies' poets."

The poetic culture of the Silver Age thus encouraged the so-called feminine principle in poetry (as defined, of course, by men) while denigrating most female poets. It is easy to understand why serious and gifted Russian women poets of the time universally rejected the idea of being "poetesses" and wanted to be thought of as poets first and female poets last, if at all. In her own desire to be an ungendered poet first and foremost, Parnok was no exception.

Nevertheless, she never hid or denied her femaleness in her lyrics. Her "way of thinking" and her poetry were profoundly woman-centered and expressed the poet's lesbian point of view. In saying this, I am not trying to attribute contemporary, western, politically correct (or incorrect) attitudes to a poet who lived in a time and culture different from ours and thought about her gender, sexuality, and creativity in her own way, and more important, in a way that can at best merely be surmised. Like any reader of Parnok, all I can hope to understand and convey is her presentation of herself in her poems and other writings.

Parnok was not a political activist, and she was not a feminist in the sense that word had for her generation of Russian intellectuals. From a young age, however, she exhibited spontaneous feelings of alienation from what she called "patriarchal virtues." She also easily discerned and deplored all forms of male posturing, condescension, and smug authoritativeness. Everything indicates that she accepted her lesbianism as a natural disposition and that her relationships with women, both sexual and nonsexual, were the creative and ultimately spiritual center of her existence.

Parnok had to struggle to express her soul's existence lyrically, in part because neither the language that she loved nor the poetic culture in which she wrote, for all their richness, expressiveness, and ardent aspiration to call things by their proper names, has a proper (nonpornographic, nonmedical) name for what she was and what she wanted to write about.

She did eventually find her words, but just as she found them, she was forced into poetic isolation by her "cruel century" and its "warriors," and thus became totally inaudible in the "inn" of Russian poetry (to borrow the metaphor of one of her late lyrics) where she so wanted her voice to be heard.

I had a sense of the sort of inaudibility that Parnok must have suffered when doing the research for this book in Russia over the past five years. Although my Russian colleagues have been generous and supportive of my work, they consider the poet's lesbianism neither "interesting" nor "relevant" to an investigation of her poetry. This attitude also explains why Polyakova's informants in the seventies—among them some of the poet's closest friends and even lovers—maintained a studious silence on the poet's sexuality, and in some cases, tried to distance themselves from the subject in order, evidently, to avoid guilt by association.

Lesbianism is still taboo in Russian scholarly and critical discourse. The taboo is rationalized as respect for a poet's privacy and status as a serious poet, even while it reinforces her inaudibility and invisibility. Painful as it is, I must confront the possibility that

Parnok herself might have shared her compatriots' discomfiture over what they would/will sometimes consider the "too personal," western, and "sexological" nature of my approach to her work.

On the other hand, I remind myself that Parnok was not closeted. Moreover, she consciously nurtured her "mutinous" creative spirit. In one early poem she wrote that she "wanted to shout, but did not dare to," and in a later one, she acknowledged the enormous cost of having acquired the boldness to shout. By middle age she knew who and what the "Chimera" was that had "stifled [her] deep voice," and, at the end of her life, she realized that her voice was purposefully ignored by her peers because it "dared to speak out loud" what they hid even from themselves.

If Parnok was proud of one thing in her "unmiraculous" poet's life, she was proud of her idiosyncrasy. This meant, as she wrote in one lyric, that she and her Muse rejected the path of "venerable male masters" and went their own way. Theirs may have been, she conceded, a "narrow" path, and it was certainly not a straight one, but it had one inalienable, supreme virtue: it was their own.

Parnok obviously and vocally took pride in her difference. She wrote from a different perspective in a new and different, authentically colloquial, poetic language, and she created, knowingly, a space of difference and for difference in Russian poetry, the space occupied by her and her soul. The issue between Parnok's and my understanding of her verse's politics is purely semantic: my definition of what lesbian means is much broader than hers was, and not at all pejorative. What I call her lesbian difference is the unique personal, emotional, spiritual existence she affirmed in her poems without naming it.

Courage marked her creative deed. The Silver Age allegedly freed Russian literature and culture from Victorian prudery and the nineteenth century radical intelligentsia's subordination of art to social issues. Decadence and symbolism opened Russian literature to themes that had previously been considered inappropriate to serious poetry. Sexuality and female eroticism in particular aroused serious philosophical, aesthetic, and spiritual interest and debate in Russia at this time. Artistic and intellectual society in Moscow and St. Petersburg even expressed a certain tolerance of the "idiosyncratic tastes" and "predilections" of its largely closeted homosexual members, especially if they lived discreetly.

Nevertheless, the Silver Age was no haven for lesbians either in life or in art. Chekhov's antilesbian attitudes were probably not that rare, even among well-educated, liberal-minded people who may have numbered lesbians among their close friends. For enlightened Russians of the *fin de siècle* "lesbian love" signified primarily a medical or psychological abnormality and sexual inversion, an object of largely male scientific desire and probing. For old-fashioned upholders of "patriarchal virtues," it was a sign of moral degradation associated overwhelmingly with peasant and lower-class women. Medical studies on lesbianism linked it with prostitution, female criminality, and hermaphroditism.[6]

Next to prostitutes, the Russian women most readily identified with lesbianism were, of course, actresses. The "persons" of whom Suvorin had written to Chekhov, eliciting the latter's repulsion, were in fact St. Petersburg actresses. And Chekhov, as Parnok's life amply demonstrates, was quite deluded in thinking that Moscow did not have them. Yet his belief in a lesbian-free Moscow is significant. Nowhere is the Russians' oft-noted pride in their innocence and simple-heartedness more evident than in their insistence that "diseases" like lesbianism are foreign in origin and cannot thrive in real Russian places such as the mother city, Moscow. Petersburg, on the other hand, has always been perceived as an imported, foreign environment, a western-style sin city, hence, its vulnerability to plagues of cholera and lesbian love.

Parnok found plenty of lesbian activity in Moscow's so-called low life and in its so-called intellectual high life where it thrived under an assumed name, or no name. One of the most pleasant aspects of researching her life has been discovering just how unforeign lesbians have been and are in Russia and Russian culture—

not that such a discovery was at all unpredictable. But confirmation of one's inner knowledge is always sweet.

Parnok, then, must have lived with the inner knowledge that she was not alone. Far from resenting those of her intimates and friends who would or could not acknowledge their difference openly as she did, she probably took pride in knowing what was not common knowledge, or knowing for certain what was generally only suspected.

Where she did suffer a desperate sense of aloneness was in her poetic life. Even in the liberalized atmosphere of the Silver Age, it was unthinkable to publish lesbian poetry without some mask for its variant contents, such as a male lyrical speaker or a conventionalized, decadent style that rendered the lesbian body and its desires aesthetically acceptable, if bookish. Both tactics significantly reinforced prevailing *fin de siècle* medical, social, and literary stereotypes of lesbians as damned souls and/or women who defined themselves by the "abnormal" desire to be men. Whether a lesbian poet of the time herself believed one or the other of these verities merely serves to demonstrate the inescapability of internalized homophobia.

Parnok's perhaps unconscious process of liberating herself from internalized homophobia constitutes one of the most interesting and important aspects of her creative development as charted in this book. Early on she realized that if she wrote about her lesbian experience in the decadent style that was favored by her times but alien to her "life-creating" poems, she would betray herself. But if she wrote about female same-sex love authentically, in her own prosaic, colloquial style, she feared destroying what she herself initially accepted as the standards of good taste in art. As a young poet she consequently often felt paralyzed by her inability to find her words, especially in her love lyrics.

Gradually, she became aware of the huge gap between the poetic tradition available to her as a reader and that available to her as a lesbian writer. She found herself in a literary soil, native and foreign, that burgeoned with paternal blooms but lacked maternal nutrients. How would her gift ever flourish when the only food it received perforce came from her self, whose living body seemed so tasteless at times to her highly refined taste?

Throughout Parnok's creative life her muse visited her intensively but sporadically, so that monsoons alternated with dry spells. Most of her creative surges can be linked with important women in her life, usually lovers, but also platonic intimate friends. To a certain degree being in love helped Parnok to write, but since an excess of passion often interfered with her ability to refine her "night verses" in "the cold light of day," it would be more precise to say that *loving* helped her to write. The wellsprings of her creativity lay in her yearning, her anguish, and its expression both of passionate and nonsexual love of particular women, including her own soul.

As Parnok herself realized, like good wine she improved with age. One of her last and greatest poetic achievements was the cycle of love lyrics, "Ursa Major," that she dedicated to her last lover, and called in one of the poems a "seven-star" of verses. The seven bright stars that comprise the constellation Ursa Major are sometimes known as the Seven Sisters, and the constellation itself was thought to represent the celestial animal incarnation of the goddess Artemis Callisto, the Beautiful She-Bear and guardian of the pole star.[7] Seven was also the number of the goddess Sophia, whose Christian symbolic significance as the female Holy Ghost Parnok revered—she called her given name the "most sacred of all names" and believed it was what had summoned her to her creative deed.

As if by a kind of sympathetic magic, Parnok's life seems to divide naturally into seven parts, and this book ended up a "seven-star" of chapters. Sometimes, the natural breaks between stars feel like great divides of black sky, such as the unstarred nights of 1904 (between chapters 1 and 2) and 1912 (between chapters 2 and 3).

Other breaks are rhythmic and seem to mark the pauses in the music that Parnok lived and died to. They accompany beginnings or endings, or those unsettling syncopations just *before* something happens. Parnok called the latter "pre-kiss" moments, and she savored them as a person whose blood, she wrote, was penetrated by "the poison of anticipations." Such syncopes occurred just before Parnok and Tsvetaeva broke up (between chapters 3 and 4); in the aftermath of Parnok's spiritual rebirth in Sudak and return to Moscow (between chapters 4 and 5); just after she realized that she had entered the "polar circle" of creative isolation (between chapters 5 and 6); and just before her great she-bear began to illumine the axis of her world (between chapters 6 and 7).

Finally, this book attempts to convey symbolically my belief that Sophia Parnok's star was the Star of the Seven Sisters. Within her emotional, spiritual, and creative universe she mingled her radiance with seven companion stars in particular. Their names were Nadezhda (chapters 1–2), Lyubov (chapters 2–3), Marina (chapters 3–5), Lyudmila (chapters 4–7), Eugenia (chapters 4–6), Olga (chapters 5–7), and Nina (chapter 7). Some of these sister stars shone brightly for a specific period and died out, while others emitted a steady, continuous light that was at times stronger, at times weaker.

This life of Parnok is based by design on her own retelling of it in her lyrics. Her poems should be read as her lyrical autobiography. I have arranged them in chronological order, as nearly as it can be determined, and supplemented them with biographical information and interpretive comments. The resulting lyric-biographical counterpoint narrates the story of how Sophia Parnok created an existence for herself and her lyrics in a poetic taxonomy that knew no "beasts" like her, and perhaps wished to remain ignorant (and innocent) of the genus she comprised.[8] Her will to outstubborn "patriarchal virtues" in Russian poetry has resulted in its permanent enrichment, and her biography, told here in English for the first time, has been and will continue to be found in what happens to those who read her.

The voice of a book tells me a lot about the fate of its author.
                    EUGENIA GERTSYK

I.

"That Marvelous Female Tenderness..."

At the turn of the twentieth century, the sleepy, whitewashed southern town of Taganrog on the inland sea of Azov had a population of about 61,000 inhabitants, the majority of whom were involved in trade and commerce. A century earlier, Taganrog had been a major Russian port, but its economic importance had steadily declined until it ranked only tenth in exports and eighth in imports among the port cities of imperial Russia.[1]

The city's multinational population included many Greek and Turkish subjects whose cultures contributed to Taganrog's exotic, un-Russian atmosphere. In the port area, with its ever-present Turkish feluccas and Greek ships, the air smelled of ship tars and salt. The sea changed color with the seasons—greyish-blue in spring, bright green in the peculiar amber yellow of Taganrog's summer sunsets.

Most of the houses in the city had terraces and balconies; "the gardens and public parks were full of tea roses, lilacs, and heliotrope. Planted with white acacias and pyramidal poplars, the shapely streets seemed like a park in themselves." In summer, the wealthier sections of Taganrog exuded a sweet fragrance. From the "Greek monastery, its Doric columns showing white against the sky, came the mournful sound of evening bells." After the oppressive heat of the day, the town's young people would come out to meet one another in the municipal park or the harbor. "Red, lilac, yellow, and orange scarves wafted in the breeze from the shoulders of the young Greek women. The evening kept the secrets of young lovers. Suddenly, an empty street would exude the sweet smell of perfume as a bronze-skinned Greek woman in a white dress darted around the corner and vanished into the night." The Greek letters on the ships in the harbor and on the hairdressing salons in town were "redolent of a mysterious antiquity," which acquired a distinctive sound in the prayers of Greek Orthodox believers sitting and telling their rosaries "as the long hot summer days stretched on indolently."[2]

On July 30, 1885,[3] it was oppressively hot. There had been a brief shower early in the day, but the "measly drops" of rain it provided could "not slake the thirsty earth that had gone all cracks and crevices."[4] The horizon seemed to be melting in the intense heat. As the "cicadas crackled and chirred" outside the open windows, a young Jewish physician, Alexandra Parnokh, struggled in the throes of her first labor:

> Now falling back, now on her elbows raising
> herself again, digging her nails into
> her palms, biting her mouth till it bled,
> plaintively and ardently a mother
> did her female deed; the vein beneath the hollow
> of her temple beat, beat under cooled sweat.
> Her depths cracked, like the earth from the heat,
> the cicadas seemed to crackle in her ears—
> and on that day of drunken witches' rapture
> to me, the newborn girl, was given a sacred,
> the most sacred of all names.
> Like a call to deeds, it summons me—SOPHIA ... (#85)

Alexandra and Yakov Parnokh's first daughter, Sophia (Sonya), was born into the exact middle of one of the bleakest decades in Russian history. The reigning tsar, Alexander III, had come to the throne upon his father's assassination in 1881 proclaiming his faith in the power and right of autocracy.[5] His dedication to turning the clock back twenty years was only increased by his belief that the reforms promulgated by his father in the sixties and seventies had ended in treason. Out of nostalgia for the *ancien régime* he fostered the traditional political alliance between the autocracy and the nobility, which, "together with the forward drive of industrial capitalism . . . constituted the principal source of policy in [his] reign."[6]

Industrial expansion became the tsarist government's economic priority and was achieved rapidly, but at the expense of industrial workers' well-being. Taganrog's growth was fairly typical in this regard. It received its initial boost in 1896 when Belgian capitalists began construction of a metalworks and boiler factory in the city. As soon as it went into operation, malfunctioning equipment and the absence of safety regulations resulted in a large number of accidents. Gradually, a whole "army of invalids and maimed men" grew up in the working class districts around the plant.[7]

Those neighborhoods presented a sharp contrast to the wealthier parts of Taganrog. Most workers did not earn a living wage and had to buy food and necessities on credit from local merchants. This forced them into a cycle of permanent indebtedness. Sanitary conditions in the poorer districts of Taganrog were appalling, and epidemics of plague and cholera swept the city in the early nineties.

Tsarist political repression increased in severity throughout the eighties and nineties and continued through the first decade of the reign of Nicholas II, who came to the throne in 1894. Russian universities, which Alexander III had considered, with some justification, to be breeding grounds of revolution, had lost their autonomy at the beginning of his reign. Between 1881 and 1905, the year of the first Russian revolution, there were few parts of the empire where ordinary laws were not at some time abrogated in favor of government by tsarist decree.

18   "THAT MARVELOUS FEMALE TENDERNESS . . ."

The official policy of russianizing non-Russian populations in the empire led to the open persecution of national and religious minorities—Poles, Ukrainians, Armenians, Russian Orthodox dissenters, Transcaucasian Moslems, and especially Jews. Under Alexander III and Nicholas II, the Pale of Settlement, within which most Jews were forced to live, was further restricted. Jewish peasants were forbidden to acquire land, and Jewish enrollment into schools, universities, and professions was limited by quotas. An official anti-Semitism prevailed. Wealthier and well-educated Jews, particularly in the two capitals and other large cities, tended to assimilate into the dominant Russian culture. They experienced less overt and less violent anti-Semitism and ceased to identify, in most cases, with the great mass of poverty-stricken and persecuted Russian Jews.

Taganrog was outside the Pale of Settlement and far from the centers of Jewish population in Russia. It was also one of the few places in the empire where there had never been any Jewish pogroms, although "in a neighboring town the pogromists would routinely stop male passersby and forcibly unbutton their trousers, looking for 'the cut ones.' "[8] Sonya's younger brother Valentin (Valya) remembered hearing the adults at home talk endlessly about "residence permits," and he never forgot overhearing someone once say, "Soon a Jew will no longer have the right to cross the street."[9]

The Parnokh family spoke Russian and was completely assimilated, as were the majority of Jewish families in the town. Yakov Solomonovich, a pharmacist and the owner of an apothecary, was one of Taganrog's five hundred "hereditary honorary citizens," a title conferred on persons not of gentle birth for good citizenship and services rendered to the state. Though sensitive to anti-Semitism, he was indifferent to religion, never attended synagogue, provided no religious instruction for his children, and gave frequent voice to his dream of leaving Russia and living in Western Europe.

The Parnokh children were brought up to think of themselves as Russian first and Jewish second, if at all. But, as often happens with children in nonreligious homes, they developed a passionate interest in religion, although they were stirred by different faiths.

The level of culture in Taganrog was not considered to be very high. In 1897 only 1.3 percent of the population possessed a higher education, a mere 10 percent were high school graduates, and 68 percent of the women and 57 percent of the men were illiterate.[10] The monied aristocracy constituted the cream of local society, but its members were not especially well-educated or interested in cultural pursuits. Their life centered around the two main social clubs in town with their perpetual round of balls, coming-out parties, arguments over seating arrangements at formal dinners, and eternal card games.

The Greeks, Italians, English, and other foreign inhabitants also contributed little to Taganrog's cultural life, since their education, for the most part, did not exceed bookkeeping and business correspondence in foreign languages.[11]

The city did take justifiable pride in its first-rate Italian Opera Company, which merchants had financed in the 1860s and 1870s. Well-known singers, actors, and other performers from larger cities regularly visited Taganrog on tour.

Anton Chekhov, the city's most famous native son, had a very low opinion of cultural life in his hometown, which he left in the late seventies in order to study medicine in Moscow. When he visited Taganrog in 1887, he noted the town's "brutish" living conditions and atmosphere of "universal laziness."[12] Things had not improved in his opinion seven years later, when, during another visit, he told a reporter for the local newspaper that the press "should be more assiduous in reminding the townspeople of how neglected their city was, of its lack of plumbing and a decent public library."[13] Chekhov himself worked tirelessly for the creation of a municipal library, which, due largely to his efforts and gifts of money and books, finally came into existence in 1903.

The Parnokhs were no doubt considered part of Taganrog's intellectual elite. As in other Russian towns, they led a life entirely separated from the masses and their problems. Alexandra Abramovna was an exceptionally well-educated woman for her time, one of the first generation of women doctors in Russia. Her husband also valued education and provided his children with an excellent one at home that prepared them well for the gymnasium. As was typical in affluent Russian homes of the educated classes, the Parnokh children learned to read at a young age, were taught to speak French and German by native-speaking governesses and tutors, and studied music. Sonya and Valya both began writing poetry in childhood, she at six and he at nine.

Sonya was the only one of the three Parnokh children to have lived with their mother. In the almost six years before the birth of her brother and sister, she did not bond especially closely with her mother and grew up with the sad feeling that she had never known her. As a little girl she was closer to her father, but her younger brother apparently replaced Sonya in his father's affections. Pride forced her to hide her resentment. Later, she rechanneled it into a studious indifference to her father and cultivated her distance from him.

She forgot, repressed, or, at the very least, did not care to record her childhood memories. Her lyrics contain virtually no childhood memories to speak of except for one striking memory of the blazing, crimson sunset she would contemplate outside the west-facing window of her nursery. According to one of her poems, it often evoked in her ambivalent "learned" daydreams of the kind of "bloody death that befits a hero" (#157). Valya remembered having similarly violent childhood fantasies of heroism as he daydreamed constantly of becoming the liberator of the Jews.[14] Both children's daydreams were fed by books. Valya's favorite was called *Wars of Liberation*—it narrated the freedom struggles of the Italians, Greeks, and African-American slaves. Sonya eagerly read stories from Greek mythology and the Old Testament.

Much later, Parnok recalled her earliest childhood "dreams," before she learned about the bloody deaths of heroes, as innocent, "springlike," and "carefree" (#2). But she came to feel cut off from those "carefree dreams" by a "thorny path" that had been overshadowed by "misfortunes" (#2).

The first of these misfortunes was no doubt the death of her mother. In 1891, when Sonya was about to turn six, Alexandra Parnokh succumbed after giving birth to the twins, Valentin and Yelizaveta (Liza). The loss of her mother left a permanent wound in Sonya.

In the poem she wrote about her birth, a portion of which was quoted earlier, she tellingly portrayed her birthing mother as doing her "female deed," while she, the daughter and poet, felt summoned to an ungendered "deed" in the service of her "sacred name, Sophia," the Mother Wisdom. Apart from "July Thirtieth" (#85), Parnok remembered her mother only once in her poems, as a personality utterly different from herself, who, she surmised, would probably have disapproved of her daughter's life. She always cherished the hope that her mother would have loved her, but she apparently never knew whether she had.

The second misfortune of Sonya's childhood followed rapidly upon the first. Shortly after Alexandra Abramovna's death, Yakov Solomonovich married his children's German governess, with whom he had apparently been having an affair. Nothing is known about the Parnokh children's stepmother, not even her name, except that she aroused strong negative feelings in all of them.

Valya nurtured a virulent hatred of his stepmother, which later expressed itself in his violently misogynistic detestation of Russia: "Russia is eternal slavery, the eternal stepmother . . . scum of the world . . . a very broad peasant-woman monster with an inordinately small vagina!"[15]

Sonya's feelings for her stepmother seem to have been more diffuse, ambivalent, and therefore, perhaps, more confusing and troubling. She probably resented her for captivating her father, whose weakness she scorned while empathizing with what she felt to be his victimization by a power-loving woman. At the same time, the sexual charisma she perceived her stepmother to wield probably attracted her. Sonya viewed her stepmother primarily as a seductress and dominatrix. She felt less persecuted by her pseudo-mother than challenged to conquer and out-mother her.

Sonya's main issue in growing up was her own motherlessness, and it ultimately expressed itself in her attitudes toward Russia, too. But where Valya rejected Russia as the false, evil, sexually unaccommodating stepmother, Sonya sought comfort in her as the true, good, all-embracing mother and self. Her view, unlike Valya's, specifically contradicted her pro-European father's outlook.

Parnok's childhood was thus spent in a materially secure and even privileged environment that was emotionally wanting and treacherous.[16] In many respects her adult life reversed this imbalance: she found herself chronically in need of money, but never wanting for the love and support of women.

Like many Victorian families, Parnok's presented a proper appearance to the world that probably covered up its share of dark secrets. One fact is obvious and compelling. The poet carried away from her childhood the strong feeling that she had had no childhood, that she had emerged into adulthood at too young an age. As a young adult she attributed her persistent sense of being too old for her years to being a Jew.[17] Perhaps her too-Jewish understanding of the world can be seen in the expression of her pensive, sad, aged-child's eyes in the one surviving childhood photograph of her.

Shortly after Nicholas II ascended to the throne, Parnokh entered the Empress Marie Gymnasium for Girls in Taganrog, where she would complete her formal education over the next eight years.[18] The curricula of all the Marie gymnasia were the same and all subjects except music were compulsory.[19] Parnokh therefore studied religion, Russian, French, German, mathematics, history, geography, physics, science, drawing, needlework, gymnastics, choir singing, and dancing. Her school year extended from the beginning of September through mid-June, and she was in school from nine in the morning until three in the afternoon, six days a week. While school was in session, she wore a uniform to classes and in all public places. She had two weeks' vacation for Christmas and Easter, and her class was limited to forty girls.

During her last three years at the gymnasium Parnokh entered puberty and began writing poetry intensively. She collected her poems into notebooks: only one poem (J-1) and the table of contents remain from the 1900 "Notebook of Poems."[20] The forty-nine poems (J-2–50) in the other group cover the period from April 1901 through mid-May 1903. Most of them are dated exactly (a few even with the hour they were written), a practice Parnok did not always follow later on. Taken together, these fifty poems constitute a kind of lyrical laboratory and diary of Parnok's teenage years as well as the only surviving source of information about her life during this crucial time.

At the time Parnokh was writing her juvenilia, the decadent-symbolist movement was in full swing in Russia and had brought to life a new great age of poetry. Parnokh naturally read the newest Russian poets with their modernist experiments with form, their art-for-art's sake rallying cry, and in some cases, their shocking themes. Yet her adolescent poems revealed no organic, or even imitative, connection with the decadent-symbolist style that dominated her poetic environment. By comparison, her brother's juvenilia from a few years later show a young man who, by his own admission, had been utterly poisoned, as so many of his peers were, by the poetry of Alexander Blok, Russia's greatest symbolist poet, whose star was at mid-heaven in the first decade of the twentieth century.

Most of Parnokh's (extant) juvenilia concern sex and love, specifically, her burgeoning lesbian sexuality and her first flirtations, infatuations, and love affairs. On one hand, she obviously used her writing for emotional therapy, as many adolescents do, and was intent upon expressing her feelings and fantasies with little thought for art. On the other hand, she was serious about her poetry, constantly (and rather harshly) criticizing herself and measuring herself against friends who also wrote, or wanted to be poets, as almost all young people of the educated classes did in Russia at the time.

In writing about her first lesbian sexual experiences, Parnokh did not turn to any of the few available literary models, although she had linguistic access to Baudelaire, Verlaine, and their followers, the poets who have been credited with inventing "literary lesbianism" at the end of the nineteenth century.[21] Ignoring, or ignorant of, the decadent lesbiana of her time, she created her own lesbian poetic speaker from within herself and out of her own experiences, and she wrote about her and them, at times colloquially, but more often in the traditional language of Russian and German heterosexual love poetry. Her juvenilia thus have far more psychological than artistic interest, although their literary and cultural significance, if viewed as they should be from the standpoint of lesbian writing in Russian, is greater than has been acknowledged.

Psychologically, Parnokh's initial self-creation in verse fulfilled her need to come out to herself and to bolster her confidence in an atmosphere she perceived to be alien to her. From the perspective of Russian literary history, the creation of a poetic speaker who was both a lesbian and a desiring female subject represented a revolution of one in modern Russian lyricism that has until now gone unnoticed.

Parnokh's earliest extant poem, dated December 1900, described one of her Saturday dance classes that met in the basement of the gymnasium building.[22] The class is portrayed dynamically as the girls practice the waltz, the allez-casse, and their favorite dance, the chaconne. One can only imagine the complicated and largely unspoken emotions Parnokh must have experienced as a sexually aware (and excitable) young lesbian at those weekly all-female (but not all-lesbian) dances.

In writing her poems she adopted the distancing perspective of a witty and acerbic observer of and participant in a scene of regimented girlish mayhem. Her rhymed couplets gave cameo portraits of herself and her friends: "charming Sophie Krissan," who may have been a special friend, considering the several poems dedicated to her in the table of contents of the nonextant notebook; Miss Radomskaya, "graceful as a poplar tree"; "divine Miss Popel, shining like a star in the sky"; Yelena Kompaneyskaya and Marianna Sokolova, young devotees of decadence, who chat about "how life decays" while Kompaneyskaya listens to her neighbor, Miss Kulik, delivering a "learned treatise." Miss Zimont, "red as a poppy," dances as if she were a perpetual motion machine; Miss Grishina grabs Miss Yovets's sleeve so hard the latter starts to move backwards; Miss Freimann and Miss Fleischer are described as "hens." The poetess Panomarenko, "rapture in her light blue eyes, discourses on progress," to which her partner Katyusha exclaims, "Ah!" and is so excited that she "seems ready to carry Panomarenko off in her arms." Miss Parnokh dances the chaconne with young "cranelike" Miss Rozhnova who whispers breathlessly,

"Just look! How good life is!"
And Parnokh, serious to a fault,
replies, importantly unclear:
"It is, but it is not my lot
to grasp the local atmosphere!" (J-1)

Parnokh was obviously aware of being different, but she took her alienation as a sign of superiority and coped with it proudly. If she had negative feelings or doubts about her sexuality, she did not express them in her poetry, even in those early poems clearly written for her eyes only. She encouraged her own idiosyncrasy and managed to develop early on either a genuine sense of self, or almost impenetrable defenses that could not be destroyed by hostile criticism or social disapprobation, of which she would encounter her share.

Unfortunately, it is extremely difficult to know how she really felt about her sexuality, or what perceptions she had, if any, of lesbians. If she was curious about her orientation, and most young lesbians who acknowledge their difference are (and were, even in the late Victorian era), there were books she could have consulted.

The corpus of late nineteenth century German medical literature on inversion was available in Russian translations from the 1890s, and in any case, if Parnokh were aware of it, she could have read it in the original.[23] The period's major Russian work on lesbianism, *Sexual Perversion in Women*, by a gynecologist, Dr. Ippolit Tarnovsky, had been published in St. Petersburg in 1896. The word "lesbian," and the terms "sapphic love" and "lesbian love" had all entered the Russian language by the turn of the century, but they were not in general use, even by lesbians themselves, in polite conversation and social intercourse. "Lesbian" was and still is regarded as a medical term.

Parnokh appears from her poems to have accepted her sexuality as an innate disposition. She felt her desires were similar to those of heterosexuals, only stronger than most people's.

Her apparent lack of fear or moral consternation about her attraction to women has to be understood, however, in the context of her late Victorian Russian social environment that accepted as natural and "normal" expressions of affection and intimacy between women, particularly schoolgirls, that would strike many westerners today as decided departures from the norm. Parnokh's independence and lack of romantic interest in young men no doubt raised more suspicions and, ultimately, condemnation from her family than her schoolgirl "crushes" on other girls.

According to her gymnasium poems, she had her first love affair during the summer of 1901, which she spent with her family in Balaclava in the Crimea. At that time, the Crimean peninsula had not yet been russianized and seemed like "a little corner of

Turkey."²⁴ Minarets towered over the landscape and the days were punctuated by the muezzins' summonses to prayer. Tartar languages were in use, and "the whole peninsula was filled with the smell of hot Turkish bread, magnolias, and olive trees. In between the cypresses one caught glimpses of the dazzling sea and heard its thunderous surf."²⁵

The fragrances, sounds, and seascape intoxicated Sonya as much as her younger brother, and she developed a lifelong love for middle eastern (Turkish, Tartar, and Persian) cultures. In August, in the city of Alupka, she wrote a stanza in which she tried to convey the stimulating effect that the "smell of magnolias," "the mysterious sound of the Black Sea," and the "intoxicatingly pure air" produced in her; it all "aroused a swarm of sweet thoughts" (J-10).

Her Balaclava girlfriend has remained unidentified, but the source and power of her attractiveness found its way into a poem. In late July, Parnokh wrote that her lover's "enchanting, excited, tender voice" had lured her into "an enchanted world of pleasure" and had "penetrated [her] soul," seeming to say: " 'You'll feel like you're drowning in raptures of love as / you'll live a fast life by my side!' " (J-8).²⁶

The following spring Sonya immersed herself in a lyrical "Reminiscence" of her happy summer in Balaclava. She imagined herself waiting for her lover's kiss as she used to do while sitting on the balcony of her house and looking through binoculars at "a little white house in the hills" (J-23). At the same time someone would be observing her from the windows of that house. Later, she would walk in the hills, meet her lover, and they would spend time in the little house so that the "hours seemed like seconds." When Parnokh would regretfully return home for dinner, she would leave knowing there would "always be tomorrow." She concluded her "Reminiscence" by comparing her tomorrowless state in the present (April 1902) with the "dream" and its "music of tomorrow" that she had actually lived the previous summer.

Music played an enormously important role in Parnok's emotional and creative life, and if she had been more ambitious and diligent about her formal musical education, she might have become a professional musician. (As a young woman she admitted that in choosing a literary career, she had merely followed the line of least resistance.) Music stood next to anguish (the untranslatable Russian word *toska*) at the core of her being, and she apparently could not listen to music without becoming visibly affected. Her poems tend to be very musical, with a great deal of attention paid to rhyme, rhythm, and sound texture—stylistic qualities that are impossible to convey accurately in English translation. Some of her late lyrics reveal her attempt to create a purely musical, and specifically female, poetic language.

As an adolescent in Taganrog, Parnokh attended concerts and operas as often as she could. The powerful, seductive operatic heroines, like Cleopatra, Delilah, Isolde, and especially Carmen, stimulated her romantic fantasies, and she frequently became infatuated with the divas who sang these roles.

In October 1901 she attended a performance of *Samson and Delilah* that simply overwhelmed her and inspired the poem "To Delilah," an acrostic "dedicated to the singer and actress Seluc-Rasnatowskaya." The poem constituted a confession of love both for the pagan seductress Delilah and the performer who embodied her and created the model of the *femme fatale* that informs the poet's early lyrical evocations of many of her lovers:

> So strong, like death, seductively-superbly,
> Each part of her whole being powerfully,
> Lovingly enticed us all to her.
> Unbounded passions of the southern girl
> Came forth, it seemed, in all her singing,
> Resplendent, hot, and powerful Delilah!
> Acknowledging the celebration's start,
> She slithered, like a snake, around her prey . . .
> Not feeling love, she unrestrainèdly

And passionately gave herself; —for god,
That god whom all her patrimony's sons,
Oppressèd slaves, adored and owed obeisance.
With zeal she tried enticing Samson into
Seductive snares, not feeling any love.
Kalypso-like, what power she put into her acting!
And with your furious and forceful passion,
You have infected certainly not Samson
Alone, it seems to me, Delilah! (J-11)

The next day she wrote another passionate poem on a musical theme. Entitled "Anita," it represented her "interpretation" of Tchaikovsky's popular piano piece "Chant sans paroles" (Op. 2, No. 3), and overwhelmed the haunting, simple song with a storm of violent words that seemed to come, quite literally, from another opera.

The poem told of Anita, who held a nameless and submissive male lover in thrall for a year. Despite his attempts to kill his passion, he found himself sickly in love with this "invincibly powerful" woman who merely laughed at him. As poet-interpreter of Tchaikovsky's music, Parnokh condemned Anita's behavior and urged her not to laugh after her victim had finally expired from his unrequited passion. Yet the young poet's sympathy with Anita's victim could not overcome her own attraction to the woman. At the end of the poem she admitted that although Anita's laughter might anger God, it was positively "infectious, and full of beauty!" (J-12).

The uninspired routine at the gymnasium obviously had nothing to compete with the exciting life Parnokh lived in her imagination. To make matters worse, some of her teachers were shockingly unqualified. She particularly scorned and mocked one of her Russian language instructors, who had been transferred to "contemptible" Taganrog from his "native Penza province" (J-14). This "wise pedagogue" routinely misaccented Russian words and insisted that his students "correct" their pronunciation to conform to his mistakes.

Writing increasingly became her refuge from Penza pedagogues, school tedium, and the ravages of her frustrated sexuality. She began to take a more critical approach to her creativity, too. In March 1902, after reading over her long poem about the dance class, she rejected it and scribbled the words "stupid little poem!" at the end of the manuscript.

Then, in "To a Young Poet," she revealed a similarly negative self-assessment, as well as a lofty opinion of poetry and the poet's calling. "How I envy you (though envy is a vile feeling)," she wrote to her addressee, a fellow poet, "for being able to plumb the hidden recesses of the most sacred art . . . for having the gift of reaching people's hearts—for sowing good in them with the word and destroying with the word their evil!" (J-16).

Her respect for words, her belief in the moral power that words could wield, in the obligation talent placed on the poet, and in the primary, communicative function of poetry, remained the foundation of her artistic credo throughout her life. By sixteen she knew exactly what she wanted to achieve creatively, and she set lofty goals for herself, but she did not know how to attain them or how to find her way into poetry's "hidden recesses."

Spring "seized" Parnokh in 1902 "with its terrible force, the terrible desire for love" (J-21). She fell in love with one of her schoolmates, a certain Zhenya. One day at school Zhenya happened to laugh in her "childishly naughty" way at something Sonya said, and the poet suddenly felt that Zhenya was not indifferent to her. That evening, she dashed impulsively over to Zhenya's house "to catch a glimpse of" her, but her hopes for the tryst she had fantasized about were not realized.

Alone in her room later that night she wrote out her disappointment in a poem, "To Zhenya" (J-22). It was the first time she dared to write the name of the woman she desired and to present herself not as an observer of other people's passions, not as a sympathizer with the male victims of passion, but as a young woman who desired another woman. She had begun writing dangerously and had taken an important step toward enabling herself "to plumb the hidden recesses" of her creativity. Her excitement spurred her on through a half-sleepless night as she comforted herself with her "Reminiscence" of her Crimean romance the previous summer.

By the end of the month she was feeling alienated and trapped by the "local atmosphere" and gave herself some rebellious lyrical advice:

> Leave here as soon as possible! Oh, faster!
> I'm smothering; I'm growing dull;
> I'm becoming malicious and nasty;
> I now shun everyone . . .
> I don't feel at all engaged with other people.
> Their happiness gives me no joy . . .
> I despise all people . . .
> Animals are a hundred times dearer to me. (J-24)

Two months later, however, she had attained some teenage wisdom that directly contradicted these misanthropic feelings. She decided that it was vain "to despise people," and, although they were not worth loving, "one had to pity them, so that one would oneself be pitied" (J-18). Possibly, her change of heart reflected a new influence in her life—Christianity. She concluded the poem by exhorting herself not to make fun of her "pitiable surroundings" and reminded herself of the example of "Jesus, who did not strive for his goal with mockery and hatred." This is the first Christian reference in Parnok's extant writings.

On the same June day she wrote another poem in an utterly different, comic-ironic key, called "Portrait of Ilichka Rediktin." The young male hero of the title may have been drawn from a real-life model, either herself or a young man in Taganrog in whom she saw resemblances to herself and with whom she may have enjoyed the first of numerous romantic rivalries she would have with men. According to the poem, Rediktin, like Parnokh herself, was eager for Sophie Krissan's attentions.

Ilichka Rediktin seems to have been almost a male double of Sonechka Parnokh. A "victim of passion" who had been in its "all-powerful vise" since childhood, he is described as merry, carefree, talkative in the company of young women, up on the latest argot, but unable to find anything to talk about with his father "beyond grades." The emphasis on the spotty communication between the young lover of women and his father is particularly suggestive in view of Parnokh's "distant" and uncommunicative relationship with her father throughout her youth. Finally, Ilichka Rediktin is portrayed as having the same wisely innocent attitude to sex that Parnokh manifested at this time: "horribly chaste," he "freely admits to loving the female sex" (J-26).

"Portrait of Ilichka Rediktin" and, even more, the long, unfinished "Correspondence," written the next day, show that Parnokh was not yet entirely comfortable writing as a young woman about her sexuality. After taking the plunge into direct expression of her desires in "To Zhenya," she retreated for a while to the safety of male doubles and masculine discourse about sex. This was not surprising, since in her day female sexuality continued to be the almost exclusive province of male interpreters, both in science and in poetry. Furthermore, lyrics that had female desiring-subjects were extremely rare in Western and Russian poetry. Parnok's earliest native poetic influences were all male: Pushkin, Baratynsky, and, especially, Tyutchev.[27]

"Correspondence" was composed of lyrical letters between two male friends that narrated a rudimentary, novelistic plot: a sixteen-year-old boy writes to his older, jaded friend that he has finally fallen truly in love, something he realized only when he overcame his nearly uncontrollable desire and did not force his beloved "Charmochka" to have sex with him out of "respect" for her. His friend, who does not believe in love outside of "sexual instincts," replies that a man who "respects" a woman is simply a fool. He advises his friend to be daring and take what he wants. The boy in love is insulted by his friend's cynicism and writes to announce his marriage and to break off their relationship forever.

The poem seems to be a rich if elusive source of clues to the psychology of the young poet who wrote it. The two narrators appear to represent her youthful and cynical selves as she debated the issue of "going all the way" with a girlfriend she had fallen seriously in love with. The young man's experience strikes one overwhelmingly as having been Parnokh's own:

> When I was kissing her and feeling
> as if completely high,
> and over her whole body wandered
> my rapt and greedy eyes,
> When I, beside myself with passion,
> was fondling her breasts,
> Then . . . (not believing in your power),
> I respected her.
> And pushed back by her feeble gesture,
> I, suffering as I loved,
> in love, and painfully resentful,
> I did control myself. (J-25, "The Young Man in Love to His Friend")

The older man responds that his young friend is merely the victim of a passing illness; he was the same at sixteen, constantly assuring everyone "with tears in [his] eyes" how he "respected" women. But now he knows that was all a fantasy. Respecting a woman's virtue simply means losing time. "If you had been bold," he writes, "you'd now have it all," and concludes:

> Fire in the blood,
> *that*, friend, is love!
> Books, notes, sweet words,
> trust me, absurd—
> just keep in mind,
> you are a man—
> short is your span,

don't live amiss,
live fast and kiss. (J-25, "The Friend to the Young Man in Love")

Perhaps, with this tough talk, Parnokh was trying to encourage herself to be more aggressive with her new girlfriend. By then having her chaste persona reject the advice of her cynical one, she was able to separate herself from her "sexual instincts" and neutralize the anxiety they caused her, probably because they did not seem so "repulsive" as they were supposed to be.

Parnokh's sexually cynical "older friend" resembled Pechorin, the Byronic hero and ladykiller of Mikhail Lermontov's classic psychological novel, *A Hero of Our Time*. Later poems of Parnok's, written when she was the age of the "older friend" in "Correspondence," reveal that in several of her love affairs her female poetic speaker identified with Pechorin. There is some lyrical evidence, then, that Parnok became the sort of lover and "Petersburg ladykiller" that she claimed to despise at sixteen.

The reader of "Correspondence" senses immediately that the adolescent author was not indulging in a bookish debate on the meaning of true love; nor was she merely affecting a cynical attitude in order to keep the debate going. She was trying to come to some conclusion on a question of vital importance to her and on which she clearly was of two minds. The chaste, moral sixteen-year-old in her was struggling with her own too-cynical self. But the question remains: What, or who, had put Parnokh so in the power of her older self that her greatest need, when she finally fell in love, was to assert her innocence and embrace the bourgeois morality against which she later rebelled wholeheartedly?[28]

By the end of June, Sonya had fallen into an almost suicidal depression, the reasons for which she merely alluded to in a poem which began, " 'What is life if it lacks enchantment?' " (J-27). The purpose of the poem was to encourage herself to find a goal in life which would enable her to escape the "stream of sufferings and misery" that her ordinary, unmagical life in Taganrog seemed to her to entail. She resolved in the poem "to seek enchantment in everything—art, learning, embraces, sweet kisses, and feeling" (J-27).

Shortly after she wrote this poem, she left to spend the summer in the Crimea. She appears to have been accompanied there by her "Charma," that is, her first true love. The young woman's real name was Nadezhda Pavlovna Polyakova (Nadya, Nadyusha). Nothing else is known about her except that her "enchantment" filled Parnokh's emotional life for at least five years and inspired her most focused adolescent love lyrics. Polyakova was the first of Parnokh's muse-lovers, and, as a poetic image, she embodied what most excited the young poet in women sexually and creatively.

On July 7, in Gurzuf, Parnokh wrote her first poem to "N.P.P." She compared Nadya to her tormenting and fickle muse who had the habit of appearing suddenly, making her "drunk with pleasure," then leaving her just as abruptly without any assurances that she would ever return (J-28).

At the end of August, on her way home to Taganrog, Parnokh stopped in Rostov-on-Don to visit relatives. During her visit her thoughts were completely centered on her new love. On August 29 she wrote three poems to Nadya, all of which convey the intensity of her passion and her feeling of being victimized by her lover, who, she wrote, gave her "all the raptures of paradise" while "pushing [her] into hell with her own hand!" (J-31). Nadya's "mad caresses" made her "drunk," but she could not depend on them and, in effect, accused Nadya of being a tease. In "Love is gone. The tuberoses have faded," she complained that Nadya did not really love her and wanted most of all to make her suffer. That was why she "love[d] and suffer[ed] without end, curse[d] the day of [their] first meeting, and sob[bed her] nights away." Pride kept her from showing her tears to Nadya, yet, as she admitted at the end of the poem, her capricious lover had only to hint at a rendez-vous, and she could torment her as much as she pleased.

She invoked Nadya more mysteriously in "Elegy," an allegorical fairy tale about black roses and white lilies that grow in a southern garden.²⁹ On the day before her wedding, a princess picks the roses and lilies. She puts the lilies in her hair and pins the roses over her bosom to hide her small but noticeable breasts—a charming detail from the very real life of a typically self-conscious teenage girl. Sniffing the black roses, the princess goes to a magic castle where she and her prince make love. The roses remain on her rumpled clothes, but the dewdrops on them dry. As for the lilies, they fade, no longer needed by the princess. After adorning her soft, warm bed, they have lost their fragrance.³⁰

However tormented by Nadya Sonya may have felt, however deeply in love she believed herself to be, she pursued other women throughout the course of their relationship, exhibiting a type of nonmonogamous behavior characteristic of her until her thirties. By the beginning of the new year, she found herself attracted to three different women at once and wrote poems to them all. The first was E. T. Veisberg, "the bacchante," whose special attraction lay in her "brilliant, marvelous, fantastic eyes" (J-34). Then there was E.D.S., possibly an older woman, who liked to give Parnokh "moral lectures" on her waywardness. This "stern Femida" hardly made Sonya weep for her sins, however. Once she realized the lectures were an instance of "the pot calling the kettle black," all she wanted to do after hearing them was "to kiss [E.D.] all over." She got some satisfaction from the fact that her moralist's admonishments were inevitably followed by "completely different words," "that marvelous female tenderness," and a look in E.D.'s eyes that expressed genuine feelings, "albeit good ones" (J-32, "To a Woman").

Not all her flirtations at this time were lighthearted. Her repeated attraction to tyrannical, spoiled women made her vulnerable to hurt from one "cold and playful" girl who, she wrote, toyed with her as if she were a pawn. She seemed to Parnokh to embody Fate herself, a girl-child who enjoyed smashing one life to pieces only to replace it with another (J-35, "Fate"). This poem reveals

Parnok's penchant for lyrical allegory, a tendency she would develop in the verse of her immediate post-gymnasium years.

In a self-critical mood that winter, the adolescent poet gave a telling assessment of her own work at the beginning of "Reply to a Letter," another of her numerous verse epistles. This one was addressed to a local bon vivant and "prolific author" who had possibly shown an interest in her poems:

> My poems breathe
> neither inexplicable charm,
> nor tender, floral scents,
> nor irresistible beauty.
> They contain no marvelous harmony,
> their diversity of hues pains the eye;
> and they lack that charming purity
> which the heavens gleam with.
> But one can, though merely by chance,
> sparkle in meager luxury.
> All the more so since I simply
> can not be in anybody's debt. (J-36)

She already took pride in her nonindebtedness to others. Like a good mother, she embraced her poems despite their manifold weaknesses because they were her own. Even the most appealing and beautiful poems she might adopt and make part of her brood would always have alien blood running in their lines and would be merely her "step-poems," so to speak.

As Sonya entered her final months at the gymnasium, she increasingly became a source of disturbance to her father. Although her grades were excellent, she showed no inclination for further study and seemed to lack focus and ambition. All she cared about was poetry and music, but as far as Yakov Solomonovich could see, she applied herself to neither.

More worrisome to him were her "tastes." She had a lot of male friends; a couple of them, including the son of their friends the Iofs, had even made marriage proposals to her, but it was plain that none of them appealed to her romantically. Her persistent crushes on older women and her intense friendships with other girls concerned him—they no longer seemed perfectly normal. He found it impossible to talk with his older daughter, however. She was rather like him in some ways—passionate, proud, obstinate. But she appeared to bear him a grudge and not to care about him at all.

Parnokh and her father began to have words about her irresponsibility, impatience, impulsive behavior, and mostly, one imagines, about her lesbianism, although no doubt the word was never mentioned. Perhaps, after one especially unpleasant row at the end of February, Sonya withdrew to her room in proud and angry silence and poured out her rage in the poem "To My Judges." Her complaints, arguments, and defenses came out helter-skelter as one line artlessly interrupted the next:

> I'm in pain. I lack the strength to speak . . .
> Perhaps I *am* pathetic, perhaps I *am* worthless . . .
> I can't keep you from thinking that . . .
> But judges! The accusation is false!

After this first outburst, she began, almost unconsciously, to reverse the balance of power between herself and her "judges." Instead of trying to answer their accusations, she began to question her accusers:

> But are the surges of my passions,
> their profundity, known to you?
> And do you have the ability to desire
> something as strongly as I?

Suddenly, it seemed to her that the power of her "judges" over her was an illusion:

> No, no! Not I, it's you who are powerless!
> And is it for the likes of you to judge me?! . . .

Having recovered her self-possession, she gained some insight into her weaknesses and also her potential strengths:

And if I, *pathetic creature* that I am,
could meld some patience with the force of my desire,
then I, *pathetic creature* that I am,
would subdue the world entire. (J-37)

During the spring prior to her graduation, if we are to trust her poems, Parnokh led the sort of fast and furious romantic life that her first lover in Balaclava had introduced her to and that the cynical "older friend" in "Correspondence" had recommended. It was a life that combined a series of "reigning women of the moment" (J-41) with her continuing passion for Polyakova, the flames of which appear to have been fanned by Nadya's absence. One March lyric began:

The colder your letters are,
the longer your silences,
the harder the waiting,
the more tormentedly I love!
Your image floats up before me . . .
it recalls a storm of caresses . . .
and it arouses my passion,
and I love more tormentedly. (J-42)

A few days later she must have finally heard from Nadya after a long, nearly unbearable silence. Excited and enraptured, she stared in amazement at Nadya's picture and pondered lyrically, "Why do I love you, do you know?" (J-43). She focused on an aural memory of "the whisper of a sleepy wave" because it brought her fantasies to life and helped her to remember the way she and Nadya had been the previous summer in Gurzuf. Ever since then, her poem continued, "the rapturous languor of moonlit nights" intoxicated her like wine because she had "seen that languor shining at the bottom of [Nadya's] eyes," and to her it was "more beautiful than stars, and hotter than fire. It caressed [her] so marvelously at times."

Yet her renewed passion for the absent Nadezhda continued not to inhibit her wanting other women who were nearer—for example, L., to whom she dedicated a poem on May 16 that began, "The force and passion of your kiss / propel me into joy and misery" (J-46). After L. kissed her, she couldn't "sober up," and wanted only one thing—to be kissed again. L. was another woman with a "powerful gaze," who "intoxicated" Parnokh and made her "submissive." Once "passion's merciless blaze" had flared up in her, she could not put it out.

In the spring, a new, nonsexual passion found an expressive outlet in Parnokh's poetry: her love for Russia, which she perceived, symbolically, both as self and as other (mother). In the first of two poems entitled "Russia," she personified "enormous Russia" as an unreasonable child whose inner space, like her own, was full of "homeless thoughts" and "mad impulses," and who, like her, had not really awakened yet, or realized her potential (J-44).

In the next poem about her homeland, she compared Russia to a sleeping beauty awaiting her savior prince, a prince who was faraway and oblivious to the moans of the beauty's "embattled Truth" (J-47). Both "Russia" poems expressed the "sleeping" poet's underlying desire to have her course directed and to be saved from her dormant state.

Indeed, Parnokh's persistent aimlessness and indolence would become constant refrains not only in her poems, but in her letters to intimates. She was painfully aware that she had emerged into young adulthood "in love [only] with liberty," "directing her flight merely for the sake of flight" (#120). By comparison with her more goal-oriented peers, she felt impulse-driven and began to wonder if she did not need to be saved from herself. She must have conveyed this need to others, especially to people she loved, since so many of her close friends and lovers appear to have felt challenged to be her savior prince or princess.[31]

At the end of her school years, however, Sonya often doubted that Russia's and her own savior would come. The poetic speaker of her first "Russia" poem therefore prayed to God to make the stars speak to the prince and tell him that Russia's "misfortune was nigh," that her enemies had "gone off and buried our truth somewhere / and crookedness rules the land" (J-44). She was becoming impatient with savior princes and their wretchedly long latency periods.

As Sonya's love and empathy for Russia intensified, so did her brother Valya's hatred for his homeland. In the spring of 1903, he was almost twelve and completing his second year at the Taganrog Boys' Gymnasium. Valya had viewed getting into the gymnasium as the first difficult hurdle on his way to fulfilling his dream of attending St. Petersburg University. He later recalled: "There was a set of gymnastics rings in our stable, and I thought of the entrance exams as gold rings on which one had to do the most difficult, acrobatic tricks. I accomplished the first 'acrobatic act,' I spent eight years at the gymnasium, and during those whole eight years I was the only Jew among the Russians and Greeks in my class."[32]

Valya's school experience made him feel much more alienated ethnically than Sonya's did—but then, she was by far not the only Jew in her class. Yet they shared the bond of growing up with an awareness of being different. She probably understood her brother better than anyone else in the family (they were apparently very close as children), while at the same time she was competitive with him (they were both gifted in writing, music, and languages). In adolescence, when she was struggling with her own alienation, Sonya had little compassion for Valya's sufferings. She thought he was "neurotic" and prone to exaggerate the degree of anti-Semitism he experienced.

She herself manifested as intense an identification with Israel as with Russia. Judging by the poem "To the Jews" (J-45), she perceived Israel as Russia's opposite, yet an opposite that was part of her self, too. Russia was a child while Israel was "old and long-suffering." In some ways the Jews represented her model of difference; they were "immortal by virtue of their humility, incomparable in the sadness of their fate." Like Russia, she thought that Israel "was slumbering." Its awakening, however, would not come from the kiss of a (possibly tardy) fairy prince. Rather, "intensified humiliations and oppressions [would spark] Israel's dimming star" (J-45).

Parnokh graduated from the gymnasium with a gold medal, the equivalent of our summa cum laude. The last three poems in her notebook, all occasional pieces from May 1903, suggest a typically up-and-down graduation mood of looking ahead and saying goodbye. In mid-May, with Tchaikovsky's piano piece "Autumn Song" in mind, she wrote a "little ditty" of her own in the album of one of her friends, Liza Danziger:

> Twilight time autumnal. Greyish all around . . .
> Sparse and thinning forest, river, naked ground.
> Earth is hidden under a yellow covering,
> Dusky like the song, the ditty that I sing.
> I don't feel like singing songs as bright as day,
> I don't feel like singing in general anyway . . .
> Twilight time autumnal. Greyish all around,
> That, my dearest friend, is how our life is bound. (J-48)

The conclusion to Parnokh's juvenile writings, "Impromptu. To My Information Bureau," is in a similarly comic-ironic vein. Parodying the form of the classic poem of farewell—of which she would become a masterly and serious exponent at the end of her life—the eighteen-year-old poet said "thank you" and goodbye to a "dear friend," whose words and faithful image she would recall "whenever disaster strikes!" (J-50). That friend was her "information bureau," a reference book or encyclopedia of some sort, perhaps, which "explained a mass of diverse matters" and was "useful in many ways."

Parnok's juvenilia gave little indication, at least technically, of the poet she was to become. Only here and there do individual lines provide an inkling of her lyrical potential. Thematically, however, the juvenilia are better predictors of the future Parnok. Love was the adolescent poet's favorite theme, and love lyrics would continue to be one of the mature Parnok's most important genres, ultimately constituting more than a third of her entire known output. Although she drew upon literary (heterosexual) models (mainly from German Romantic poetry) in several of her juvenile love poems, from the beginning her best efforts were autobiographically inspired and open about her lesbian orientation. Her obvious desire to write her own love life into Russian poetry made the issue of her affectional preference crucially important to her creative development. In order to become the poet she was capable of becoming, Parnok would have to challenge the artistic and moral norms of her national poetic tradition and culture.

Parnok's early identification of her muse with one of her lovers, Nadezhda Polyakova, also demonstrated how closely her sexuality was linked with her creativity. Her artistic and erotic interaction with Polyakova established the type of relationship Parnok would enjoy throughout her life with her creative spirit and self, one in which the poet felt both bound, or leashed, to her muse by the bonds of love and inspiration, and bound for her muse by the yearning to find a poetic home in which to create her being.[33]

2.

"Love Summons Me, and I Won't Contradict Her..."

After Parnokh's comic poem of farewell, all traces of her vanish for two years. It is unlikely that she stopped writing during this time, but whatever she did write has been lost. It is equally unlikely that she spent the whole two years in Taganrog, but where she might have gone is also a matter of supposition. Since she had an uncle in St. Petersburg, it is possible that she spent some time visiting him in the capital.

She may also have lived in Moscow during part of those two years. Toward the end of her life she once happened to reminisce about the time in her late teens when she and another girl lived in Moscow under the patronage of a well-known prima ballerina, Yekaterina Geltser, who had been dancing at the Bolshoi Ballet since 1898. Geltser was a remarkable dancer, but apparently a jealous and tyrannical patroness. Parnok recalled that when she herself was not dancing, she would take Sonya and her other charge to sit with her in her loge at the Bolshoi. Neither of the girls dared to praise any of the other ballerinas' dancing in Geltser's presence, however, for if either of them simply could not restrain herself and burst out in applause or praise for another ballerina,

Geltser would silently pinch the offender out of "malice and jealousy."[1]

Nevertheless, Parnok's love for the ballet was kindled under Geltser's patronage, and she genuinely admired her patroness's art. As an adult she enthusiastically attended Geltser's performances, and after one of them, in October 1915, she wrote a poem, "To Yekaterina Geltser," in which she compared the prima ballerina of the Silver Age to the leading Russian ballerina of Alexander Pushkin's Golden Age (#31). Parnok's extensive collection of photographs included two of Geltser, from 1914 and 1926, inscribed, respectively "To dear and loved Sophia Yakovlevna" and "To dear and loved Sonya Parnok."[2]

Parnokh's youthful relationship with Geltser appears to have been another instance where being loved brought the young poet pain as well as pleasure. Still, it seemed preferable to life in her father's house in Taganrog, where her lack of financial independence forced her to return, and where, it seemed to her, she received pain without love. By 1905 the misery of her situation there had intensified, and she sought a more permanent escape. She managed to persuade her father to send her to Europe, convincing him that she wanted to study music in Geneva.

Yakov Solomonovich probably did not know that his wayward older daughter had fallen in love with an actress and that her main reason for leaving her "paternal threshold" was to pursue this latest infatuation.[3] Many years later, in the lyric, "Why, oh why from my paternal threshold" (#95), Parnok acknowledged that her first trip abroad seemed to her to have initiated a pattern of having been "abducted" out of Russia "by love" on the eves of fateful historical events:

> Why, oh why from my paternal threshold
> when a fateful happening was brewing
> was I led away beneath some foreign
> sky by you, my fearsome tourguide, Love? (#95)

Parnokh settled in Geneva—it is remotely possible she had relatives there[4]—and at the end of May when Russia endured its humiliating defeat from the Japanese at Tsushima, she found herself "closed in by Alpine summits" (#95). The news of Tsushima "offended" her patriotic, Russophile heart, but could not dampen her high spirits and the exhilarating sense of freedom that made the year she spent in Europe "a splendid time," one of the happiest times in her adult life (#197).

During her time abroad Parnokh corresponded regularly with Vladimir Volkenshtein. The "celebrated Vovochka," as Sonya hailed him in a 1903 "Impromptu," was himself an aspiring poet. By 1905 he had become Sonya's best friend as well as the first person she had known who took an active and informed interest in her writing.[5]

Volkenshtein was two years older than Parnokh. His father was a close friend of a well-known writer whose house in Petersburg had been a meeting place for people in literature and art since the mid-nineteenth century. The Volkenshteins belonged to an intellectually high-powered set, the prerevolutionary, largely liberal, Russian-Jewish Petersburg intelligentsia, whose members had completely assimilated into mainstream Russian culture and who bent their considerable academic and creative talents to fostering that culture. Several of them were Russophiles. Some, like Volkenshtein's maternal grandfather, who died in 1904, had converted to Russian Orthodoxy.

One of young Volkenshtein's closest friends at this time was an aspiring composer, Mikhail Gnesin, a Jew from Rostov-on-Don. He and Vladimir were the same age and had met in 1901 when they were both beginning their student careers, Volkenshtein in the philology department of St. Petersburg University and Gnesin at the conservatory. Volkenshtein introduced his friend from the provinces into the various and often competing circles and salons that played an integral role in encouraging the rich intellectual and artistic life of the capital.

Like most of his friends, Volkenshtein was not only well educated, but also well traveled. In the summer of 1904 he and Gnesin made an adventurous trip through Italy and the Mediterranean. Having little money, they traveled fourth class from Rostov-on-Don to Venice, spent a month in Italy and returned by sea from Naples to Odessa. On their way they made stops in Sicily, Crete, Athens, Smyrna, Khios, and Constantinople. Volkenshtein later recalled, "The ship's hold, where fourth-class passengers were assigned plank-beds, was dirty and stifling, and we preferred to sleep on the deck. We were awakened at five in the morning when they washed the decks down. They fed us on beans. But it was an unforgettable journey. Seething life, the ruins of classical culture, the Aegean landscape, thousands of islands."[6]

For his part, Gnesin later recalled Volkenshtein in youth as an "extraordinarily merry" fellow who suffered from an exorbitant fear of death. "Sometimes," the composer wrote, "he would sink into the most intense gloom and could not get out of it for weeks at a time."[7]

By 1905, one of the leading symbolist circles in St. Petersburg gathered weekly around a reputedly bisexual couple: the classical scholar and poet Vyacheslav Ivanov and his writer wife, Lydia Zinovyeva-Annibal.[8] Gnesin, who had been cool to the so-called first generation of decadent poets that burst on the scene in the 1890s, developed a passionate enthusiasm for the more mystically oriented second generation of symbolists, and he became a frequent visitor at the Ivanovs' apartment, which was known as "the Tower." Volkenshtein, however, did not care for symbolism and went to the Ivanovs' only rarely.

Parnokh shared his antisymbolist viewpoint and found in him a friend whose intellectual interests and artistic tastes were nearly identical to her own. They were similar in other ways too. Both had a good sense of humor, enjoyed parodies, puns, and prankish escapades. Both loved music and felt comfortable in the company of musicians. In short, they were extremely compatible. Looking back on the positive side of her friendship with Volkenshtein, Parnok wrote: "We were splendidly suited to one another in terms of intellectual and moral development and artistic tastes, and precisely for that reason we should never have spoiled our relationship by getting married."[9]

Volkenshtein's intellectual polish must have impressed Parnokh, and with reason, but she may not have realized at first that intellect and poetic talent are two very different things. Volkenshtein possessed a considerably smaller natural gift for poetry than she, and the poems he was writing in his student years were in no way superior to hers. He was the last person in a position to give her advice on becoming a poet. (Eventually, he gave up poetry and turned to playwriting.)

Parnokh's personal liking for Volkenshtein and her respect for his superior education blinded her to his weaknesses as a poet. She believed she genuinely liked his work. Worse, she looked to him for advice in improving her own writing, about which she felt increasingly doubtful and insecure. (She made a similarly unhappy choice of literary advisor in Gnesin, whose criticism she sought for years, despite the fact that he was not even a writer.) Only much later did she realize that Volkenshtein's "authority oppressed [her] in all ways."[10]

In 1905 she was a long way from this insight. Volkenshtein seemed to be a savior of sorts, who liked her, accepted her sexuality—or, at least, claimed not to be bothered by it—nurtured her talent, and was eager to help with practical advice and, later, with what influence with editors he possessed. While Parnokh was abroad, she regularly sent Volkenshtein what she was writing and filled her letters with detailed discussions of her poems and his.

Her lyrics from this period, almost entirely unpublished, differed greatly from the technically less proficient poems she had written in her gymnasium years. Most strikingly, the various human subjects who had filled the world of her juvenilia—the poetic speaker, her female friends and lovers, the actress Seluc-Rasnatowskaya, the Penza schoolteacher, Zhenya, Ilichka Rediktin, Nadyusha—disappeared entirely from the poems of her early "Volkenshtein period." They were replaced by abstract and allegorical entities: Indifference, Dispassion, Audacity, Intellect, Beauty, Death, Thought, and, especially, Life.

For the most part, her poems of this time (most of which are undated) also lacked specifically lesbian contents. This was not a coincidence. Although Volkenshtein probably never consciously tried to discourage his friend from writing about her sexuality, he did guide her in the direction of his own less life-based lyricism. Eager for his approval, she followed his lead, probably as unconsciously as she had earlier followed her own inclination for autobiographical lyricism.

A certain suggestion of female same-sex interactions can sometimes be discerned in Parnokh's allegorical poems, however. It obtains from the poet's frequent personification and animation of abstract nouns which act like lyrical female impersonators, in their relationships with one another. One of the most important such female impersonators in the allegorical world of Parnokh's early verse is Empress Life. Several poems meditate upon her (Life's) relationship and struggle with her powerful female archenemy, Thought. When Thought conquers Life,

> hopes and passions don't exist, and
> the skeleton of empress-life,
> once proud and powerful, arises
> in all her shameful nakedness
> and stands before impartial thought.
> A crowd of blind men mindlessly
> and dully follows after her:
> and thought severely eyes them all,
> and life appears to her absurd
> and ruthlessly monosyllabic,
> and she no longer can descend
> from her great height to earth.[11]

Some of the masterpieces of Parnok's mature poetry reveal that allegory was not in itself uncongenial to her talent. Her best allegories were usually rooted in her specifically lesbian "way of thinking,"[12] however. Another early example is the poem "Life," written in 1905. Though not a good poem, it did reflect something that came from within the poet and defined both her attitude toward life and her erotic relationships with women as she had illustrated them more spontaneously and concretely in many of her juvenile poems:

> Life is a woman. Merely by her own seductions
> intoxicated, she will stand above her victim.
> The more unhappy is the soul that lies before her,
> the fuller she all is with unrestrained desire.
> How often her mysterious gaze has hovered over
> my soul with powerful inquisitiveness,
> but merely had my soul to quiver in responding—
> and silently, with unconcern, she sought the distance.[13]

During her Volkenshtein period Parnokh treated her poetic speaker differently as well. After being constantly onstage as a living actor in the gymnasium poems, she retreated modestly behind the scenes. Whenever she emerged for a brief appearance, she let her soul upstage her. Parnokh's new spotlight on her soul reflected a serious process of looking inward as well as a fervent desire to bring her soul out into her poetry:

> Perhaps because I wished to fall in love with being
> with so much obstinate avidity,
> I felt more vividly how bottomlessly
> dispassion for it had come over me.
> But what of now? Can I be captivated
> by life in an enraptured rush I do not understand?
> My soul luxuriates in boundless freedom,
> as if inhaling life for the first time.[14]

The theme of the poet's soul, and her (the soul's) separate life both within and alongside the poet's body, proved to be the most creatively productive seed of the many which Parnokh scattered in her Volkenshtein period. The harvest from that soul-seed lay some twenty years in the future, but the poet seemed to sense its potential for creative growth in the lyrical advice she gave herself in this early October 1905 poem:

> Just listen, how amidst inspired dreaming
> the soul will suddenly lay bare its secret curves.
> Let your thought illuminate them brightly
> with creation's breath in an audacious surge.
> You will see, then, how the endless distance
> so easily and wondrously removes its haze,
> and there upon a lofty pedestal of marble
> the depth of worlds feels Beauty's silent gaze.[15]

By the end of the year Parnokh and her actress friend were apparently no longer together, and the poet found herself in more sober company. She was still in Geneva, but now living at the Plekhanovs, the family of the Marxist theoretician, Georgy Plekhanov. They were part of the large Russian expatriate community in Switzerland, which was composed mainly of revolutionaries escaping persecution in Russia.

Although the majority of Parnokh's Petersburg friends, including Volkenshtein, Gnesin, and Yulia Veisberg (a young composer, like Gnesin, in the Rimsky-Korsakov circle), had taken an active part in revolutionary student politics, she herself was not politically engaged. Her Russophilism, an attitude often associated with the Russian right wing, was essentially a matter of personal politics. Ideologies, war, and violence alienated her whether they were promulgated by the tsarist government or later by the Soviet regime. She instinctively saw them as having nothing to do with patriotism, which she considered, characteristically, a form of love that one either had or did not have in one's blood. Perhaps because she did love Russia, she later felt somewhat guilty about spending the fateful year 1905 away from her "native fields" (#95), pursuing the amorous pleasures of her happy, carefree, young life.

52 "LOVE SUMMONS ME, AND I WON'T CONTRADICT HER..."

In mid-December her travels took her to Florence where she went with the Plekhanovs. In the third stanza of the autobiographical poem "Why, oh why from my paternal threshold" (#95), she portrayed this trip as the second of her romantic jaunts with her "fearsome tourguide, love"—

> Why, oh why not earlier, not later,—
> but the day when Presnya was rebelling,
> not a fugitive and not an exile,
> was I walking over Tasso's land? (#95)

The spirit of these lines rather contradicts the reality of travel with the Plekhanovs, whom she described to Volkenshtein as "interesting types, but endlessly boring in actuality."[16] Perhaps she used a little poetic license in the poem so that all her travels would illustrate a pattern she had discerned in her life. Alternatively, she may have had an Italian romance about which nothing is known.

By the middle of January she was back in Geneva and experimenting with new forms of self-expression. A letter to Volkenshtein from this time contained part of a piece called "Dream," which, she wrote, was "something still less finished, but more interesting from my point of view in terms of thought. It's not prose and not verse."[17]

"Dream" narrated an allegory of Parnokh's ongoing interaction with Life. The poetic speaker addresses a woman standing in a crowd of gapers and watching Life, who is "dancing a wild dance." Then the addressee vanishes, and the speaker does not know where she has gone. The lost Other (or self) eventually comes to the sea, to which she screams out her anger as it rolls on "in supreme beauty and dispassionate magnificence." Unfortunately, the remaining pages of the letter that contained the dream's conclusion were lost.

Before leaving for Italy, Parnokh had finally enrolled in the Geneva Conservatory of Music, but her term of study there was shortlived. Something happened in the middle of the spring semester that led her to change her plans radically and return to Russia.

It is possible that general political conditions at home played a role in mandating her return. In the wake of the Presnya rebellion in mid-December, which is generally considered to mark the end of the 1905 Revolution, the tsar began to strike back at the revolutionaries and initiated reprisals against them. In 1906 Volkenshtein became one of hundreds of students expelled from the university for having participated in strikes and disorders. More active radicals were exiled, persecuted, and driven underground or out of Russia. Gradually, Nicholas II retracted most of the constitutional rights he had granted the previous October.

By the beginning of May, if not before, Parnokh was back in Moscow and apparently living with Nadezhda Polyakova in a private house on Tverskoy Boulevard. When she first arrived, she thought of trying to get published in the prestigious symbolist journal *Golden Fleece,* but precisely the symbolist orientation of the poems she read in the journal put her off. Doubts that she could get her poems accepted in such a high-powered journal must also have daunted her. She was not satisfied with her work and seemed to be having a crisis of confidence: "I have only one moment of love for what I write," she confessed to Volkenshtein, "when I imagine what I think as written. But later, after I have already written it, I am dissatisfied, annoyed, or worst of all, indifferent." [18]

Her dissatisfaction stemmed in large part, ironically, from her almost religious awe of words. They seemed to her to be something "precious and dangerous"—so much so that she felt as if she were committing a sin "to speak them without seeking, i.e., without first having gone through all the anxieties of looking for the right ones." [19]

She also turned to Gnesin for advice and criticism in her initial efforts to get published. At the end of May she sent him two poems, one of which expressed her lyrical predicament: her intense creative desire usually ended in silence for want of her own words:

> I so want to reflect my whole soul in my words,
> I so want to discover them in my soul's depths,
> what they say should not be accidental.
> But my impulse for searching's rebelliously-weak—
> I lack know-how in finding my words,
> and that's why I have made my soul subject to silence,
> and I hear in the silence her ebbings and flowings—
> I so want to shout out—I don't dare to.[20]

As summer came on, the general state of things grew worse. Parnokh and Polyakova were still in Moscow and did not know if they could manage to get away somewhere to the country.[21] Nor had they decided where to go. They were considering a trip to Poltava province "if nothing interfered," but something apparently did come up that canceled even these vague plans, and in June Parnokh suddenly returned alone to her "paternal threshold" in Taganrog.

Before she left Moscow, she reconsidered the possibility of publishing in *Golden Fleece* and asked Polyakova to go to the editorial offices of the journal and find out if they were interested in a few of her poems and a translation she had done of a French article on Ibsen. Polyakova's mission ended in defeat. The head of the literary section told her that the journal did not accept translations from the French. During their conversation Volkenshtein's name came up, and the editor launched into an attack on his poetry and called it unoriginal, banal versifying. After that, Polyakova decided that nothing was to be expected from *Golden Fleece* and left without showing the editor Parnokh's poems.[22]

The news of this first publishing defeat reached Parnokh in Taganrog. Although she had not seen her father for over a year, his reception of her was far less than a wished-for homecoming, and their difficult relations resumed where they had left off. "In my father's eyes," she wrote to Volkenshtein, "I'm just a crazy, wayward girl and nothing more. My way of thinking and my tastes offend his patriarchal virtues and he condescends to me."[23] Yakov Solomonovich defended his "patriarchal virtues" by putting Sonya on a strict and reduced allowance.

After the freedom and glamour of Europe, and the pleasures of life with Polyakova in Moscow, Taganrog must truly have seemed to Parnokh a lonely and provincial hell. She summed up what it felt like to live at home that summer by quoting to Volkenshtein two lines from an epigram he had once written about her father's apothecary: "But there is silence all around, a customer is heard / Abruptly entering the drugstore to buy himself a purge."[24]

Parnokh used her Taganrog captivity to make a serious effort to get published. She was motivated in part by wanting to prove to her father that she was not the crazy wayward girl he took her for, and in part by the need to earn some money to supplement her small allowance. Her unhappy experience with *Golden Fleece* had convinced her that it was impossible for an unknown provincial poet even to think of getting published without personal contacts. Since Volkenshtein was a member of the permanent staff of the Petersburg *Journal for Everyone,* she turned to him for advice and assistance in approaching the editor, Viktor Mirolyubov.

She had decided to break into print with her poem "Life," and when she sent it to Volkenshtein at the end of June for his preliminary criticism, she had made a second, important decision: "If Mirolyubov accepts it, have him print it under my name—Sophia Parnok (I detest the letter *kh*)."[25] Her reason for choosing her pseudonym appears whimsical unless her parenthetical comment about detesting the letter *kh* had esoteric meaning for her and Vladimir. The fact that she bothered to give any explanation for such a minor change, however, suggests that it had significance for her, a significance, moreover, that she may not have wished to discuss, even with her best friend.

Women writers do not choose their pseudonyms idly, and it would be an error to dismiss Parnok's as merely caprice, or worse, an attempt to hide her Jewishness, as some critics have suggested.[26] In deciding to write under a pseudonym, Parnokh was "creating an alter ego, another possibility of female destiny."[27] Her need for this other possibility had arisen from her father's paternalistic condescension to her creativity. It is significant that she considered her pen name to be *her* name as well as a name that distinguished her from her father and her chosen destiny from the destiny he wanted her to follow. At the same time, her pen name was as much her father's name as hers could be while still being different from his, almost as if she were accepting as her own everything of her father's except the final guttural element that she detested.

Like the typical neophyte, Parnok was obsessed over the proper forms to be followed in submitting her poem for publication. She asked Volkenshtein for detailed instructions as to what she should write in her cover letter to Mirolyubov, whom she should address in the letter, how she should address him, and even how she should address the envelope. More importantly, she added, "It goes without saying that I won't send Mirolyubov a single poem that has not got your preliminary okay."[28] Volkenshtein responded by essentially rewriting her poem (his edited version of "Life" is unfortunately not extant). This put Parnok in a quandary: "My poem in your edited version," she replied, "is incomparably more finished, but I don't know if it's still mine. I don't think it is, and therefore I can't make up my mind to send it to Mirolyubov."[29]

The poem "Life" never did appear in print. Either Parnok decided not to submit it, or she did and it was rejected. In the end, the first poem she succeeded in publishing was a nature lyric, "The Autumn Garden," that appeared in November:

> In mournful luxury of trees that have been gilded,
> in tiredness of branches bent without a quiver
> is Autumn's quietude. Deserted and so pale
> the distance that has dimmed; and in the night the play
> of stars is cold; and a discerning silence
> stands guard, or so it seems, to see if some weak sobbing

will not break out, a last enfeebled groan
from fading foliage. The air, though, is made thick
with fog ... and it appears that the exhausted garden
wants to sigh, but doesn't dare; and strangely blazes
among the tree-tops, colorlessly gold,
a single ruby leaf, as if with blood engorged.[30]

The autumn garden that wants to sigh but doesn't dare sounds like the poetic speaker of "I am still, for I fear," who wanted to shout out, but also lacked the courage to do so.

Nature lyrics similar to "The Autumn Garden" were fairly numerous in Parnok's verse until 1916, and certain trees (poplars, birches), flowers (roses, tuberoses, carnations), and natural phenomena (rivers, sandbars, wind, storms, snow and ice, intense heat, night) remained constant motifs throughout all her poetry. She believed, however, that her view of nature was another thing that alienated her from "normal" experience. She was chronically ill (with Grave's disease, evidently) from her youth and despaired that she had never and could never perceive nature with the eyes of a healthy person.[31] Possibly her lyrical fondness for autumn and her emphasis on nature's feebleness, tiredness, and withering reflected her empathy with the aspect of nature that seemed to externalize her frequent symptoms of exhaustion, muscular weakness, and emaciation.

In 1906, however, Parnok's health was far from being her major creative issue. Rather, she continued to doubt that she could find words to express what seemed inexpressible:

How can one write about the quiet fading
of vivid rushes deep within one's soul?
About how thought, far off in sunless exile,
in morbid meditation or joyless sleep
looks lifelessly inside herself, exhausted,
and slowly drowns in her own feebleness,
how can one write?
How can one write—about the golden-textured
ray thrown lazily upon the emerald waves?

58   "LOVE SUMMONS ME, AND I WON'T CONTRADICT HER . . ."

> The play of hues on strange and wondrous sea shells
> and lightning's whimsy, and the thought of thunderclouds.
> The loving tuberose's drunken fever,
> and the weeping willow's lonely tears—
> how can one write?!³²

The three last lines of this poem may have encoded significance. The "loving tuberose" probably alludes to Nadezhda, whom the poet had associated with tuberoses in her juvenile love lyric, "Love has gone. The tuberoses have faded" (J-31). This suggests that the "weeping willow" represented the poetic speaker here, as it would occasionally in much later poems. Thus, Parnok addressed indirectly the issue of writing her lesbian love affair into her poetry as part of the general problem of finding words for the inexpressible.

Because she shied away from direct treatment of her sexuality in her poems of this time, it is difficult to find such allusions to her continuing relationship with Polyakova (or to any other love affairs she may have had after she graduated from the gymnasium). Nadya, however, would appear to be the lover-addressee of this undated, unpublished love lyric from 1905–6:

> I know profoundly well—you've shown me everything,
> the breathing of the skies, and speech of mighty billows
> and twinkling of the stars within the depths of air,
> and lightning's vivid laugh in gloomy quietude
> you've given me with you in brilliant consonance.

This brief poem could be read as the poet's unconscious reply to her own query of how to write the unwritable, for it shows her underlying realization that she was writing about the inexpressible when she wrote with the knowledge she had received through the body of her woman-lover.

Highly sexed and easily aroused, the poetic speaker of Parnok's early love lyrics cannot resist the temptation of love, no matter what suffering and loss she knows each new love will inevitably bring her, as she makes clear at the end of the poem, "Soon the leaves of the green poplars."

So let that farewell cry, as always, sound above me!
I have a heart so that it can be broken!
I know too well that last, that grievous moment,
when happiness can't help but be forsaken—
but through the garden joyfully I'll go!
So what if a new loss lies in my future,
—My heart's so happy in its secret fever:
love summons me, and I won't contradict her.

Repeatedly, the poet-lover feels she cannot control or controvert her need for love, and therefore she "does not love love because [her] powerful and willful thought is submissive to love, and submission is alien to her [thought]." An impassioned reader of Nietzsche, like so many of her generation, Parnok believed her thought was both a creative and quintessentially destructive force that had to murder ruthlessly all "phantoms" that threatened her. The one "phantom" the poet's Thought could not destroy was Love, because only Love equaled her Thought in strength and implacable desire. This poem, "I do not love love," and Parnok's early verse in general, reveals that while the poet conceived of her creative Thought as wholly female, she represented Love as polymorphous ("eternally dressed in something new") and androgynous—a female being ("love" is a feminine noun in Russian) with a concealed (phallic) weapon:

Oh love! You stand before me, and I'm afraid of you.
I know inside your breast you hide a gleaming dagger,
you'll wound my thought with it and thus renew yourself,
to give to drink with blood your living body—[33]

The sexual fantasy underlying this poem expressed the female poetic speaker's attraction to and fear of a rapacious female vampire.

In real life Nadezhda Polyakova was the first lover to make Parnok's Thought submissive to her for a long period of time. She was the young musing poet's first "guiding Genius/Demon," the first woman who put Parnok "in Touch with her Creative Spirit," provoking her to want to find a way of expressing her sexuality in poetry and yet to despair of expressing it. Nadezhda was also, paradoxically, the first lover and muse who almost convinced Parnok that love was fatal to her creative thought (when virtually the opposite was true). In view of Polyakova's importance in Parnok's emotional and creative life, it is indeed unfortunate that so little is known and knowable about her, including the circumstances that finally led to the breaking of her spell over the poet, sometime, one supposes, in the early part of 1907.[34]

Parnok felt very bitter in the aftermath of this love affair. Several months after Polyakova and she broke up, the poet was riding home in a cab from a store in Taganrog and happened to catch sight of her ex-lover. Polyakova returned her glance briefly and quickly shifted her eyes, pretending not to have seen her and to be immersed in reading the shop signs. The women did not say hello. "Just think," Parnok wrote Volkenshtein, "and that's what I gave up five years of my life to."[35]

Her bitterness over the failure of this relationship must only have made her home situation more unbearable and her financial dependency on her father more oppressive. "Things are very bad for me, Vovochka, in my father's house," she complained in a letter to Volkenshtein at the end of May 1907. "I arrived yesterday morning; I've been here a whole twenty-four hours and have not exchanged a single word with my father, not a single word. He's probably afraid I'll ask him for money.... I feel just as awful here as I did two years ago."[36]

As far as Parnok was concerned, her father was tight-fisted, but she must have realized that his stinginess toward her was in part punitive. He had obviously had enough of supporting her in a way of life that offended him and which he now realized was not a "passing phase." When Sonya could not be persuaded to give up her "tastes," he began threatening to cut her off entirely if she did not marry and settle down.

It was time for her to do some serious thinking about what she wanted to do with her life. She was twenty-two years old and had accomplished almost nothing. She had plenty of pride, but no particular ambition and no academic or intellectual aspirations. She wanted to be a poet, but lacked confidence in her talent. Besides, she was constantly undermining her own efforts with self-criticism that came, she supposed, from her sense of good taste. She had experienced enough rejections to realize that it would not be easy for her to break into mainstream Russian poetry. Taganrog offered no possibility for creative stimulation, her family gave her no support, and living with her father and stepmother had become impossible.

Now that Polyakova was out of her life, the only person who seemed to care about her was Volkenshtein. He was very fond of her, maybe he even loved her—at any rate, he had made it clear that he would like to marry her. He knew her fairly well, seemed not to mind about her "tastes," and probably wouldn't interfere with that side of her life provided she was discreet.

Sonya liked Vladimir and respected him. He was very intelligent and some of his poems appealed to her. Perhaps she could inspire him; perhaps she had something he needed. They thought alike about most of the important things, had many friends in common, and had almost grown up together. Wouldn't living with him simply continue and maybe even deepen their friendship? And she would be in Petersburg, meet interesting and talented people, make new friends, and be at the center of things.

True, she was not in love with him. She had never been in love with any man, although her natural ebullience with men had sometimes made them think she was interested in them romantically. Gnesin had once thought so, as recently as the end of the previous summer. No, she had only been in love with women. But she was very fond of Vladimir, and the idea of intimacy with him did not put her off. And besides, she would like to have a child. . . .

• • •

All things considered, getting married seemed the best thing she could do at this particular time. It would insure her some emotional support, provide an escape from her father, and make happy her siblings, Valya and Liza, who, she always thought, had been uncomfortable about Polyakova, although they did not really know what that was all about. Most important, it would be a chance for a new life that might, finally, give her a focus.

In September 1907 Parnok and Volkenshtein were married in a Jewish ceremony. Shortly afterward they were invited by one of Vladimir's acquaintances, the writer and critic Lyubov Gurevich, for a visit to her country estate in Revyakino. They were joined there by Mikhail and Nadezhda Gnesin, who had been married in June and had recently returned from their honeymoon in Bavaria.

Lyubov Gurevich was nearly twenty years Parnok's senior and came from the same generation of Russian women intellectuals as the poet's mother. To a limited degree, she played a maternal role in Parnok's emotional life. More important, she became an intellectual mother for the young poet, and one who wielded authority. A committed feminist and political activist, Gurevich was "the most important female journalist in Russian history [and] a vital presence in Petersburg's *fin de siècle* intellectual life."[37]

Gurevich's personal life was also considered to be unorthodox—she never married, but had a daughter, Yelena, to whom she gave her surname. Parnok, who apparently learned after her marriage that she could not, to her despair, have children, took a maternal interest in Gurevich's daughter and was inspired by her to write children's fairy tales.

The motherless poet herself developed an immediate daughterly attraction to Lyubov Yakovlevna. Like a young girl, Parnok wanted the older woman to pay attention to her and to find her more interesting than Volkenshtein. Her desire for Gurevich's attention made her reserved and unlike her naturally expansive self. As she later admitted to Lyubov Yakovlevna, she felt jealously competitive with Vladimir: "It seemed to me that you found his company more pleasant and interesting than mine, and that made me miserable. It's stupid, but I remember having a long, diplomatic conversation with Sophia Isaakovna [Chatskina] in order to try to find out whom you liked better, Volodya or me, and I was as agitated as a schoolgirl,—the first case of jealous rivalry in my life."[38]

As Parnok had expected, her circle of acquaintances and literary contacts broadened considerably after she settled in the capital. Among her literary society friends she counted Sophia Chatskina, who, together with her husband, Yakov Saker, a well-known lawyer, presided over one of the most brilliant literary salons of Petersburg. In the prewar period, Chatskina and Saker were co-owners and co-editors of the liberal literary journal *Northern Annals*. Parnok was also introduced to many of the leading poets of the period—Alexander Blok, Mikhail Kuzmin, Vyacheslav Ivanov, Fyodor Sologub, and Maximilian Voloshin. She later became especially friendly with Voloshin, and their friendship lasted until the end of his life. She also occasionally went to Ivanov's Tower, more for the spectacle than the poetry, and made the acquaintance of the young Anna Akhmatova, who was only just beginning to appear in Petersburg poetic circles.

Volkenshtein encouraged his wife to pursue her education. In 1908 she attended the Bestuzhev Higher Courses for Women at St. Petersburg University. At first, she thought about studying in the history and philology department, but she switched to the faculty of jurisprudence, not because she had any interest in law, but because "like many people at that time, [she] wanted a higher education that would not put excessive demands on her."[39] Although she felt insecure about her lack of education, she continued to have little desire for serious study and confessed to her husband in a letter that she was "not used to studying alone" and hoped to find "a diligent woman student to study with. To be frank," she concluded, "I am not keen on being a student and am doing so from a sense of obligation."[40]

Married life turned out to be not quite what she had expected. She continued not to be in love with her husband, but found that she was sexually responsive to him. Her active participation in conjugal relations must have flattered Volkenshtein's masculine vanity, but it may also have surprised and confused him. Aware (and accepting) of his wife's lesbian preference, he may not have anticipated or inwardly even have desired her more than passive participation in their sexual relationship. Problems could also have arisen because Parnok might have been more sexually experienced than her husband. She was accustomed, moreover, to playing the initiating, traditionally "masculine" role in sex. One incident reveals the gender-role challenges and complexities that their intimate relations called into play. At some point in the brief marriage, Volkenshtein apparently fell ill with a nervous disorder and was told by his doctor to refrain from sex. When he wrote Parnok of the necessity for abstinence until he recovered, she responded with her characteristic mixture of frankness, gallantry, and sincere comradely feeling: she offered to move out of the house temporarily so as not to be a temptation to him.

Indeed, good fellowship seems to have been what Parnok most desired and needed in her intimacy with her husband and with male friends in general, whom she appears to have responded to at times without conveying any consciousness that they belonged to the opposite sex. This evidently confused her male friends, some of whom mistook her lack of "feminine" reserve as a sign of sexual forwardness.

Volkenshtein was most likely Parnok's only male sexual partner. The handful of heterosexual love lyrics she wrote (all of them published in her first book, *Poems*), as well as scattered lyrical allusions to men as lovers, are probably based on her experience with him. Her poems suggest that however willingly or actively she had engaged in marital relations, sex with her husband did not satisfy her or answer her need for intensity, "splendor, and fatefulness in a romance" (#39). In a few of her poems, her female poetic speaker notes that men, especially young men, are typically impatient and finish too quickly to be good lovers.

The previously quoted 1912–13 poem, "In a romance I like" (#39), offers Parnok's most clearly expressed view of the shortcomings of a heterosexual relationship, perhaps of hers with Volkenshtein. The female speaker's coupling with her male lover seems to her to belie the feeling of true conjugality that she has experienced, by implication, with women. After "clinging to one another," the speaker notes that she always remained "alone" and so did her male addressee. At the end of the poem she makes her point: "And is there a mystery more boring than ours and simpler: / the nonmerging of one soul [feminine noun] with another soul [feminine noun] beloved by her." The implication is that the merging of two souls in sexual union is the antithesis to what happens between the separate woman and separate man in the poem and can in the poet's mind (and in her grammar) take place only between two women.

As far as Parnok was concerned, the mutually stressful emotional complexities and shortcomings of namely her sexual relationship with Volkenshtein gradually undermined and damaged their friendship irreparably. Later, in trying to explain the problems in the marriage to Gurevich, she wrote euphemistically: "All those feelings and experiences that are inevitable in conjugal life were utterly superfluous and harmful for us both and for our relationship."[41]

Socially, married life also turned out to cut both ways. Surrounded by educated, artistic people who "spoke [her] language," Parnok felt herself become somewhat spoiled by a pleasant and made-to-order social life that demanded no effort from her. On the other hand, it left her with very little free time to devote to any serious pursuit of her own. This was debilitating because she lacked the self-discipline to make time for herself.[42]

Contrary to her expectations, after her marriage her writing began to slacken off. She later attributed part of the problem to her own lack of ambition, and part to being married to a "smart husband" and a poet who had more ambition and vocation than she:

> I have so little ambition that only if I were to become the ambition of some other person and that person's vocation were to make me the biggest thing possible, only in that case would I become more ambitious; with Vladimir Mikhailovich my last drop of ambition vanished. I was more occupied with what he was writing than with my own work; while I need the sort of person, who with himself could have helped me to feel myself, my strengths, my will, my personality.... I think if I found someone like that, I would be happy.[43]

Marriage obviously did not provide Parnok the best soil for cultivating her lesbian muse. Since the time when she had begun looking to Volkenshtein for advice and direction, that muse had been virtually silent except through the mediated language of allegory, but unexpectedly, she spoke softly and distinctly in two of four lyrics Parnok published in the spring of 1908. These two poems suggest that the poet had or wanted affairs with women while she was married, and that these relationships nurtured what little poetic "ambition" she possessed. The poems also heralded the reappearance of the poetic speaker whom Parnok had created for herself in her juvenilia, the desiring (or yearning) female subject who expresses herself in direct address to the woman she desires, or who desires her.

In "I'm afraid of my heart as never before," the female speaker both wants to start a relationship with her addressee and yet, does not dare to. She feels oppressed by her fate of not being able to love, or live, without ruining the lives of others—thus, she advises her would-be lover to steer clear of her:

> Of everything I've said
> just one thing's worth believing,
> Begone! . . . Let my desire, tormenting me alone,
> die out in stern unreciprocity.[44]

In "Look—the moon, a weaveress of wiles," which appeared in June, the speaker describes a moonlit walk with a female companion that ends in an erotically suggestive nature image of "mossy paths that twine in and out as they creep into the sleepy center" of a grove of trees.[45]

In the spring Gurevich invited Parnok to coedit a Russian translation of Baudelaire's *Petits poèmes en prose*. The translation represented a joint effort of several women translators in Petersburg, including Sophia Chatskina. Parnok, who knew French perfectly and adored Baudelaire, evidently translated several of the pieces herself. The names of the translators, following standard practice at the time, did not appear in the book.

Late that spring Parnok began suffering digestive problems, frequent in cases of Grave's disease. Her doctor prescribed a special diet of milk products and a complete rest in the country. She and Vladimir rented a dacha in Sorochintsy, a village in the Mirgorod district of Poltava province, Ukraine. This was a part of Ukraine celebrated in the early stories of Nikolai Gogol, and Parnok was not unaware of the area's literary fame. Although she appreciated the peace and beauty of the countryside on the banks of the Dniepr River, the locale did not captivate her as she had thought it would from Gogol's descriptions.

She tried assiduously to remove any and all "obstacles to good digestion." She and Vladimir led a lazy country life, relaxing, walking barefoot, "thoroughly going to seed," and entertaining, in classic Russian fashion, a steady stream of guests. At the end of July, her brother and sister, both of them about to enter their last year at the gymnasium, came for a visit. "My brother and sister have arrived," she wrote Gurevich on July 22, "I love them so much, they're amusing and extremely dear to me. My brother writes poems *à la Blok* while my sister has the same opinion of poetry as Lev Tolstoy; hence, some very entertaining clashes."[46]

At the beginning of the summer the Baudelaire project had run into all sorts of difficulties. The publisher who had originally agreed to do the translations backed out. Another publisher indicated an interest but did not pay the translators the advance the first one had agreed to. This particularly upset Parnok since she had borrowed money from Gurevich against the advance she had counted on receiving. Gurevich, moreover, had decided to edit the translations without remuneration, so Parnok, painfully aware of her lack of a literary name, felt she could not ask for money either. The whole thing had turned into a headache for both women, and Parnok later referred to it as her "unfortunate experience with Baudelaire."[47]

She greatly missed Gurevich over the summer and expressed affection and longing for her in her letters. At one point she wrote: "It would be good if you and I lived in Moscow; I've been dreaming of Moscow for a long time. If only we could make a trip there together. I'd like to very much."[48]

Parnok was feeling very dissatisfied with herself. She was not doing much work. Her reading did not go beyond Hans Christian Andersen's fairy tales, and the only thing she was working on were rhymed fairy tales for children. Gurevich wrote trying to encourage her young friend to work, to which Parnok replied:

> I'm in a very difficult situation. I'm not reading anything and I know how dangerous that is for me, more dangerous than for anyone else. I'm way too much of a Jew for my work to be naive. If I do have a natural gift, then it's the kind I won't be able to develop without education. But I began thinking seriously about becoming a poet before I had read almost anything. My taste has been developed at the expense of everything else. The things I should have read I can't read now, they bore me. I'm emotionally and morally much older than a beginning writer needs to be. I could devote myself only to what conforms to my moral-emotional disposition. And the results are pale and anemic. If there is a thought in what I write, it is nurtured by nothing except itself. And one fine day one finds oneself without a penny to one's name and writing fairy tales and nothing else. My taste is sufficiently developed for me to know precisely what I should want, and that's about all I have going for me. I'd be

better off without it. It's a sad spectacle and one which will not inspire you to save me. I think only disappointment lies in store for you. Dear Lyubov Yakovlevna! I have no idea why I've written you all this. I still won't accomplish anything. You see the depths to which I've sunk. I'm ashamed that I'm writing you all this, and I think I have because your attitude to me makes me endlessly happy and I can't understand why precisely you are so well-disposed to me. Perhaps it's merely because you think better of me than I am.[49]

The day after her twenty-third birthday, Parnok wrote another letter of self-criticism to Gurevich. Until recently, she wrote, she felt she had lived an utterly passive intellectual existence, as if she were the proverbial "empty box that one has only to stand somewhere and in a few days someone will throw something into it." Her only point of pride was that she had at least freed herself "from [her] own and other people's trash," but her "triumphant" emptiness made her indifferent and, consequently, lazy. She knew that the time had come for her to take responsibility for her life: "There comes a moment when one has to focus, or else one never will be focused. I hope I haven't let that moment slip by."[50]

Parnok anticipated that the winter ahead would prove both "difficult and important" for her. She planned to pursue an intensive program of reading and writing, but decided that first she had to "get hold of [her] life from the other side."[51] The "other side" could have included being in a marriage that was killing her ambition and bringing increasingly less inspiration and gratification to both her and her husband.

By the summer of 1908 Gurevich had become an intellectual and personal role model for Parnok, a new chance for "salvation," and the older woman's charisma had obviously outstripped Vladimir's. Gurevich also represented a female survivor whom life had not beaten down. "Dear Lyubov Yakovlevna!" Parnok concluded her July 31 letter, "I'm endlessly grateful to you for your letter; it is extraordinarily important for me to know that after such a complicated life as you have had, you exist as the woman you are.

I don't know anyone who is better and dearer than you. I am very fond of you. Write me. I kiss you firmly, your S. Parnok."

For the remainder of the summer Parnok wrote almost nothing, and commented in a note to Gnesin (August 3) that she didn't feel like writing. Her silence continued into the fall and early winter, which brought the difficulties she had anticipated. She and Vladimir began to quarrel, and the "struggle of wills" between them drained her energies. She began to sense that Vladimir did not need her after all, that there was nothing she could do for him. She could not inspire him, or, as she later wrote, "make a library out of [herself]," and he "did not need moral inspiration."[52] At the same time, she sensed that her own needs were not being met by a husband who was absorbed in his own creative process.

Things suddenly and unexpectedly came to a head in the first month of the new year. As she had the previous year, Parnok went to Moscow for the Christmas holidays. She wrote her husband from there on January 8, apparently with the intention of returning to St. Petersburg shortly, since she mentioned her plan of finding someone to study with once she arrived home. Yet during the next two weeks something happened in Moscow that made her decide not only *not* to return, but to leave her husband and ask him for a divorce. In her long, explanatory letter to Gurevich of February 2, she did not give any details, but simply said, "Here, after lengthy reflection, I made up my mind not to return; I did not simply *remain*. I *decided* to make a new start." This "new start" may have involved either a new relationship with a woman, or the revival of an old one—with Nadezhda Polyakova. Volkenshtein believed his wife had left him either for a specific woman or for the freedom to live an unfettered lesbian life.

Parnok had no illusions about the social censure her decision would provoke: "I know that my leaving you won't bring me anything good in the sense of public opinion," she wrote Volkenshtein on January 25, "but I also know very well that as soon as I have my first real success, everyone who has turned their backs to me will turn again and acknowledge me with polite smiles on their faces. Therefore, I really don't care whether I see their backs or their faces."[53] She began her new life by taking a room in a residential hotel on the Petrovka, called, ironically enough, the Hotel Decadence.

Gurevich must have heard of her young friend's decision from Parnok's other Petersburg friends or from Volkenshtein himself. Knowing the high regard Parnok had for Gurevich, they, or he, might have hoped that Lyubov Yakovlevna could try to persuade Parnok to reconsider and come home. Unfortunately, Gurevich's letter is not extant, but from Parnok's reply, it is clear that the older woman did express certain qualms about the poet's action. She wondered if Parnok were not just a "wandering soul" with a hankering for "the element of undefined, slithery impressions and fleeting contacts." In other words, she feared Parnok was incapable of making a commitment to a relationship.

Parnok was overjoyed to receive Gurevich's letter and replied in a spirit of wanting and needing to have Lyubov Yakovlevna understand her:

> There is no one whom I could value more than you and whose good feeling could be dearer to me than yours. Ever since I made your acquaintance, in moments of the most interminable emptiness that overcomes me when I'm in the company of people close to me and not, the consciousness that you exist makes me feel grateful (namely grateful, I don't know what else to call it) to you, and more to the person you are, than for anything you've done, which I can't define. I've thought about writing you several times in order *to answer to you* so that you would interpret my action in the right way, but each time I stopped myself with the thought that I didn't know if you would ask me although I felt as if you already had asked, or even if you hadn't, I had to answer namely to you.[54]

The marriage had foundered, Parnok went on to explain, because she had found it impossible to reconcile her will with her husband's. "This struggle (in the broadest sense of the word, of course) consumed way too much of my energy for me not to reject it out of a sense of *self-preservation*." She had also begun to chafe under Volkenshtein's literary authority, which hampered her own creative development. "If I had stayed with Vladimir Mikhailovich, I would have dabbled in writing forever, but now I will either write, or give up writing entirely; it's better this way." In leaving her husband, she had quite simply taken a risky but necessary and courageous step toward becoming her own person.

In answer to Gurevich's doubts about her ability to make a commitment, she replied that she did desire committed companionship, but had not found it yet. "I've wasted a lot of time and energy on searching [for the right person], and now I want to try and see if I won't profit more from the company of books with which I've had little contact."

Her health had been worrying her greatly, and she considered it the crucial factor in the success of her new start. From this time on her poor health became a recurrent theme in her correspondence and later in her poetry, as she suffered periodically from tachycardia, nervousness, depression, headaches, digestive disorders, and insomnia.[55]

In *answering to* Gurevich, Parnok had separated from her adopted mother and asserted the integrity of her own life. As a result, the women's relationship changed in the direction of true collegiality. Gurevich welcomed the change and began to be more open about her own needs, professional concerns, and especially creative doubts. Earlier, Parnok had felt too insecure and uneducated by comparison with her famous friend to presume to comment on her work. But Gurevich's reply to her letter of explanation encouraged her to take the first step toward a new peer relationship in the creative sphere:

> My dear, dear, most esteemed Lyubov Yakovlevna, I've never talked with you about your work for fear of being importunate, but now your openness gives me the chance to say what I have thought about it. I had an idea of a new literary form, i.e. of the possibility of your creating it. Here's what I thought: the one thing you need [in your

writing] is space to unfurl your leaves, and for that you need a form which you could feel was least of all a form per se.... It would be endlessly precious to me if you shared with me what you're writing at present, if that's possible, of course. As for me, for the time being I can't get away from fairy tales. I wrote one more; I'm finishing a fourth. Soon I'll have a whole volume. I want to send Lyulya the new fairy tale, for her and your criticism. When I finish my ill-starred story, which little resembles a story, I'll send it to you, with your permission.[56]

In the immediate aftermath of moving to Moscow, Parnok led a fairly reclusive life. The few people she saw regularly and the habit of socializing itself gave her no pleasure and actually made her anxious. As a married woman, she had taken her social life for granted. Being on her own left her with a lot more free time and forced her to take responsibility for her own entertainment. She often found herself alienated from the doings of the famous literati of her time. After attending a meeting of the Literary Artistic Circle, she wrote to Gurevich:

> A splendid assortment—all the poets and philosophers with their facial tics. Andrey Bely was hysterical and positively elegant in his stupidity; Krechetov has a forehead no higher than a centimeter. Out of respect, Abramovich arranged to have a tic on his face too, Berdyaev's tongue was hanging out of his mouth; everything smacked of scrofula and onanism. Ivanov compared Blok with Nekrasov; it would all have been funny if it weren't so disgusting. To the public's glee it ended with a scandal. I haven't seen any other spectacles, and I won't be going there again. It's disgusting.[57]

Parnok began to work and read more, but continued to feel very pessimistic about her writing. At the end of the winter she sent Gurevich the first poem she had written in a long time:

> Oh mistress Anguish! You, the muse of incantations,
> make one bright moment show from all the recollections
> of my superfluous, unhappy, boring days!
> And that unbounded moment, when, as in a graveyard,
> the soul by the deserted silence is bewitched,
> and cemetery visitors, the pangs of conscience,

will dig the past up from the bottom of all graves—
may you and I be reconciled in that moment,
and may the aimless lot I've drawn be bound with life,
as rainbows brightly unify the earth
with the heavens' inextinguishable blue.[58]

Anguish/Yearning *(toska)* would become a major theme, or even the primary music, in Parnok's poetry. It/She represented a powerful and inspirational female being in the poet's personal mythos. The poem, which was called "Prayer," also contained the first mention of "that last unbounded moment" before death, another recurrent motif in her poetry.

By mid-March she was living much the way she had when she was married, though she felt calmer and "more normal." She still felt she suffered from "an excess of superfluous feelings," however.[59] Apparently she wanted to live on a less emotionally intense level and was dissatisfied with her inability to keep feelings out of her life. "Superfluous feelings" of animosity and reproach also accompanied the intensifying conflict with Volkenshtein over the divorce.

From the beginning, he did not want a divorce, either because he still loved Parnok or wanted to punish her for leaving him. He resorted to various stalling tactics, broke appointments they set up to discuss the terms of divorce, and tried to make things as unpleasant for her as he felt she was making them for him. They argued endlessly about financial arrangements. At the end of March, in a desperate maneuver aimed at trying to turn Parnok's siblings against her, Volkenshtein told Valya and Liza that their older sister was a lesbian and that she had left him to return to Polyakova. Parnok wrote Volkenshtein to assure him that his attempt at emotional blackmail would not have the desired effect:

> I did not anticipate, Volodya, that you would drag the children into our private affairs and upset them for no reason. You won't spoil my relationship with them, all you'll do is make things unnecessarily unpleasant for them. Of course, it's your business, you can do as you please, I'm only expressing my surprise: the children haven't

done anything bad to you, why did you want to upset them? For two weeks they've been miserable because they think I'm back with Polyakova and haven't dared to write me about it.[60]

Embattled in divorce proceedings that became more and more ugly, and that she repeatedly urged Volkenshtein to expedite, Parnok drew closer to Gurevich, if only by mail. She expressed great concern about the older woman's health, urging her to go abroad for a rest and trying to get her to stop smoking. It seemed to Parnok that she loved Gurevich both as an individual and as a "model of a genuine human being," whose good opinion was invaluable to her:

> It is absolutely essential to me that you consider me a good person; in art I stand on firm ground, but in life I need support and you probably don't realize how important your attitude to me is for me. My reasonableness doesn't keep me out of complete chaos, and I need a true and constant guiding light, which is immovable, so that I can see it shining irrepressibly from out of any delusion [I may be in]; even if it's a burden on me at times, I have to have something *to return to*. And the fact that you are not my fantasy, but a real, an actual image—is so new and splendid for me that there hasn't been a moment when I could think of you without enraptured astonishment, and the most respectful affection.[61]

Parnok valued Gurevich as someone "completely honest" who possessed the rare gift of saying exactly what she felt. In the poet's eyes, this distinguished Lyubov Yakovlevna from the majority of people, who "talk[ed] about their feelings exactly in the way they never fe[lt]." Gurevich also embodied Parnok's ideal of genius, which lay, she believed, in a writer's ability to express the simplest feelings in the simplest words, and in so doing, to duplicate "the most artless speech of a human being at those rare moments when she is not thinking of herself." In her mature verse Parnok aimed precisely at such simple, unself-conscious, "artless speech."

At the end of April one of the poet's Petersburg acquaintances paid her a visit on her way through Moscow and told her that all her Petersburg friends already considered her "a woman perished" and had begun offering condolences. At first, this pricked Parnok's vanity, but soon she found herself merely irritated by the thought that any man "could dare to think he was essential to [her] survival." She got to thinking about how her poor health had permanently affected her life. The next day she wrote, movingly, to Gurevich:

> If I were very proud, I would be roused by a desire to prove everyone wrong. And perhaps I am proud, only I lack the physical strength to nurture my pride. You can't imagine what I feel when I see healthy people. I've never envied anyone anything like wealth or success, but I'm madly envious of health. It rivets me irresistibly. And the thought that I couldn't even bear a healthy child from the healthiest man, in a word, that I will never be able to create anything healthy, or big, causes me despair. I don't know if you have experienced the desire to be strong, the kind of woman who could lift any weight, walk for hours without getting tired, and be brutally strong, like a laborer, so that no work would tire her. Sometimes that desire comes over me, and I suffer.[62]

Characteristically, at the end of the letter she apologized for sounding maudlin and morally weak.

In the late spring Volkenshtein at last acceded to Parnok's wish, and the couple was divorced. By that time they had come to hate each other. Although their resentments naturally dissipated over the years, their friendship never revived. As Parnok had feared, marriage had ruined it forever. For her, divorce marked the end of any pretense to a socially acceptable heterosexual, or even bisexual, camouflage, but it also liberated her to new possibilities of a "more normal" life that she would want increasingly to express in her writing. Her process of self-creation proceeded slowly, agonizingly, and, as she would later describe it, "unmiraculously." She knew precisely what she wanted to achieve in her poetry. Her desire and will to achieve it were strong, but it often seemed to her as if the creative organs that would satisfy her desire were crippled, or even lacking, and her "soul rushed about in . . . anguish."[63]

Her soul was not the only part of her seized by restlessness. In the two years after her divorce she quite literally rushed from place to place, changing her address in Moscow five times, thus establishing a pattern of "nomadic existence" that characterized her life until the 1917 Revolution. In part, her frequent moves were a consequence of her straightened circumstances—she lived mainly in transient quarters and furnished rooms. But the nomadic life also clearly suited her disposition at this time and reflected her rebellion against domesticity and "patriarchal virtues" as she gave herself over to alternating bouts of "lechery" (her own word) and monkish celibacy.

She continued to feel annoyed and depressed by her persistent physical weakness. Nevertheless, during the summer of 1909, she indulged her fondness for riverboating, traveling by steamer down the Volga and then going to the Crimea and the Caucasus.[64] Two poems she published the next year appear to have been written under the impact of her experiences there. The first of these Crimean lyrics, "Excerpt," expresses a new dimension to the poet's ongoing affair with Life. The poem contains allusions to Knut Hamsun's best-selling novel *Pan*, which Parnok had read the previous spring and which made her weep, she wrote to Gurevich, "because all of that is inaccessible to me, closed forever, and it never was open. I've never seen nature as it is seen by healthy eyes, and I never will see it that way."[65] The poetic speaker of "Excerpt" is "possessed," as in the past, by the majesty of the mountains (mountains have a similar effect on the hero of Hamsun's *Pan*). She is filled with "jealous yearning" when she ponders the mystery of the "mountains' . . . power over a powerful soul." Her jealousy originates in her envy of healthy, strong people; unlike them, she feels trapped in the restricted capacity of her body as if she is enclosed "in a small box imported from the East." She imagines how "simple" and "intoxicating" the awareness of lightness and health must be, and then ponders the "strange duel given [her] by life . . . [and] the acute silence of [her] already harvested fields, where Death roams softly and hides in a gully."

Life seems to be standing in front of the vanquished speaker "like an unquaffed cup," despite the fact that her "deeply open, sad eyes" are "already drunk on the anguish of all passions." Her only comfort comes from the knowledge that "all is vain—both life and death."[66]

The other poem from this period with faint Crimean overtones was "Romance," which appeared in the June 1910 issue of the *New Journal for Everyone*. The third of Parnok's "how-can-one-say" poems, it is addressed to an Asian or Eurasian beloved and attempts to express in lyrical form the urgent creative issue of the relationship between the poet's sexuality and her creativity:

> In words, in their cold interlacing,
> your movements' melody and pacing
> how can I say?
> Your raptures' whims, your passion's slumber,
> your power, and the way you tremble
> can I convey?
> The misty North has not made cooler
> your mouth's vermilion, or your golden,
> deep suntan's stream;
> the sun's warmth, live and animating,
> flows on in you without abating,
> my very dream.
> All of the East's intoxications
> I drink in the deep undulations
> of your night eyes.
> Your spicy smell, can I convey it?
> My drunken heart, how shall I say it?
> Oh love of mine!

Although the form, imagery, and language of this poem remained conventional, it was an improvement over the first two in this series because here Parnok succeeded in giving concrete expression to something inexpressible that was specific to her "moral-emotional disposition" as a lesbian and a poet of love. The poetic speaker of "Romance" asks not only how she can put her love into words (all poets face that problem), but also how she can convey her specific female lover's sensual allure for her with a poetic language that has no words for her kind of love ("Oh love of mine!") and denies it a name in poetry.

Parnok's romance continued into the fall and early winter in "the misty North." The poet evidently spent several months in St. Petersburg and returned to Moscow and the Hotel Decadence only at the beginning of 1910. There, at the end of January, she read an article of Gurevich's (on the popular dramatist Leonid Andreyev) and suddenly "felt the upsurge of a creative mood, something that had completely abandoned [her] for such a long time." It seemed to her that her friendship with Lyubov Yakovlevna had deepened: "When I read you, I think what happiness it is that I know you, that I see behind the lines your so beguilingly intelligent, honest, stern eyes, and I am seized by the hugest hopes. Don't forget me, my dear, my endlessly precious friend *[drug]*—you will allow me to call you that, won't you?"⁶⁷

Gurevich's new importance to Parnok was not lost on Gnesin, who himself aspired to the role of Parnok's chief mentor and "serious" friend in the aftermath of her divorce. Gnesin condescended to Parnok's platonic friendships with women, and when Parnok mentioned her "very friendly correspondence" with Gurevich, he scoffed at it, saying, "You probably just write each other all sorts of nonsense," by which he meant personal rather than "useful" things. Parnok tolerated his patronizing attitude because she needed his friendship, too. Their relationship was complicated, however, and had in the past endured ambiguous moments caused by Gnesin's consternation at Parnok's lack of restraint and desire for nonromantic intimacy with him, and by his unacknowledged ambivalence to her lesbianism. Her sexuality both titillated and disturbed him. He appeared to encourage her personal confessions while chiding her for wasting her time writing him "frivolous" letters about personal problems. At the same time he flattered himself that her desire to confide in him indicated a romantic interest in him.

At the beginning of February, Parnok was going through a bad time emotionally. Needing a shoulder to cry on, she wrote to Gnesin "in a foul mood." She acknowledged that the reasons for the mess she was in would probably make Gnesin "wrinkle [his] brow" in distaste at her "complete *U-turn*." Probably she was alluding to her turn away from heterosexuality after her divorce, or her turn back to a nonmonogamous way of life. She did not want her letters about her personal affairs to upset or scare him with the thought that she desired a more intimate relationship with *him*. In order to end the ambiguity, she proceeded to come out to Gnesin gently, but in no uncertain terms:

> Dear Mikhail Fabianovich, you once told me that you thought I was in love with you; probably because my letters seemed too personal to you; don't think it now either, for goodness sake. Volodya once told me that when I really like a person, I talk with him in a way that a man might dare to think I was in love with him. I have never, unfortunately, been in love with a man, and so I don't know how I would talk if I were, and whether Volodya was right. I am very fond of you and think of you with great affection, and besides that, my personal affairs have made me sad at the moment; that's why I'm writing you this letter, my first useless one. I beg you, for goodness sake, not to think I am in love with you because I know that if you imagined that, you could get scared, or not want to write to me, and I desperately wouldn't want that to happen.[68]

The muddle in Parnok's personal life ended in a major depression that proved impossible to talk about. Then her health broke down, and she was ill for several weeks. By mid-April, she wrote to Gnesin that she felt "awful, and not in the mood for verses or vice."[69] She could not be more forthcoming in a letter, she explained, because he generally responded in a way that made her feel that everything that was most important and sad for her seemed not significant enough to tell him about.

In April, much to her relief, she finally moved out of the Hotel Decadence and took a room until the beginning of the summer in a house on Krivokolenny Lane. After a three-month silence, she wrote to Gurevich and apologized for not having written for so long:

> I've had so much trouble and sadness in my personal life that I simply lacked the strength not only to write, but even to talk. I know that many people make confessions to you, and I don't blame those who do because I too have experienced your irresistible attractiveness, but you aren't to blame for being a magnet to people's hearts, and I'm sparing you.[70]

Parnok evidently felt constrained even with Gurevich, although with Lyubov Yakovlevna, she at least did not have to justify or belittle the significance of her emotions.

Very gradually, her poems were beginning to appear in the more prestigious journals. She was pleased that *Messenger of Europe* apparently intended to publish her work. After "Excerpt," she had three more poems accepted there. The first appeared in the June issue and was one of the first of several lyrics she wrote throughout her life in which her poetic speaker fell under the spell of a woman's voice. In the last two lines the speaker expressed a cherished wish, to die to the sound of her beloved's voice, a wish she echoed in several future lyrics: "Sing to me! I could listen, listen constantly, / and quietly expire, to your elated voice." The previous winter Gurevich had mentioned Parnok to Peter Struve, the eminent editor of the journal *Russian Thought,* and he apparently encouraged the poet to submit something, which caused her to enthuse to Lyubov Yakovlevna at the end of January, "Struve seems to me like the good fairy in a very pleasant fairy tale. Suddenly she appears and asks, 'Do you want to be tsar?' And the next day, or even that very instant, it turns out that you really are a tsar."[71] Because of her debilitating personal problems and illness that spring, she did not get around to writing to Struve until the end of May, when she submitted two poems to *Russian Thought*. Then she left Moscow and spent the summer in the Saratov area.

Struve's magic did not work so quickly or effectively as Parnok seemed initially to think. He was slow in responding to her first submission, and the response itself may not have been entirely positive. Not to be daunted, as soon as she returned to Moscow at the end of August, she sent him three more poems together with the briefest of cover letters, at the end of which she wrote, "I shall be extremely grateful if this time you do not take so long in responding."[72]

His answer came in about three weeks. He could accept only one of the three poems she had submitted, and his own choice fell on the lyric, "Whose strange and savage will." The head of the poetry section, Valery Bryusov, did not agree with his choice, however. Parnok responded that she agreed with Struve (indeed, even five years later she still recited "Whose strange and savage will" at public readings) and added this characteristically proud comment: "I am not in a hurry to publish and I don't have anything against my poem appearing in the April or May issue of *Russian Thought*. In order not to disturb you further, *I shall write to Bryusov myself* about this matter."[73]

"Whose strange and savage will" finally appeared in the July 1911 issue of *Russian Thought*. It treated frankly, but again in traditional poetic language, the alienating aspects of sex in the absence of love.

> Whose strange and savage will had cast a spell on us,
> at that despondent, that night-time hour deep—
> was I tormenting fate, was I by fate tormented,
> who came and stood your life in front of me?
> Our hearts are still replete with our night's madness,
> but there's a lifeless wrinkle by your mouth;
> the needless words we speak are more abrupt and crueler,
> an emptiness has frozen in our eyes . . .
> Oh ominous design! Paints that have been poisoned!
> What has the artist of this canvas done

to paint two solitary, tragic masks like ours,
and merge two strangers' bodies into one?

The depiction of sexual passion as distinct from love and more akin to hate, as well as the notion that sex can be violent and alienating, informed many of Parnok's love lyrics at this time. She portrayed the duel of sex with particular animus in another poem, "To Him," in which the genders of the lovers are ambiguous. The speaker is most likely female, but she addresses a quintessentially androgynous lover whom she calls both her "enemy" (a masculine noun and the likely *he* of the poem's title) and her "passion" (a feminine noun and the likely *she* on whom the addressee was modeled). Although the language of this poem was once again undeniably bookish, there was autobiographical authenticity in the depiction of sex as a power struggle and in the aphrodisiac effect that despair tended to have on Parnok.

> To one another we're condemned
> by love, as by an oath of vengefulness,
> our pleasure always is replete
> with terror and a sense of desperateness . . .
> Oh what a fateful duel it is!
> Two hearts made burning hot eternally
> by hate that can't be satisfied—
> two bodies loving intertwinèdly.

In 1911 Parnok began publishing in yet another journal, *New Life*. The March issue contained "Prayer" (about the poet's "mistress Anguish"), which had been written two years previously, and an important lyrical meditation of more recent vintage that the poet herself was fond of:

> At times our premonitions, at times our recollections
> uncover to our souls a world beyond our knowledge:
> we like the features of the faces we have dreamed of,
> the voices and the hues that make our hearts responsive;
> and often all our lives, we yearn for them in secret.

> We can't resist a thing that resonates their music;
> we seek them in all things, the fleeting and eternal,
> in pictures, poems, and in our belovèd women. . . .
> Is that not why, my darling, you have me in your power?
> What voice has made your voice become its repetition?
> From whose curved lips have yours retained their obstinacy?
> Whose arms encircle me when I'm in your embraces?

Despite her feeling that this poem was a success, Parnok had fallen into a depression by the time that it appeared in print. She missed Gurevich and found herself "daydreaming" about her. She wasn't writing much and did not know if what she did write was good. Her stalemated literary career and the endless melodrama of her love life weighed heavily upon her. She wrote to Gurevich, "The life I'm composing for myself is more talentless than my poems," and went on to analyze her "main misfortune" as a deficient instinct for self-preservation.[74] She believed she too often allowed other people to take her time and energy until they were exhausted. Her sacrifice of energy, moreover, had yielded no positive results to herself or others and was interfering with her writing.

She had approached another crossroads in her creative journey. Two years had passed since she had broken away from Volkenshtein in order to make a new start. The lyrical fruits of those two years had been sparse and, in her own judgment, "talentless," while her romantic escapades had proved more numerous and, in her eyes aesthetically tasteless. In March, though suffering from one of her Grave's related headaches that made it hard to find the words she wanted, she wrote of her dissatisfaction to Gurevich as straightforwardly as she felt she could (and, in a very talented way):

> When I look over my life, I feel awkward as one does when reading a cheap novel: it has a five-story intrigue and venomous women and so much of the most French blather and falsity that it makes me groan from shame. Everything that I find utterly repulsive in a work

of art, that can never be in my poetry, is evidently in me somewhere and seeks embodiment, and so I look upon my life with a fastidious grimace the way a person with good taste looks upon other people's tastelessness. But the tastelessness is not somebody else's, it's my own. Should one be completely frank? I remember how the game ended that Ferdyshchenko invents in *The Idiot*. But I'll say it anyway. I think that if I were to find myself in the best, most desirable society, of which I dream ceaselessly, in a few months I would again create on the side some sort of utterly intolerable melodrama, after which I would feel nauseated just looking at myself.[75]

Parnok's quandary evolved from the fact that her life experience was her primary lyrical inspiration, but the kind of life she led seemed incompatible with the patriarchal standards of good taste in art that she had internalized and insisted on enforcing upon herself. Yet she had finally mustered the courage to accept her putative tastelessness as her own. This unqualified self-acceptance proved to be the first significant step in modifying her aesthetic standards in order to give her moral-emotional disposition the poetic embodiment it rightfully demanded.

When she wrote her confession to Gurevich, the seeds of transforming her life were already germinating: "You ask about my external life: it is the most humdrum imaginable and in it, unneeded by anyone, I'm becoming a grumbler. I dream about a great journey as a means toward rebirth, but I think that's a self-deception."[76] The thought of escaping from the temptations of Moscow continued to seduce her, however, and she also desired to see Gurevich. As had happened the previous year, when Lyubov Yakovlevna passed through Moscow in late May, Parnok happened to be out of town, and they missed each other by hours.

By this time the poet had moved again. Her new room in Kozitsky Lane was rented only until June 20, however, and on June 4 she wrote to Gurevich to ask whether Lyubov Yakovlevna might be able to find her a room with full board in the neighborhood of her country estate in Revyakino so they could be together for the summer.

If Parnok did spend any part of her summer with Gurevich, it was probably in August. At the beginning of July she arrived in Marienhof, near Riga, for a vacation by the sea that appeared to have been decided on at the last minute.

During the summer her dreams about a great journey of renewal, self-deceptive as they may have seemed, moved toward realization. In August she sent Chatskina four poems that she wanted to publish in *Northern Annals*. After receiving them, Sophia Isaakovna wrote to Gurevich, raving about Parnok's talent and saying how she would like "to lure" her to Petersburg.[77] Her enticements evidently succeeded. In September, Parnok moved back to the capital and remained there, in an apartment on Vasilevsky Island, for at least half a year.

Shortly after arriving, she learned of the newspaper *Russian Talk* and went to see the head of the literary section, Boris Sadovskoy. "He made a most unfavorable impression on me," she wrote to Gurevich a year later, "he carries himself as if he were an official on special assignment for a ministry of literary affairs; he's a fussy man, a 'diplomat' and indecently worldly . . . ; he's extremely observant of praise and criticism and as sensitive as a beautiful woman surrounded by men. I think he lacks impartiality."[78]

After two meetings with Sadovskoy and his passing remark during one of them that he was "very greedy" and did most of the work for the literary section of *Russian Talk* himself, Parnok decided that it would be "indelicate" to offer him her services. She also cooled on the idea of writing for a newspaper. The pace frightened her, and she did not like the thought of appearing as a writer in "dishabille," which Sadovskoy had told her "in an authoritative tone" was natural in newspaper writing.

A more personal attraction of living in Petersburg had been the chance to see Gurevich regularly, but this proved more difficult than Parnok expected, for Lyubov Yakovlevna was overwhelmed with work, and although both women visited Chatskina, their visits never seemed to coincide.

As winter came on, Parnok herself became busy and sequestered herself at home. Finally, at the end of October, she wrote Gurevich to find out when Lyubov Yakovlevna would next be at Chatskina's so that she could plan on meeting her there. She needed advice on an article she was writing about Théophile Gautier. She also was looking forward to working on Flaubert's correspondence, but had to put this major project off for lack of time to do the necessary reading. "At the moment," she concluded, "I feel indecently talentless and depressed."[79]

Two of her poems appeared in the December issue of *New Life:* "Like the image of a divinity," which had been written the previous year, and "Madrigal," a conventionalized portrait of one of her lovers. This woman embodied the poetic speaker's ideal of beauty and held her "spellbound" with her "mournful speech," "childishly joyful, cruel mouth," "skilled languors," "inhuman radiantly black eyes," and "marvelous smile in which all [was] permitted ... and paradise [was] forever reconciled with hell." Lyrical shades of Nadezhda Polyakova.

Parnok had come to Petersburg in order to concentrate on her writing. "Ever since I arrived here from Moscow," she wrote Gnesin toward the end of the year, "I've thought constantly in my work of delighting you at last with something completely worthy of your attention." Although she did indeed "live like a monk" in Petersburg, her hopes remained unrealized, and her journey proved to be the "self-deception" she had feared.[80]

The beginning of the new year found her "in the most joyless mood" about her work and "terribly upset" about how things had turned out with *Russian Talk*. She had apparently overcome her pride and agreed to work for Sadovskoy only to realize that her freedom to write on the poets she wanted was limited because he had first choice of books to review. She wrote to Gurevich, saying she needed advice and "cheering up," for she had become frightened at her own "despondency."[81]

Three months later she left Petersburg unexpectedly with borrowed money. Judging by a letter she wrote to Gurevich from Moscow, the ten roubles she owed Lyubov Yakovlevna "tormented" her, and she was abashed and annoyed that the larger sum of a hundred roubles she had borrowed from someone else could not be paid back immediately. Due to the red tape involved in transferring the money from the Taganrog bank to her Moscow account so that she could forward it to her creditors in Petersburg, they would have to wait a few days longer than she had expected. The seemingly trivial delay in repaying the loan appeared to upset her greatly. All her life she manifested an almost neurotic horror at being in anybody's debt, not only literally, but also symbolically and creatively.

The issue of the hundred roubles may have upset her at this time especially because the facts of her financial situation were staring her too obviously in the face—namely, she had to work for pay in order to support her writing. "My dear," she wrote to Gurevich from Moscow, "everything is turning out most depressingly.... Thank you, my friend, for arranging for me to write reviews for Lyatsky. No doubt, I'll like the work. But at the moment I'm utterly exhausted. Nothing makes me happy; it's obvious that without a salary I can't support myself no matter where I might go, even to heaven. It's horribly tedious."[82]

After this letter all traces of Parnok seem again to have been swallowed into a black hole. Like 1904, the year 1912 appears not to exist in her biography. All that can be surmised from subsequent events is that she spent some time in Taganrog during that year and that she witnessed there a "spectacle" (her own word) that made an indelible impression on her and significantly changed her understanding of life and her approach to her work.

3.

"Oh, Steal Me Away from My Death..."

I was very distant from my father, so for me his death was not the death of a loved one, but death as such. And I saw that spectacle for the first time. I don't understand it, and I didn't understand it even when I witnessed the whole process, but at moments the sense of obliteration reaches such intensity, such clarity, that it overwhelms all other feelings.

Parnok wrote this to Gurevich at the beginning of January 1913 after she had received a letter from Lyubov Yakovlevna that "made a very strong impression" on her. Gurevich had once again expressed her faith in Parnok's poetry and had asked why she had decided to leave Petersburg and the career she had finally begun to make for herself there. Parnok replied that she had become aware of a profound change in herself. Almost without her noticing it, her "consciousness had been reborn," and everything that had seemed necessary to her before had now become unnecessary. She linked the change to her father's death, which had made her realize that she lacked a vocation. She realized that literature had been merely an occupation which she preferred to others and had taken up because other careers were less appealing. Her feeling that all occupations were superfluous had a deleterious effect on her work. In going to Petersburg she had thought, wrongly, that what wasn't coming *from inside* could be summoned by external stimuli. Her decision to return to Moscow therefore seemed to her "an act of the most elementary conscientiousness." Of course, her Petersburg friends and well-wishers, including Yulia Veisberg, did not agree. They told her that in leaving the capital, she was signing a warrant for her own bankruptcy. Parnok realized very well the financial consequences of passing up a journalistic career in Petersburg. "Yes, I did sign my name to insolvency," she wrote Gurevich, "because my pride meant more to me than my vanity."[1]

From another standpoint, though, Yakov Parnokh's death was an unforeseen boon to his oldest daughter. It freed her from his immediate presence and thus allowed her to begin the process of coming to terms with her "distant" progenitor, whom she had loved, long ago, in her nearly forgotten, "carefree" infancy (before her mother's death), but with whom, since then, she had stubbornly refused to admit any spiritual kinship. Because she so assiduously reinforced and asserted her father's absence in her life, it had continued to be too painful a wound within her. When she went home to witness her father's dying, it felt to her again as if she were not related to him, and not a member of his family, neither a loyal son, like her brother, nor a dutiful daughter, like her sister, but merely a spectator at a public event. She denied his death's relevance to her, claiming it was not the death of a "loved one," but "death as such," a spectacle from which she had been separated, as a member of the audience is separated from events on stage. At the same time, her need to bridge the distance from her father, which his death had made permanent, seemed to increase. However one chooses to interpret them, psychologically or spiritually, Parnok's turn toward God and her spiritual searchings were obviously a direct consequence of her father's death.

A far more mundane but symbolically related and immediate consequence was her change of heart about working for *Russian*

Talk.[2] When Gurevich, who wrote drama reviews for the paper, invited Parnok to review for it at the beginning of 1913, the poet demurred. She did not like the literary section because she thought it suffered from *"modishness*—a foreign disease, alien to the Russian spirit, but nonetheless extremely dangerous to it." Moreover, she did not believe Sadovskoy was so eager for her services now as Gurevich claimed, and she suspected that he had probably agreed to her writing for *Russian Talk* at Gurevich's urging. "In a word, dear Lyubov Yakovlevna," she concluded, "this is my answer: in principle it's possible for me, but I don't know yet if it will be possible in fact; two reviews of 100 lines each per month suits me, but I must know *exactly* what area the paper is assigning to me."[3]

Parnok's quandary over writing for the newspaper naturally disturbed Gurevich less than the poet's morbid conviction that life was pointless in the face of death. She tried "to infect" her young friend, "if only for a moment," with a sense of the reasonableness of death[4] and counseled the wisdom and sweetness of humility in submitting to death's inevitability. What impressed Parnok most, however, was Gurevich's openness in communicating her private thoughts on "the most important thing." It seemed to herald a greater intimacy in their relationship, which made Parnok want to respond with equal candor, though to write about such matters was "very difficult" for her.

> The wisdom of humility that transforms the horror of death into a mystery of salvation is alien to my whole spiritual make-up. I understand humility from hopelessness, or from the consciousness of the futility of one's will; I'm familiar with the *bitterness* of humility, but its *sweetness* is beyond my comprehension. Savioress or violatress, death is our consciousness of the unavoidable end, and the more acute that consciousness is, the more aimless life seems. If death is the beneficent destroyer of life's difficulties, then what's the point of life, what's the point of striving? Is our whole existence nothing more than a way of passing time? I feel that such an interpretation of life cannot help but end in complete demoralization, and that horrifies me.... If one looks at life as merely a way of passing

time, one can sink into complete "spiritual dishabille." . . . Only by denying death through faith in immortality can one attain recognition that life is something reasonable. Until the day I saw a man die, I did not understand that death is annihilation. But now I realize that it is, and everything has become superfluous.[5]

Parnok was predisposed to believe in immortality if only in order to find some purpose to her life. Her father's death had mysteriously planted in her the seed of faith, although at first the opposite appeared to be the case, and she remained consciously unaware of this mystical transfer.

In mid-January Gurevich unexpectedly replaced Sadovskoy as head of the literary section of *Russian Talk*. Sadovskoy's departure surprised Parnok, since she felt the paper needed critics like him to keep its circulation. "The public likes chic," she wrote Gurevich, "and you'll probably want to keep him as a gourmet offering. I have no doubts that the literary section that you'll head will be superb; needless to say, in thinking that, I mean that once you've become convinced of my bankruptcy, you'll drop me from the staff of permanent critics."[6] She concluded these self-deprecating remarks with a serious communication: "I have some poems, but they are too intimate to be published in a newspaper."

Illness prevented Parnok from meeting the deadline for her first review. She sent it to Gurevich a few days late with a cover letter in which she justified the harshness of her criticism on the grounds that "chatterboxes should not be encouraged to publish their idle chatter," even though she had no faith that she would be able to discourage them "since stupidity is an incurable disease."[7] Some of the sarcasm and severity in her reviews may have stemmed from her insecurity about her right to be a critic. At the same time, she obviously wanted to be taken seriously by her readers. That may have been one reason why she chose to write her criticism under a male pseudonym—Andrey Polyanin. In making this decision she followed the practice of scores of women reviewers of her day who sought the authority conferred by masculinity in their male-dominated literary culture. Far more suggestive was the Russianness of the pen name she chose for her criticism, which epitomized her critical point of view. The adoption of a special pseudonym for her journalism also served to separate it from her poetry and symbolically, perhaps, to preserve the latter from infection by "newspaper dishabille."

In submitting her first review, she gave Gurevich permission to make any changes she deemed necessary and expressed a disarming impatience to see her words in print. She was also unabashedly eager for her honorarium, joking, "My pocket is even more empty than my head."

She was upset when her review had not appeared by the end of the month. Its lengthiness and hostile tone apparently displeased Gurevich, although she did not say so directly. But Parnok got the message: "Although you wrote that you 'want [my] reviews terribly,' I sensed in your letter a dissatisfaction with what I'd written. But the material I was sent to review was so poor that it was hard for me to say anything important about it."[8]

The review finally appeared in the February 27 issue and within a week Parnok gratefully received her honorarium along with some other good news. At her request, Gurevich had broached to Struve at *Russian Thought* the subject of Parnok's new asking price for her poetry—she had decided to raise it from twenty five to thirty kopecks per line—and Struve had agreed to pay her "pris courant."[9]

Parnok made her debut as a poet in the pages of *Northern Annals* in the February 1913 issue, and two months later her first review article for that journal appeared. Entitled "Noteworthy Names," it dealt with recent books of verse by Klyuev, Akhmatova, and Severyanin. In her first major critical article, Parnok-Polyanin emerged as an antimodernist whose praise for contemporary poets was limited to their technical achievements only. She upheld the classics—Pushkin, Goethe, Dante. They exemplified for her "the spirit of the poet," which she defined as the supreme conjoining of mind and heart, something she found generally and regrettably lacking in modernist poetry.

Her literary conservatism seemed at odds with her way of life and flaunting of public opinion. In this respect she resembled her European contemporaries Radclyffe Hall and, to a lesser degree, Natalie Clifford Barney, who both tended to conservatism in all things except their openness about their lesbianism. Most of Parnok's criticism was written, of course, before she realized her potential as a poet and began forging her own modernist style and point of view. They too would differ, however, from *fin de siècle* modernism in Europe and Russia, which owed a larger debt to decadence than Parnok was prepared to shoulder.

In her next article for *Northern Annals,* "Seeking the Path of Art," she continued her antimodernist attack, this time against the antisymbolist, modernist poets who called themselves acmeists. The issue also contained a poem of hers dedicated to Lyubov Gurevich:

> A light profound, a light endearing,
> you passed along this soul of mine—
> your ray plunged under fields to shine
> on cornshoots, previously fallow.
> And then I dreamed—of blossoming,
> and bounteous harvests in my desert,
> and in my heart, blue and calmly,
> streamed morning from my years of spring.[10]

This poem revealed the maternal nature of Parnok's creativity as well as her need to be penetrated and fertilized by female wisdom (light). The poetic fertilization Parnok had received from Gurevich had been purely spiritual; in her other relationships with creative women, it would be rooted in carnality. The poem to Gurevich also typified Parnok's use of traditional agricultural imagery to write about her creativity, her frequent employment of the color blue to express positive, spiritually exalted moods, and her fondness for speaking of her life, again traditionally, in terms of seasons and times of day as well as for looking back on her infancy ("years of spring") as the only purely happy time of her life.

The more turbulent side of the poet's life was reflected in the "Sonnet" that appeared in the May issue of *Russian Thought*. The poem is noteworthy for the fact that the lovers in it, the speaker and her addressee, are both marked (grammatically, through the second- and first-person singular past tense forms of the verb "became" in line 4) as being female:

> We hadn't noticed what the dusk was up to,—
> the muslin curtains suddenly looked grey,
> the carpet deepened, the armchairs' outlines softened,
> and you became—not you, and I became—not I.
> A total stranger dropped her hand in sorrow
> upon the place your hand had been till then,
> and suddenly we knew our love was joyless,
> and bloomed while hiding its own lack of strength.
> Day's plashes had died down outside the windows
> when oddly sharp, your voice began to speak
> unnecessary words we both found strange;
> when you got up, your shawl around your shoulders,
> and rustling, your silks said their "so-long,"
> when leaving, you gave me the merest nod.[11]

None of the love affairs Parnok had during the four years from her divorce until the spring of 1913 appear to have been long-lasting, and none of her lovers from this period left their names in her poetry. She obviously was not looking for a permanent partner, and, despite the alienation and misery that some of her love affairs brought her, she enjoyed her bachelor existence. Eventually, however, the energy demanded by falling in and out of love began to take its toll physically and creatively.

In the spring of 1913, she met and fell in love with Iraida (Rayechka) Albrecht, the socialite daughter of a wealthy Moscow family, who was thought to be a great beauty. The women spent the summer together in Butovo, a country place outside of Moscow, where Parnok, buoyed by her new love, plunged into creative activity, unusual for her in the summertime. She returned to her novella *Anton Ivanovich*.

Her desire for work did not abate in the fall nor did her desire to continue living with her new woman friend. For the first time in her life she rented herself an entire apartment, an action full of symbolic significance, as she wrote to Gurevich:

> I was very happy to get your letter. What pleasure it would give me, if, right now, I could run up the stairs to your office, see that devastating NOT IN sign on the door, ignore your stern Tatyana's instructions, go in, hear a year-and-a-half's worth of you, and "catch up on the time we've been apart." But at present, I don't think I'll be able to get out of Moscow for a long while. However one runs from time, it catches up to one—I'm evidently getting old and no longer up to my former nomadic way of life, and so I've become the possessor of an apartment. I'm renting a whole apartment, have even acquired some furniture, and now, as a result of luxury far beyond my means, I'm a stay-at-home in Kolokolnikov Lane with my girlfriend and a monkey, who, by the way, despite her considerable monkey charm, is rather unbearable as a housemate for humans. So much for the external side of my life.[12]

Ironically, domestic happiness, perhaps because it too was a first in Parnok's life, took some getting used to. It seemed to contradict the gloomy view of her poetic life that she continued to believe was her fate: "There are no miracles in my life, and it's obvious that something very sad and gloomy is going to come out of me. And no doubt it was not to have been otherwise."[13]

In the early fall Parnok and Maximilian Shteinberg, a colleague of Gnesin's and the brother-in-law of Yulia Veisberg, decided to write an opera together on a subject from the *Arabian Nights*. Parnok, with her usual enthusiasm, set to work immediately and quickly finished the text for the first scene. Shteinberg was somewhat abashed at her ardor and asked her not to begin the next scene until he had found musical material for the first. Nevertheless, as soon as she received the libretto back from him in mid-November, she began writing the second scene. Her hope was that

Shteinberg would be inspired by seeing the libretto in its entirety. "The impression I got from our conversation," she wrote him in November, "has left me thinking constantly of ways I might be able to *entice* you into this project. You are not at all sanguine about its success while I have already fallen in love with our heroine and hero and so want to *hear* them that I'm taking the risk of becoming a nag."[14]

The fall brought her more success in her journalistic career. In late October Gurevich offered her a permanent staff position on *Russian Thought* which she tentatively agreed to accept, assuming that it would not interfere with her reviewing commitments to *Northern Annals*. When she informed Chatskina by telephone of her decision, Sophia Isaakovna became upset. She explained that she and Saker had wanted to offer Parnok the same sort of position, but had not done so because they did not want to take her away from her writing. Parnok realized she could not hold the same position on the staffs of competing journals and decided to take the position at *Northern Annals* because, as she explained to Gurevich, "*Russian Thought* is alien to me as it is to you; at *Northern Annals* the possibility of making an important creative contribution appeals to me. Besides, in turning down *Russian Thought*, which in essence is not yours, but somebody else's, I'm not offending you in any way while I would seem to be 'offending' Sophia Isaakovna and Yakov Lvovich if I turned them down."[15]

Parnok wrote only four lyrics that can be dated to the fall of 1913. Three of them appeared in the December issue of *Northern Annals*, along with her review of a collection of short stories. She devoted her creative energy that fall to her libretto and novella. Chatskina reported on the latter's progress to Gurevich who was ill during the early winter. When she was on the road to recovery, Parnok herself wrote to her, "Sophia Isaakovna has told you about my novella. It's my first big work, so I'm sure you can understand how anxious I am for it. It consumes all my thoughts and all my time. If it's not too much for you, write me about yourself, my dear, if only a few words. In the greatest affection I kiss your dear, lovely hands, Your S. Parnok."[16] This is the last of Parnok's extant letters to Gurevich until the mid-1920s. Whatever correspondence they may have had with one another in the ensuing decade has been lost, and unfortunately, the manuscript of Parnok's "first big work" met the same fate.

What might be called the "Gurevich period" in Parnok's life had spanned all the major passages of the poet's youth: her marriage, divorce, postdivorce "chaos," her father's death, her existential and creative crisis, and her settling down in a permanent relationship and in a permanent journalistic position. During the turmoil and searchings of those years, Gurevich had been the guiding light that Parnok had wanted and needed her to be.

In the early spring of 1914 Parnok and Albrecht left Russia for an extended tour of Europe. They traveled abroad for five months, making their first stop in Italian Switzerland at Ascona, near Lake Locarno. From there Parnok sent a postcard to Shteinberg apologizing for her long silence and reporting that various events in her life had kept her from work on the libretto, but she was now returning to it.[17]

While in Ascona, Parnok must also have worked on her long review article about Andrey Bely's novel *Petersburg*, which appeared in the June issue of *Northern Annals*. Bely's innovative work, now considered one of the masterpieces of European modernism, did not, as might be expected, please Parnok at all. To her it exemplified the grave error made by writers who were attempting to revive Russian prose through technical brilliance and formalist experimentation alone. She accused Bely of not being worthy of his epic theme (the Revolution of 1905), of disdaining all his characters and mocking them for the reader's benefit. To her mind he lacked respect for the sanctity of genuine feelings and abused irony to deleterious effect. She made her point in a self-revealing metaphor: "Irony has never been the mother of a large-scale work of fiction: a large child can't be carried to term in a small pelvis; thus, what has happened was inevitable: a large child has appeared prematurely, and Andrey Bely's *Petersburg* makes the kind of unnerving, unnatural impression that a giant premature baby would produce."[18]

Later in the spring Parnok and Albrecht went south to Italy, visiting Milan, Rome, and Venice. In Forte dei Marmi outside Venice, the poet wrote one of her strongest poems from this period, in which she contrasted her impressions of two of Italy's most famous churches: the Milan Cathedral and Venice's San Marco. The speaker begins by stating her dislike for

> churches where the architect
> speaks more audibly than God,
> where genius, vying with the Father's will,
> neither merges with it, nor is lost. (#7)

She prefers "smooth Byzantine cupolas" to "sharp Gothic spires," and her gendering of the two architectural styles makes an encoded statement about her affectional preference. At the end of the poem she describes the spiritually orgasmic impact on her of San Marco's smooth lines that convey "the sacred power of the Lord's will," and wavelike cupolas whose "fluid-smooth force lifts up [her] soul" "like a fulsome goblet, filled to the brim by God" (#7). San Marco makes the poetic speaker want to prostrate herself before God like a nun.

From Italy the women friends traveled north through Germany up to Hamburg, and from there they sailed to England and the Isle of Wight. They stayed in Shanklin, one of the island's most popular tourist resorts, at Napier House, located twenty yards from the sea.[19] On July 1 Parnok sent a postcard to one of her and Raya's poet friends, Konstantin Lipskerov, in which she noted that she hadn't "been in the mood for poetry the whole time" she had been abroad.[20]

The "stupefying news" that war had begun in Europe reached Parnok and Albrecht in London, and the women made plans to return home immediately. As soon as Parnok was back in Moscow, she tried to get in touch with her brother and sister. In the hope of learning some news of them, she wrote to Gnesin in Rostov: "If you know anything about my brother Valya, be so kind as to share it with me.... Just a few days ago I learned that Liza is in Berlin and I sent her money there. I imagine Valya is also penniless and I'm very pained by not being able to help him out immediately."[21]

As it turned out, Valentin had left Russia in July on a journey to Palestine. After his graduation from the university, where he matriculated in 1909, he had stayed on in Petersburg, pursuing his poetry and esthetic interests in the Russian avant-garde movement. In 1913–14 he regularly attended Meyerhold's experimental theater workshop. Unlike his older sister, he was a modernist through and through, and, unlike her as well, he had grown up to be an impassioned Zionist. He spilled over with rage against Russia and the anti-Semitism of the tsarist government. Nor did he have any use for the assimilated Russian Jewish intelligentsia: "My life in Petersburg bred in me a repulsion for the education provided in Russian universities, a conviction in the worthlessness of the tsarist professorial class, in the falseness of the legend of a revolutionary student movement, and disillusionment in Russian culture."[22] His journey to Palestine was thus an attempt to recover his ethnic roots and to escape from his hatred of Russia. The news of the outbreak of war reached him when he was in Beirut.

By the time Parnok found out where her brother was, he had already reached Jaffa. She telephoned the bank in Taganrog about wiring him funds, only to learn that it was impossible "for the time being" to transfer money there. In the meanwhile she had received information that Liza had returned to Dresden where the military commander happened to be a friend of her fiancé (a young man from Taganrog named Tarakhovsky). "Aside from what you told me," Parnok wrote Gnesin on September 19, "the only thing I know about Valya is that he asked his friend Tarakhovsky to send him some money, but it came back undelivered. I wrote to Valya, but have no hope of getting a reply. I also wrote to Liza twice: once through acquaintances in Sweden, the second time through acquaintances in Italy. But I haven't heard from her."[23]

Upon her return to Russia, Parnok moved into a new apartment on Myasnitskaya Street. Aside from worries about her brother and sister, her life during the early fall was calm and uneventful. It proved to be the proverbial calm before the storm.

One of Parnok's closest women friends in Moscow was Adelaida (Ada) Gertsyk, a memoirist, translator, literary critic, and poet whose only published book of verse, *Poems,* had appeared in 1910. Adelaida had a younger sister, Eugenia, born circa 1881, who had matriculated in the Higher Courses for Women at Moscow University in 1900. Eugenia enjoyed sisterly intimacies with several of her more famous male contemporaries, including the philosophers Lev Shestov and Nikolai Berdyaev and the symbolist poet Vyacheslav Ivanov, with whom she was particularly close in the years 1906–9. These famous "brothers" and soulmates constituted the focus of her published memoirs along with her older sister, who was their "father's pride" and the emotional center, apparently, of Eugenia's life.[24]

Adelaida had been withdrawn and "unaffectionate" as a child, divorced from the life around her, and living in a fantasy world that excluded adults. "I don't remember," she wrote in her reminiscences, "when precisely I became disenchanted with adults. Gradually, the conviction took root in me that nothing new or important could be expected from them, but, on the contrary, one had to protect everything one valued and loved, hide it, and save it from their touch."[25] Adelaida's first childhood love was for her girlfriend Grunya, the daughter of a workman, whom she imagined to be a Georgian princess abducted from her native land and forgotten in early childhood. In her youth Adelaida had a passionate love affair with a young man that ended tragically when he died in hospital literally before her eyes. The trauma made her partially deaf.

At the age of thirty-four she married the son of a prominent military family, Dmitri Zhukovsky, and the following spring she gave birth to the first of two sons. The Zhukovskys settled in Moscow in Krechetnikovsky Lane and began building a new house in Sudak. Like her sister, Adelaida was extremely attached to this Crimean town on the Black Sea near Feodosia.

During the prewar period, Adelaida's Moscow home became a gathering place for young women poets. Her sister recalled her in two "domestic" roles, supervising the education and upbringing of her sons, and "listening with an absentmindedly affectionate smile to the outpourings of some young female-poet who had become attached to her. There were several of them in those years around Adelaida,"[26] including Marina Tsvetaeva, who lived virtually next door, in Boris and Gleb Lane, Marina's sister, Anastasia, and Maya Kudashova (née Cuviller), the illegitimate daughter of a French governess and a Russian midshipman who had perished at Tsushima. Parnok apparently also frequented Adelaida Gertsyk's circle.

At the beginning of 1915, Eugenia came to live with her sister and brother-in-law. She later recalled the war years in Moscow as, strangely enough, "a happy oasis" in her and Adelaida's lives when they both "wanted simply *to be*, to see, to give ourselves to creative work and tender friendship."[27]

During the war years Adelaida immersed herself in the work of the German Romantic writer Bettina Brentano von Arnim. She was particularly drawn to von Arnim's *Correspondence* with her romantic friend, the poet Karoline von Guenderode, which, along with other von Arnim works, she translated into Russian.[28] For Gertsyk and the female poets in her circle, Bettina von Arnim became a cult figure, a symbol of feminine, "Amazon" genius. Gertsyk was particularly fascinated by the eroticism of female friendship as expressed in von Arnim and Guenderode's intimacy.

In addition to a mutual interest in female creativity, both Gertsyk sisters had spent years on "spiritual searchings," not so much in a quest for faith, but for the faith that best answered their respective yearnings. The war years brought a resolution of Adelaida's "spiritual torment" when she quietly "went over to Russian Orthodoxy." Secretly from her sister, and without seeking a well-known confessor, she simply "rejected the oppressive untruth of Lutheranism and became, in the end, completely at home in the Moscow churches she had come to love."[29] Since Parnok's equally quiet conversion to Orthodoxy most likely took place at this time, the Gertsyks may well have provided her with spiritual support and encouragement.

Adelaida played just as significant a role in Parnok's romantic life of the war years, if perhaps unconsciously. In mid-October 1914 Sonya attended an evening party at the Gertsyks where she met Adelaida's young romantic friend and surrogate "daughter," Marina Tsvetaeva. The only details available of this fateful first meeting are contained in Tsvetaeva's lyrical recollection of them the following January in the tenth poem of the cycle of lyrics she wrote to Parnok and eventually titled "Girlfriend."[30]

Tsvetaeva remembered Parnok from the moment she entered the drawing room, wearing a simple, black-knit jacket with a wing collar. A fire was crackling in the grate, the air smelled of tea and White Rose perfume. Almost immediately, someone came over to Parnok and said there was a young poet whom she had to meet. She got up, inclined her head slightly, and put a finger to her lips in a characteristic pose. As she rose, she noticed, perhaps for the first time, a young woman with short, curly blonde hair, dressed in an almost gold-colored faille dress, who was getting up to meet her with an unforced movement.

The other guests surrounded them, and someone said jocularly, "Get acquainted, gentlemen!" Parnok extended her hand, which Tsvetaeva recalled in her poem as "a sliver of ice that lingered on [her] palm affectionately." Sensing some sort of ironic comment from a guest who had been watching out of the corner of his eye, Tsvetaeva sat down semiprone in an armchair and began playing nervously with her wedding ring. Then Parnok took out a cigarette, and Tsvetaeva, instinctively slipping into a courtly role, offered her a match.

Later in the evening, Tsvetaeva remembered clinking glasses with Parnok above a blue vase. As they toasted and locked glances for a moment, she thought to herself, "Oh, be my Orestes!" Spontaneously, she took one of the flowers from the vase and offered it to Parnok.

She remained acutely conscious of her Orestes's presence the whole evening. Once, hearing Parnok's soft, deep, throaty laugh nearby, she wondered if the woman she was already in love with might be laughing at one of her witticisms. She looked over and watched as Parnok slowly drew a handkerchief out of her black suede bag and let it drop on the floor.

When Tsvetaeva met and fell in love with Parnok, she was twenty-three years old, married to a young student, Sergey Efron, and had a two-year-old daughter, Ariadne (Alla, Alya). Parnok was her first lesbian lover, though not her first same-sex infatuation. She considered herself bisexual and had been attracted to women since childhood.[31]

The combination of womanliness, boyishness, and strength that she perceived in the twenty-nine-year-old Parnok attracted her irresistibly, not to mention the dark, romantic, sinful aura that the older woman's reputation had inevitably created around her:

> And your powerloving forehead
> under the weight of a reddish helmet
> —Not a woman and not a boy,
> But something stronger than me! ("Girlfriend," #10)[32]

In wishing Parnok to be her "Orestes," Tsvetaeva most probably was indicating her desire for a homoerotic friendship along the lines of the Greek male friends Orestes and Pylades.[33] Emotionally, she had grown up with a strong need to be mothered and receive maternal love (her own mother, who died when she was fourteen, had wanted a son and had apparently been cold, possessive, and capricious with her daughters). At the same time, in her intimate relationships, Tsvetaeva wanted to wield the power of a mother, illustrated in her heterosexual preference for boyish, weak, "feminine," and often semi-invalid men.

Despite her own motherhood, when she met Parnok, Tsvetaeva considered herself a child. She had apparently never experienced real passion or been capable of orgasm. Tragically for her and Parnok's relationship, she was enormously invested in retaining her pure, childlike persona, and simply could not come to terms with the adult sexuality Parnok aroused in her and satisfied.

Many Tsvetaeva scholars have interpreted her and Parnok's relationship along stereotypical, implicitly homophobic lines. They see the "real lesbian," Parnok, as the active, mannish, evil seducer and the "normal" woman, Tsvetaeva, as the passive, sex-denying, innocent victim of seduction. To a certain degree, Tsvetaeva's own internalized homophobia facilitated this view. In some of the "Girlfriend" poems she portrayed Parnok as a "dark lady" and "tragic heroine, whom sin hovers over, like a thundercloud" (#1). Indeed, that decadent aura of the Baudelairean *femme damnée* excited Tsvetaeva and must have made her feel deliciously dangerous in loving Parnok as if she had taken the risk of plucking her own personal *fleur du mal*.

By attaching a decadent literary image to her antidecadent lover, Tsvetaeva belied her innocence, at least in the lyrical sphere. In the same poem in which she cast Parnok as the dark lady, she revealed a sophisticated awareness of her own stereotyping procedures by delighting in the "ironical enchantment" that her romantic you-addressee was, for the first time, "not a he."

More important, the "Girlfriend" poems demonstrated that Tsvetaeva perceived *herself* as playing the active, male lover's role in her relationship with Parnok. Tsvetaeva consistently portrayed herself as a boy, a page, a courtly lover of a powerful being who was "neither a woman, nor a boy"; she saw herself as a knight who wished to perform heroic, romantic, and reckless deeds in order to win her "dark lady's" favor. Tsvetaeva's lyrical self-portrait had a basis in real life. She did set her cap for Parnok and succeeded in wooing her away from Iraida Albrecht.

Tsvetaeva's poems to Parnok also show that she became ambivalent about her feelings, primarily after she began to want the passion that threatened her and her cherished image of herself as pure "Spartan child." She felt she was losing control of the relationship, and she became hateful. From that moment, her animus drove her more intensely than her love.

Parnok's feelings for Tsvetaeva were slower to crystallize and express themselves and are much harder to guess at. She immediately recognized Tsvetaeva's giftedness, fell in love with it, nurtured and cherished it, and never ceased to love it. The less generous side of her must have envied her young lover's poetic gift, but she managed somehow to conquer her envy and wisely refrained from vying directly with Tsvetaeva in the poetic arena. She rejected the loathsome role of Salieri and endeavored to be a "Salieri who loved his Mozart,"[34] deferring to Tsvetaeva's desire to write their love into Russian poetry in the "Girlfriend" poems.

Tsvetaeva was the second (and last) poet with whom Parnok had an intimate relationship, and the only poet she was ever in love with. In her marriage to Volkenshtein she had become bored "playing the role of muse," and had, by her own admission, "played it vilely, without either inspiration or benefit, in a word, [she] failed in that role."[35] With Tsvetaeva, Parnok played the role of muse and did so superbly: she inspired her "Bettina Arnim" — as she called Tsvetaeva in one lyric — to new creative achievement and elicited from her arguably some of the best poems of her early period. Simultaneously, she began, slowly, writing more herself, especially in 1915.

But while avoiding, or neutralizing, a "duel of wills" with Tsvetaeva in the poetic arena, Parnok took up the challenge in the sexual one, a challenge, if not a provocation, she won handily and gloried in unabashedly.

Thus, the women challenged each other to break out of the images that each had imposed on herself; they forced each other to take risks. Such risk taking could not possibly make for a smooth relationship, and probably even exacerbated deep hostilities and needs that were difficult to confront and resolve. Theirs was an earthquake of an affair, and the aftershocks lasted much longer than the main upheaval. Tsvetaeva felt them and denied them with a vengeance much stronger than her love had been, until the end of her life (she committed suicide in 1941), and Parnok realized the creative seeds of Tsvetaeva's love only in the last year and a half of hers.

A day or two after their first meeting at the Gertsyk-Zhukovskys, Tsvetaeva made her first lyrical confession of love to Parnok in a contentious spirit, as if she were giving in by being the first to admit she was in love:

> Are you happy?—You won't admit it!—Hardly!
> And it's better thus!
> Methinks you've kissed too many people. Hence your
> Melancholiness.

She declared her love boldly at the beginning of the poem's fourth stanza and in the remaining ones enumerated the "reasons" for her love, ending with the most shocking, and perhaps most important:

> Because this trembling because of—is this really
> All a dream?—
> Because of the ironical enchantment that
> You aren't—a he. ("Girlfriend," #1)

A week later Tsvetaeva reflected lyrically on her first experience of making love with a woman, which she called "the dream of yesterday." It happened in her house on Boris and Gleb Lane and was witnessed by her "Siberian cat." The newness of it troubled her, she did not know what to call it, and wondered if love were involved. The heterosexual roles she was used to did not apply, everything, she wrote, had been "demonically in reverse." It had seemed to her like a "duel of wills," but she had no idea who had won. She felt regretful and at the same time wanted more.

> And still—
> what happened, really?
> What do I so regret and want?
> And I don't know: did I conquer?
> Was I overcome? ("Girlfriend," #2)

By the next day her feelings had mellowed. She had "sobered up," "calmed down," and found it easier to breathe. From this she concluded, at the end of her third "Girlfriend" poem:

> My heart has already mastered
> Oblivion's tender art.
> Some big block of feeling
> Thawed today in my heart.

At the beginning of the relationship Tsvetaeva perceived Parnok as playing cold and hard to get. When Tsvetaeva invited her over late one night, Parnok refused, saying she felt too lazy, and it was too cold to go out. Tsvetaeva took playful lyrical revenge for this rebuff in the fourth poem of "Girlfriend," saying that in refusing to come out and play with her, Parnok had lost her chance for "merriment" and was letting her youth slip by.

The next evening, "between seven and eight," Tsvetaeva's poetic speaker caught sight of Parnok and "another woman" (probably Albrecht) speeding by in a sleigh, sitting "eye-to-eye and fur-to-fur." She perceived the other woman as "someone desired and dear, desired more strongly than I," but accepted this as part of the natural order of the fairy-tale dream she was in, as if she were "little Kay, almost frozen to death" in the thrall of her "Snow Queen" (#5).

Considering the whirlwind start of their love affair, it is strange that November passed without leaving a trace in either woman's poetry or biography. Perhaps Tsvetaeva, who, after all, is virtually the only source of information about the beginning of the affair, simply exaggerated the intensity of her own and Parnok's feelings. Perhaps both women were distracted by their respective family concerns: Tsvetaeva with her husband, who was also having an extramarital affair and suffering from tuberculosis that had him in and out of the sanatorium at the end of the year; and Parnok with her brother, who had returned to Petersburg from Palestine in November.

Parnakh had become disenchanted with Palestine, where, he later wrote, he "suffered from the justifiable hatred of the local Jews for their stepmother Russia." His inability to become part of the Jewish community in Palestine only increased his antipathy for the assimilated Russian Jews of Petersburg: "I was greatly disturbed by the indifference of many Jewish intellectuals to the fate of their fellow Jews who had been killed by the tsar's army and new inquisition. I found the loyal-subject aspirations of these privileged people of the capital especially vile."[36]

Although Parnok was a pacifist and against the war, she definitely shared the patriotic attitudes of the Petersburg Jewish intellectuals whom her brother despised. In addition, by the time he returned to Russia, she had moved spiritually closer to Russian Orthodoxy. Brother and sister, so similar in many ways, seemed headed on a political and religious collision course.

After a six-week silence, Tsvetaeva's poem of December 5 to Parnok made it clear that the affair was escalating. The poem rang with Tsvetaeva's boyish swagger and suggested, in its final stanza, that she, as a "thoroughbred" racer, had decided to enter the race for her mare with the sparkling pupils (Parnok), that is, win her away from her "fellow-travelers" (other women friends), who were, by implication, not thoroughbreds:

How your pupils sparkle brightly
From beneath your heavy mane!

Are your fellow-travelers jealous?
Thoroughbreds can really race! ("Girlfriend," #6)

As she put it in a later poem, Tsvetaeva had perceived that Parnok's heart "had to be taken by storm" (#9), and her decision to do so changed the course of the relationship. In mid-December Parnok quarrelled with Albrecht and moved out of her Myasnitskaya apartment, taking her pet monkey with her, and renting a room near the Arbat. Shortly afterwards, Tsvetaeva went away with Parnok for a few days and would not tell any of her friends or intimates where she was going. This caused them great concern, especially Yelena (Pra) Voloshina, the mother of the poet Voloshin.

Voloshina had known Tsvetaeva for years and nurtured maternally protective, jealous feelings for her. According to Eugenia Gertsyk, Pra "spoke in a bass voice and dressed like a man."[37] She was then living in Moscow, not far from the Gertsyks, and acting as the head of an apartment-commune of free spirits, young artists and writers. Like most of Tsvetaeva's friends, Pra was hostile to Parnok, and possibly jealous of her.

She believed, or wanted to believe, that Tsvetaeva had been the helpless victim of an evil spell. At the end of December she wrote to her friend Yulia Obolenskaya, a sculptor:

> As regards Marina things are rather frightening: her affair has become deadly serious. She went off with Sonya for a few days and made a big secret of it.... All of this upsets and disturbs me and Liza [Efron] very much, but we don't have the power to break this spell.[38]

Tsvetaeva and Parnok had gone to the medieval city of Rostov-the-Great. After their return to Moscow, Tsvetaeva wrote an enraptured description of one fantastic day they spent there.[39] With snowflakes sparkling on their fur coats, they began the day by roaming through the local Christmas fair, where they shopped for the brightest ribbons they could find. Tsvetaeva gorged herself on unsweetened waffles and welled with tenderness every time she saw a chestnut-colored mare. Reddish-coated salesmen plied them with worthless wares, cursing them for not buying anything, and "the peasant women gaped and marveled at such strange and fancy Moscow gals."

When the fair crowd began to disperse, the girlfriends found an old church and went inside. Parnok's eyes were simply riveted by an ornately framed icon of the Mother of God. Gasping, "Oh, I want her!" she let go of Tsvetaeva's hand and went up to it. Tsvetaeva watched as her lover's "cultivated, opal-ringed hand," the hand that held her "whole misfortune," lit a candle and placed it in front of the Holy Mother's image. In a typical outburst of recklessness, she promised Parnok that she "would steal the icon" for her "that very night."

At sunset, in blissful high spirits, feeling like "nameday girls," the girlfriends stomped through the doors of the monastery-hostel where they were staying. They finished the day in their room at one of their favorite pastimes—playing cards and telling fortunes. And when the king of hearts showed up in Tsvetaeva's cards three times in a row, Parnok "became furious."

The game excited them both. Sonya came and stood in front of her beloved "small girl"; she took her curly, cropped head between her hands, and pressed it gently, "caressing and kissing every curl," as Marina felt the coolness of her lover's enamel brooch against her lips.

Later, Tsvetaeva recalled "sleepily drawing [her] cheek across [Parnok's] tender fingers" as Sonya whispered endearments, gently "teasing [Marina] for being a boy" and letting her know she "liked [her] just like that."

The love affair reached its peak in the first part of the new year. Being with Tsvetaeva finally provoked Parnok, whose muse had been very quiet for almost a year, into writing poetry again, and for the first time since her adolescence she began to date her poems exactly. This marked a creatively healthy move back in the direction of historical specificity and autobiographical inspiration, which always had been, and would be, the wellspring of her best poems, no matter how much she had regrettably chosen not to tap into it, for long periods in her poetic apprenticeship.

Even in 1915 and 1916 Parnok continued to vacillate between the native poetic sources of her life and body and the foreign, bookish, but tastefully inoffensive aesthetic ones that constrained her native element. Tsvetaeva also felt constrained by the aesthetic mores and silent censorship of Russian literary culture that did not admit the depiction of real-life lesbianism, as opposed to literary lesbianism, in serious poetry. Her poems about their affair were bolder than Parnok's in large part because she did not write them for publication, while Parnok always had publication in view.[40]

Perhaps in compensation for submitting to Victorian literary norms, Parnok and Tsvetaeva enjoyed flaunting their affair in literary society. One contemporary recalled seeing them at "two very strange parties" at the home of Parnok's friend, Yulia Veisberg and her husband, Andrey Nikolaevich Rimsky-Korsakov. "At that time," the spectator later wrote, "Marina Tsvetaeva was considered a lesbian, and I saw her there twice at those parties. She came with the poet Sophia Parnok. They sat with their arms around each other and took turns smoking the same cigarette."[41]

Proud of her poet lover, Parnok introduced her to her other friends and colleagues, including Chatskina and Saker. From January 1915 *Northern Annals* became the main outlet for Tsvetaeva's lyrics. Since she did not like to take money for her poems, Chatskina and Saker paid her with gifts and entertainments.

In the winter of 1915 Parnok's sister, Liza, came to live with her in Moscow. They rented two rooms in an income building on Khlebny Lane, just around the corner from Tsvetaeva's house. Tsvetaeva came to visit frequently. She and Parnok, sometimes joined by other women poets, would read their poems to each other and tell fortunes. In Liza's opinion, offered in her unpublished *Reminiscences* when she was already an elderly woman, Tsvetaeva gave little thought to her husband or daughter.[42]

Sometimes Tsvetaeva brought her daughter along with her, as Ariadne Efron herself recalled years later:

> Mama had a friend, Sonya Parnok—she also wrote poetry, and mama and I sometimes went to visit her. Mama would read her poems to Sonya, Sonya would read her poems to mama, and I would sit on a chair waiting to be shown the monkey. Because Sonya Parnok had a real live monkey who lived in the other room and was kept on a chain.[43]

Three of Parnok's poems appeared in the January issue of *Northern Annals,* but none of them had anything to do with her new love. The most substantial of the three was the lyric "As if you've resurrected / my very first days, spring," a generalized and meditative scan of her life in which the poetic speaker addressed the issue of her prodigality. Despite her carelessness, she felt that her "soul had remained one with God" and believed that her poems would tell Him that. Again, the poet seemed to be projecting her tragically unresolved relationship with her father into her attitude to God.

As for Tsvetaeva, that winter she was lyrically immersed in Parnok and wrote three ecstatic poems to her in January alone. On the tenth she evoked the whole of her girlfriend by focusing on specific details of her appearance: her "tender sprout" of a neck, the "weak and whimsical curve" of her "unpainted lips," "the blindly dazzling ledge" of her "Beethovenesque brow," her prominent, moonlike eyes, "lightly shadowed by bright brown rings," her "touchingly pure, oval face," and finally, her hand,

> A hand that ought to hold a whip,
> Its opal, silver-rimmed.
> A hand whose wrist is swathed in silk,
> A violinist's hand,

A hand that's unrepeatable,
A hand that's elegant. ("Girlfriend," #8)

Four days later Tsvetaeva wrote her ninth "Girlfriend" poem, in which the expression of her passionate love reached its peak and revealed her greatest need in the relationship:

Right away my heart said: "She's the one!"
At random, I forgave you everything,
Knowing nothing—not even your name!
My only thought was, "Love me, love me!"

Perhaps in this winter rapture originated Tsvetaeva's impossible if psychologically understandable desire to have a child with Parnok. She rationalized it to herself as an expression of her "normal" maternal feeling, but it is not hard to see her rationalization as stimulated by guilt over the pleasure her "abnormal" love was giving her. Her desire for a child also masked her will to power in a relationship where she felt increasingly powerless.

Almost twenty years later, when Tsvetaeva was living in emigration on the outskirts of Paris, she wrote an antilesbian tract in French, "Lettre à l'Amazone." It had two addressees and constituted a double-pronged revenge upon two women whom she believed had spurned her—not given her what she wanted—in utterly different ways: Natalie Clifford Barney, the Amazon of the title and the external addressee, whose Paris literary salon had not recognized or welcomed Tsvetaeva; and Parnok, her Amazon of bygone days, the unnamed internal addressee, news of whose death (in 1933) apparently evoked bitter memories of what Tsvetaeva always felt, after their affair had ended, was Parnok's unfair rejection of her.[44]

Again playing on the Baudelairean tradition of *les femmes damnées*, Tsvetaeva argued in "Lettre" that lesbian relationships had one major shortcoming, which "cursed" and invalidated them—

they could not produce a Child (Tsvetaeva's capitalization) and therefore could not satisfy the "normal" maternal desires of "the younger" partner in the relationship. Her idiosyncratic projection of a "typical" lesbian couple in fact belied any standard of typicality and revealed that her general case was based largely on her own personal one.

Tsvetaeva had several other affairs with women after she and Parnok broke up, but since the description in "Lettre" of a typical lesbian couple echoed numerous moments and phrases from her "Girlfriend" poems, one concludes that it was modelled primarily on the author's experience with Parnok. Thus, Tsvetaeva's example in "Lettre" of a conversation between lesbian lovers on the child issue resonated with the fantasy she must have started verbalizing to Parnok in 1915:

> At the outset it sounds like a joke.
> "What a nice child!"
> "Wouldn't you like one like that?"
> "Yes. No. By you—yes."
> But . . . it's all in fun, in jest.
> The next time it's already a sigh.
> "How much I would like to . . . "
> "Yes, what?"
> "Oh, nothing."
> "No, no, I know . . . "
> "Well, if you already know. But only—by you."
> Silence.
> "Are you still thinking about that?"
> "If you say so."
> "But you're the one who keeps saying . . . "[45]

More important than whether such conversations ever took place between Tsvetaeva and Parnok is the inner truth of how much Tsvetaeva's fantasy must have hurt and horrified her lover, especially in view of Parnok's despair over not having been able to have children herself. Tsvetaeva indirectly acknowledges Parnok's pain when she goes on to describe the "older" lover's fear of losing the "younger's" love and her jealousy of any men who cross the "younger's" path.[46]

As early as the spring of 1915, Parnok apparently began to accuse Tsvetaeva of wanting to leave her, and of inevitably doing so because she (Parnok) could not give her what she wanted. Her jealousy came to focus, as might be expected, on Tsvetaeva's husband, and it revealed her vulnerability, which in turn fed Tsvetaeva's unbridled will to power. Her impossible desire soon became an obsession.

While Tsvetaeva's repressed "feminine" self desired a child from Parnok, her "masculine" self felt challenged to the role of Pygmalion-like revealer of her Galatea's hidden genius. Here her will to create her woman-lover (so reminiscent of Virginia Woolf's desire to invent her lover, Vita Sackville-West, in *Orlando*) came up against Parnok's equally strong will to create herself.[47] Although she had still achieved only modest results in the realization of her poetic potential, Parnok did not want to hand over the Pygmalion role to her young poet-lover. She never had been able to bear the thought, after all, that anyone would dare to presume he had "discovered" her. The last stanza of the ninth "Girlfriend" poem, in which Tsvetaeva climaxed her rapture over her girlfriend by asserting herself as the discoverer of this "fair stranger" for Russian poetry (the "us"), must have evoked ambivalent feelings in Parnok:

> Parrying all smiles with my poems!
> I reveal to you and the world-at-large
> Everything in you that lies in store for us,
> Fair stranger with the brow of Beethoven![48]

By the end of January Tsvetaeva's worried friends and family had given up hope of saving her from her passion. "Marina's love affair," Voloshina wrote to Obolenskaya, "is developing apace, and with such uncontrollable force that nothing can stop it. She'll just have to burn herself up in its blaze, and Allah knows how it will all end."[49]

On January 28 Tsvetaeva seemed to second Voloshina's opinion in her lyrical reminiscence of her first meeting with Parnok (in the tenth poem of "Girlfriend"). The remaining five poems in the cycle, however, expressed a greater or lesser degree of hostility to Parnok because of her "thrice-cursed Passion," and they showed that by spring, Tsvetaeva was beginning to recover from her burns and, consequently, feeling pain.[50]

For Tsvetaeva, who distrusted and devalued physical love, the most positive, and eternally beautiful, aspect of her love for Parnok was its maternal-filial eros. Some of Parnok's previous lovers had also stimulated her maternal emotions and others would in the future, but Tsvetaeva was special in that she apparently led Parnok to confront long-buried feelings about the loss of her own mother. Perhaps she sensed a bond of orphanhood or, rather, motherlessness, with Tsvetaeva, who had lost her mother relatively early in her life, too, and, more important, at the critical moment of puberty.

In the poem "The Letter," which appeared in the February 1915 issue of *Russian Thought,* Parnok expressed some of the complicated feelings she had about her mother. Their brief, emotionally unsatisfying relationship had left her with the sense that her mother was a woman she had not known; yet she had been a mother for many of the women she had known, including her current lover. Parnok was inspired to write about her mother when she apparently came across an old letter that Alexandra Parnokh had written to her sister (Parnok's aunt) after a visit to the latter's house:

You wrote your sister, "What a pity!
I forgot my sleeveless cloak."
Your fine script helps me track the features
of a soul I did not know.
You were incapable of trusting:

> your o's and a's are tightly spaced.
> I try in my imagination
> to sketch the outlines of your face.
> You were quiet, uningenious,
> like your lines, formed modestly.
> And everything my heart cherishes
> you would malign as vanity.
> I cling, though, to the tempting dream
> that all the same, you would have loved me:
> the flourish ending your delicate,
> small "I" is just so lovely. (#16)

Memory, a frequent motif in Parnok's work, also figured prominently in the first love lyric she wrote to Tsvetaeva, probably in February 1915 (she was later unsure of the date), after Tsvetaeva had already written ten poems to her. The lyric was inspired by Sappho's fragment, "Like a small girl you appeared in my presence ungracefully," and was Parnok's first Sapphic poem.[51] As such it heralded a new stage in her creative evolution and signaled a new strategy she would employ in writing her lesbian experience into Russian poetry.

Parnok's discovery of Sappho coincided with the beginning of her affair with Tsvetaeva, so it is not strange that her first Sapphic imitations expressed aspects of that love relationship. Had she possessed a better sense of timing and literary faddishness, she would have published her collection of Sapphic poems, *Roses of Pieria,* which came out only in 1922, before the 1917 Revolution. During the war years there was a minor rage for Sappho in Russia that followed the appearance, in 1914 and 1915, of two poetic translations of the Lesbian poet's "complete" fragments and poems.

The poem "Like a small girl" (#59) had two addressees, Sappho and Tsvetaeva, and dealt with three interlocking love affairs: Sappho and Atthis (the "small girl" addressed in Sappho's line); Sappho and Parnok's poetic speaker (who has been "pierced" by Sappho's one-line fragment and made to desire Sappho through emulation); Parnok and Tsvetaeva (Parnok's "small girl" and lover).[52]

In Sappho's possession, the poetic speaker falls to musing on her sleeping lover as she cradles her in her arms:

> "Like a small girl you appeared in my presence ungracefully"—
> Ah, Sappho's single-line shaft pierced to my very core!
> During the night I leaned over your curly head pensively;
> motherly tenderness stilled passion's mad rush in my heart—
> "Like a small girl you appeared in my presence ungracefully."

Sappho's ancient line becomes a lyrical refrain that cradles the poetic speaker's memory of different moments from her and her lover's affair: "I recollected your dodging my kiss with some subterfuge," "I recollected your eyes, pupils incredibly wide" (a reference, perhaps, to the October 22 rendezvous when Tsvetaeva had felt everything was "demonically in reverse"). Then there was Tsvetaeva's girlish pleasure in her new "possession" on the day she first came to Parnok's apartment: "Into my house you came, happy with me as a novelty: / colorful slippers, a sash, maybe a new string of beads." And finally, Parnok's most recent memory, repeating countless others, of Tsvetaeva's ungirlish "malleability" and post-orgasmic sleep:

> But, beneath the mallet of love you are gold—and so malleable!
> Leaning, I cradled your face, pale in our passion's shade,
> where it appeared death had passed like a snowy white
>   powder-puff...

The poetic speaker concludes by thanking her "small girl" for being hers and for being in her life: "I'm also grateful to you, sweetness, because in those days / 'Like a small girl you appeared in my presence ungracefully.'"

The rhapsodic mood of this poem contradicted the unharmonious reality of the lovers' ongoing relationship as Parnok expressed it in two other poems she wrote in the winter of 1915: "Embroidery has covered up my windowpane" and "That evening was blazing dimly."⁵³ On February 5 Parnok sent copies of both poems to Tsvetaeva's sister-in-law, Liza Efron, who had asked for them after hearing Parnok read them.⁵⁴ Neither poem specified its addressee, but both contained details of the Moscow neighborhood where Parnok and Tsvetaeva lived at the time of their affair: that shopsign GEORGES BLOK (#56) was visible from Parnok's apartment on Khlebny Lane, and the Union Theater, mentioned in "That evening was blazing dimly," was (and still is) located at nearby Nikitsky Gates.

Both these poems are early examples of what would become Parnok's forte—the treatment of lesbian love in romantically heightened, but nonliterary, colloquial language. They constituted a stylistic and thematic contrast to the stylized and, unfortunately, anachronistic Sapphic treatment of the same theme in "Like a small girl."

"Embroidery has covered up" expressed what can easily be imagined as one of Parnok's morbid moods after she and Tsvetaeva had quarreled and broken up for the umpteenth time:

> Embroidery has covered up
> my windowpane. Oh day of parting!
> I press my anguish-ridden hands
> against the glass's unsmooth surface.
> My devastated eyes look out
> upon the frost, first gift of winter,
> the way the icy moire melts down
> and then dissolves away in teardrops.
> The fence is buried in a drift,
> the rime is fluffier, more like terry,
> the garden under silver fringe
> and tassels—like a brocade coffin . . .
> No walkers and no cars are out,
> my telephone is cruelly silent.
> With letters on the sign GEORGES BLOK
> I play at guessing odds or evens. (#56)

In "That evening was blazing dimly," urban nature also seems to express the emotional situation of the lovers who have had a spat after making love. The alienating effects hang over them at the movies afterward, where they go at the addressee's wish.⁵⁵

The poem narrates how they entered the theater and sat down in silence. The speaker was immersed in amorous memories of the network of veins on her lover's hands that still felt "weak from happiness," but were "purposefully covered in gloves" that made it impossible for the speaker to touch them. Throughout the movie the speaker was more aware of the movements of her lover beside her than the moving images on the screen—how she (the addressee) would move tormentingly closer and then away again, as if remembering that they were fighting. The speaker wanted to make up but felt she couldn't find the right words. "In the darkness your distant, brown eyes . . . ," she started to whisper, but was cut off by the sound of waltz music. Scenes of Switzerland flashed on the screen—a tourist in the mountains, a goat. The speaker smiled, but getting no response from her lover, she resigned herself to another stalemate and caressed her sleeve softly and surreptitiously.

The day before Parnok sent these two poems to Liza Efron, she received an unexpected visit from Voloshina, whose worry about Marina had finally forced her to approach directly the woman who, in her eyes, was responsible for her and Marina's distress. She came away from the meeting feeling somewhat differently than when she arrived, as she reported to Obolenskaya the next day in a letter:

> Yesterday I was at Sonya's and she and I had a long talk lasting hours, and there were many gaps in what she said that grated upon me, and there were moments in the conversation when I was ashamed of myself for what I had said about her to other people, when I had condemned her or coldly pronounced irreversible sentences on her that were worthy of an executioner.⁵⁶

Two days later Parnok wrote a short lyric that foresaw "unavoidable destruction" for the poetic speaker in the stormy course her heart had set:

> Again we have the signal to depart!
> On a wild midnight we left our moorings.
> My heart—a captain who's gone mad—
> sets sail for unavoidable destruction.
> Whirlwinds have set the moon-ball dancing
> and stirred up heavy breakers all around . . .
> —Pray for us, the unrepentant,
> oh poet, companion of all seekers! (#60)

Parnok had once described herself to Gurevich as a "seeker" who had "wasted a lot of time and energy on searchings" for the right person to satisfy her need for a committed relationship.[57] It seems she realized by early February 1915 that Tsvetaeva would not be that person either.

By the end of the month Tsvetaeva was also beginning to express ambivalence about the relationship. Her eleventh "Girlfriend" poem fairly bristled with spoiled-child hostility. If Parnok suffered because of Tsvetaeva's devotion to her husband, her obsession with a Child Parnok could not give her, and her willingness to flirt with men, Tsvetaeva was jealous of Parnok's other women friends and even more of her nonmonogamous reputation—her "inspired seductions," as she had put it in the first "Girlfriend" poem. She suspected Parnok of taking other lovers while they were in love, although there is no evidence that Parnok did so after she left Albrecht. In her eleventh poem, Tsvetaeva revealed her desire to best Parnok in the art of betrayal:

> In the sun all eyes are searing,
> Tomorrow's not today,
> I'm speaking to you in the offing,
> If I should betray.

At the same time, she wanted Parnok to know that "no matter whose lips" she "might be kissing in the throes of love," she was totally faithful to her, as devoted as Bettina von Arnim had been to Karoline von Guenderode. In the last stanza of the poem, she quoted Bettina's oath of devotion to her romantic friend: "Come and whistle beneath my window."[58]

The stormy relationship continued through the spring as the two poets' lyrical duel also heated up, Tsvetaeva, as before, offering the majority of thrusts, Parnok parrying mainly with silence and once in sonnet form. Parnok's sexual demands oppressed Tsvetaeva, and she was enraged by her submission to her own newly awakened desire for "burned and burning fateful mouths," as she put it in a poem she wrote on March 14.[59]

According to her twelfth "Girlfriend" lyric from the end of April, she wished in some ways that she had never met Parnok, whom she both resented and respected for her proud aloofness and sexual possessiveness. Yet, in the same poem, she insisted that even "on the eve of breaking up"—she also foresaw the end of the relationship almost from the beginning—she would be able to repeat that she had loved Parnok's haughty gaze, "which didn't give anyone the time of day," and her "powerful hands."

It was at this time in her love affair that Tsvetaeva developed the image of herself as a "Spartan child"—robust, resilient, unpampered—completely in the power of an older, fateful woman "with a name like a suffocating flower" and an Amazon "helmet of red hair" ("Girlfriend," #13). Tired of hearing Parnok's accusations that she would leave her for a man who could give her the Child she was obsessed with, Tsvetaeva began hurling her own accusations at Parnok. They expressed fear and the negative prediction that her "tragic, Shakespearean heroine" would inevitably move on in fulfillment of her restless, homeless destiny (#14). She tried reading mirrors to learn what that destiny held and magnanimously blessed Parnok on her way to meeting it (#14).

After one of their frequent quarrels, she lashed out at Parnok and everyone else who was putting emotional demands on her in a May 6 poem that she originally intended for the "Girlfriend" cycle, but later excluded:

> Remember: one little hair of my own head
> Is dearer to me than all other heads.
> So go away ... You too,
> And you too, and you.
> Stop loving me, all of you stop loving me!
> Don't watch over me in the mornings,
> So that I might be free to go out
> And stand in the breeze.[60]

Tsvetaeva's stream of lyrical hostility finally evoked a response from Parnok, if a controlled one, in her "Sonnet" written on May 9:

> You watched the little boys at all their games,
> and showed indifference to smiling dolls.
> A superfluity of energy propelled you
> from your cradle straight astride a horse.
> Years have passed, by their ominous shadow
> your power-loving outbursts have not been
> blotted out in your heart—how little I mean
> to it, Bettina Arnim and Marina Mniszek!
> I gaze upon the ash and fire of your curls,
> upon your hands, more generous than a king's,
> the lack of colors on my palette defeats me!
> You, passing by to your own fate!
> Where does the sun rise that is your mate?
> Where is your Goethe, and where your False Dmitri? (#28)

Parnok loved the Bettina in Tsvetaeva, that is, her genius, and had accepted her superior giftedness with sufficient equanimity to wish her well on her creative journey to her poetic equal (Goethe). She felt much more bitter about the Marina Mniszek in Tsvetaeva. The seventeenth-century Polish noblewoman, whom Tsvetaeva celebrated as her historical alter ego, had played a powerful and, from the Russian viewpoint, perfidious role in Russian history after her husband, the so-called False Dmitri, a pretender, seized the Russian throne with Polish and Jesuit backing in 1605. By comparing her Marina to Marina Mniszek, Parnok both identified the addressee of her sonnet and implied that Marina's treachery to her, just like Mniszek's betrayal of Russia, would involve her loyalty to her husband, whom Tsvetaeva had the habit of addressing in her poems as both her "sun" and her "tsar." From Parnok's point of view, it was her married lover, not herself, who behaved nonmonogamously and treacherously throughout their relationship, in being unable to choose between her two loves.

Despite all the contraindications to domestic harmony, the lovers decided to spend the greater part of the summer at Koktebel, where Voloshin and his mother, Pra, had a famous summer colony for artists, poets, and intellectuals. Tsvetaeva had been summering in Koktebel off and on since she was a teenager. It was there that she had met Sergey and decided to marry him virtually at first sight. Parnok had never been to Koktebel, and considering Pra's less than warm feelings for her, she could not have helped sensing that this was not the most auspicious time for a first visit and that she was somehow penetrating enemy territory. Not to be hopelessly outnumbered, she brought her sister, Liza, along with her. Tsvetaeva had a more impressive retinue comprised of her daughter, Alya, and Alya's nurse, her sister Anastasia (Asya) and her little son, and his nurse.

Because of the war, Koktebel had fewer summer residents than usual in 1915. "People are afraid of the Turkish women," Voloshina reported in a letter to Tsvetaeva's other sister-in-law, Vera Efron, adding that she had "reserved four rooms for Marina, Asya, Sonya, and Liza."[61] The four women left Moscow by train on May 20 and arrived in Koktebel six days later.

On the surface Parnok and Tsvetaeva's two-month stay in Koktebel was a model of peaceful domesticity with Tsvetaeva playing the role of "wife" and including Parnok in her family. The lovers evidently shared one of the four rooms reserved for Tsvetaeva's party, and some miraculously preserved domestic detritus (including a laundry list on which Tsvetaeva recorded her and Parnok's blouses before sending them to be cleaned) provides concrete evidence of Tsvetaeva's putative wifely concern for her lover.[62]

Little Alya may have resented, however, that she didn't see much of her mother, because, as she told her in one of their few private exchanges, "I was with nurse, and you were with Sophia Yakovlevna."[63] And at the other chronological end of the Koktebel "family," Voloshina had reservations about the summer. Her problems began after a married couple arrived, with whom three of "the poetesses" did not want to socialize. She wrote to Liza Efron:

> They [the poetesses] became depressed and started discussing ... whether they should join the whole company for meals or eat separately. They chose the latter course, and only Asya has joined us. The others have contact only with me, and infrequent contact at that. I regret their absence, but can't do anything about it. Yesterday one more poet joined us, Osip Mandelshtam. We're in high spirits, a lot of conversations, laughter, declamations.[64]

Mandelshtam soon added a new complexity to the emotions seething beneath the jollity at Koktebel when he developed a crush on Tsvetaeva. He began openly demonstrating his jealousy of Parnok by dismissing her poetry and raving about Tsvetaeva's. Then, one evening, the assembled company "played a joke on him," as Liza Parnokh Tarakhovskaya recalled. "We read some of my sister's poems and told him they were Tsvetaeva's. He began praising them to the skies. When he found out he had been praising my sister's poems, he was angry at all of us for a long time."[65] This may have been one of the behaviors that convinced Parnok that Mandelshtam was "simply stupid."[66] On the other hand, she was not indifferent to his open flirtation with Tsvetaeva however foolish it made him look.

Mandelshtam's brother, Alexander, was also at Koktebel, and as the summer wore on, the sisters of Tsvetaeva and Parnok spent more and more of their time with the Mandelshtam pair. Both brothers were sickly, especially Osip, who was on a special diet that interfered with his always joining the others for dinner and drinking parties. Asya Tsvetaeva willingly fell into the role of Mandelshtam's sister-nanny, "while Sonya Parnok's sister Liza," she recalled, "began nursemaiding Alexander. Liza and I would share many amicably ironic laughs about our roles and would give each other friendly support."[67]

Pra continued to dislike Parnok while simultaneously developing a fondness for Liza: "Sonya is completely alien to me, I have no relations with her; Liza and I are on friendly terms," she wrote to Liza Efron in June. In mid-July she reiterated, "I have no interest in Sonya and complete indifference to her. Liza is simple, nice, and I like her."[68]

While Parnok was in Koktebel, she wrote only three poems and devoted her energies to the libretto for the opera she and Shteinberg were still working on. At the end of June she sent him the entire first act and promised the second scene of the second act in a month. She suggested calling the opera *Abductress of the Heart*, noting, "It has a genuinely oriental ring to it and comes from one of the stories in *1001 Nights*. In order to speed up our work we must communicate with each other more frequently and more intensively. I intend to be in Petersburg in the fall and listen to the music you have composed so far."[69]

That summer brought another turning point in the life of Parnok's brother. He left Russia and eventually settled in Paris, not to return to his "stepmotherland" until she was much changed, in 1922. Once again his Russophobia had compelled him to emigrate:

> When the German army penetrated the borders of the Russian Empire, even the Petersburg Jews began to be threatened with exile from the capital. Rumor of this new abomination swept the entire country three times. It seemed time had gone backwards. The specter of the inquisition arose before even the most sober, imperturbable people. "This will end in another Spain," they said. The year 1492, when the Jews were driven out of Spain, seemed to have been resurrected in 1915 in Petersburg.[70]

By the time Valentin left Russia, he and his sister had become totally estranged. The exact reasons for and circumstances surrounding their falling-out remain mysterious, however.

When Valya had returned to Petersburg in November 1914, he was much changed—so much, that upon seeing him again, his older sister, who resembled him physically, could only marvel at how strange his familiar features seemed to her. The change Valentin must have found in Sonya was even more profound, and went to the very core of her being. She was seriously considering converting, or perhaps had already converted, to Russian Orthodoxy—the religion of the enemy, from Valya's point of view.[71] Valentin may have questioned the reasons, and even the sincerity, of Sonya's new faith. His refusal to understand her spiritual needs naturally stung and offended her, and she may have expressed her hurt and anger in this undated lyric published in *Poems* (1916):

> What do I care for the scorn on those cruel lips!
> Tell me, valuer, on what scales have you weighed
> everything I live by and in which I unhesitatingly believe?
> With what measure have you measured a living soul?
> Were you here when my soul was conducting her affairs
> in silence? (#46)[72]

There was gossip from a source close to Parnok that in addition to their religious and political differences, the poet and her brother had become interested in the same woman, and their romantic rivalry over her had led to their estrangement. Another of Parnok's undated lyrics, which was first published in the November-December 1915 issue of *Northern Annals,* could be read as lyrical evidence in support of this gossip, providing one understands the "brother" addressee mentioned in the last line to be Parnok's biological (rather than metaphoric) brother.

In the poem the female speaker acknowledges that she and her "brother" (romantic rival) were too similar in their difference not to avoid clashing "on the same path." As is typical for internally mediated triangles, their mutual hatred proved stronger than the love either felt, and they discovered that they were Dostoevskian doubles, complementary opposites:

> Isn't the reason why our hatred was more mutual
> and more passionate than love, and juster than love by far,
> that we discovered our doubles in each other? Tell me,
> in chastising you, my brother, am I not chastised myself? (#45)[73]

After their rift, whenever it happened, Valentin and Sonya were out of contact for several years.

On July 22 Parnok and Tsvetaeva left Koktebel and went to spend the last three weeks of their summer at friends of Parnok's in Svyatye gory, Kharkov province, Ukraine. From there Tsvetaeva wrote her sister-in-law a frank and moving letter about the impossible emotional situation she found herself in. Her surroundings, with their "pines, sand, heather, coolness and sadness" reminded her of Finland. Things were particularly depressing in the evenings when they sat alone by a kerosene lamp hearing the pines rustle and pondering the bad news about the war that filled the newspapers. Marina had been completely out of touch with her husband for over a week—he was serving as a male nurse at the front— and felt hopeless about getting any reply to her letters. At the end of the letter she summed up her quandary:

> I love Seryozha for my whole life, he is my own, I shall never leave him. I write him every day, or every other day, he knows my whole life, only I try to write him as little as possible about what's saddest. I feel a constant weight on my heart. I go to sleep and wake up with it there. Sonya loves me very much and I love her—and that's eternal, and I won't be able to leave her. I feel torn apart from the days I must divide [between two loves], my heart continues to combine jobs and hold two offices. It seems I will never have simple happiness and in general, it's not in my nature to have it. And complete joy has also eluded me. I can't hurt other people and can't help hurting them.[74]

Parnok expressed the pain she was suffering from the relationship indirectly in three lyrics she wrote in Svyatye gory. On July 31 she vented her need to rebel against the domesticity that had engulfed her in her last two relationships and had failed to make her feel happy or cared for:

> All ablaze, the clouds fly by,
> the sky city lies in ruins.
> My step is obstinate and light,
> the wind has spread a willful windlass.
> Who blessed me as I headed off?
> Who murmured, "Have a happy journey"?
> Let the winds not cease to blow,
> to urge me from my threshold.
> To the devil for his use
> I throw the past—my fateful burden.
> Up above my homeless head
> blaze on, nomadic heaven! (#13)

Tsvetaeva had once teased Parnok that her youth was passing her by. Now, on the day after her thirtieth birthday, seeing that her youth (Tsvetaeva) would never be wholly hers, Parnok seemed to have embraced again the only thing that she always knew would be her own, her nomadic persona. Tsvetaeva herself perceived Parnok to be a wanderess, though she gave the word a more specifically amorous and hence pejorative value than Parnok, and had asked her, in the last poem of "Girlfriend," who her next destination would be: "Your third woman was / dear to you in another way ... // What will remain of me / in your heart, wanderess?"[75]

Tsvetaeva may have worked subconsciously to encourage Parnok's wanderlust, seeing in it a natural way out of her own dilemma, a way of passively forcing Parnok to break the bonds of love that she felt she would not be able to break. After all, from the very beginning, she had perceived her *gynekouros* as "something stronger than [she]." Certainly, the prolonged demise of the love affair suggests that the lovers were vying with each other to see who could hold on to the relationship the longest.

On August 1 Parnok continued the lyrical expression of her

fantasy plans to hit the road, almost echoing the question Tsvetaeva had asked her in June as to who her next lover would be:

> The cranes have flown southward.
> I'm leaving too for faraway.
> Where shall I meet her, a girlfriend,
> a mistress who will be my fate?[76]

At the end of the poem, the speaker asserted that she was seeking "not Manon, not Cleopatra / not Carmen, and not Isolde!" Parnok had evidently had her fill of fatal, operatic heroines, but whom was she seeking? If she really did still love Tsvetaeva "very much," as Tsvetaeva thought, then this poem could be read as a tacit acknowledgment of loving her too much to tolerate only half of Tsvetaeva's love in return. Thus, the poem pinpointed the moment in Parnok's turmoil over Tsvetaeva when she realized she had to move on and take up the search again for the woman who would command her whole fate, not the one who was passing on (or returning) to someone else.

Four days later Parnok wrote her second poem specifically addressed to Marina. It had the ring of an epitaph before the fact and was stimulated, ironically, by the poet's contemplation of an icon of the Holy Mother in a local church:

> Blindly staring eyes of the
> Holy Mother and Savior Child.
> Smell of incense, wax, and oil.
> Sounds of soft weeping filling the church.
> Melting tapers held by young, meek women
> in fists stiff with cold and roughskinned.
> Oh, steal me away from my death,
> you, whose arms are tanned and fresh,
> you, who passed by, exciting me!
> Isn't there in your desperate name a
> wind from all storm-tossed coasts,
> Marina, named after the sea! (#9)

Parnok acknowledged that Tsvetaeva had in essence already passed out of her life, and the excitement she had aroused, and continued to arouse, was all that remained of their relationship. But the fallout from that mutual excitement was still a strong bond, and its virility enabled Parnok to ask her "desperate," youthful lover—or the part of her that had once recklessly vowed to steal an icon for her lady "that very night"—to save her from death, just as the weeping women around her in the church prayed to the Mother of God to protect their menfolk at the front.

By a strange coincidence, a few days before Parnok wrote this poem, Sergey Efron arrived unexpectedly (and safely) in Koktebel. He stayed there until the end of the month and then went to spend the winter somewhere outside of Moscow and return to his studies.

Her anxiety about her husband's safety resolved, Tsvetaeva was able to return to Moscow in a calmer frame of mind. She and Parnok were back in the city by August 18 and were "inseparable" after that. Immediately upon their return they began giving private readings to their women friends of the poems they had written that summer.[77]

The July-August issue of *Northern Annals* contained Parnok's review of a collection of short stories by Alexey Remizov *(Spring Powder)* that she regarded highly and that seemed to her to illustrate her own conviction that compassion was a greater emotion than love. Remizov's work had the same effect on her, she wrote, as the "soul-searing, morbid, unbearable fullness" produced by the sound of the organ. Her review also expressed her apocalyptic belief that "Russia [was] a country with a dreadful fate and ought to be protected with a reliable veil,"[78] and reflected the specifically Christian religiosity that had become much more noticeable in her lyrics and her thinking at this time. She also noted Remizov's "marvelous gift for unbinding spells" and the way he "orchestrated his sentences with the art of a genuine musician, . . . succeeding in conveying not only his voice, but its most subtle intonations too." She obviously desired the same musical refinement for her own voice.

In the fall and early winter of 1915, the lyrical record shows that Parnok and Tsvetaeva's love affair was in its death agony. Their final breakup was especially painful because both of them struggled against the inevitable end: neither wanted to be the first to let go, and, most painful of all, they continued to love and want each other.

At the beginning of September, however, Parnok was feeling the strains of love: her lips were "happy to be nobody's," and she delighted in her empty apartment where she could immerse herself in "coldly fiery Stendhal." She positively resented her lover's visits: "Why do you come, you whose name / brings me the winds of all roads?" (#37).

According to a poem Tsvetaeva wrote two days later, "In the fog, bluer than incense," Parnok, the poem's likely addressee, was seeing another woman. Tsvetaeva called her a "rival," but without particular animus.[79] She apparently no longer felt threatened by potential rivals, so caught up was she, like Parnok, in "the gypsy passion of separation," in which both of them, as she wrote in an October poem, emerged true to themselves only when they were being treacherous to each other.[80]

During their "gypsy passion of separation," Parnok suffered more from jealousy than Tsvetaeva. After finally meeting (or seeing) Tsvetaeva's husband, she wrote a viciously ironic and embittered poem to him in which she called her seemingly victorious male rival "a veritable Adonis." Acknowledging that her addressee (Efron)[81] had bested her in youth and beauty, the poetic speaker resigned herself to the bittersweet comfort of knowing she had bested him as a lover:

> As I press myself to my beloved woman's lips,
> I cheer myself with this sad thought:
> it was not you, young man, who broke the spell on her.
> When her next lover marvels at the fire from these lips,
> oh, you who had her first, not your name will he
> jealously recall—but mine. (#53)

At the end of November Tsvetaeva described one of her and Parnok's typically estranged cab rides home in the lyric "Full moon, and bear-fur lap robe," which she concluded by saying: "I'm starting to dream—of the Lord, / I've stopped dreaming—of you."[82]

Parnok unconfidently attributed three poems to November 1915, all of which would appear in *Poems,* which she was then preparing for publication. In "Fortune telling" (#36), dedicated in the autograph to her friend Konstantin Lipskerov, the female speaker reads a paranoid and dire fortune in her cards. By signifying herself as the queen of hearts (cups) and noting that the other three queens were conspiring against her, she acknowledged that she was responding to the world in terms of emotion alone and psychologically excluding the alternative responses of action, business, or intellect (the provinces of the three other queens):

> I am the queen of hearts. The others, all three,
> are concluding a secret alliance against me.
> Take a look—the ace of spades points down like a spike
> over the nine, the card of love,
> a piercing dagger raised above the heart.
> You see: the alien kings hold wands,
> only the red king bears a single sword,
> his eyes gaze with malice the others know not . . .
> Love will be a duel of two wills.
> Who is he, who is he, the menacing king? (#36)

The mood of the poem and the prediction it contained seemed in tune with the general music of Parnok's love life at the time, and it may have expressed her unconscious knowledge that some man threatened her and Tsvetaeva's future, either Efron or some other "menacing king." When she cast her cards and/or wrote the poem, she may have recalled the blissful night at the monastery hotel in Rostov-the-Great just about a year before, when she and Marina had read their cards, and the king of hearts had turned up in

Left: FIG. 1. "I cherish the alluring dream / that all the same, you would have loved me."

Alexandra Parnokh, the poet's mother.

Right: FIG. 2. "I was very distant from my father."

Yakov Parnokh, the poet's father.

FIG. 3. "I learned to daydream / that a bloody death befits a hero."

Sonya as a little girl in Taganrog.

FIG. 4. "Life's good, but it is not my lot / to grasp the local atmosphere."

Sonya as a gymnasium student in Taganrog.

FIG. 5. "We should never have ruined our relationship by getting married."

Parnok *(center)* with her future husband, Volkenshtein *(standing)*, Volkenshtein's brother *(on left)*, and an unidentified woman *(on right)*, circa 1905.

FIG. 6. *Left to right:* Gnesin, Volkenshtein, Chapygin (a writer and friend of Parnok's), Gnesin's brother.

FIG. 7. "Each wicked finger's shape disseminates / a woman's tenderness, a boy's impertinence" (Tsvetaeva).

Parnok during the time of her marriage to Volkenshtein. By permission of the Amherst Center for Russian Culture, Amherst College.

FIG. 8. "Sad eyes, so deeply open, / drunk on the anguish of all passions."

Parnok seated behind her desk, circa 1910.

FIG. 9. "I'm now a stay-at-home in Kolokolnikov Lane with my girlfriend and a pet monkey."

Parnok circa 1913.

FIG. 10. "Overpowering the face,/ the eyes, like double moons" (Tsvetaeva).

Parnok during the time of her love affair with Tsvetaeva.

FIG. 11. "Mama had a friend, Sonya Parnok—she also wrote poetry" (Ariadne Efron).

Marina Tsvetaeva *(on right)* and her daughter Ariadne, 1915.

FIG. 12. "The . . . rosiness, goldenness, / and pearliness of face, and silkiness, . . ./ And the coldness of serpentine wiles."

Marina Tsvetaeva, 1916.

FIG. 13. "Oh my passionate friend,/ my insatiable one!"

Lyudmila Erarskaya *(standing)* and Parnok on the veranda in the Gertsyks' garden, Sudak, September 1918.

FIG. 14. Erarskaya *(center)*, Parnok *(right)*, and an unidentified woman *(left)* in Sudak.

FIG. 15. "Oh dark, dark, dark road, / why are you so dark and long?"

Parnok at the time of her return to Moscow, 1922.

FIG. 16. [———] "Again I gaze at your steep-browed profile."

Valentin Parnakh, Parnok's brother.

FIG. 17. Lev Gornung as a young man, 1920s.

FIG. 18. "Interchanges of our dreams / and secrets, mine, yours."

Parnok and Olga Tsuberbiller in their room in Moscow, 1920s.

FIG. 19. "Sin, have fun, and blossom with the years!"

Parnok *(on right)* and Faina Ranevskaya, 1920s.

FIG. 20. "And truly, one cannot predict, / who in the world will be one's reader."

Parnok in the late 1920s.

FIG. 21. Parnok and Tsuberbiller *(on the left)*, their landlady's son *(center)*, their landlady and an unidentified woman in the garden of the dacha they rented in Maloyaroslavets, summer 1931. Photograph by Lev Gornung.

FIG. 22. Parnok *(on the right)*, Tsuberbiller, and their landlady's son *(in the tree)* in Maloyaroslavets, summer 1931. Photograph by Lev Gornung.

FIG. 23. "Thank you, my angel, for being you, / and for being next to me."

Parnok and Tsuberbiller in the garden of their rented dacha in Maloyaroslavets, summer 1931. Photograph by Lev Gornung.

FIG. 24. "I want to dance! . . . Zurnàs, your wailing / inspires my stormy exaltation!"

Maria Maksakova as Almast in the opera *Almast* (end of Act III) for which Parnok wrote the libretto.

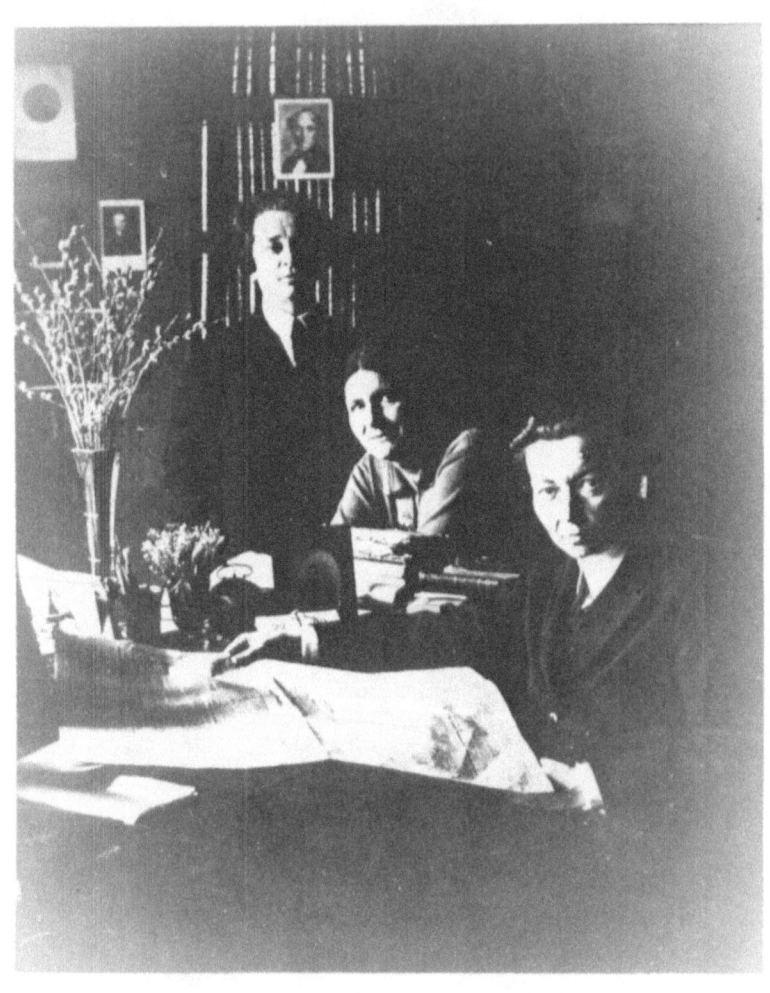

FIG. 25. A complex triangle of mutual need, love, and obligation. Parnok *(standing)*, Erarskaya *(center)*, Tsuberbiller *(right front)* in Moscow, 1932. Photograph by Lev Gornung.

FIG. 26. "A head of silver grey. And youthful features. / And Dante's profile. And a wingèd gaze."

Nina Vedeneyeva, 1932.

FIG. 27. "Now, without rebelling or resisting, / I hear how my heart beats its retreat."

The last photograph taken of Parnok, by Lev Gornung.

Marina's cards three times in a row. Whatever may have been the autobiographical basis for the poetic speaker's prediction in "Fortune telling," events in the next three months proved it to be correct.

The poem "How light the light is today" (#11), on the other hand, contradicted the ominous atmosphere surrounding Parnok at the time it was allegedly written. It concerned the power of naming as invested in Adam by the Creator—the poetic speaker pictured herself in Eden, hidden among the other creatures to be named. The poem began with an evocation of a primeval spring when the "earth [was] no years old"; perhaps its joy and "bubbling" creative energy provided a respite from the darkness and sorrow that were threatening to engulf Parnok in reality.

Finally, "I love you in your expanse" (#24), a love lyric to Russia, revealed that Parnok both empathized and identified herself with Russia in a way that gave a spiritual dimension to her own wandering. The poetic speaker evoked her motherland as a "much-loving wanderess" who was "moving toward Christ in a great aloneness."[83]

During the fall Parnok began suffering intensified but familiar symptoms—headaches, insomnia, fatigue, and tachycardia. As always, thoughts of death accompanied this onslaught of symptoms. The knowledge that death often occurred unexpectedly and instantaneously for sufferers of Grave's may have contributed to the poet's lyrical obsession with last moments. One example was her prediction of the single "boundless moment" before her death in the poem "Rondeau," which appeared in the November-December issue of *Northern Annals:*

> I'll remember everything. In one boundless moment,
> the obedient herds of all my days will crowd before me.
> On the paths I've trodden I shall not overlook
> one track, like the lines in my reference book,
> and to the evil of all my days I shall softly say "yes."

> Are we not summoned here by the whim of love—
> love, I have not endeavored to break your chains!
> And without fear, without shame, without despair
> I'll remember everything.
> Even if my toil has yielded me a pitiful harvest,
> and my barns are full of wormwood rather than corn,
> and even if my god has lied, my faith is firm,
> I won't be like some contemptible defrocked monk[84]
> in that endless moment, the last moment, when
> I'll remember everything. (#42)

Nine years had passed since Parnok had broken into print. Despite often leading the sort of life she had once felt could "never be in [her] poetry," she had managed to write and publish scores of poems that gave at least an idea of her life and affectional preference. She was certainly no longer a "young" poet, either in age or in outlook, if, indeed, she had ever been one in the latter sense. Yet at the age of thirty, she still had no book of her own.

Her proud comment to Struve in 1910 that she was "in no rush to publish" must have seemed more and more of an ironic understatement as the years passed. No wonder that she often tormented herself with undermining thoughts of talentlessness, creative penury, pitiful harvests, and threshing barns filled with bitter wormwood. No wonder, either, that her lack of ambition had made her, as Tsvetaeva had so correctly perceived, a "fair stranger" in Russian poetry with a Beethovenesque, or revolutionary, potential that far too few people had heard. The musical editor who recalled seeing Parnok and Tsvetaeva sitting in each other's arms at the Rimsky-Korsakovs' "strange parties" seemed to sum up Parnok's prerevolutionary poetic status in the eyes of her contemporaries when he ended his impression with the disparaging and homophobic remark, "Which of them dominated? What had Sophia Parnok written? I don't know."[85]

Unfortunately, it is difficult even to guess at the reasons and circumstances that finally made Parnok decide to harvest a first major crop from her fields. All one can say is merely the obvious—

she felt she was ready at last to publish her first book. She gathered together sixty poems she had written and, in many cases, already published, from 1912 through 1915 (roughly the period covered in this chapter). She rejected everything she had written prior to 1912 and thus consigned a substantial body of her work to oblivion.

Obviously, she felt that any earlier work deserved death. Equally obviously, she chose 1912 as the chronological beginning of her first book because of its personal, rather than creative, value. The year 1912 had had no particular importance for her writing as such—in fact, as far as one can tell, she wrote almost nothing that year—but, as the year of her father's death, it must have had powerful, perhaps unconscious, psychological significance. A similar pattern of death followed by creative renewal can be observed at subsequent stages of her poetic journey.

Parnok's first book, called simply *Poems,* was divided into five sections of unequal length, each of which had a certain thematic, rather than chronological, cyclical, or formal, unity. The sections dealt with: wandering (thirteen poems); death (seven poems); Russia and the war (four poems); love and poetry (thirteen poems); and love and remembering (twenty-three poems). The love lyrics, which comprised roughly a third of the book, introduced the first openly lesbian poetic speaker and desiring subject ever to be heard in a book of Russian poetry.

Parnok declared herself in a revolutionarily nondecadent, life-based lyricism. Although Tsvetaeva was mentioned by name (Marina) in the book only twice, several of the love poems, perhaps the majority, were clearly inspired by Parnok's relationship with her (##40, 52, 57, and 58, in addition to the ones discussed). The remaining love lyrics evoked episodes and lovers from Parnok's casual relationships prior to Albrecht, including a particularly intense encounter with a prostitute (#47).

The lesbian contents of *Poems* shocked some critics and forced more sympathetic ones, like Adelaida Gertsyk, Lipskerov, Khodasevich, and Voloshin, to find delicate circumlocutions for them or pass over them in silence. There was still no critical language for dealing with lesbianism in Russian literature, just as there was no appropriate way to talk about it in polite society. The poem that raised the most consternation among Parnok's reviewers turned out to be "Like a small girl you appeared in my presence ungracefully."[86] Part of the reason it aroused particular notice must have been that it assumed a lesbian Sappho; but in Russian poetry of the Silver Age, Sappho was considered to be a great *heterosexual* poetess. Overall, the reviews were positive, but they sent Parnok an ambiguous message by welcoming her as a fair stranger while avoiding her difference.

4.

"There's No Way Back, for You, Me, or Us..."

At the end of the year Parnok and Tsvetaeva went to Petrograd for about two weeks, and stayed at the home of Chatskina and Saker. It was Tsvetaeva's first trip to the capital and her introduction to literary society there. Among the many new people she met were the Kannegisers, the family of an eminent naval architect. They took her on a whirlwind tour of the city that left her with lasting impressions of "freezing cold, multitudes of monuments, fast-driving sleighs ... and huge marble fireplaces," where it seemed "whole groves of oak" were incinerated. But the main thing that remained in Tsvetaeva's memory of her visit "was the poetry of Pushkin and Akhmatova."[1]

In January the Kannegisers held a big evening party at their home to which Tsvetaeva and Parnok were invited, along with all the leading lights of literary and artistic Petersburg. The featured attraction was the celebrated poet Mikhail Kuzmin, who was to perform his songs. Unfortunately, Parnok did not feel well and could not go, which caused a quarrel between her and her lover, as Tsvetaeva recalled in dramatic detail several years later:

I had just arrived. I was with a certain person, i.e. it was a woman. Lord, how I cried! But that's not important. Well, to be brief, she really did not want me to go to that party and therefore made a point of urging me to go. She herself couldn't go—she had a headache—and when she had a headache—and she always had one—she was unbearable (our dark room, the dark-blue lamp, my tears . . .). But my head didn't ache—it never aches!—and I absolutely did not want to stay home (1) because of Sonya, (2) because Kuzmin would be there and was going to sing.

"Sonya, I'm not going."
"Why not? Certainly not because of me."
"But I feel sorry for you."
"There'll be lots of people there, you'll cheer up."
"No, I feel very sorry for you."
"I can't stand pity. Go, go. Just think, Marina, Kuzmin will be there, he'll sing."
"Yes, he'll sing, and when I get home, you'll never let me forget that I went, and I'll cry. I won't go for anything in the world."

Of course, she did go. And, unexpectedly, one of the multitude of guests there turned out to be Mandelshtam, whom she had not seen since she left Koktebel the previous summer. Both he and Tsvetaeva read their poems at the party, and for the first time they "realized each other's literary importance."[2] Their meeting at the Kannegisers initiated a new stage in their relationship, which has been described variously as a poetic friendship, a romantic flirtation, a mutual admiration of each other's talent, and a full-fledged, if brief, love affair.

The poetic, and perhaps amorous, excitement of meeting Mandelshtam and of her own success at the party naturally delighted Tsvetaeva, but also apparently made her feel guilty about enjoying herself in the absence of her lover. She decided to leave before Kuzmin sang, and made her excuses by telling everyone "in a business-like tone, 'I have my girlfriend at home.' " Kuzmin himself prevailed upon her to stay, and Tsvetaeva replied,

"You don't know me at all, but take what I say on faith, I've never wanted to stay so much in my life as I do now and never had to leave so much as I do now." . . .

"Is your girlfriend ill?"
"Yes."
"But, after all, you did leave her and are already here, so...."
"I know that I'll never be able to forgive myself if I stay, or if I go...."

She left after one or two songs. When she got home, Parnok had gone to bed.

The lovers returned to Moscow on January 19. Four days later they were both scheduled to participate in an *Evening of Women Poets* at the Polytechnic Museum, but neither of them attended. Ironically, Tsvetaeva's poems may have been read at the evening by an actress who was destined shortly to play a fateful role in the young poet's personal life. This actress was Lyudmila Vladimirovna Erarskaya.

A tall, dark-haired, Eurasian woman in her twenties, Lyudmila (Mashenka, Milochka) lived in Moscow and had two sisters with whom she was close. She worked in a private theater company, the Nezlobin Theater, named after the director and actor who had founded it in 1909. Unfortunately, nothing is known of how, when, or where Parnok and Erarskaya met, but by January 1916, they had "become close."[3] A mysterious, undated poem at the end of Parnok's first book that begins "A seed can't bloom in infertile soil" (#52) concerns an amorous triangle between the female speaker (Parnok), her present, but imminently unfaithful, passionate, and coldhearted lover (the addressee), and another, "third woman," who, the speaker warns her beloved, "already stands like a shadow between us." If Tsvetaeva were the intended addressee of this poem and Erarskaya the "third woman," then it could be read as a lyrical warning from Parnok of what Tsvetaeva would later call the "first catastrophe" of her young life.[4]

Erarskaya's appeal for Parnok is far easier to surmise than the details of their first meeting and involvement. She was as different from Tsvetaeva as a rebound lover could be (and often is): dark and statuesque where Tsvetaeva was rosy-golden and slender;

womanly where Tsvetaeva was boyish; worldly and reserved where Tsvetaeva was disingenuous and bold. Erarskaya was not a poet, desired no creative "duel of wills," and Parnok found her beautiful and seductive.

At the beginning of February, Mandelshtam unexpectedly arrived in Moscow to see Tsvetaeva and, in her words, "to finish the conversation" they had begun in Petrograd.[5] This "conversation" took up two days, during which Tsvetaeva introduced Mandelshtam to Moscow and shared poems with him. This time their literary importance for each other made her forget entirely about her "sick girlfriend," who was home suffering from almost continuous headaches, but who was also having conversations of her own with Erarskaya. According to Tsvetaeva, the two days with Mandelshtam was her first unexplained absence from Parnok "in ages," but she believed they were to blame for everything that followed.

After Mandelshtam left, on February 6, she went straight to Parnok's apartment, burst into the room, and then froze at the sight of "another woman" sitting on Parnok's bed in her usual place, looking "very large, fat, [and] black."[6]

In an instant Tsvetaeva sensed that she had been replaced in her mother-lover's affections by a serious rival, and the realization traumatized her. A few days later, she struck back with a hurtful blow of her own, apparently demanding that Parnok return her letters and the notebook of the "Girlfriend" poems. Parnok responded to this "blasphemy" in a proud and angry poem:

> To blush for poems that you wrote,
> demand that I return your letters,
> your gift is sacred, independent
> of those blasphemous hands of yours!
> What can I return? Here, catch
> your notebook full of written pages,
> but the fire, moisture, and wind in murmurs
> of love can not be given back.
> Aren't they why my night is black,
> my eyes—vacant, my voice tender,

but do I know which ear of corn has
arisen from the seed you've sown? (#82)[7]

Despite her burgeoning relationship with Erarskaya, Parnok appeared to be as emotionally devastated as Tsvetaeva by the death (black night) of their love, but unlike Tsvetaeva, she accepted the finality of what had happened on February 6 and its aftermath. Her "To blush for poems" suggests that she compensated for the loss of Tsvetaeva's "sacred gift"—the one thing of Marina's that she had cherished without qualification—by making herself believe that she had not, and could not, ever lose it. She had absorbed her poet-lover's seed, the elemental fire, air, and water of her love, and believed that seed would not die, but would "bring forth much fruit," according to the mystery spoken in the well-known lines from St. John (to which her poem clearly alludes): "Except a corn of wheat fall into the earth and die, it abideth alone, but if it die, it bringeth forth much fruit." In the mother-daughter context of her personal and creative relationship with Tsvetaeva, Parnok's "To blush for poems" could also be read as a reworking of the Demeter-Persephone myth.

When "To blush for poems" was written, Tsvetaeva's seed had just died in Parnok, and she did not know what fruit it would produce. But she knew she had come away from the relationship permanently enriched. The sense that she had gained something lasting from "the eternity promised by love" (#52)—and by her mutable genius-lover—left open the possibility of forgiving Tsvetaeva and remembering her with love.

Tsvetaeva, on the other hand, must have perceived her failed relationship with Parnok as a total loss (at one time she considered calling the "Girlfriend" cycle "A Mistake"). Subconsciously, she made several attempts at compensation for the loss. First, she returned to her "tsar" husband. Second, she promptly became pregnant during the summer of 1916.[8] Then, three years later, she had a love affair with another Sonya (the actress Sophia Holliday) in which she played the older, "maternal" partner. But she could never make up for the defection of her original Sophia, and harbored a grudge against Parnok for the rest of her life. She looked back on their love as the time when she had "suffered under Sonya Parnok."[9]

In the immediate aftermath of their February break, however, Tsvetaeva did not believe the relationship was over. At the beginning of March she noted down a brief exchange she had had with Ariadne, in which she said she felt sad because she "had only two friends—you and Sonya."[10]

Part of her sadness must have come from her sense that Parnok was already in love with Erarskaya. Indeed, at the end of February, Parnok wrote her first love lyric "to Mashenka" (one of her pet names for Lyudmila Vladimirovna), "Oh my God, I am unworthy of this!" (#151), in which she expressed the intense but complicated emotions that her new lover's "desperate tenderness" had evoked in her. She felt unworthy of Mashenka's love and hopeless about it, yet blissful in her despair. She feared for Mashenka's vulnerability and capability to withstand the force (wind) of her passion.

It is possible that Tsvetaeva and Parnok continued to see each other through the spring. By the end of April some further rupture had occurred to which Tsvetaeva responded with resignation and an upsurge of nostalgia for their love that inspired her to write one of her most beautiful poems to Parnok, a valedictory to their "sunsetless days of yore."[11] It was her last poem to her "tragic heroine," whom, as it turned out, she had not been able to save— for herself.

Ironically, the April-May issue of *Northern Annals* carried Parnok-Polyanin's review of Mandelshtam's *Stone*. She praised his work in the highest terms, calling the volume "a singing stone," the essence of real poetry. Six years later in a poem she would speak of the "singing stone" of her own stanzas. Perhaps because she had perceived Mandelshtam as a romantic rival, Parnok was particularly sensitive to any traits or tastes they had in common, such as their mutual adoration of Tsvetaeva's genius. The hostility his often rude (but apparently typical) behavior evoked in her must have been exacerbated by her seeing him in some ways as a negative double, or shadow, of herself. Her later relations with Mandelshtam bore the unmistakable stamp of such Dostoevskian doubling and were similar to her relationship with her brother.[12]

After the emotional turmoil of the past year, Parnok was exhausted and desperately in need of peace and quiet. Perhaps with the encouragement of the Gertsyks, she decided to spend the summer in Sudak, where she rented a room with board in the cottage of a local priest.

One of her main correspondents that summer was the poet Vladislav Khodasevich, with whom she had recently become friends and who was spending his summer in nearby Koktebel. In addition to liking Khodasevich's poems, Parnok considered him "a secret brother who doesn't know he's mine." Khodasevich became important to her after the emotional defection of her biological brother and her rivalry with the "bad" brother poet, Mandelshtam.

Parnok empathized with Khodasevich's chronic poor health and took an almost semiprofessional interest in his medical problems. That summer he was recuperating from tuberculosis of the spine. After receiving a letter in which he described his symptoms, Parnok suddenly feared that he might have a sarcoma of the spine, but he quickly disabused her of that awful thought.

Khodasevich, for his part, was very fond of Parnok and liked her poems. He kept her informed of the comings and goings of other guests at Koktebel that summer, including Tsvetaeva and her husband, who made a brief visit in early July. Later that month, after several weeks of exposure to Mandelshtam "strutting about" and acting "simply stupid" (as he wrote his wife in June), he came to share Parnok's opinion of him:

> You're right, you know, Mandelshtam is not smart. But he's unhappy, one feels sorry for him. His literary self-esteem is frustrated.

Petersburg ruined him. Well, what kind of a poet is he? And, you know, he's "in for a penny, in for a pound." That's oppressive, i.e., I want to say that he'll write good poems, if he sits down and does a little work, but still, he's not a poet. It's unfair, but true.[13]

The September issue of *Northern Annals* contained four poems by Parnok: "Sonnet" (#118); "Sapphic Stanzas," later retitled "The Return" and published in *Roses of Pieria* as part of a trilogy; a poem she had written to Khodasevich in June; and her second love lyric to Lyudmila Erarskaya, the first poem she had ever published with a dedication to a specific lover-addressee.[14]

> *To L.V.E.*
> Can a lynx ever really be tamed,
> so why play the kitten with me?
> How you soften your fateful face
> with that smile so skillfully!
> Thus an actress should play saucy girls:
> training her gold, gypsy eye
> from beneath sultry lashes downcurled
> to look *at* you while looking aside.
> Oh that ominous calm before storms:
> it is just like the quiet was when
> Don Jose said, "You're the devil himself,"
> and Carmen replied, "I am." (#138)

The image of Erarskaya in this poem differed significantly from the vulnerable "little stalk" and godsent "light" that Parnok had perceived her to be in her first poem to her. Here she seemed more the powerful woman with "fateful features," a type that had attracted Parnok since adolescence. Apparently, Erarskaya did not merely act but in fact possessed the "double" personality (wild/tame, lynx/kitten) that Parnok perceived in her not long after they became lovers. Thus Parnok's portrayal of her in this poem: Erarskaya's serene, sophisticated, extremely controlled exterior hid a wild soul that seethed with dark emotions—anger, hatred, fear. She must have evoked Parnok's own personal demons as well as her capacity to love compassionately and maternally.

Erarskaya was the other half of Parnok's longest, most committed, and in many ways, most all-encompassing love relationship. During the course of their constantly evolving intimacy and friendship of sixteen years, they explored and experienced all the possibilities, dangers, and dead ends of human love. As Erarskaya wrote to Eugenia Gertsyk a month after Parnok died: "Yes, we lived through so much that it's hard to tell about it! So many moments that I shall absolutely remember my whole life!"[15]

Parnok attributed four poems to the year 1916 without indicating specifically when they were written. "The heat is doubled by the lack of wind" (#101) probably dated from her summer in Sudak. The occasional poem "Acrostic" (#102) was dedicated to Lipskerov, her friend and poetic "discovery," whom she hailed as her "brother by fate and the lyre." "At the Concert" (#134) recalled a concert she had attended with a male friend (perhaps Volkenshtein) who was both dear and alien to the poetic speaker. Finally, "Again, just like a bird who's wounded" expressed Parnok's recurrent gypsy anguish that made her and other "homeless folk" sisters of gypsy singers:

> Torment me, tear me, gypsy voice,
> and with your song sing me to death—
> one shouldn't let the soul keep struggling
> against herself! (#140)

The sisterhood of black angels, gypsies, and homeless souls in this poem represented a community of female outcasts that offered a kind of homeopathic therapy for the poet's soul when it had become too chafed by "the religious fetters of love" (#42).

Parnok's restlessness and yearning also reflected one side of the ambivalent mood that had gripped many Russian intellectuals and poets toward the end of 1916. Eugenia Gertsyk later recalled the two sharply contradictory attitudes among Russians on the eve of the February 1917 revolution: "Some were trying optimistically to reconcile all self-evident contradictions, others consciously exacerbated them as if wanting to hasten catastrophe."[16] Parnok's yearning for catastrophe also contained a strong religious, apocalyptic element, which may have been influenced by Eugenia Gertsyk. In the fall the poet, who still had not realized the spiritual potential of her new faith, drew closer to Eugenia.

At the beginning of the revolutionary year, Parnok wrote to Gnesin that she and Eugenia had become friends. She hoped that when Gnesin came to Moscow, he would have time to meet her at the Gertsyks. She had told them about his latest composition and generally had sung his praises so that her friends urged her "to lure [Gnesin] to their house, if only for an hour."[17]

Another old friend, Yulia Veisberg, acquired new creative importance for Parnok at this time, when she invited her to write a libretto for an opera she had begun on the subject of *The Little Mermaid*. Work on the opera with Shteinberg had apparently ground to a halt.

Parnok and Erarskaya were now living at 2 Sukharevskaya Sadovaya Street. The poet was in wretched health: "I feel so awful," she wrote Veisberg, "that the doctor has been a far more frequent visitor than my muse. (It's the same old neuralgia and enlargement of my heart caused by my thyroid gland, and the result is that I'm at death's door.)" After discussing details of the *Mermaid* libretto, Parnok turned to a song Gnesin had just written to one of her poems:

> I like the "Romance" Mikhail Fabianovich wrote to my poem very much. . . . In my view, something generally good has happened to [him]: he evidently has begun to believe in himself more and therefore has relaxed the constraints on his originality. He allows himself to be banal, i.e. human, and that is a pledge of a greater creative flow. I think something similar is happening with me.[18]

Finally, Parnok was beginning to relax the aesthetic censor in herself that had always been so wary of her "banal" life as a subject for her poetry. Her new "greater creative flow" was also spurred by the "deadly mood" that had recently overcome her and everyone else in Moscow. "It's impossible to live," she wrote to Veisberg, "therefore I have rather a lot of poems. I'll send them to you somehow. And for the time being, here are eight gloomy lines:"

> They won't come and it's really no matter,
> —they'll recall me in joy or in wrath;
> in the ground I shall not be more homeless,
> than I was when I walked on this earth.
> And the wind, my unhired mourner,
> will twirl up over me snowy lees . . .
> Oh my path, sorrowful, distant, somber,
> predetermined uniquely for me. (#147)

"All that's left," she signed off, "is for me to kiss your sugary lips. Your Sophia."[19] The poem expressed no faith in immortality, no faith in human caring, no faith in anything—just the awareness of her aloneness in death as in life and a belief in her idiosyncratic, "dark" destiny.

Spring came early to Moscow that year, but "everything [was] so hopeless" that it just made Parnok feel sadder.[20] By the end of March, however, her mood had changed as radically as the government of Russia—the tsar had abdicated and a provisional government headed by Alexander Kerensky was in power. No longer "at death's door," Parnok now felt not only "alive, but even in a kind of ferment." Caught up in the revolutionary spirit, she prayed that the overthrow of tsarism would turn out to be a "fairy tale with a happy ending."[21] In some sense her hope was cynical, namely, that people would act out of self-interest where they should have acted out of patriotism. Russians as a people seemed to her to be distinguished by their "inability to love their fatherland. . . . The old [tsarist] government," she wrote to Veisberg, "nurtured in generations [of Russians] a lack of respect for their homeland, but no disenchantments can cure one of love—because love is in one's blood—and if Russians have been cured of love for Russia, then that can only mean that they had no love for her to begin with."[22]

The February revolution had an immediate financial impact on Parnok if only because it forced the closing of *Northern Annals*. Her last article, a long and scathing attack on Bryusov's poetry, had appeared in the January (and final) issue. With the demise of *Northern Annals,* Parnok's five-year professional association with Chatskina and Saker came to an abrupt end, and a major source of her very modest income dried up. In order to support herself, she went to work in an office.

In June she and Erarskaya went to Milino village in Tula province, where they stayed as guests of the Knipers. The situation she observed daily in the village killed her hopes for a "happy ending" to the revolutionary "fairy tale." "Things are pretty awful in the countryside right now," she wrote to Voloshin; "hardly a day passes without the peasants coming with new demands; their faces have a mystically vacant look, and with every day I gain a better understanding of the saying, 'The more I see of people, the more I like dogs.'"[23]

With this letter Parnok enclosed a poem she had recently written to Erarskaya. It appears to have been composed at one of the many times Parnok was convinced she did not have long to live, and Erarskaya, whom she again evokes as a "delicate stalk," was herself either depressed, or unwell:

On its delicate stalk droops a flower . . .
Oh belovèd, all I have ever loved
and will leave on this earth when I go,
finish loving, belovèd, in place of me,
these petals as soft as a kiss,
this fire splashed over the heavens,
these tears (which only a poet
understands!)—the anguish of bliss.
And a lonely grave-mound in the steppe,
and majestic singing of verses,

but the gypsies' wild tambourines
love in this life no less . . .
In the twilight the cupolas pink
as the pigeons fly out over Moscow.
Oh belovèd, please love above all
the bells tolling eventide! (#142)

Parnok had heard from friends in Petrograd that Voloshin had reviewed her book *Poems,* and in her June letter from Milino she asked him for a copy. She received it only after she was back in Moscow, working in her office, "dispatching and filing papers." The work exhausted her and left no time for writing so that her muse had become "unfriendly."[24] But there was nothing to be done. Famine had followed in the wake of the winter's political upheavals, and the provisional government's failure to end the war with Germany had resulted in mass desertions of Russian troops and complete chaos. By August there was hunger in Moscow.

Voloshin reviewed Parnok's first book in the context of a larger article he had planned on the subject of the "unforgettableness" of a poet's voice, an idea that Parnok, of course, found "very appealing." His article had ended up focusing, however, on the voices of just two poets, Parnok and Mandelstam, and for all its enthusiasm about both of them, Parnok's voice was made to sound more attractive. The review delighted her, and she wrote him of her gratitude:

> Without even mentioning how I value praise from the lips of such a master of verse as you, I was made endlessly happy by your unfeigned, human friendliness toward me, which I value more than anything else, perhaps because I have been so little spoiled by it in my life. I am not only flattered, but touched to the core by your poet's and human being's attention to my book.[25]

Erarskaya's health had worsened over the summer, and she was advised to leave Moscow before winter. Parnok could not bear to be separated from her, especially in such chaotic and difficult times. Besides, her own health was not good, Moscow and her office job had become detestable, and her closest female friend, Eugenia Gertsyk, had been permanently ensconced in Sudak since the spring.

At the end of August or beginning of September she and Erarskaya left their apartment in the care of Lipskerov and his brother and set out for Sudak. Once there, they found a place to live in the cottage of a local Greek. Parnok immediately relaxed and felt better, glorying in the marvelous weather and tranquility of this "unforeseen vacation," as she put it to Voloshin.[26]

One day, not long after the women's arrival, there was a soft knock at the door of their cottage. Parnok was not at home. Erarskaya opened the door and saw a man of shorter than average height. He had glasses and "grey eyes that peered kindly from under his grey hat." He introduced himself as the composer Alexander Spendiarov. Erarskaya asked him to come in and sit down, and introduced herself. "It can't be!" Spendiarov exclaimed joyfully. "I'd been told that you were seriously ill, and I find you a woman in the bloom of life! I'm so glad I decided to ignore what the doctor said, come make your acquaintance and invite you to participate in a concert I am arranging as a benefit for indigent students at our gymnasium." When Parnok came in, Spendiarov rose and, coming over to her, said, "You have no idea how happy I am to make your acquaintance. It is my great good fortune that you happen to be living here in Sudak precisely now when I am thinking of writing an opera." He handed her a manuscript and followed the expression on her face as she read it. "It's a very interesting theme," Parnok said. Spendiarov became animated. "I'm so glad you like it, Sophia Yakovlevna, because I would like you to write a libretto on that theme."[27]

Parnok began work on her libretto immediately, using as her source Hovaness Tumanian's epic poem, "The Taking of Tmuk Fortress." The poem retold a legend from the life of an eighteenth-century Armenian princess, Almast, who betrayed her husband, Prince Tatul, to the Persians in order to satisfy her political ambitions for the Persian crown. She herself was then tragically betrayed by her lover, the Persian shah, and executed for treason.

Parnok worked on her libretto "with enthusiasm," creating it as a lyric-dramatic narrative poem in its own right. She often recited parts of it at public poetry readings, both in Sudak and later back in Moscow. The work had deep personal significance for her, since Erarskaya served as the inspiration for Almast, and Parnok expressed some of her own emotional experiences in their love affair in the words of Almast's lover and, particularly, her husband. Many of Tatul's enraptured words in praise of his wife's beauty and the "fragrant darkness of [her] hair" could only have been written, it has been argued, by someone "who had buried her face in her beloved's hair, inhaling its fragrance, and whose eyes had been covered by its abundance."[28]

The terribly cold winter of 1918 gave way to a spring of escalated warfare and almost daily changes of power in Sudak. Months after Parnok had finished the libretto of *Almast,* Spendiarov at last began writing the music. His work began in earnest that hot, sultry summer, the summer that Parnok realized she and Erarskaya had passed a point of no return in their relationship and in their lives:

> Shade from the windmill
> creeps along the vineyard.
> Mysterious anguish
> bewitches my heart.
> Again a dark circle
> has closed in above me,
> Oh my tender friend,
> my implacable one!
> Cicadas' rasping chirrs
> fill the sultry silence.
> There's no way back
> for you, me, or us—
> a hot, languid spirit
> hovers over the earth . . .
> Oh, my passionate friend,
> my insatiable one! (#114)

Parnok's poems from her years in Sudak, none of them precisely dated, provide fleeting glimpses of this emotionally, spiritually, and creatively significant period in her life. In 1919 she published a rather large group of lyrics in an obscure almanac. Some of this group had been published previously, but a few of the new poems testified to important changes in her spiritual outlook that were already underway at the beginning of her sojourn in the Crimea.

In the spring of 1918 she was more immersed than ever in reading Sappho and developing a personal and poetic relationship with her. Being in the Black Sea area, the putative homeland of the Amazons, stimulated her to remember her ancient Lesbian creative roots:

> Thus, on other shores, by another melodious sea,
> a millennium later, in just such a young spring,
> calling to mind her own ancient childhood,
> a maiden pensively drew her finger over her strings.
> She feels the breath of Ellada in a breeze from beyond the sea,
> a breeze, unsensed by other people, stirs her heart:
> it seems to the maiden she will dream out your dreams, Sappho,
> she will finish your songs, which have not reached our ears. (#68)

While Parnok was discovering a poetic sister in Sappho, she was realizing a sister "by heavenly blood" in Eugenia Gertsyk. Because of her mournful disposition and reclusiveness, Eugenia seemed like a widow to Parnok. Most important, she perceived Gertsyk as a "sibyl" who prophesied, and a "godmother" who presided over her spiritual rebirth.[29]

Gertsyk's own faith changed as a direct result of her experiences in Sudak during the Civil War: "The years of the horrors of war, of persecutions and hunger, dried up my former faith, that is, all the moisture and sweetness were steamed out of it."[30] Parnok was also struck by the Sudak winegrowers' practice of putting the young wine out in the sun to quicken the aging process that produced drier wines, and it became a personal symbol of the spiritual process she underwent during her Sudak years. In one poem, "Into the most savage sun" (#115), she wrote metaphorically of carrying her spiritual self (her young wine) out beneath the "most savage, fire-winged arrows" of the sun, and begging it, her "fateful, merciless, intoxicating friend," to dry up her sweetness and "cleanse [her] spirit with fire."

Despite her impatience and desire to age spiritually, she never, unlike her sibyl, completely lost her sweetness, or became "dry, like old wine" (#236). She also continued to be driven by her "dominatrix, Fate," to recall another lyric of this period, "from a monk's cell / straight to a witches' sabbath," where too often she would hear in "the din of debauchery" some "long-tailed" devil call her "a loathsome name" (#124).

Nevertheless, the Gertsyks' house and garden in Sudak became a hallowed place for Parnok. She recalled, lyrically, one magical evening there, when "such tranquillity [stood] over" the assembled company that it seemed they were no longer sinners, and "a light blue tabernacle [had] covered everyone." A "tender, navy-blue sky" was becoming evening as it descended above the gardens "so that no one in the world might be homeless." The footsteps of Adelaida's young sons could be heard "rustling over the gravel," Eugenia's "widow's weeds [swayed] gently in the sea-breeze. To our great and celebrated infamy," Parnok concluded, "clearly, Lord, Thou condescendeth with love" (#113).

Unconsciously, Parnok still sought to bridge the seemingly insurmountable distance she felt from her father, which his death had intensified. It was important to her that in her intimacy with Gertsyk, she believed she had found an earthly love that was agreeable to God, and, symbolically, her father:

> So softly and so wonderfully
> the roses have not ever bloomed:
> your breath is here, and you are lovely
> with all the earth's sad loveliness.
> How softly has the sky above you
> stretched out its tender covering!

> And the world's first evening wasn't
> so blissful as these evenings here . . .
> And there, above us two, THE STERNEST
> is trying not to knit His brow,
> but He and all the lesser godlings,
> have fallen in love with our love. (#106)

Parnok's relationship with Gertsyk helped the poet to begin liberating herself from the power of "the fearsome tourguide, love" who had ruled her since youth and had disempowered her psychologically while making her feel sexually powerful. With a little help from her increasingly ailing body, Parnok began to break what might have been an addiction to "love." The first signs of this change can be seen in an undated lyric she addressed to her amorous Memory:

> No, today I do not want you,
> Memory, so just hold your tongue,
> you, vainglorious procuress,
> don't procure me anyone.
> Don't seduce me down dark alleys,
> to the places left behind—
> to the bold or to the timid
> lips I've kissed so many times.
> Sacrilegiously inspired,
> I have ploughed my heart soil up,
> rooting out the names of lovers
> from my sacred calendars. (#104)

In a typically oxymoronic metaphor, Parnok compared the whorehouse of her carnal memory to church calendars of past loves, or "saints," whose feasts she celebrated by worshipping their memory. On the day in question, however, she rebelled against this faith and, "committing sacrilege," dug down to the bottom of her heart and tore out all her saints' names, thus breaking the power of her own submission to them.

Such fits of emotional iconoclasm, and the inner rage against "love" that they expressed, could not help but have an effect on her intimate relationship with Erarskaya. Feeling at times like "enchanted denizens on some forgotten island," the two women would sit in the moonlit night, watching the "fading clouds drift through the dark-blue fields" as Erarskaya's "swarthy hand [would] just barely wave its ostrich-feather fan." Parnok memorialized one such moment of boundaryless intimacy as she addressed her beloved:

> You bend your head toward mine,
> so we may think a single thought,
> and the doves coo more tenderly,
> cradling your languid peace. (#123)

At other times they would quarrel violently. Then, Parnok would again feel like a homeless traveler cast into the godforsaken midnight, alone except for the moon flying by over her head, "like a cat dashing across the road." Such occasions made her poetic speaker long for "nooses, poisons, and triggers" as "surer, more caustic, and quicker ways" to end it all. She didn't know "whether to sob or to sing from [her] permanent anguish," and her heart had "no one to fly to under the fleeting October moon!" (#144).

The rift alluded to in this poem appears to have caused Parnok and Erarskaya to separate for awhile. Parnok went to live at the Gertsyks' where Adelaida assumed a silent, "maternal" guardianship over her younger friend's troubled love life. Addressing Parnok, Adelaida wrote:

> From behind my white shutters,
> I keep watch over your life,
> waging a silent struggle
> with your ancient enemies.
> I like your voice's undulations,
> I watch you walking barefoot,
> drying your auburn hair
> in the garden beneath my window.
> I watch the insatiable passion
> that moves your avid brow.

> Ah, only through my prayer
> can your love be saved.[31]

A year had passed since Parnok had finished the libretto for *Almast,* yet Spendiarov was having great difficulty making progress with the score. The magnitude and genre of the work, both new to him, apparently daunted him, and he began to lack confidence in his ability to write an opera that would pass muster. Parnok tried to encourage him:

> Yesterday, the strains of *Almast*'s music reached me when you were playing and singing downstairs, and I was very sad that I could not go down and listen properly. The more I listen to *Almast,* the more it captivates me. I'm very sad that there's no one in Sudak whose musical judgment you could value. I'm sure that if you had one of your colleagues nearby, you would immediately take heart and come to believe that you are capable of composing first-rate operatic music.[32]

Thus began Parnok's long, laborious mothering of her and Spendiarov's "brainchild," her "big work," and poetic testimony to her love for Erarskaya.

Lyudmila, she felt, had already taken her beyond her capacity to love, but in 1919 she began making a stubborn effort to reawaken her feelings:

> Every evening now I pray
> God to let me dream of you:
> I have loved you to the point
> where I can no longer love.
> Every day I walk myself
> past our now deserted rooms,
> trying to arouse my memory,
> but she won't remember you . . .
> And I stubbornly repeat your
> name again, and once again,
> softly and with angry lips to
> try to resurrect my love. (#122)

Despite the crisis in their relationship, Parnok and Erarskaya were constantly thrown together through their shared professional and creative work. The creative activity of the Sudak intellectual community intensified in response to the chaos of civil war, changing governments, and even famine. Many years later, Parnok recalled "the productions [they] mounted in Sudak when the Crimea was cut off from Russia and Sudak led a detached, but very creative life, [when they] had to create everything [them]selves, without any outside resources at [their] disposal, when in order to have sets and costumes [they] were forced to beg furniture and clothes from kindhearted acquaintances."[33]

Everyone participated in the semiprofessional productions. An all-arts spectacle in September featured songs sung by the Gertsyks' cook; Beethoven sonatas played by a professional pianist; Parnok's *sprechgesang* recitation to one of Spendiarov's songs; the performance of a scene from Gogol's *Inspector General*; and music from *Almast*. Later in the fall Spendiarov arranged an *Evening for Children* for which Parnok wrote a verse play, and he composed the music.

Unfortunately, the composer's philanthropic activities took precious time away from his work on the opera, and despite Parnok's efforts to speed things up, the pace of composition became agonizingly slow. Erarskaya recalled the following conversation from the summer of 1919:

> Once we were coming from the post office and suddenly spotted Alexander Afanasyevich walking in haste toward the town. He became embarrassed when he saw us and asked very gaily: "And where might you be coming from?" Sophia Yakovlevna pointed to the post office and said, "We're coming from there, but where might you be coming from? I thought you gave me your word yesterday that you were going to stay home in the mornings and work?" Alexander Afanasyevich gave Sophia Yakovlevna a serious look, slowly drew a notebook out of his side pocket, and read a long list of "urgent matters" that he said required his attention before he could sit down to work with a clear conscience. He had to help

a widow with many children to buy a cow, visit a sick pupil, etc., etc.[34]

At the time Erarskaya and Parnok were apparently living together again, but a great deal of ambivalence remained beneath the calm surface of their relationship, as revealed in Parnok's last lyric of that year, written on December 24:

> If you should cry out in your sleep,
> and your voice should begin to sound angry,
> I'll gently take hold of your finger
> and whisper, "Come, talk about me,
> just tell me, my love, how you love me,
> just tell me, my dove, how you touch me."
> And doors which were shut until then
> will burst terrifyingly open,
> the pain lying hidden and dormant
> will gush in a torrent of words,
> and your heart as it weeps will be shaken
> at the furiousness of its hatred. (#146)

Erarskaya became a member of the secretariat of the Feodosia Art Workers' Union while continuing to work, along with Parnok, in the Sudak office of the ministry of education. As head of the theater section there, Erarskaya organized plays and concerts for the local proletariat.

Fighting intensified in the town during the first half of the year, but despite the hard times Parnok and Spendiarov continued their work on *Almast*. "They often worked at our place," Erarskaya recalled. "Spendiarov would come over when we were out on the terrace, settle himself on the sofa, and, without taking his eyes from the view of the evening landscape, would say, a broad smile on his face, 'Well, then, Sophia Yakovlevna, let's get down to our two tasks: working, and admiring the sunset.' "[35]

A summer of drought created food shortages all over the country, which was in the last throes of the Civil War. To combat the economic crisis, Lenin introduced the New Economic Policy, or

NEP, a return to limited private enterprise and capitalism. The benefits of NEP did not reach Sudak, however, in large part because fighting toward the end of the war was fiercest in the Crimea, the base of the last of the White armies to be defeated.

Even the special rations with which civil servants were paid (and which had long since replaced money in the country) could not guarantee survival when food disappeared from the stores and the surrounding countryside. Parnok recalled in a poem, "Kitchen Garden" (#110), written four years later, how stubbornly she worked to make a vegetable garden grow from the "dry, scabby, saline soil," full of "twisted, writhen roots of vines that once had flourished [there]." The sole of her foot began to bleed from leaning on the shovel, her hands, unaccustomed to physical labor, became red and calloused. It seemed to her that the earth, like a recalcitrant woman lover, "put up quite a fight against [her] and resisted [her] with a kind of ancient vengefulness." But she vowed, characteristically, "to outstubborn [her] stubbornness." As she bent over her pick, she dreamed of the "sprightly peas," "high stalks of corn," "monstrous, big-bellied pumpkins with Gorgon tresses," and the "first spring cucumber" that would emerge from her garden:

> The sharp fang of my pick shone in the sun,
> around me clumps of earth bobbed up and crumbled,
> a seabreeze blew, the sweat ran down my back
> and cooled, an ice-cold, slender little snake—
> and never had the sweet bliss of possession
> burned through me with such piercing pride
> and unbeclouded fullness. (#110)

Such moments made the Sudak years special for Parnok and her cosurvivors. As Eugenia Gertsyk later wrote, "And those years in all their difficulty and joylessness were so significant inwardly, that I would not refuse [to relive] them. Both the joys and the pain—it was all the most real thing, and not words, words, as it had often been before."[36]

During the summer Erarskaya and Spendiarov organized a Grand Evening of the Arts to benefit the Sudak Public High School. Parnok read three of her gypsy poems; Erarskaya performed the title role in an "oriental drama" that Eugenia Gertsyk had written, and also directed and choreographed a performance of the oriental dance and chorus from Borodin's opera *Prince Igor*.

In September, the critical moment in the fighting for Sudak arrived. The night before the final battles, Erarskaya acted the lead in a play at a restaurant in town for an audience that included many officers on leave from the front. "The next day," Marina Spendiarova recalled, "there were pitched battles in Sudak between the Whites and combined Reds and Greens. I recognized among the corpses left after the fighting those of officers who had been at the performance the previous evening. Fighting took place in our garden too. Spendiarov would locate 'safe zones' (from the bullets coming through the windows) and hide the whole family in them."[37]

By November, British and French ships were evacuating 100,000 military and civilian opponents of the Soviet regime from the Crimea. On November 14 the Red army occupied Feodosia, and by December the White armies in the south of Russia were defeated.

That winter both Adelaida Gertsyk and Parnok were arrested, together with most Crimean intellectuals who had not actively supported the Reds. Gertsyk spent a month or more "in the cellar," as she referred in her fictionalized memoirs to the basement of the building in Sudak where she and others were held. The dates of Parnok's arrest and imprisonment are unknown, but she was released by the end of March.[38] On the twenty-third she, Spendiarov, Erarskaya, and Butkova, an actress from the Bolshoi Theater, wrote a joint letter to the writer Maxim Gorky (who was close to Lenin and enjoyed his confidence) in which they "urgently requested" him to assist in creating conditions in Sudak favorable to "peaceful work."[39]

Shortly after this, Spendiarov was arrested. According to his daughter, the townspeople staged a protest demonstration at the jail, threatening to break it down if the composer were not released. When she went to deliver a message to her father, she was told by the trade union secretary that the workers had decided "to send a telegram to Lenin requesting him personally to have Spendiarov released."[40] Parnok joined his family in welcoming him home when he got out of jail on April 10.

In the spring Parnok was in a train accident and escaped death by a quirk of fate. Before the train departed, she asked the man who was sitting opposite her to change places so that she would not have to ride backwards. He was happy to oblige. When the train crashed, he was killed, whereas she escaped without a scratch. This tormented her for the rest of her life, and she did not like to remember it.[41] Unfortunately, no details of the accident are known, and even the time when it occurred is a matter of surmise. Certainly it was an event in Parnok's life that contributed to the poet's inveterate fatalism and confirmed her perception of fate as an all-powerful, incomprehensible, often malevolent and capricious force. The train accident may also have enhanced Parnok's sense of having been marked somehow for a special destiny, yet a destiny that she could not understand. Finally, like many Russians of her generation and Russophile bent, Parnok expressed negative feelings about trains. In one poem, "Nobody ever has anything" (#148), the speaker identifies speeding, "firebreathing trains" whose "iron rapid patter" beats "in time with the tachycardia of the world" as harbingers of the apocalypse.

The deprivations of the war and her brief imprisonment had taken their toll on Parnok's already poor health, and she developed tuberculosis. Through his massive network of friends, Voloshin managed to find jobs for both her and Erarskaya in Simferopol, but in mid-May Parnok wrote him that she was too ill to make the move and did not think she had the stamina to live in the city, given "the current level of nutrition." She thanked him for his "genuinely comradely regard" and added, "I've already made up my mind to die in Sudak. Lyudmila Vladimirovna also thanks you, but her health prohibits her from leaving Sudak too."[42]

Conditions in the area worsened. The second summer drought in a row brought famine in its wake, and starvation threatened the whole Crimea in the coming winter. Moscow colleagues and friends of the Crimean writers initiated relief efforts in their behalf. In late November, Tsvetaeva, who had spent the Civil War in Moscow alone with her daughter, reported to Voloshin that she and Volkenshtein had written to the commissar of education in an attempt to get special food parcels for their Crimean friends. As was her habit, Tsvetaeva described the scene of writing the letter dramatically, in telegraphic phrases: "V [olkenshtein] prompting me over my shoulder. I'm in a bad mood. 'Sonya! Don't forget Sonya!' he whispers. I reply: 'Dammit! Max is more important to me!' 'But S[ophia] Ya[kovlevna] is a woman and my former wife.' 'But Max is also a woman and my actual (present indicative) friend.' "[43] Tsvetaeva ended up writing on everyone's behalf, one letter for the Sudak writers, and one for those in Koktebel.

Parnok and Erarskaya had already realized that they would not be able to survive the winter in Sudak, and they decided to return to Moscow, although the trip back was daunting. Trains were impossibly overcrowded, and travel was not only expensive, but dirty and dangerous, especially for unaccompanied women. They first went to Feodosia, the nearest urban center, where Marina Spendiarova said good-bye to them at the end of November 1921, and remained there until, with Voloshin's help, they received safe conducts to travel on a special hospital train to Moscow.

En route to the capital, Parnok wrote Spendiarov a long letter filled with advice about the parts of *Almast* that remained unfinished. The composer greatly regretted that he had not managed to complete the opera before his librettist and collaborator left. He often needed to consult with her and knew he would feel her absence even "more intensely when composing the musical interlude and the fourth act."⁴⁴

Parnok reached Moscow in January. She was assisted by the poet Vladimir Mayakovsky in becoming a member of the Writers' Union and getting a room. It was located on Fourth Tverskaya Yamskaya Street in the heart of what had been Moscow's red light district. During her first months back in the city, she dedicated herself to raising money for the friends she had left behind in Sudak whose plight had become dire. At the end of January, Spendiarov wrote that he and his family continued to be plagued by robberies, almost all their chickens had been stolen, and locks were no longer a deterrent to thieves. In view of not having enough to eat himself and not being able to help anyone out with food, he was very upset about the "intense hunger of several friends and the death from starvation of several Sudak inhabitants."⁴⁵ His family was helping the Gertsyks and others as much as they could.

Parnok came up with the idea of writing courtly sonnets to the hostesses of various Moscow literary salons in return for donations of money for her Crimean friends. "I couldn't write a line to get something for myself," she wrote to Voloshin, "but in this case, I seem able to bake sonnets from dawn to dusk. Unfortunately, not everyone has a weakness for them."⁴⁶

One of the people who did have a taste for Parnok's sonnets was Eudoxia Nikitina, the founder of one of Moscow's biggest poetry circles, the Nikitina Saturdays. Parnok described her as "a young, healthy woman with a turned-up nose, ruddy complexion and short haircut, a swell coachman who drives with swagger a whole team of literary horses of the most diverse breeds. Her ambition is a salon and indeed, she has enough will to have one."⁴⁷

Parnok wrote a sonnet (#105) in honor of Nikitina's birthday on January 31. "With this piece of flattery I made a conquest of the dear coachman," she reported to Voloshin. Nikitina agreed to organize a 'Tauride Evening' for the benefit of the Crimean writers.

It raised 14 million roubles in the highly inflated currency of the time. "That means," Parnok joked, "I earned a million per line, an honorarium heretofore unknown even in Soviet Russia!"[48]

After being ill for much of February, she redoubled her efforts on behalf of her Sudak friends, and finally succeeded in obtaining free transportation to Moscow in a hospital train for the whole Gertsyk family, Butkova, and Butkova's mother. In addition, she buttonholed a colleague at one of the Nikitina Saturdays and badgered him until he swore "on his life" that he would get academic ration cards for everyone. Parnok did not know whether to trust in this promise or not. At the beginning of April she wrote to Voloshin:

> I don't want to lull myself with hope and am continuing to act here on my own—I am collecting money and will be sending it via messengers although I realize how worthless the sums are. Thanks to the million [you have already been sent], I now feel at peace on your account, at least as far as money is concerned. I would feel okay about the Gertsyks too if there were fewer of them because they have many good friends; Eugenia Butkova worries me the most—due to their insufferable personalities, she and her mother have contrived to live in the world as if it were an uninhabited island, and I'm the only person on earth who feels sorry for them and worries about their fate.[49]

As soon as Parnok had arrived in Moscow, she went to see the editor of Campfires Press and submitted on Voloshin's behalf the manuscript of his poetic cycle "The Burning Bush," which dealt with the Revolution in unabashedly religious terms. Like other editors she had approached, this one rejected Voloshin's work because of its religious contents, but he agreed to include excerpts from the cycle in an almanac he was publishing. He also offered to publish a book that Parnok had put together of her poems from the period 1916 to 1921.

She left him the manuscript and began dropping by the office regularly in the hopes of learning its fate. The editor was never in during his office hours, and the secretary kept urging her to come again. By then she had seen two volumes published by Campfires and found them "sloppy, tasteless, terribly dilettantish!" She became angry at the futility of running to the Campfires office for nothing. Finally she requested payment of the seven million they owed her in one lump sum rather than installments, and was told that if she wanted a lump sum payment, she would have to lower her fee. She riposted that there was nothing to lower her fee to, took back her manuscript, and sold it to another press that she considered a slight improvement over Campfires because, she wrote Voloshin, it published "with love and all the 'luxury' that can be had in Moscow nowadays."[50]

All through the spring and summer Parnok was writing poems that would form a new volume, *The Vine*. She also wrote an important critical article, "Days of the Russian Lyric," that appeared in the second issue of the almanac *Dogrose* (1922). The article treated books of verse by Akhmatova, Khodasevich, Sologub, and Bryusov, but more importantly, it gave Parnok the opportunity to express her views on the relationship between man and God and on the religious significance of the 1917 Revolution. The article began with Parnok's view of human beings as eternal debtors before God:

> The creative work of all humankind in all areas of the spirit has been, is, and will be the repayment of that debt obligation. The worldwide, national, and individual worth of a person is determined on the scales of eternity by the degree of his or her spiritual capacity to pay. The God-Son redeemed the debt of an entire nation. Every spiritually alive person is duty-bound, to the limit of his capacity, to pay God back for what he has been given by Him.[51]

One cannot help but be struck by Parnok's obsession with indebtedness as the essence of the human condition and the meaning of creativity, as well as her conception of an individual's life as an off-stage play for an audience of one, God the Father. In her view, those who had experienced and survived the Revolution had been given "new credit" with God and new indebtedness to Him. The article concluded with the poet's thoughts on what insured God's justification for the word: "(1) when the word is uttered not before people, but before God"; "and (2) when it is uttered at the last moment."

God was also the focus of two poems of Parnok's that appeared in 1922, in *Lyrical Circle*. In one of them, later republished in *The Vine*, the poetic speaker expressed her yearning for face-to-face communication with God:

> The Lord has not heeded my yearning,
> has not delighted me with coldness,
> has not led my exhausted
> flesh out of the circle of flame.
> And people drink of my lips
> though their last heat is not yet drunk.
> Like centuries-old mead, my blood is thick—
> oh, my sultry captivity! My Egypt! . . .
> But I dream, from hollow depths
> arises a light-blue stream,
> and I'm borne aloft, and there alone
> I am face to face with Thee. (#94)

The second stanza of this poem may allude to the beginning of a new love affair sometime in the spring or early summer of 1922, a love that happened despite Parnok's "exhausted flesh" and desire for "coldness." By the beginning of the following year and possibly before, the poet was living with a new female companion, whose identity, unfortunately, remains unknown.[52]

The other religious poem from the *Lyrical Circle* group (#107) also had an Old Testament context. In it Parnok reimagined "youthful Jehovah" at the moment when "Eve had only just fallen," her "depths foaming with seed," and "the world was God, and God was passion."

> He wore [it] out with His jealousy,
> pouring fire straight into the blood . . .

> Israel, can you really have drunken
> up all of the Lord's first love? (#107)

The God of Parnok's lyrics is the Old Testament Jehovah, jealous, stern, passionate, and fiery, a Creator whose nostrils are pleased by the smoke of his people's sacrifices to Him (#131). God "remembers" the poet twice. First, He makes her aware of Him by lighting the divine spark in her soul and causing her to find a spiritual guide (possibly, Eugenia Gertsyk) in whom she will be reborn.

> For long I lived in love with liberty,
> with no more thought of God than has a bird,
> directing my flight merely for the sake of flight.
> And the Lord remembered me—and so,
> like heat lightning, the soul in me was sparked,
> everything lit up. And I found you,
> to die in you and to be born again
> for other days and for other heights. (#120)

Second, God conferred upon the poet the power of naming, which formerly she had abused by writing dead, rather than living, words:

> The Lord has made note of me too,
> I dream of mysterious sounds:
> for names I do not search in books,
> I carry my calendars in me.
> I baptize in a sacred font,
> —the one I had hurt with a nickname,
> I haven't endeavored to try
> gold locks with a burglar's lockpick.
> My world may be sparsely settled,
> but I have my godchildren with me,
> and in the eternity of names
> the name I have given blossoms. (#96)

The power to name was granted to Parnok's poetic speaker by the Creator, but according to her own creative cosmogony, that power originated in her personal intimacy with Anguish, the primeval female element that was in nature before God created the world and had inspired Sabaoth to His own creative act (#80). In another lyric from this time, Parnok's poetic speaker portrayed herself as full to bursting with the waters of anguish that had been dammed up for centuries:

> Oh, the unconquerable heaviness
> of these waters silenced
> behind centuries-old dams!
> Oh Lord! Still the same for me, hard for me,
> with my heart full to overflowing,
> with a muse who's untalkative. (#108)

Trying to resurface in the mainstream of Russian poetry, which was no less patriarchal and homophobic than it had been before the revolution, Parnok felt like a pregnant woman with her waters just about to break. Her heart was filled to the brim with woman-identified experience, both her own and her Amazon race's, but her muse remained "untalkative."

By the beginning of August she had had her first experience of the new crackdown on religion, which mandated first of all that the word "God" be decapitalized. When the proofs of her article "Days of the Russian Lyric" came back with this change, she assiduously restored each capital "G." When Gosizdat (the State Publishing House) offered to publish her book *Centuries-Old Mead*, she was thrown into a quandary: on one hand, she desperately needed the money from the sale of the book (the State Publishing House paid significantly more than private, cooperative presses), but on the other, she could not stand the thought of "god" in her book instead of God. She did finally sign a contract with Gosizdat, but her book never appeared. The censor obviously realized that its religious contents went deeper than spelling conventions alone.

The need for money forced her to return to office work, which left her "totally exhausted." She felt alienated from Moscow literary life and hurt by the lack of interest in her work. "Dear Maximilian Alexandrovich," she wrote to Voloshin on August 3, "you can't imagine how I value your fondness for my poems, especially now when nobody has any interest in them. . . . Literary Moscow, like any Moscow, is hateful to me at the moment, and my life here has no purpose as far as I'm concerned. What pleasure it would give me to exchange Moscow for Feodosia if I could only be guaranteed a salary to support myself there."[53]

A month later her situation and mood had worsened. "Life in Moscow is incredibly hard and I don't know whether I'll be able to struggle for existence like this for long. I'm tired and everything has become loathsome to me to the nth degree. If I were guaranteed a salary in Feodosia that I could live on, I would leave Moscow without a moment's thought."[54]

By early September she had finished all the poems that would go into *The Vine*. She gave the notebook containing them and everything else she had selected for publication from 1916 to September 11, 1922, to Gertsyk, who was returning to Sudak after spending six months in the north.

About a month later, Valentin Parnakh returned to Russia and Moscow after an absence of seven years. The pogroms during the Civil War had confirmed his worst fears about the Bolsheviks' attitude to Jews, and he still had not forgotten the anti-Semitism that had greeted him in Russia upon his return from Palestine in 1914. Nevertheless, in his self-imposed Parisian exile, he had become homesick, especially for Taganrog, "whose whiteness had lit up [his] childhood."[55]

Parnakh's return initiated a minor cultural revolution in the new Soviet capital, since he brought from Paris a suitcase full of jazz instruments, including a saxophone, which had previously been unknown in Russia. During his Paris years, he had developed a passion for African-American jazz that was as fanatic as his Zionist ardor.

In their musicality, Valentin and his sister also turned out to be perfect Dostoevskian doubles. Parnakh once wrote that "the substance of music attacks a human being, rises to his throat and overwhelms him with horror,"[56] and his older sister described music's effect on her soul similarly as "a sense of unbearable fullness" and "horror of sweet bliss" (#78). But while Sonya loved Beethoven and the Romantic composers of German-dominated nineteenth-century western music, Valya "was not possessed by the Beethovens, or the Bachs, or the Chopins, Liszts, or Wagners." He "loved the animal plaint of the East, its intermittent singing that vomits anguish, saving a poor human creature from his misery."[57]

In March, Valentin had inscribed a copy of his first book, *Simoon*, which had come out in Paris in 1919, "to dear Sonya. The author's first book." The gesture may have signalled his desire for renewed contact. But details of their relationship after 1915 are scarce and vague. However Parnok felt toward her brother after his homecoming (which ironically coincided with her own), she apparently did not try to see a great deal of him in the three years he lived in Moscow before leaving again in 1925.

They must have been aware of each other's presence at the same gatherings, however. In late 1922 Liza brought her twin brother to one of Nikitina's Saturdays. Parnakh had already become something of a celebrity for his jazz dances, and when Volkenshtein spotted him in the audience, he passed a note to Nikitina: "Yelizaveta Yakovlevna has come with her brother (and Sophia Yakovlevna's), Valentin Parnakh. Ask him to read his poems!" Nikitina scribbled on the back of the note in response: "He looks like an idiot. I'd rather he did a jazz dance, his specialty."[58]

Parnok's muse fell silent after the creative surge that produced *The Vine*. The publication of *Roses of Pieria* in September (1922) brought her no joy. The poems in it now left her cold, she confessed to Gertsyk,[59] and it annoyed her that her anthological volume had come out before her other two. "After a six-year hiatus (and such a stormy one!)," she wrote to Voloshin, "this small anthological collection looks somehow 'too esthetic' and that upsets me very much."[60]

She had already parted emotionally and creatively from Sappho, whose presence dominates *Roses of Pieria*. Sappho's eternal but bookish "roses" had been replaced in Parnok's affections by Eugenia Gertsyk and the grapevines of Sudak that inspired *The Vine*. Yet these two volumes are intricately interconnected in Parnok's creative life. They both emerged from her Sudak renaissance, and they both tell a great deal about her evolution as a poet over the six turbulent years that separated them from her first book. *Roses* represented a look back on that experience, while *The Vine* revealed what Parnok took from it for the future.

Parnok was too dismissive of her Sapphic poems. Far from being merely aesthetic exercises, they represented a unique contribution to the Sappho tradition in Russian poetry, a tradition that had begun in the mid-eighteenth century when Sappho's two surviving poems were first translated from the original Greek into Russian prose.

During the first third of the nineteenth century, the first Russian Sapphic imitations and fictions appeared, often translated from French. Sappho's popularity in Russia at this time reflected the classical and Grecophile tastes of Napoleonic Europe in general and Tsar Alexander I in particular, and may also have been connected with the emergence of Russian women poets, of whom two were called "the Russian Sappho" by their male contemporaries. As in western Europe at that time, Sappho was considered a heterosexual poet.[61]

The second Russian vogue for Sappho began around 1890 and did have demonstrable ties with the Russian women's liberation movement as well as the vastly increased presence of women writers in Russia. One ambiguous and humorous indication of this connection was expressed in an epigram by the philosopher and symbolist poet Vladimir Solovyov: "The solution of the woman question / will, truly, come to us from Lesbos."[62]

The decadent culture of the nineties, when Parnok was at the gymnasium, hailed a new Russian Sappho, Mirra Lokhvitskaya.[63] Like the old Russian Sapphos, she lacked authority or desire to name herself, as the original Sappho of Lesbos had, or to empower herself creatively in Sappho's name the way western lesbian poets of the time were doing. Lokhvitskaya did not receive her epithet because of her lesbian preference or her personal poetic association with Sappho, about whom she wrote only a handful of imitative anthological poems. She acquired her Sapphic notoriety for the old reason that she was a female poet, and for a new Silver Age reason—she wrote unabashedly erotic lyrics that shocked the bourgeoisie and were perceived by some of the intelligentsia "as an attempt to use the poetic word to stand up for a woman's right to her own feeling, her own voice, not only in literature, but in society."[64] Yet Lokhvitskaya's allegedly own female voice ironically was called "masculine" because it sang of "physiological" love—sexual rather than spiritual.

Lokhvitskaya's Sapphic persona, the woman poet burning with strong, "masculine," heterosexual desire, produced a seemingly endless stream of imitators, both male and female, and soon became a cliché. In the first decade of the twentieth century Sapphic doggerel filled the pages of Russian provincial journals, focusing apparently inexhaustible attention on Sappho's legendary suicide from unrequited love for the young boatman, Phaon. By contrast, *fin de siècle* Sapphic fictions in the West were asserting a homosexual Sappho both as a cultural model of decadent modernism and, in the work of some poets like Renée Vivien and Natalie Barney, the original, woman-identified poet. But Russian Silver Age Sapphic fictions, outside of Parnok's, remained virtually silent on the subject of lesbian love.[65]

This silence can be attributed largely to two things: the culture's adoration of poets as quasidivine lovers of the Word who must be above such lowly, human (physical) activities as sex; and the influence of Russian philologists, whose view of Sappho took shape in the mid-nineteenth century and drew heavily on the theories of the eminent German Hellenists, Johann Gottlieb Welcker and Ulrich von Wilamowitz-Moellendorff. Their authority on Sappho remained unquestioned well into the twentieth century in Europe, and holds sway even now in Russia.

Welcker's influential work on Sappho was, ironically, not so focused on her as on the issue of Greek (platonic) male homosexuality and its status as a moral ideal crucial to the building of nation states. For Welcker, Sappho was the spokeswoman for the companion ideal of female platonic eros and chastity.[66] Wilamowitz rearticulated the theory of Sapphic chastity at the turn of the twentieth century in an effort to defend Sappho from the decadent French poets who asserted and (in his opinion) abused her sexuality. He developed the hypothesis that Sappho was the leader of a religious community and school for girls and that her relations with the young women in her fragments contained nothing sexual, but reflected her special pedagogical and spiritual role in their lives. Following Welcker and Wilamowitz, Russian philologists affirmed the presence of female same-sex love in Sappho's poems while vociferously denying it the name "sapphic" or "lesbian."

There was one voice—albeit medical, not philological—coming out of Germany at the turn of the century that seemed to counter the implied antilesbian prejudice of most German and Russian philologists. That voice belonged to Otto Weininger, whose book *Sex and Personality* caused a sensation in Europe and was translated into Russian in 1908, arousing a similar furor. One reviewer of the Russian translation of Weininger's book quoted the author's argument at length:

> The philologists have tried zealously to cleanse Sappho from suspicions that she had amorous relations with women and have argued that they were merely an expression of extraordinary friendship: as

if the accusation, if it were true, would in fact lower a woman morally.... That is utterly untrue.... Homosexual love does much greater honor namely to a woman than a heterosexual connection. ... A woman's tendency toward lesbian love is a manifestation of her virility, which is a condition of her giftedness.[67]

Weininger's "prolesbian" stance, unfortunately, depended on his misogynistic view that creativity was essentially a "virile" or masculine province. Indeed, the notion of Sappho's virile genius seemed to separate her from real-life female poets both in Europe and in Russia. In his 1916 review of Parnok's *Poems*, Khodasevich made a point of distinguishing her—ironically, in order to praise her—from those of his female contemporaries whom he considered inferior, "ladies'" poets and "youthful offspring of Sappho."[68]

Russian interest in Sappho culminated when the first poetic translations of her "complete" extant poems and fragments appeared. Vyacheslav Ivanov's flamboyant and decadent "translation," which augmented many of the fragments beyond recognition, appeared in 1914 and became Parnok's main (and mediated) source for the Lesbian poet.[69] Ivanov had studied with Wilamowitz in Germany. In the introduction to his *Sappho and Alcaeus*, he revoiced his teacher's theory that Sappho was the head of a religious community and school for aristocratic young women. He explained Sappho's strong but chaste "erotic feelings" for her "female pupils" as the central component of her "idiosyncratic, purely Hellenic understanding of her educational task, a task at once moral-religious, artistic, and erotic."[70]

The popular writer and amateur Hellenist Vikenty Veresaev published a second poetic, but far more literal, translation of Sappho in 1915. Considering Parnok's enthusiasm for Sappho, it seems likely that she at least glanced through his translation, but if she did know it, her own Sapphic poems show that she preferred Ivanov's version.

Veresaev's view of Sappho drew mainly on the work of Welcker, and exemplified the characteristically Russian denial of the word for Sappho's love in the name of love for Sappho's word. Veresaev dismissed the idea that (uppercase) Sapphic love, which he defined as Sappho's "passionate love for women and lack of erotic feeling for men," was the same love as the "unnatural perversion" that was called (lowercase) sapphic, or "lesbian" love. He argued that Sappho's alleged homosexuality was just as scurrilous a "myth" about the great poet as her fatal, unrequited love for Phaon and the "gossip" that "she sold her love to men for money."[71]

The Sappho that Parnok discovered in 1914 thus came embedded in cultural accretions, contradictions, sexual ambiguities, and creative pitfalls and potentialities. Added to the Russian attitudes about the original Lesbian poet were the French "sapphistries" of Baudelaire, Verlaine, and Louÿs, all of whom Parnok had doubtlessly read and absorbed.

Unlike that of other Russian women poets, however, Parnok's interest in Sappho had a personal dimension that struck to the core of her own creative identity.[72] *Roses of Pieria* represented her first attempts to write her experience of female same-sex love into Russian poetry through emulation of and desire for her distant, creative Other (the original Lesbian poet herself). As such, it remains a unique treatment of Sappho in Russian literature and one of a small number of other, western uses of Sappho that affirm the original woman poet as a great poet and an active (sexual) but nondecadent lover of women.

The volume contained twenty poems, written at various times from 1912 through 1921 and divided thematically into three groups: "Roses of Pieria" (eleven poems); "Penthesilea" (a trilogy), and "Wise Venus" (six poems). Sappho figured most prominently in the first group; the trilogy "Penthesilea" represented Parnok's artistic reworking of the mythological duel between the Amazon queen and Achilles; "Wise Venus" catapulted the poetic speaker, the main unifying presence in the collection, to the lofty position of goddess of love, dispensing advice to lovelorn worshippers. The three sections of the book thus gave stylized artistic expression to three facets of a modern lesbian poet's existence: her relationship with the original Lesbian poet; her amorous competition with men for lovers; and her wisdom about women and love that made her not the competitor, but the intercessor for unsuccessful lovers of both sexes.

In the first poem of the book (#61), Parnok invoked Sappho as her "sister of a single faith" in women and poetry. The kinship of their temporally separated poetic speakers introduced the notion of Parnok's parity with the original Lesbian poet. The next poem (#62) retold the Greek myth of the birth of the lyre from a tortoise shell and ended with a vision of Sappho, the Tenth Muse, coming "across the centuries into the Pierian garden to pick the eternal roses." As in Sappho, roses in Parnok's collection symbolize poems and beloved women.

Here Parnok seemed to be inspiring herself through belief in the eternal coming of Sappho to her co-religionists in posterity. Like other European lesbian poets of her generation, she sensed that being a lesbian privileged her relationship with the Tenth Muse. It put Sappho in the special relation to her that Aphrodite occupied in Sappho's life.

The third poem in the "Roses" group continued with the theme of the religious meaning of poetry as implied by Sappho's fragment: "'You did not feel like gathering the roses of Pieria'" (#63). Parnok's later coldness to her Sapphic poems may have been explained in part by her conversion to Orthodoxy that took place in the years between the writing and publishing of many of her Pierian roses.

The next two poems in the *Roses* group expressed what the discovery of Sappho had originally meant for Parnok. The idea of Sappho's school had stimulated her imagination, which in turn warmed her orphaned creative spirit with thoughts of Sapphic community and collective creation. (Similar fantasies inspired Renée Vivien and Natalie Barney in France at the turn of the century.)

> Once I hear the song of the Aeolian lyre,
> I catch fire, I do not walk, I dance—
> mimetic my voice, nimble my hand,
> music in my veins.
> I try not my pen, I tune my strings, preoccupied
> with an inspired care, to
> pour out of my heart, release into freedom
> sounds of ringing strings.
> Clearly in this life I have not forgotten
> unforgettable raptures from unforgettable songs
> that of old, my companion lovers sang
> in Sappho's school. (#38)[73]

From the ancient community of companion lovers, the fifth poem focused on one special, latter-day companion-lover who had shared Parnok's enraptured discovery of Lesbos:

> The whole of me was drunk on recollections,
> feeling weak from happiness, I said:
> "Lesbos, cradle of lyrical song,
> last stopping place of Orpheus!"
> My soul was avid with wonderful avidity,
> we left the muses no spare time.
> In that land I was not alone,
> oh splendid companion-lover! (#64)[74]

In the next two poems, a dyad entitled "Dreams of Sappho," Parnok assumed the identity of her mentoress. First, she wrote out the dream that Sappho mentioned she had had and "told to Cyprian" in one of her fragments (#65). In Parnok's fantasy, the speaker (Sappho-Parnok) dreamed of running for a long time in a strange place. She called out to her favorites and companion-lovers, but they did not answer. Her step was heavy and her lyre burdened her; the dawn, the sea, the grasses, herbs, and flowers were all different from the ones she had known in her "native meadows." Even the face she saw reflected in a stream was unfamiliar to her. Clearly, she was in the land of death.

The second dream was inspired by one of Sappho's most famous fragments, "Believe me, someone in the future will remember us," and revealed Parnok's awareness of the controversy over Sappho's sexuality. It made clear that she saw no basis for it: in Parnok's perception Sappho incontrovertibly preferred women to men. Before falling asleep, Parnok's Sappho sinks on her female lover's breast. In her dream Aphrodite appears to her, smiles, and says (with gentle irony): " 'Here is fame, Sappho: people arguing who you addressed / your eternal—rapture of the gods!—love songs to, youths or maidens?' " (#66).

Following Sappho's dreams were three lyrics, all of them previously published in *Poems*, including the "Alcaean Stanzas" Parnok had written to Sergey Efron in October 1915 (#53), and "Like a small girl" from February of that year, in which she used Sappho's love affair with Atthis to write about her love for Tsvetaeva. In the Tsvetaeva poem she also illustrated the complexity of her poetic speaker's relationship with Sappho: how Sappho, in effect, took the Parnokian poet as her timeless poetic lover while enabling Parnok to be a lover and a poet in her image.

A similarly complex relationship between Parnok and Sappho on one hand, and the Parnokian poet and her lover on the other, underlay the poem "You sleep, my companion-lover." By writing out Sappho's fragment, "Sleep on your companion-lover's breast, sleep on her tender breast," Parnok put herself in the position of Sappho's addressee and her companion-poet in posterity.[75] Simultaneously, her poetic speaker executes the command Sappho issued in her fragment and reenacts Sappho's post-orgasmic and creative languor:

> You sleep, my companion-lover, just like
> a child on the breast of its mother!
> How sweet: for you to fall asleep,
> for me to lack strength to awaken,

since, tell me, is this not a dream,
this bed abounding in rapture,
the sonorous twilight, and you,
and you in my peaceful embrace?
Oh delicately winding tendrils
on your moist temple! Oh violets!
The same as the ones which would bloom
for us in our native meadows.
The two of us wove floral wreathes,
and where there were wreathes there was singing,
and songs came with bliss . . . Oh my last,
my sweet dream, are you finally asleep? . . .
Flow gently, Aeolian sky,
as you drift and drift up above me,
keep blazing, last sunset of mine,
keep foaming, my ancient wine! (#67)

Sappho seems present in this poem as the moving spirit behind the poetic speaker's languor, her racial memory of Lesbian violets—a commonplace in Sapphic poems—and native meadows, and the bucolic, creative pursuits that she and her lover seemed to have shared in their ancient life.

In a 1910 poetic drama about Sappho, Natalie Clifford Barney wrote out a similar fantasy of Sappho's prediction to a lover who had left her (Timas, in Barney's play), that she would be a permanent presence in her (Timas's) life. Interpreted metapoetically, Sappho's speech to Timas appeared to be directed at every one of Sappho's lesbian readers in posterity, especially to those who were also poets:

Près de l'autre, c'est moi déjà que tu regrettes!
Et m'appelant tout bas d'une angoisse secrète,
Tu verras mon regard provocant à travers
Ses yeux, tu m'étreindras dans ses bras entr'ouverts.
Comme autrefois c'est moi qui viendrai vers ta couche,
Ce sera son baiser, mais ce sera ma bouche.
Tu me désireras à travers son désir
Et tu redonneras mon nom à ton plaisir.[76]

The trilogy "Penthesilea" represented a shift in mood as Parnok's poetic speaker noted at the beginning of the first poem, "The Challenge" (#69): "I am not tuning my heart for the voluptuous mode, / I have smashed my languorous lyre to smithereens." Yet symbolically, the "deadly battle" she would sing could be construed as a battle in an amorous competition between herself, a modern-day Penthesilea with the "indomitable blood of Amazons" in her veins, and her rival, a modern-day Achilles and worshipper of the same old "masculine god more malevolent than the malevolent Erinyes!"

The duel between Achilles and Penthesilea is described in the second poem of the trilogy, "The Duel." When Achilles's first two spear thrusts missed their target, "unexpected failure merely fanned the flames of ancient fury in the hero." His third spear penetrated Penthesilea's shield "like a fateful splinter," as Achilles saw when she "quietly moved [her] shield away from [her] heart." Penthesilea's legendary death constitutes the model of Amazon courage against which the modern Penthesilea measures herself.

In the last poem, "The Return," Parnok shifts from mythological to present historical time and gives Penthesilea's fate an ironic and demythologizing twist. The wound suffered by the Amazon queen of *fin de siècle* Russia does not kill her; it merely forces her to leave the field of battle, and thus differentiates her from her model:

> I went into battle armed with a deathless rose
> rather than a deadly spear. In ancient times
> my ur-mother went against Achilles
> differently armed.
> It's the same he in murderous battle array,
> his heart full of hate. But I am anguished:
> I have not borne the ancient hatred
> up to this life . . .
> Quietly returning from the field of battle
> and cursing the evil lot of female warriors,

Penthesilea presses her hands to her breast—
and weeps. (#71)

This concluding poem in the trilogy was the most personal and was probably written first. Given the situation it describes in general terms—a male rival's victory over the female speaker in love—and the date of its first publication, September 1916, "The Return" could be read as an encoded expression of Parnok's feelings after she "lost" Tsvetaeva to her "Adonis" husband.[77]

The poetic speaker rises from defeat, however, and concludes *Roses of Pieria* with the immortal wisdom of her "deathless rose" in the cycle "Wise Venus." Adopting the *conseils à un amant* model exemplified in Pierre Louÿs's *Songs of Bilitis,* to which she alludes in one of the poems,[78] Parnok expressed a subversive sexual politics, namely that there are women who prefer female lovers, and men would often be better lovers if they loved "with a woman's hand." Parnok's Venus counsels an art of love with "many rules": take your time as you move in a long kiss from your beloved's shoulders down to her breasts; do not fall into hopelessness; if you are a man, try to hide that fact as long as possible; do not hide your amorous sighs, however; be a "slow flame," or a "tender shower," rather than a "bolt of lightning" or a "storm"; be patient, do not hurry your lover's pleasure; and once you have fallen in love, act on your desire.

These were the poems in *Roses* that obviously made the greatest impression on the readers in Parnok's immediate Moscow circle. An acquaintance by the name of Vazlinsky was inspired by one of the wise Venus poems (#72) to write a parody of it, which began by quoting the second (and most piquant) line of the original:

"Some intractable girls find a girlfriend more dear than a boyfriend."
Not for masculine hearts have my arrows been sharpened by Love.
So she sang in Piéria (on the Fourth, on Tverskaya Yamskáya)
The sister of Sappho, a daughter of Lesbos true-blue.

> Well, one can't argue tastes. Blest she who embodies the feat
> Of the girlfriend of girlfriends here on Tverskaya Yamskaya Streets.[79]

Perhaps Parnok suspected that the parodist's good-natured joke rested as much on his titillation by her amorous achievements as on his admiration for her poetic ones. That sort of response may have increased her own doubts about *Roses of Pieria*. She had turned to anthological stylizations because they seemed to offer an acceptable way of writing her sexuality into Russian poetry, which accepted homoeroticism in stylizations because they affirmed the distance in cultural time and space that Russia wanted to maintain between itself and female same-sex love.

Parnok, of course, wanted not to maintain her distance from Sappho, but in every way to overcome it by "finishing" Sappho's songs, by interacting with Sappho lyrically, by asserting her ancient Lesbian creative roots, and affirming the intoxication to a modern lesbian poet of the Tenth Muse. In addition, Parnok wrote several personal relationships into her Sapphic poems—with Sergey Efron, Tsvetaeva, Erarskaya, and other lovers whose names remain unknown, but who made Parnok's poetic speaker wise in love.

The problem was that stylization was as strange and alien to Parnok's talent as the land of death seemed to Sappho's shade in Parnok's fantasy. She could not force her native voice through an ossified, "too aesthetic" lyricism. Perhaps she sensed that this artistically unsuccessful book would, ironically, be read as her ultimate Sapphic statement, and thus undermine the most important things about creativity, community, and loving that she had to say. She already knew, when *Roses of Pieria* appeared, that the forthcoming *Vine* said those things better, more directly, and in living words.

The Vine, Poems of 1922, represented the first vintage of Parnok's "old wine." The twenty-three thematically interconnected poems in the book (##77–100) related the poetic speaker's life as a poet and lover of women from her birth in Taganrog through her spiritual and creative rebirth in Sudak. The psychological framework and summary of this lyrical autobiography was provided in "Why, oh why from my paternal threshold" (#95), which formed a kind of life-within-a-life in the volume's structural plan.

After her several real and symbolic journeys from her father's threshold in Taganrog, Parnok had discovered a "homeland" in Sudak under the aegis of a "godmother," "sister," and "sibyl" whose ministrations and spirit made possible the lyrical retelling of her life in *The Vine,* and who is invoked in the first, dedicatory, poem of the book:

> My homeland is the place where my spirit rose,
> as a vine in that saline soil; where my troubled
> blood ceased boiling, and my ear took wing,
> and my body delighted in its weakness.
> That place is where I heard the music of light in
> cicadas' chirrs, and rustles of the heat-cracked earth,
> that place is where you brought me cooling grapes
> to soothe my feverish lips—a sacred eucharist...
> And if all that was just a dream, lest I
> forget an unforgettable dream forever,
> oh my beautiful and splendid godmother,
> at least appear to me in dreams, Sugdalian Sibyl! (#77)

The "unforgettable dream" of Gertsyk and Sudak had replaced the "unforgettable songs of unforgettable blisses" of Sappho's school. Once back in the Moscow inferno, however, the poet pined for Gertsyk's presence. "Suddenly, at the wave of a magician's hand," her vision of the garden in Sudak vanished, Eugenia wasn't there, "the waters had dried up," and "cicadas again chirred in [her] veins" (#92). This reference to cicadean music also seemed to allude to a new love affair that began in Moscow in 1922. Parnok sought her godmother with "outstretched hands," but they "grabbed hold of—emptiness," and she began to doubt the reality of her and Gertsyk's Sugdalian love.

By ministering to Parnok's spirit, Gertsyk had nurtured the poet in her, the poet whose lips had first been opened in adolescence by the anguished sonority of an organ. She recalled this ecstatic moment in the autobiographical second poem of *The Vine*:

> I remember, remember the service,
> foreign church, ceremonial voice.
> I'm a teen. In the sun my hair is
> like fire, and my step is firm.
> Getting weary of prayerful faces,
> of the alien, grand sacred things,
> I was leaving, but then she thunders,
> from the choir a new Latin rings . . .
> Who are you, dark, glad congregations?
> I'd not known paradise makes one sad.
> Is it from some enormous anguish,
> or from bliss that they sing like that?
> And what kind of a sparkle had punctured
> through the rumbling-thundering gloom?
> I had shut my eyes tight. Thus Isaac
> in submission awaited his doom.
> And 'twas then that a fiery seed fell
> on my soul, that the organ was seized
> by its ultimate frenzy, leaping
> in an outburst of full-voiced joy.
> And not I began shouting—a poet
> for the first time had open her lips
> that sense of unbearable fullness,
> that horror of sweet bliss. (#78)

Parnok looked back on the birth of the poet in herself as a moment of sacrifice and an orgasmic reception of Mother Anguish's fiery seed. She chose the Old Testament sacrifice of Isaac as a symbol of the sacrifice her creative insemination entailed and thus eschewed the poet-Christ identity that the majority of Russian poets of her generation adopted. By visualizing herself as an adolescent Isaac, moreover, she seemed to show her unconscious awareness of the critical role played by her absent father—given that Abraham is missing in the poem—in facilitating, albeit negatively, her creativity at its beginnings. At the same time, in casting herself in the role of Isaac, she might have been externalizing a wished-for self-image as a God-fearing, submissive, and beloved son, quite the opposite of the wayward daughter she had been to her father in life.

Several other poems scattered throughout *The Vine* lyricized moments in the poet's creative evolution after she had received the "fiery seed" in her adolescence. They formed the book's inner cycle that traced Parnok's self-perceived poetic life from the turn of the century through the time of the book's composition. In "Anguish" (#80) the poet acknowledged what had been implied in "The Organ" (#78), that the female wild element, Anguish, was her creative element as it had been Sabaoth's. Anguish's organ, she wrote, "sobbed in the darkness over the abyss" before God created "our vale of tears," and Anguish had "summoned [God] to creation" (#80). Addressing Anguish, Parnok concluded: "And in me your ancient flame is burning / and you make the singing stone of these / stanzas sing" (#80).

The next turning point in Parnok's poetic life, according to the lyrics in *The Vine,* came when a poet and lover (Tsvetaeva) inseminated her with a "grain of corn" that contained the "fire, wind, and moisture of [her] love" (#82). For a long time, however, Parnok did not take the poet in herself seriously: she looked upon poetry as a game and upon poems as things one tossed off with as much romantic aplomb as one could muster. Only after Sudak did she realize that being a poet was a serious, passionate vocation:

> A song's not an act, or skimmed from the top:
> blood makes the deathless rose purple!
> I do not want the young wine,
> it cannot quench my spirit—
> give me the ancient, fateful kind,
> noble and dry like passion. (#83)

Once she began to take her vocation seriously, Parnok felt that the Creator "took note of [her]," and she began to "dream secret sounds" (#96). She no longer had to look for names (words) in books; rather she consulted the "vital calendars" within her. (Were they the same, one wonders, that she had torn out of her heart in Sudak on that day when she rejected the lures of her amorous Memory [#104]?) Her lack of poetic productivity no longer bothered her because the spirit of her "godmother" had made it possible for her to bear "god-children" (her poems).

Finally, Parnok expressed her poetic life as a modern variant of the myth of Bellerophon and the Chimera (#97). She rejected the delusive authority of the patriarchal myth by doubting its veracity in her unheroic age. To counter the myth, she presented her poetic speaker as a necessarily failed Bellerophon whose aim could not always be true, who could not slay the eternal Chimera that confronted her.[80] At the end of the poem she asserted her own kind of poetic heroism in her unflinching, unsentimental acceptance of her life and her continued confrontation of the unnamed enemy who had stifled her voice:

> But I look my life straight
> in the eye without tears,
> and I see the claws of that
> same ancient, that same [creature],
> and I know by whom my deep
> voice has been smothered
> and who has breathed molten
> darkness into my soul. (#97)

The unifying theme of *The Vine* was the life of the poet's body, its sufferings and raptures. Parnok suggested that the vagaries and whims of her body were in part responsible for her manic-depressive experience of life. Her illness apparently so weakened her at times that she felt, as her poetic speaker says in one poem, that she was "hardly flesh," that her veins were filled "with sky rather than blood," and that she had no desire "for bread" (#91). But at other times, her physical appetites were insatiable and her body seemed to her "like a pregnant wife" with unsatisfiable cravings (#91). At those times, the heat of her exhausted body could not be drunk up (#94). In fevers of desire, she longed for "coldness"; she wanted more than anything to become spirit and rise out of her Egyptian captivity (#94), which seemed like a slow torture as she waited "until a lazy fire would burn through to the bone" (#91).

The poetic speaker of *The Vine* is a passionate woman who has used "love" at times as an easy way to gain the illusion of intimacy.[81] Her dependency on "love" led to a kind of addiction, or captivity, that was not so easy to break. Her body struggled with itself as bouts of incapacitating illness intermittently released it from its more exorbitant desires. But physical incapacity was not liberation. At the age of thirty-seven, her spiritual sisterhood with Eugenia Gertsyk notwithstanding, and weary from love's battles as she was, Parnok's poetic speaker still had to acknowledge her kinship with sisters of a different sort, whom she could pick out immediately in any crowd:

> You came in just as thousands have entered,
> but the doors for an instant breathed fire,
> and I realized: your hand has been hewn with
> that selfsame, prophetic sign.
> Yes, I know it, the ring—of Venus
> marks your palm in the very same way:
> for your walk is entirely too measured,
> and the light far too dimmed in your gaze,
> and your face powder covers up tear stains,
> and your lipstick is smeared over blood—
> yes, my sister, I know, that's precisely
> how she chokes you with kisses—love! (#81)

Though Parnok already felt at times that she was in the early winter of her life, that her "house" (body) was "icily tranquil" and wrapped "in a snowy winding-sheet," she still could not "endure music without tears" or take her eyes off a woman's "slender fingers" (#89).

The paucity of specifically addressed love lyrics in *The Vine* reflected Parnok's unsettled and intermittent romantic life at the time the book was written. The poetic speaker of the collection speaks in one poem of her need for a lover whose heart did not conceal in its recesses (as Erarskaya's had) her "own horror," her "own night," and who would not suffer the poet's kind of "chronic anguish" (#86). Perhaps she had found such a "dove" in the unnamed addressee of "To suddenly glimpse in your other's heart":

> You warm your feathers as if in the sun . . .
> And my trembling will not scorch you,
> may my dark spirit pass you by,
> and not get its hooks in your soul,
> and may your idle chatter be
> the last sound I hear as I die. (#86)

Nevertheless, during her tachycardiac nights when death seemed near, the speaker desired the lover who had once lain on her breast (probably Erarskaya):

> "What time is it?" "The mad hour. Come take a look:
> eleven o'clock, midnight, one, two, three!
> A moment and the hand will come full circle.
> Is this feverish thumping in the clock or in me?
> It makes my heart beat faster, and faster still
> in furious rapid patters of its own . . .
> Ah yes, I know—soon I'll also rush about
> just like that pendulum which has gone mad,
> and dimly-dimly will the night-light glow,
> and in despair my clockmaker will spread his hands,
> my heart will start its beating, and wheeze, and groan,
> and on my chest the sheet will bobble up and down . . .
>
> And at that midnight hour, where will you be?
> You who once slept on my breast, come, come to me!" (#87)

The last two poems of *The Vine* left a strikingly ambiguous impression of the poetic speaker's spiritual condition. The penultimate poem, "A spider has spun my dark hinged-icon" (#99), showed the speaker in a deathly mood, unable to pray, and cynically convinced that she would die without any sense of exultation.[82] At times like this she predicted death would come to her,

> not as music, not an aroma,
> not as a darkwinged demon,
> not as inspired silence—
> rather, a dog will start to howl,
> or an automobile will screech,
> a rat will slither in its hole.
> That's how! Neither good, nor evil,
> that's the music that I've lived to,
> that's the music to which I'll die. (#99)

The last poem of the book, however, expressed the poet's faith in prayer and in the flame that could still baptize her spirit:

> My heart will burn to ashes,
> my spirit rise from them.
> I pray to all the martyrs
> that the flame won't dim.
> Rage, my blizzard-fire,
> in your thicket black,
> until my spirit finds a
> baptismal font inside the
> blaze of seething fire. (#100)

5.
"While My Other Self Roams in the Wilds..."

After Eugenia Gertsyk left Moscow in September 1922, Parnok went into a prolonged physical and spiritual decline. Illness forced her to stop working for the last two months of the year. She described her state as a "fainting fit of the spirit" that made it impossible for her to see or hear anything. "Even music doesn't reach me!" she wrote to Gertsyk. "I haven't written a single line of poetry since the day you left. I am dead and *malevolent,* repulsive. I'm sick almost all the time—bronchitis and constant stomach problems. I'm utterly miserable about the poverty and exitlessness that I see in the lives of the people close to me; I try, but can't do anything to help them. I've never felt so powerless, and that has made me hysterical."[1]

In January of the new year she corrected the proofs of *The Vine.* She already knew that her next book had been "frozen" at Gosizdat and suspected the reason was that it contained "too much about God," because "the persecution of God [was] getting more and more intense."[2] Two review articles she had written, on Anna Akhmatova and Abram Efros, also did not pass the censor, and she expected the same fate awaited her article on Khodasevich, written the previous year.

With every passing day life in Moscow seemed harder, and Parnok dreamed of going away somewhere, all the while knowing "there [was] nowhere to go." Erarskaya had tuberculosis in her right lung and was "getting terribly thin," and Parnok felt she could not leave her. It seemed to the poet that if Gertsyk were in Moscow, things would be easier for her (Parnok), and she "would come back to life. But the way things [were], it [was] all hopeless."[3]

Despite her creative slough, she continued her participation in Moscow poetry circles. She became a regular at the Poets' Guild that met in the Bryusov Lane apartment of Anna Antonovskaya and was in competition with Nikitina Saturdays for poets and literary lights. At one February meeting of the Poet's Guild, Parnok met a young amateur poet by the name of Lev Gornung. They soon became friends, and Gornung's largely unpublished, anecdotal journal and reminiscences are the main outside source of information about Parnok in the 1920s.[4]

At the beginning of the year, Voloshin's mother died. As soon as Parnok heard the news, she wrote her condolences, but Voloshin never received her letter. When, months later, she learned from a third party that Voloshin had been surprised, and obviously hurt, not to have heard from her, she wrote again immediately to set matters straight and say that she too had been surprised at his long silence. In the same letter she reported: "I think your book *[Selva Oscura]* will freeze at Gosizdat just as mine will, and for the same reason: they now demand a 'Soviet orientation,' and have begun an open, frenzied attack against anything mystical."[5]

One of Parnok's mystically expressed and cherished convictions was that creativity represented a kind of "beautiful profit, the penultimate delight of the spirit," intimately connected with carnality. The artist who ceased to love the flesh disenabled him or herself and could no longer incarnate the Word (#161). In expressing these thoughts in a poem she dedicated to Gertsyk, Parnok seemed to want to remind herself that it was not a good sign if a poet lost her libido entirely. Her own lack of interest in the flesh may have made her fear abandonment by her muse. In point of fact, she wrote very little for the next two years.

At the beginning of this period, she met and became friends with Olga Nikolaevna Tsuberbiller, an instructor of mathematics at Moscow State University, and the author of the standard math text used for decades in Soviet high schools. Olga Nikolaevna was slightly older than Parnok and had begun her teaching career in 1903. She had been married before the Revolution, but the Civil War apparently left her a widow. Behind the camouflage of widowhood she lived quietly and undemonstratively according to her lesbian preference. Tsuberbiller was "even-tempered, serious, and good-hearted, but possibly lacking a sense of humor," the temperamental opposite, according to Gornung, of the "energetic, impulsive" Parnok "who had a marvelous sense of humor."[6]

In September Parnok inscribed a copy of *Poems* to her new friend with a stanza that stopped just short of being a declaration of love:

> Like music I love your sadness,
> your smile, so similar to tears,
> like the tinkle of cracked crystal,
> like the fragrance of December roses. (#109)

The exact nature of the women's friendship and gradually deepening intimacy, especially in its initial stages, and whether or not they were ever lovers, is impossible to determine. Parnok's poems and other references to Tsuberbiller leave no doubt that Olga Nikolaevna came to occupy a unique place in her emotional and spiritual life and was far more to her than even a closest friend. They also make it clear that the source of Tsuberbiller's ultimate and enduring appeal was not sexual. While Parnok's poetic speaker often perceived the hands of her lovers as instruments of passion, givers of pleasure and pain, she celebrated Olga Nikolaevna's "palm" as an "amulet" that protected her from the ravages of sexual love and her own desires.

As she neared forty, the poet began to have negative feelings about sexual passion in general and went so far as to condemn it in a few poems as merely an illusion of love and less important than friendship. Yet she remained susceptible to this particular illusion, as this 1923–24 poem indicates:

> It's not passion's bed that is sacred,
> but bread a guest breaks over victuals
> at moments of being friends.
> Forgetful girl, fond of good eating,
> from whose hands have you only not nibbled,
> my chirruper, tidbits of seed?
> Yet, as in a church for a feast day,
> at home I lit all of the candles
> the night you came flying to me . . . (#145)

In the early fall Parnok and a small group of poets broke away from the Poets' Guild and formed a circle of their own that met in the two-room basement apartment of Pyotr Zaitsev in Starokonyushenny Lane. Parnok became active in this group. Gornung recalled her at the September 27 meeting as she conversed with Zaitsev and smoked: "She was not young, but very appealing. She had light hair with a reddish tinge. Her voice was slightly hollow and hoarse. There weren't many people there. Before leaving, she read a few of her poems."[7]

A month later she gave a more extensive reading that was followed by comments. One listener said that her poems suffered from being "too good" and advised her to break up her meters and strive for free verse. Another annoyed her by calling her lexicon "luxuriant." At the next meeting Parnok spoke impassionedly about the death of the acmeist poet Nikolai Gumilyov, Akhmatova's husband, who had been shot for alleged counterrevolutionary activities. Later in the evening the question of new members came up, and someone proposed that they invite Mandelshtam to join their circle. Parnok protested, saying that she had had a quarrel with Mandelshtam and did not want to socialize with him.

In private she explained to Gornung what had happened: she and Mandelshtam had been sharing a cab to a common destination. When the cab drew up to the entrance, Mandelshtam leaped out and disappeared through the front door of the building, leaving her to pay the fare. This incident had obviously been the last straw for Parnok. In addition to all the unpleasantness she had suffered from him in the past, not to mention their romantic and poetic rivalry over Tsvetaeva, she may also have resented his recent friendship with her brother, who was then living with Mandelshtam's brother and another man in a filthy, squalid, cold room on Tverskoy Boulevard.[8]

By comparison Sonya's room on Tverskaya Yamskaya seemed almost comfortable. When she held poetry readings there, it even radiated a certain austere warmth and intensity, at least as Gornung remembered it:

> Her large, square room was lit by an unshaded electric light that hung from the ceiling. A large, four-cornered table stood in the middle of the room; a few chairs and a couch were pushed up against the walls. I found a place on the very edge of an ottoman near the door. There was rather a large crowd; all the seats were taken, and the rest stood in the doorway and even the vestibule where many of the men were smoking. Sophia Yakovlevna also smoked a lot. She sat at the table and read from a leather-bound notebook. After she finished, people made comments and gave their impressions.[9]

As soon as Parnok was more or less settled and marginally solvent, she gave up her office job and relied on free-lance translating for her main source of income. The work became increasingly hateful to her, particularly team-translating jobs when the text was parceled out to many translators in order to give as many people work as possible. Nor was translating particularly well paid. Her average salary at the end of the decade rarely exceeded a hundred roubles a month.

She sought refuge from daily life in dreams that provided a private, spiritually enhanced reality and a creative stimulus:

> I haven't died yet,
> I still can sigh,
> just let me listen
> to all this quiet,
> catch this faint babble
> slipping away,
> see off this sailboat
> floating away . . .
> Ducklings dive into
> watery blue,
> quiet the sandbar,
> still through and through . . .
> Yesterday's passing
> left no regrets.
> Just one more minute,
> don't wake me yet. (#155)[10]

It was becoming as difficult for Parnok to publish her criticism as her poetry, and in March 1924 she wrote what turned out to be her last published critical article. Originally titled "Today's Day in Russian Poetry," it focused on the work of Boris Pasternak, which Parnok treated in the context of a distinction between "today's day" and "the eternal day, in the name of which true art lives."[11] At the end of the article she scorned the epigones of Pasternak who, she punned, had begun to "pasternacize" their writing and "out-pasternacize" each other with such a vengeance that they would soon "pasternacize themselves out." Then, suddenly, she turned to two poets, Mandelshtam and Tsvetaeva, who had more than passing interest for her. Affecting real concern for what she perceived as the first signs of a "flight to Pasternak" in their work, she concluded with an encoded, autobiographically revealing perception of them:

> Mandelshtam and Tsvetaeva en route to Pasternak! Why this flight? Lovers, in the very heat of love, who have torn themselves from the good and kind arms of their beloved. Why, whenceforth this astounding lack of faith in art? How could they, so generously endowed by poetry, have doubts in her? I value these poets too much to suspect them of empty connoisseurship.[12]

Parnok read her article at the April 2 meeting of the Zaitsev circle, and it was published as "Pasternak and Others" in the second issue of *Russian Contemporary,* along with two of her recent lyrics. The first of them, "Nobody ever has anything" (#148), expressed the poet's alienation and cynicism about the possibility of making human connections in a world of speeding trains and "no time," an apocalyptic world that pulsed to a tachycardiac beat and seemed to externalize Parnok's hyperthyroid condition.

The other *Russian Contemporary* poem summed up her creative life to date. Calling it her "unleavened chunk [of bread]" and "unmiraculous deed," the poet implied that her physical and creative existence had become a kind of permanent exodus with "a bodiless body," "a deaf-mute muse," and no promised land in sight. Switching at the end of the poem to Christian imagery, the poetic speaker exclaimed:

> Oh Lord! What happiness
> to kill this soul of mine,
> and for a Castalian stream
> exchange the Eucharistic wine! (#149)

Parnok seemed to recognize in this poem that the sources of her *creativity* were elemental, and until she realized the potential of her pagan stream, her muse would remain deaf-mute. Her very conception of her muse as a deaf-mute woman seems fraught with significance for the plight of a lesbian poet in a patriarchal, homophobic poetic culture. Even if Parnok intended "deaf-mute" in the metaphorical sense, meaning "utterly unresponsive," there is a punishing and almost grotesque self-irony in the notion of a poet, whose life, soul, and creativity were imbued with and empowered by music, being bound (or "leashed," as she put it in another poem) to a deaf-mute inspirational source. A "deaf-mute muse" is in itself almost a logical contradiction (like a "bodiless body"). At the same time, it suggests that Parnok felt her poetic gift was crippled, handicapped, or in modern terms "creatively challenged." Inwardly her muse could hear (as the deaf Beethoven did), but she could not communicate her inner music to outsiders in the usual way. She required a new expressive language, since the traditional poetic one was often burdensome to her. Similarly, the poet needed a new body since the one she had when she wrote this poem had been used up by a chronic, debilitating disease.

In the early spring Parnok gave a poetry reading at the Cythera Society, a group dedicated to the study and propagation of the work of Annensky. When Gornung went to pick his friend up to accompany her to the reading, he found her cleaning soot from the walls of her room. Earlier that day she had bought tongue and wanted to delight everyone in the apartment with this delicacy. It was an enormous piece of meat, but, as it turned out, no one in the apartment liked tongue. Forced to cook it for herself, Parnok set it to boil on the kerosene stove in her room, then got involved in some work, and completely forgot about it until soot had covered the walls.[13]

Parnok and Gornung were the first to arrive at the meeting, which was very slow in getting started, and the delay annoyed Parnok. When someone asked her if she intended to read her poems, she snapped, "That's the only reason I'm here." While she was reading a large selection of poems, one listener wrote notes to Gornung in which he complained about "the too-visible appearance of the soul" in Parnok's work and her "pronouncements on the poet's spiritual deed," but the response of the audience in the discussion period was generally positive.

For part of that summer Parnok managed to get away to Lianozovo. A good friend in her communal apartment, Irina Sergeyevna, relayed messages to her, and the poet herself returned to the city briefly in August in order to pick up two novels at Mospoligraf where she was working as a translator. Her old friend Lyubov Gurevich was in charge of French and German translations there.

Her translating activities expanded in the fall and early winter. In November, Nikitina included her on the staff of translators of a new publishing cooperative she was organizing as an outlet for her Saturdays. Lunacharsky, the commissar of education, was in charge of selecting books for translation, and his top priority were the works of Jean Giraudoux. Parnok managed to get a copy of Giraudoux's *Siegfried and Limousin,* and Lunacharsky agreed to publish her translation of it, prefaced by his own introductory note about the author. In December she signed a contract for the translation that specified she would receive half her fee when the censor passed the book and the remaining half when the book appeared in print. At first she objected to not being paid an advance, and to having the payment of her fee depend on the censor's decision. Nikitina overcame her objections by saying the publishing cooperative had no money for advances and that the censor would certainly pass any book that had the backing of the commissar of education himself.

Throughout the fall, trouble had been brewing in Parnok's personal life, and in December the first symptoms of a severe emotional crisis manifested themselves. "I had a fainting fit," she wrote to Gertsyk two months later. "I had gone to bed and fallen asleep; then I woke up, got out of bed, went over to the window, returned to bed, and then, I fainted. I don't know how long I was unconscious since I was alone. After that episode, all of me somehow came unglued: I have no will, cry all the time, lack money and can't work."[14] Worried about herself, she went to a doctor, who diagnosed her condition as "acute psychasthenia," a now-obsolete psychiatric term that covered a range of disturbances from mental exhaustion to neurosis marked by fear, anxiety, and phobias.

Worse was yet to come. On January 7 Erarskaya stayed overnight in Parnok's room and in the middle of the night became "angry in her sleep" the way she used to in Sudak. This time when she woke up, however, she suffered some kind of psychotic breakdown. The next day Erarskaya had to be hospitalized in an asylum in Petrovsky Park. Parnok recalled it a year later as "the most terrible day" in her life.[15]

Erarskaya's illness turned out to be emotional in origin and did not affect her reason. It was Parnok's later impression that the first month Mashenka spent in the hospital "was a period of spiritual uplift, but then she went into a decline, and a terrible depression ensued."[16] She was paranoid and believed that all her friends were enemies. Parnok especially could not bear Erarskaya's repeated accusations that her friends were happier once she had been hospitalized, that her being in the asylum made life easier for everyone. Erarskaya insisted that she had been hypnotized by someone, even by a whole group of people, who were making her act against her will. Everything she did or thought was forced on her by the will of this cabal.

Parnok was not allowed to visit her until the middle of February. During this time Olga Tsuberbiller, by then the poet's most trusted friend, visited in Parnok's place and acted as a liaison.

Erarskaya's illness occurred in the midst of an "exceptionally difficult" period in Parnok's own life and clearly overwhelmed the poet with guilt. Shortly after Mashenka was hospitalized, Sonya "left home" and began "living all over the place." It seemed to her only right that she be homeless when Mashenka also had no home. Evidently, she had taken on the suffering of homelessness as a way of relieving her guilt for her former lover's breakdown. "For the first time in my life I'm living without a kopeck to my name," Parnok wrote Gertsyk in March. "People feed me, water me, supply me with cigarettes. . . . I think something basic in me has begun to degenerate because my parasitism doesn't bother me at all."

She saw Tsuberbiller every day and used her address for her mail. To her she confided that Erarskaya's breakdown was the "greatest misfortune" in her life. She took no comfort in the doctors' generally optimistic prognosis or in any visible improvement in Erarskaya's condition, and, during the first month of Mashenka's hospitalization, she was in a state of constant tension and anxiety. She desperately wanted a "way out" for Mashenka, wanted to make her life better and felt absolutely powerless to do anything.

Tsuberbiller wrote to Gertsyk about Parnok's condition: "The main misfortune is that Sonya is dissipating her energies, has already used them up, and has no source of new strength. . . . At the moment she doesn't want to do anything for herself, can't think about herself, and takes only others into consideration while no one takes her into consideration although she needs attention no less than Milochka [Mashenka]."[17]

By mid-March Erarskaya had become entirely absorbed in herself and in obsessive reminiscences of the past. She took a perverse, self-lacerating pleasure in dwelling on all the "shameful" things that had happened to her in life, and, evidently, almost everything seemed shameful to her. She chastised and blamed herself with a vengeance. Parnok was convinced that she would feel better if she stopped constantly "working on herself." She worried that Mashenka was too controlled and noted: "If I heard that she had broken the windows, or beat up on her doctor, I'd feel better because that would mean the boil had burst."[18]

After every visit Parnok became "utterly ill," but Erarskaya did not see her pain. She believed that her own sufferings had remitted all of Sonya's pain, and that Parnok had thereby been "liberated" from her. She behaved to her former lover as she would to a stranger, and this naturally hurt Parnok more than anything.

The atmosphere in the asylum also oppressed Sonya, and she marvelled that Mashenka did not mind the other inmates or consider them insane. Erarskaya had a private room and felt best when she was alone. Then, she told Parnok, she was calmer and everything "became clear" to her. "It is unbearably hard to leave her after a visit," Parnok wrote to Gertsyk,

> and to leave her alone like that, among the mad people. Often, often when I'm having a conversation with someone I'll suddenly seem to *see* her room, every tiny detail of it, even the design on the wallpaper, and Mashenka—sitting on the couch, walking from corner to corner, standing by the stove, going up to the window—alone, alone, alone. Not physically, but spiritually—endlessly alone with all her darkness, maelstroms of darkness and illuminations no less unbearable than that darkness. My very own! I know only one thing—if Mashenka does not recover, I'll go under.

Parnok and Tsuberbiller were told that Erarskaya would recover, but it might take as long as six months, and there was always the possibility of a relapse in a couple of years. Parnok doubted the doctors' ability to understand the human soul, however, and even believed that "simple folk" knew more than they. "The doctors don't know the way into the soul," she wrote Gertsyk, "that's why they can't find a way out."[19]

Erarskaya agreed. She and her family tended to put more faith in prayer and spiritual counseling than in psychiatry. One of her sisters consulted a priest who said they should pray for Mashenka to the martyr Tatyana. Erarskaya had begun to put such great hope in the church that Parnok feared a new disappointment. Similar disappointments had interfered with Mashenka's recovery from the beginning as she would grasp at one potentially saving grace after another.

Gradually, with Tsuberbiller's support and assistance, Parnok began to regain some of her emotional equilibrium. Her nightmares stopped, as did her fear that she too would go mad. She credited her recovery entirely to Olga's intercession. "If only someone could analyze Mashenka the way Olga Nikolaevna has analyzed me!" she exclaimed to Gertsyk.[20]

By spring Erarskaya also showed signs of real improvement that even the pessimistic Parnok could put some faith in. As she got better, she became self-conscious about being a "mad woman." When someone offered to bring her some henna dye since the roots of her hair had darkened, she replied, "Mad women don't dye their hair."[21] She also manifested a compulsive desire to be useful, started sewing herself a shirt, and dreamed of going to Sudak to take care of a friend.

Parnok also would have liked to visit Sudak that spring with its "bitter wormwood" and "blossoming almond trees," the "southern homeland" she "remembered with gratitude."[22] At the moment, though, such a trip was impossible. Her straitened circumstances had forced her to apply for financial aid from the Central Commission for Bettering Scholars' Living Conditions.

At the end of May she finally finished the translation of *Siegfried and Limousin* and submitted it to Nikitina. Six weeks later, Nikitina informed her that due to a technicality, the censor had not approved it. Nikitina agreed that Parnok should still be paid in full for her work, but at its July 11 meeting, the governing board decided to pay her only half her due, the remainder to come when the book passed the censor. Parnok went to the office to get her 153 roubles, only to learn that Nikitina was on vacation and no money had been left for her. An office worker gave her thirty roubles from his own pocket.

By midsummer Erarskaya was much better, but Tsuberbiller's health had broken down, which deeply disturbed Parnok. Then, in mid-July, the poet received the news that Adelaida Gertsyk had died suddenly from a kidney ailment at her home in Sudak at the end of June. Her response to this death in a letter to Eugenia was revealing:

> I think that for the first time . . . perhaps in her whole life, Ada, in leaving this life, permitted herself to do something wholly for her own self. She accepted the grace of God, the rest she had earned through the way she had lived. To you, my dear, I cannot hide that the news of Ada's death evoked a kind of tender emotion in me.

Perhaps because I myself am also tired with a sort of ultimate tiredness, and it seems to me that death is a gift of God, not sad, but joyous.[23]

The poet's recent harrowing experiences and homeless existence had provoked a drastic change in what she thought was important in life. It was a change that would also influence the way she would approach her writing. As she put it to Gertsyk toward the end of her letter of condolence, "It is hard to grasp that the truly beautiful lies not in abstract thought, not in art, but in each day. And if one could grasp that once and for all, how much more peaceful one's soul would be."[24]

In the fall Parnok's homelessness ended. She moved in with Tsuberbiller at 3 Neopalimovsky Lane I, off Smolensky Boulevard. The windows of their room looked out on the golden cupola of the small Church of the Burning Bush (now demolished), which Parnok often contemplated when she stood looking out the window, and which she mentioned in a few of her poems.

She had decided to put off the quest for her money from Nikitina Saturdays until Nikitina returned from vacation, and she finally succeeded in contacting her by phone in mid-September. Nikitina assured her that she would do everything in her power to see that Parnok was paid in full. Two days later, sensing she was being given a classic runaround, the poet submitted a request to the governing board that she either be paid in full or be paid half and have her manuscript returned to her so that she could try to find another publisher for the translation. The governing board ignored her requests and reaffirmed its decision to pay her half the sum she was due. At first, they deliberately miscalculated the amount, but finally agreed to pay the remaining 123 roubles, informing her that she could come for her money at any time. For ten days she tried repeatedly to get her money, but received only 50 roubles. Finally on October 16 she brought an official written complaint against the press to the arbitration tribunal of the Union of Writers.[25]

Amidst this business, her muse suddenly visited her after an absence of several months. The resulting lyric, "Excerpt" (#159), dealt with the general theme of poets' relations with their peers and posterity and, specifically, with the empowering legacy of Karolina Pavlova, who had been hounded out of literature (and Russia) by a hostile public that could not accept, as Pavlova herself believed, the "abnormality" of a female poet.[26]

In the first two stanzas of "Excerpt," Parnok wrote in general about poets' failures to find love and acceptance in their own families, so to speak. In the last stanza she switched from the general rule she had illustrated with male members of the poetic family (grandfather, father, son) to her own situation as a female poet in this poetic patriarchy:

> Silence is my only confidante.
> My mournful voice is dear to no one.
> If once you loved me, my son, or peer,
> no doubt you long have ceased to love me . . .
> But, persecuted by her peers in life,
> grandmother Pavlova now is glorified. (#159)

The final two lines of the poem provide a sharp grammatical gender contrast to the rest of it: six of the nine words they contain are feminine nouns and adjectives, whereas the previous sixteen lines contain only three feminine forms.

"Excerpt," with its encouraging remembrance of female poetic triumph, initiated a major creative period in Parnok's life. It produced poems that focused on the poet's idiosyncratic voice and unique soul, which she realized had both been shunned, ideologically and in actuality, by her contemporaries. Parnok's intimacy with her soul, like her dreams in which she and her soul were closest, provided a haven from a hostile outside world of critics, censors, and literary bureaucrats. On a more political level, the poet's private relationship with her soul offered an alternative to public aggression, noise, and bustle, not only for women, but for any person who dared to open his ears to her voice.

Starting in late 1925, Parnok began dating most of her poems by month and day again, a practice she had not followed for ten years. Those poems that are specifically dated present the reader with a lyrical reality that can be fixed in time, no matter how timeless, ephemeral, or esoteric it may be, and a lyrical reality that, no matter how otherworldly, still has deep roots in the poet's life.

When put into the order in which they were written—an order not observed in the collection *Half-voiced* (1928), which contains most of the poems Parnok wrote in 1926 and 1927 (in *Collected Poems*, ##162–99)—her lyrics really do become "life creating," as she called them in a poem written shortly before her death. For her, "life creating" meant providing space for her soul to breathe. For her readers, "life creating" means giving some idea of the poet's inner biography at a time when her inner life was increasingly becoming her whole life.

At the beginning of the winter, Parnok suddenly remembered her brother, who had left Russia again the previous summer and had returned to Paris. Her memory of his jazz dancing stimulated her to write a poem to him in which she emphasized their differences. As he "overstrained" his voice, she would "listen sullenly," not believing in his "shouting-match style." Her declining years had made her "more bashful" and her ear "painfully exacting." "I don't believe in your dense ravings," she concluded, "or in your gasps, or your contortions" (#200). She rejected her brother's style on the grounds that aging had made her more modest and discriminating. Her tone of reproach suggested, however, that she was not so distant from her brother as she wanted to be and wanted him to believe.

On the same day that she wrote to her brother, she celebrated the liberating end of a relationship with an unnamed lover. Standing by her "down-covered window," the relieved poetic speaker admits that she feels neither "awful" nor "depressed" about the breakup, and murmurs under her breath: "What a fine snow fell overnight, and how my liberated soul wants to go for a sleigh ride in the new-fallen powder!" (#160).

Three more poems followed in December. The first of them was a frankly political lyric in which Parnok directly alluded to the crimes of the new regime, how it had stolen the people's wealth and exiled them to Solovki. Needless to say, this poem remained unpublished during her lifetime. The other two December lyrics constituted the final two poems in the "Dreams" cycle, which Parnok had begun two years earlier. She dedicated "I'm walking somewhere" (#154) to Sophia Fedorchenko, a writer three years younger than she, who would soon become a trusted co-worker and friend. Finally, in #156, she described a dream that seems to express symbolically a new stage in the speaker's life journey and creative evolution. The luminosity of the poem's imagery indicates that Parnok was describing a moment of epiphany that put her life and self in a new light:

> A cloud lit up from inside.
> It was suddenly light and mysterious—
> the hour when a single image is
> revealed behind chance appearances!
> I'm leaving on a narrowish path.
> It's as silent as in a cloister.
> Intoxicating and desperate,
> as it can only be from music.
> And the places are so familiar . . .
> It's been hundreds of years since I left home,
> and I've returned to the same house,
> always back to the same pure lake.
> And the water babbles. . . . Isn't that you
> calling to me in the moist babble? . . .
> The guslas weep above Lake Ilmen,
> white swans are swimming out.[27]

The poem concerns homecoming, an important and recurring theme in Parnok's late verse, and the mention of "guslas," "Lake Ilmen," and "swans" suggests that the speaker's homecoming resonated with the native folk sounds, places, and creative ethos of the Russian north. In this adopted home—Parnok, after all, had come from the south of Russia—the poet, homeless for many years, realized she had returned to an origin that was timeless and virginal.

Although Parnok was ill off and on all winter, the new year began auspiciously for her. On January 3 she joined a large group of Moscow poets in organizing a new poets' publishing artel, which would be called The Knot. Its aim was to publish small, inexpensive editions of the poetry of its members, each of whom would make a yearly contribution to cover the costs of printing all the books in that year's series.

At the first general meeting of The Knot, Parnok "gave a moving speech about the fates of Russian poetry."[28] Two days later, a smaller organizational group met to determine whose books would be published in the first spring series and to decide the length and format of the books. Parnok immediately became very engaged in the work of The Knot and wrote Gertsyk in January that it already was her "only interest in life."[29]

By now Erarskaya was completely well and had been discharged from the hospital. Parnok believed that everyone's prayers were answered, but she continued to worry about Mashenka. She made a solemn vow never to leave her and wrote to Gertsyk, "Never, even after my death, will my soul cease aching over her."[30] At the same time, she felt unworthy of having a friend like Olga. Erarskaya had also come to regard Tsuberbiller as a "saint" and "hero" in her and Parnok's "grey everyday life."[31] In the psychologically complex triangle of mutual need, love, and obligation that had developed between the three women, the poet somehow found an emotional anchor that stabilized her life for the next five years.

At the end of January, her creative outpouring of 1926 began with two poems written on the same day, one of which revealed the aim of her mature poetry:

> People treasure-hunt at midnight,
> I come in the light of day,
> I don't hunt your soul in secret,
> you'll hear me from far away.
> Thieves maraud with lockpicks, crowbars,
> but, my friend, I must disclose,
> I've no crowbar, but a word with
> which to enter in your soul . . .
> Locks and clamps can all be broken
> by the marvelous breach-grass:
> from my soul straight into your soul
> come the words that I've addressed. (#173)

The major spiritual event that had enabled Parnok finally to engage in soul-to-soul poetic intercourse, to have real words with her addressees, was a maternal deed that the forty-year-old poet celebrated in a "Song" she wrote at the end of January:

> Drowsily an agèd pine
> rustles in her sleep.
> Leaning on her coarse-grained trunk,
> here I stand and speak.
> "Little pine-tree, just my age,
> give me of your strength!
> Not the usual nine months,
> forty years I carried,
> forty years I had been bearing,
> forty years I had been begging,
> begged my heart out, got by pleading,
> brought to term
> my soul." (#178)

In one of her many undated poems (#158), Parnok revealed that she conceived of creativity in wholly feminine terms. She believed that every person had a "creative [botanical] ovary" that would eventually produce a "wingèd hour." According to her own lyrics, her "creative ovary" had been fertilized by the "fiery seed" of anguish *(toska)* in the music of the organ that had fallen on her soul when she was an adolescent and had "made [her] lips open" for the first time (#78).

In effect, Parnok acted out the same fantasy in her favorite metaphor of creativity that Tsvetaeva had once expressed in their amorous life together, when Marina wanted to have a child from Parnok—"une petite elle de toi."[32] Parnok's spiritual pregnancy lasted a biblical-sounding, but biologically real, forty years. The birth of her soul was that "Castalian spring" she had yearned, two years earlier, to receive in exchange for the "Eucharistic wine." In a sense she did make that trade, for the soul-to-soul creative communion she desired and practiced noticeably lacked any specific Christian element. Rather, as in the song of her soul's birth, it drew its energy and incantatory power from the privileged relationship the speaker enjoyed with her "coevaless," the little pine tree.

The lyrics of Parnok's first wingèd hour reflected her apparently celibate life of the years 1926–27 and often expressed a kind of "seraphic eros."[33] Many of these poems recalled or were written to Olga Nikolaevna, whom Parnok nicknamed her "little deer," and whom she embodied in the lyrical image of a deer, or stag, the constant companion of the wild, virginal, Artemis-like poet of seraphic eros. In Russian the noun for deer, *olen'*, sounds like an elision of the short form of the name Olga, *Ole*, followed by the palatalized *n'* that begins the patronymic, *Nikolaevna (Ole + n' = olen', deer)*.

On February 18, Parnok first gave lyrical expression to her and *Ole N's* intimacy, and revealed its supraverbal, "unreal," creative potential:

> I sing about the kind of spring
> which is in fact unreal,
> but in my dream, toward quiet light,
> like a sleepwalker you steal.
> The paltry music of mere words
> is now not only verse,

but interchanges of our dreams
and secrets—mine, yours...
And so the glimmering vista of
deserted lunar blue,
shows through the icelike crystal there
right in front of you. (#163)

The poetic speaker's soul (and her soulmate) replaced the "fearsome tourguide love," (#95), whom she had followed for twenty years, and they became her new guides to an "ultimate" inspirational communion:

To my little deer
A mare snorts beneath her covering
and savoringly chews her hay.
And like a blindman with his leaderess
my body follows my soul again.
Not to my proud Muse for a rendezvous—
she's not what I am yearning for—
to wordless music, to the ultimate,
lead me, darling, lead, my soul!
The door was open, we stepped out quietly.
Where have all the meadows gone?
As if on holiday, luxuriant,
tall banks of snow stand all around...
From melancholy and from tenderness
I cannot make a move to go.
And over there, off in the distances,
are deer tracks on the blueing snow. (#164)

A second poem Parnok wrote on the same date also expressed the spiritually enraptured, quiet mood that defined her *sotto voce* lyricism and the collection *Half-voiced* that celebrated its magic. Having compared the quiet word's bewitching power "to convoke secret dreams" with the "pied piper's pipe" and the "blue quicksilver of the moon," the speaker addressed her intimate friend's soul:

Half-voicèdly, hardly audibly,
I come to you and ask your soul

to rise from bed and come outside to me
and off in paradise we'll roam.
Above the lake the birds are fluttering,
the water's limpid, like a tear . . .
Your soul lifts up her eyelashes—
and gives me such a wide-eyed stare. (#165)

Just as "interchanging dreams" (#163) represented the mystical equivalent of Parnok's earlier "intertwined bodies," so her two souls roaming paradise together represented her seraphic version of lovers in an earthly garden of Eden. Interestingly, her addressee's soul in #165 responded to the speaker's invitation to stroll in paradise with the same wide-eyed astonishment that, many years earlier, her "awkward small girl," Marina, had registered after her Sappho (Parnok) gave her a passionate kiss (#59).

Parnok's memories of Tsvetaeva must have been particularly acute in March after she attended a gathering at which Pasternak read a privately circulated manuscript copy of Tsvetaeva's new "Poem of the End." Parnok thought the work was "terribly unbridled, but uncommonly talented."[34] Pasternak's own response was more extreme. After reading "Poem of the End," he deluged Tsvetaeva with letters in which he offered himself to her "as her ideal reader, ideal critic and as a man desperately in love."[35]

Parnok herself was in love that year with the beautiful winter, feeling a joy her execrable health could not mar. Despite the ever-present threat of death, she survived and wrote Gertsyk ironically: "As is my habit, I was supposed to die, but didn't die—all I did was pass the time." While Mashenka had completely recovered by the beginning of March and looked "radiant," the reverse was true of Sonya. The doctor had advised a complete rest at a sanatorium, "but that's impossible," Parnok added. "Olga Nikolaevna can't leave since her mother won't have anything to live on if she does, and I can't leave Mashenka."[36]

She was putting "an awful lot of time and soul" into The Knot. As had so often happened in the past, however, she was more enthusiastic about this undertaking than most of her colleagues. When she discovered to her chagrin that she was the only member of the board who regularly kept her scheduled duty hours, she wrote a curt letter informing the others that henceforth she had decided to reduce her office duty to the minimum as well.

One of the first books that The Knot published was Parnok's *Music,* which appeared in March. It comprised thirty-three lyrics written between 1916 and 1925, the majority of them previously published. *Music* was thus a retrospective collection, and although Parnok dedicated it to Tsuberbiller, the woman and lover most present in the poems is Erarskaya. Seven poems either allude to Mashenka, are addressed to her, or recall moments in their ten-year relationship: from the beginnings of the relationship in February 1916, to the peak of their rapture the following year, and ultimately to the ravages of love and hate that developed by the end of 1919, taking Parnok beyond her capacity to love. There is also a lyric about the music of madness (#136) that obviously alluded to Erarskaya's most recent life and the latest stage of her intimacy with Parnok. As a group, the poems to and about Erarskaya stress Mashenka's intense duality: she is both a vulnerable, "little stalk"(##142, 151) and "the devil himself, Carmen" (#138); she is associated both with "gypsy tambourines" and church bells (#142); and she loves and hates with equal intensity (#146). In dedicating her collection about music and Erarskaya to Tsuberbiller, Parnok asserted the emotional primacy of the three of them together at the time the book appeared.

The lyrical center of the collection is music, however, and music epitomizes ambivalence, an energy and a spirit that can be both destructive and creative. In one poem (#134) the major impact of a symphony concert on the poetic speaker is to fill her veins with "melodious, thousand-year-old anguish" and to make her aware of her creative and destructive potential. Anguish/Yearning frequently accompanies music in the book's poems, as does the theme of homelessness. The poet invokes music as a "dark" and "terrible spirit," which, like the magical "breach-grass," separates people from each other and from themselves (#136). Yet elsewhere, she shows that music brings people together and allows her, the alienated poet, to participate in common humanity, "to cry out [her] soul with everyone else" at the Last Judgment (#135). Submitting to the destructive laceration of a gypsy voice liberates the poet's soul from its struggle with herself (#140). Music is a "wondrous, useless, devastating rapture" (#134), a source of unequalled "hopelessness and intoxication" (#156). However destructive its power, music is the essence of a spiritually viable existence; when the poetic speaker cannot hear music, she has fallen into a "terrible fainting fit of the soul" that renders her spiritually dead (#150).

A multitude of sounds, instruments, musical performances, performers, and musical experiences fills the lyrics of the collection. Parnok had a particular fondness for string instruments: violins, lyres, guitars, and cellos. "The violin bows suck out my soul / to its most hollow depths," concludes the poetic speaker of one poem (#134); "And the cello / streams its honeyed, prolonged rapture / pampering one to death with sweet bliss" (#135), she rhapsodizes in another. Gypsy singing had a similarly potent effect on her: "Torment and tear me, gypsy voice / and with your song sing me to death" (#140).

Because the poems in *Music* were written over a relatively long period, during which Parnok's creativity changed drastically, the collection does not have the stylistic cohesiveness of the books that preceded and followed it. In this respect *Music* resembled *Poems,* although on a much smaller scale. As with *Poems,* it is sometimes difficult to understand what guided Parnok in selecting her own poems for publication or republication.

As in all her collections, however, several of the poems in *Music* do highlight moments in the poet's creative autobiography as well as stages in the development of her thoughts on poetry. *Music* begins and ends with poems about art, the artist's relation to the world and to the divine. In both introductory and concluding lyrics, art is called "profit" or "cupidity" *(koryst')* and as such it constitutes "the penultimate delight of the spirit" (#161). Thus, "the world is beautiful a hundredfold," where a mere mortal, the artist, can enjoy the profits of artistic endeavor, defined as a "mortal god's" striving "to imprint the immortal [God] with an anguishing hand" (#133).

Significantly, the artistic endeavors mentioned in the first poem of *Music* are in full swing: "The brush flies upward, the pitch of strings respires / and the pensive hammer knocks into a block of stone," but in the last poem of *Music*, the sculptor's "hand feels almost no attraction to clay," and nothing he sculpts will be realized in marble. The painter will suddenly "stop [his] brush in midstroke," and the poet "will stop [her] song in the middle of a word." Creativity stops because it is superfluous: "Whosoever falls out of love with the flesh cools to incarnation" (#161).

Everything in the world of *Music* is frightfully double-edged: the poet is caught between the tedium and hopeless desirability of her homelessness on the "great" yet "cursed" earth. She seeks a homeland as she yearns for gypsy caravans. She comes from a "home" that was at once limpid and "pure" (#156) and crimsoned with fantasies of heroic, bloody deaths (#157). She loves, equally, "gypsy tambourines," "majestic verse," and Moscow's "bells of eventide." The "melodious quiet" of dreams delights her; the silence of her peers to her poems grieves her.

Even night has two sides to it. On one hand it is the time when a "dark wave rises and assaults" the poet, liberating her soul "to outstubborn" her "daytime will" (#137). Parnok gave the title "Dark Wave" to seven poems (##13–142) that she previously had published as a cycle (in 1919 and 1922), and despite their different themes, all allude to gypsies. The nighttime gypsy mood, or resonance, combines the individual strains of an unnamed gypsy singer with very black hair (#137); Lyudmila Erarskaya (##138, 142) and Carmen (#138); the fourteenth century "queen of the gypsies," Bari Crallisa (#139); another "black angel" gypsy singer whom the poet heard in 1916 (#140); and an unidentified woman with gypsy blood (whose name began with "B") with whom the poet evidently had a relationship (#141).[37]

Night, however, is also the time of dreams and a totally different music, which comes on a "melodious wave" (#152) rather than on a dark one. This is a music in which "melodious silence" (#155) replaces jangling guitars, where the intimate addressees speak "in moist babbles" (#156) rather than wailing in "redhot, wild" voices, and where the poet hearkens to the plaintive guslas, not guitars and seven-stringed lyres. The cycle "Dreams" (##152–56) sounds the musical antipode to "Dark Wave." Dreams allowed the poet's soul the space to breathe freely (#152). Her dream world was a place where she could not hear the demands her intimates made on her (#154); yet her incapacity to respond caused her no guilt (as the impossibility of being able to help people close to her frequently tormented her in real life, especially in the case of Erarskaya). Dreams forced the poet to safeguard herself, something Parnok had often found difficult to do in her intimate relationships. In dreams the poet was separated from the despair of people who "needed" her (#155), and she could therefore act autonomously in a self-actualizing, Artemisian[38] journey *she* needed in order to recover wholeness, "that pure lake," where she could hear the native sounds of the guslas and watch the majestic swans swim out (#156).

Music attracted no attention from the official literary establishment, but it impressed many of Parnok's friends. The favorable response to the book, and especially to the "Dreams" cycle, pleased the embattled and semisilenced poet enormously. "To my great satisfaction," she wrote to Gertsyk at the beginning of the summer,

> *Music* has evoked a response in the most different sorts of people and is better liked than my previous books. That means a lot to me now as a human being more than as a poet. It excites me that now, when a voice like mine is officially unlawful, such a book appears

unexpectedly desirable. I've had the chance to give public readings of my "Dreams" several times, and every time I've sensed an enthusiastic response in my listeners. I did not expect that a voice like mine could be heard at present. The acknowledgment of a soul's right to existence is dearer to me than any literary recognition. I now look on poetry as a means of communicating with people. I'm happy that there is an eternal, extra-temporal language that can be used in all times to make oneself clear to people and that sometimes I find words everyone understands.[39]

To express one's difference, yet to be understood by the mainstream culture, is a rare accomplishment for a poet on the margins of that culture, and it is not difficult to understand why the response to *Music* made Parnok so happy. At the same time, she was pessimistic about the future: "It seems to me," she confessed, "that it's all over for poetry forever. I'm sure I won't get to publish another book: it's no time for poetry. No!"[40]

Voloshin was one of those who expressed enthusiasm about *Music,* and perhaps through him, news of the book's appearance and Parnok's penurious condition reached Tsvetaeva, who was by then living in Paris.[41] In April, Tsvetaeva wrote to Pasternak with the strange request that he try to do something to help Parnok. To explain her interest, and perhaps to discourage him from his own desperate pursuit of her, she apparently told him that she and Parnok had once been lovers, and as proof, appended to her letter one of the love lyrics she had written to Parnok back in 1915.[42] Her motives were ambiguous, to say the least, particularly in view of the poem she chose. One of the more negative and self-martyring evocations of her "Girlfriend," it was bound to create sympathy for her and hostility toward her former lover when read out of context by a man who was desperately, romantically, and "purely" in love with her.

> There are names, like suffocating flowers,
> And there are glances, like a dancing flame . . .
> There are sinuous, dark mouths

With moist and deep-set corners.
There are women. Their hair is like a helmet.
Their fans give off a fatal, subtle fragrance.
They're thirty years old. Why, oh why
Do you need my Spartan child's heart?! ("Girlfriend," #13)

If Tsvetaeva were still out for some sort of private revenge against Parnok, then she succeeded in manipulating Pasternak into winning it for her by evoking his jealous protest for the pain she had suffered. "One would have to be a glutton for punishment, a veritable Saint Sebastian," he replied on May 19, "to write about oneself as you did at the age of twenty. I am afraid even to glance at that Leyden jar of a letter charged with pain, jealousy, shrieks, and suffering."[43]

Pasternak read "the Leyden jar of a letter" in a trolley on his way to the newspaper offices of *Izvestia*. Upset for his "beloved little Spartan," as if he had just learned Tsvetaeva was in the middle of a passionate lesbian affair, rather than one that had ended a decade ago, he "rushed into the editorial office" like a "bull in a china shop."[44]

As it happened, the night before he received Tsvetaeva's letter, he and Parnok had had one of their frequent squabbles, and he had left the editorial office of The Knot in a huff, blaming Parnok for his departure. That was part of the reason, he claimed to Tsvetaeva, that he could "do nothing to help" Parnok. She and he had "never had anything in common."[45]

There is no evidence that Parnok knew of Tsvetaeva's misguided attempt to "help" her, or of Pasternak's refusal to be involved. But if she had known, she would not have been surprised, having herself experienced the hatred and betrayal of love that passion often brings in its wake. Such passion had often made her feel that she could not love without hurting herself or others. Her own violent passions had in some sense, she felt, deprived her of a father, ruined her relationship with her brother, nearly destroyed a lover's sanity, and had brought her to the brink of madness. Her strongest lyrical statement against passion (as distinct from love) came at the very end of March in response, evidently, to a visit from a former lover:

> "I loved you," "I love you," "I'll always love."
> But my guest's eyes are greedy.
> The way a woodpecker dully drums wood
> day and night, day and night, without ceasing,
> the way that a drop drips, until it will eat
> through granite; that worms gnaw at souls . . .
> Each sinner in the world has his cross to bear,
> and mine's—to hear speeches like those.
> "Please don't blaspheme!" I answer.
> "Better sing, curse me out!
> By compassion, not passion
> does love make itself felt."
> "I love you!" her mouth full of teeth repeats,
> it repeats, and her eyes stay open.
> Thus dully echoes a clump of earth
> as it's striking the lid of a coffin.
> It's quieted down, the air is dead,
> unbearable calm before thunder . . .
> "Now you're being chastised," I hear in my head,
> "the way you chastised others." (#204)

The sense of "unbearable calm" that the poetic speaker has at the end of this poem recalls the calm before the storm experienced by the poet at the end of "Is it thinkable taming a lynx?" (#138). And the preaching of her inner voice that she is now being chastised as she chastised others virtually echoes the moral lesson which the speaker of "I gaze again at your steep-browed profile" (#45) learned from her quarrel with her unrepentant "brother." Unfortunately, neither of these lyrical reminiscences of Parnok's past relationships with Erarskaya and Valentin Parnakh, respectively, solves the mystery of who the former lover might have been who declared her "eternal love" to Parnok at the end of March 1926 and received this stern, lyrical rebuff.

That year April began with the Feast of the Annunciation, one of Parnok's favorite holidays in the Christian calendar. She celebrated it lyrically by taking a holiday from her muse:

> Today the sinners in hell
> are no hotter than in Sicily,
> today I'm off my Muse's leash—
> we have set each other free. (#167)

Full of holiday religious fervor, she wrote to Gertsyk announcing her intention of fasting with Mashenka during the fourth week of Lent. In the same letter she mentioned having recently heard a peasant poet who had "sought salvation" by becoming a wanderer in the far north. Overcome with momentary wanderlust, she noted, "Now there's a place I would like to spend some time in and see the permafrost."[46]

In the spring The Knot had plans to publish an almanac if the censor permitted it, and Parnok wanted it to include an obituary of Adelaida Gertsyk and a selection of her poems, most of which had remained unpublished at the time of her death.[47] She had, in fact, wanted to publish a separate book of Adelaida's poems but could not because the regulations of The Knot stipulated that it could only publish works of its charter members.

She wrote to Eugenia asking her for material to include in a short biography of her sister. She also asked her to select some of Adelaida's poems for publication in the proposed almanac, but cautioned her to remember that "religion is the opium of the people." For the same reason, Parnok had decided not to write Adelaida's obituary herself since she could not write "in Aesopian language" and did not "want to say less about Ada" than she "desire[d] to say."[48]

A great deal of Gertsyk's unpublished poetry is intensely religious, and Parnok herself had experienced the difficulties in publishing religious lyrics even in the early 1920s. At least, she believed that her collection *Centuries Old Mead* had not passed the censor because it had "too much in it about God." Later, when God almost vanished from her lyrics, and her spiritual focus shifted to the life of her soul, she understood her unpublishability simply as a sign of the Soviet censorship's hostility to personal themes and poetry itself, and believed it was directed at and oppressed all "genuine" poets. In addition, she knew that the pessimistic tenor of her lyrics was badly out of tune with the official optimism of Stalin's early reign.

Toward the end of the 1920s official "antipoetism" and antipessimism characterized communist literary policy, and it is impossible to gauge what role, if any, the specifically lesbian contents of Parnok's personal lyrics played in determining, or enhancing, their unpublishability.[49] Unlike male homosexuality, lesbianism was not considered a crime in Russia at any time during Parnok's life, nor would most of the poems, including love lyrics, that Parnok wrote in her seraphic period have been considered "lesbian" by her contemporaries, who defined female same-sex love in the most narrow, merely physical terms. Nevertheless, both before and after the 1917 Revolution, Russian artistic norms and public morals proscribed the direct, unmediated expression of sexual love between women in poetry and, during the Soviet period, in life as well.

As a young woman, Parnok had internalized and accepted the norms of her antilesbian culture. She practiced various forms of self-censorship, which manifested itself in her obsession with good taste, her youthful belief that art and abstract thought were higher than "ruthlessly monosyllabic" life, the chronic "untalkativeness" of her muse, her awareness of writing poems "too intimate" for publication in the mass-circulation media, and her concealing the identities of many of her lover-addressees in order to protect their privacy. Ironically, the official Soviet muffling of her voice, for whatever reasons it was done, made the pressures of publishing in an antilesbian society a nonissue. It released her from the censorship she had imposed on herself—perhaps unconsciously—and thus to some extent actually liberated her creativity.

In the spring of 1926, however, "no one [was] publishing poets, not even very timely ones."⁵⁰ Despite its pressures, frustrations, and frequent disappointments, Parnok continued to be very engaged in the work of The Knot. The censorship was a constant and often insurmountable problem, and the press's lack of money also prohibited it from publishing everything it wanted to. In April, Parnok had had to write to Kuzmin, on behalf of the editorial board, that the "superb volume" he had sent could not be published in the spring series and would have to be put off until the fall for lack of funds.⁵¹

Of course, work for The Knot could not gratify the deepest longings of Parnok's spirit. Often she found herself sitting at meetings, outwardly discussing matters with her colleagues while inwardly escaping into a private world:

Cigarette after cigarette.
We have meetings, discuss, make judgments.
Amid the smoke, throughout the evening,
auburn-haired I appear to people.
While my other self roams in the wilds . . .
Light's ineffable blueness!
Every leaf on them tremulous,
sorrowful aspens shudder.
Heaven's somnolent vaults move asunder,
into view comes a luminous bee garden—
"Step-daughters of mine! Stepchildren! . . ."
respires nature. (#168)

The speaker's fantasy of being welcomed home into nature's apiary reveals the source and the nature of Parnok's "inveterate yearning." The poem may contain an allusion to the Greek mother goddess Demeter, who was addressed in her myths as "the pure mother bee."⁵² The metaphor of nature's apiary might also suggest the matriarchal judge of Israel, Deborah, who was also associated with the queen bee. Finally, Parnok's semi-invalidism had made her feel alienated from nature, and from mothers, because it kept her from being able to have a "healthy" child. Thus, the fantasy described in the poem had healing power. It healed the wound of separation of the "unhealthy" self (the daughter) from her natural other (the mother, nature). Healing was accomplished through an erotic maternal-filial dynamic: nature (mother) separated, revealing the apiary womb, and inhaled into her depths the excluded stepdaughters so that they could be reborn into the hive. The fantasy also realized that the price exacted from the orphaned stepdaughter for her reintegration was, she believed, her exclusion from the world—that was why her "other self" roamed in the wilds.

After her falling out with her brother, the only family Parnok had was her sister Liza. Apart from the Civil War years, the sisters were in constant contact from 1915 until Parnok died. Like her siblings, Liza had finished the gymnasium in Taganrog; unlike them, she lacked any particular gift for music or poetry, although she did become a writer of children's stories. She married a young man from Taganrog at some time after 1915, but she must have been widowed early since no husband appears in her life from the early 1920s on. Nevertheless, she went under her married name, Tarakhovskaya.

Parnok treated her younger sister with maternal solicitude. She provided a shoulder for Liza to cry on when the younger Parnokh encountered her first misfortunes in life, lived with her for a period in Moscow after World War I began, dedicated several poems to her, and included her in her social and literary life. Liza met most of her literary friends and contacts through her sister.

In 1926 Parnok asked Voloshin to invite Liza to Koktebel for the summer, which he was happy to do. He naturally invited Parnok also, but she replied that she did not have enough money, and even if she could afford it, she would prefer to visit him in the fall "after the summer commotion." That seemed uncertain, however, because her lack of money had become "chronic."[53]

Parnok had been writing a great deal that year in comparison with others and was already planning a new book she intended to call *Dreams*. This was evidently the first title for the book she eventually called *Half-voiced,* and it reveals the important connection the poet herself established between her *sotto voce* lyricism and her dreams.

Gertsyk had invited Parnok to come to Sudak for the summer, but the poet was afraid to go there. Instead, she, Erarskaya, and Tsuberbiller rented a cottage together in Bratovshchina outside Moscow. Arriving in the country after her and Mashenka's illnesses of the previous year, Parnok felt "like a patient the hospital has just released into the world," as she wrote in a June poem to Erarskaya, who, more than anyone, probably shared her former lover's feelings of liberation. The poet went on to describe the intensity of nature's impact on her: "the air [seemed] sharper, the sky huger, the clouds lighter, the talons on the paws of the somber spruces brighter, and the moss more luxurious" than she had remembered. Being back in nature, of which she had daydreamed during so many tedious meetings in stuffy, smoke-filled Moscow rooms, stimulated her creativity even as she still doubted the reality of this dreamed-of homecoming:

> I walk, overhearing in myself
> a line begin to build.
> A dewdrop quivers on the heather,
> exchanging a bow with me—
> and yet to me my homecoming
> still seems beyond belief. (#174)

Memories of Bratovshchina are scattered through the eight lyrics Parnok wrote in the fall of 1926 as her creative surge continued. All but one of these poems (#205) went into *Half-voiced*. The poetic speaker of them already felt at times that her soul desired independence from her body, which was imprisoned in a crowded communal apartment where "mumbling on the other side of the wall" reached her ears during her frequently sleepless nights (#179).

Back in the city and its stressful mundane reality, the poet began to suffer again from her inability to respond to the "helpless cry" of her intimate friend. Nevertheless, she tried to comfort her:

> But don't you cry, but don't be saddened,
> do not lament your love.
> I don't know where, my friend, but somewhere,
> you and I will meet again. (#177)

No longer doubting the existence of an afterlife, and remembering the quiet twilights at Bratovshchina, the speaker of this poem comforted herself by imagining the real possibility of coming back to earth "at some quiet hour, as an otherworldly (female) guest" in order to spend time with her intimate addressee (possibly Erarskaya).

That fall, Parnok also remembered her "comforting, last, blessed friend," Olga Nikolaevna, in two lyrics, both of which contain allusions to Bratovshchina. In the first she recalled Olga picking mushrooms there one day, and as she had held a *borovichòk* mushroom in her hand that seemed "like a communion wafer no baker of communion wafers could bake" and "stood mass" in a "dusky heathen temple" formed by the pine trees that "dripped wax from their green candles" (#175). Typically for Parnok's mature poetry, the spiritual essence of this lyric lay in the speaker's love for and adoration of her companion-other and in the religious experience of elemental communion that the two women enjoyed with nature and with each other.

As already noted, the poetic speaker of Parnok's seraphic love lyrics often has an Artemisian quality as she seeks intimacy with her other while maintaining her autonomy.[54] A mysterious love lyric that Parnok wrote on October 30 appears also to allude to Olga Nikolaevna in her familiar animal hypostasis (the deer). The reference in the poem to the "paws of tenebrous spruces" suggests the landscape in Bratovshchina (cf. #174). As evening "slowly-slowly descends on the quiet earth," the poetic speaker watches her deer emerge from the forest "to meet the night." Filled with "enchanted yearning," she wonders if the deer is "the precursor of a new deity" (a new love), or the "sorrowful shade of an old deity" (a former love). The notion that her deer could represent either "a friend lost by [her]" or "one being sensed in the future" recalls, strangely enough, the idea behind one of Parnok's early (1910–11) poems, "At times our premonitions," in which she first expressed her belief that people are drawn to their lovers by recollections or premonitions. At the end of #171, the speaker imitates the spruces (nature) in adoration of her deer as she honors her past and future loves (deities) in her:

> Tenebrous spruces are stretching
> toward the deer with their paws as if praying.
> Reverently genuflecting,
> I kneel and shut my eyes.[55]

The poem may have hinted at new stirrings in Parnok's emotional life in the fall of 1926, a possibility also suggested by another, equally obscure lyric from October, that begins, "A kind of barely perceptible sign" (#176). It recounts a visionary tryst between the poetic speaker and her addressee, a spectral woman who has crossed the speaker's threshold "again" (an attraction via recollection, perhaps). Through this woman "in the open door," the speaker sees the "radiance of a newly born dawn, inexpressible in words." A stanza that Parnok omitted from the version of the poem she eventually published in *Half-voiced* described the vision in the open door in more concrete and allusively erotic detail:

> A shapely alley rises into the sky,
> and the golden cupola curves sharply,
> and an apple tree, like a veiled bride,
> stands reddening, and sweetly blushing.[56]

The vision might also represent a lyrically heightened impression of the view out Parnok and Tsuberbiller's window onto the cupola of the Church of the Burning Bush.

Despite visions of radiant "new dawns," Parnok's worsening

health and pessimism about publishing her work—particularly bitter in the light of her enhanced creativity—combined to push her into another major depression by early winter. She felt that her overworked heart was "beating a retreat," and death was near:

> Is it mutiny again? Well, hardly—
> since my drummer beats retreat.
> We're done roving, we're done estranging,
> done wandering are you and me.
> My leg doesn't seek the stirrup.
> Bare the distance, dark the night.
> Time is done for us, vanished,
> other times for us are nigh. (#196)

The prospect of death caused the poet no fright, merely a "delicate chill," which would force her from her bed. She would go to the "tear-stained" window, "wipe off the panes," and lamenting death, stare out at the world. She did not see the "adjacent cross-street" or an old woman dragging herself to early mass, or the dirty, bespattered wall, consumptive dawn, or the antenna with a sparrow dozing on it, but she saw something . . .

> that I can't find words to describe—
> exaltation illuminated,
> penetrating the gloom from inside! . . .
> And a female voice, exalting,
> —alone in the bright sacristy—
> sings and sings. Hallelujah,
> hallelujah to the world in peace! (#196)

Such visions sometimes helped Parnok to overlook her bleak surroundings and the disappointments of her life.

One seemingly endless disappointment was Spendiarov's epic procrastination about finishing *Almast,* something he had been promising to do for almost five years. In October Parnok received a letter from him informing her that he had still not finished the orchestration of the last act and did not think he would get it done until the following fall. She liked him too much to get angry at him, but she did write him an emotional letter expressing her frustration and trying to inspire him to "exert all [his] will and all [his] ambition and finish the orchestration of the opera."[57]

The translating Parnok had to do to support herself was almost always a torment for her. One exception was her joint translation with Gurevich of Proust's *A l'ombre des jeunes filles en fleur*. In a way their collaboration on this project represented the fulfillment of the promise, which Parnok had made to Gurevich eighteen years before, that one day they would "translate something good together." On November 30 Parnok finished her part of the translation and sent it to her old friend and colleague along with a note expressing her "most Proustian respect and love."[58]

One remark of the invalid narrator in Proust's novel obviously struck Parnok by its appropriateness to her personal situation; it filtered into her creative consciousness and emerged six weeks later, transformed into a poem:

> My earthly day is finishing,
> without dismay I greet the evening,
> and what is past no longer flings
> back from in front of me a shadow—
> that long shadow, the very same
> which our confused-articulation
> distinguishes from its relations
> and says that "future" is its name. (#198)[59]

With such pessimistic and resigned thoughts Parnok began the new year. Her life continued as before: endless translating, frequent illnesses, labors of love for The Knot; and most important, writing poems, and increasingly sepulchral ones. The fourteen lyrics she wrote from January through May 1927 provide the only clues to her life in that period.

On January 16, she described a nightmare, in which she envisioned the world as a "den of mournful debauch" that overwhelmed her with the smell of "perfume, sweat, and anguish." An orchestra "lacerated itself," and "rhythm ruled the universe" in the style so beloved by her brother and by her, in the years of her restless "searchings" (#181).

Parnok now perceived her poetic situation as one of "ultimate loneliness," from the space of which her voice issued "not as a prophecy," but with the only "precept" appropriate to her vocation: "Do not kow-tow to your times, / but be the brow of your times, / be a human being" (#192).⁶⁰ Despite her resignation to death and the impossibility of further mutiny, in mid-February she voiced her fear that domesticity would immure her alive "inside four walls." She warned herself of the dangers of such a traditionally female captivity:

> There's no chamber for which a poet
> would exchange her homelessness—
> that's why the cuckoo cuckoos
> that she hasn't got a nest (#208)

Death continued to hover in the shadows of the poet's room well into the spring but without bringing the desired end, as she wrote self-ironically in an April poem which she dedicated to Yulia Veisberg:

> Softly do I weep and sing
> for the life I'm burying.
> Dim light cuts the semi-gloom
> from the window in my room,
> from the corner dark escapes
> taking an old werewolf's shape.
> Tediously her slippers shuffle
> and again, her toothless mouth
> mumbles its persistent snuffle,
> God knows what it's all about.
> Up against the wall she's spraddled
> and she stands behind my chair
> as a long and hunchbacked shadow,
> and she whispers in my ear,
> and she prattles on with vigor,
> and I hear the old crone snigger:

"Die? Alas, she didn't die,
all she did was pass the time!" (#185)

Parnok's hyperthyroidism made her extremely sensitive to the rush and hurry of urban life. A sufferer of tachycardia, which has been described to me as an "awful mixture of weakness and impotent energy,"[61] Parnok often must have felt that her heart was rushing away with her. Even as her "rapid heartbeat" *(serdtsebienie)* energized her, it left her too exhausted to run. At times it seemed to her, moreover, that fire coursed through her veins, and the only person who could slow its rush was Olga Nikolaevna. Quiet and free from anguish, she seemed to Parnok to be a veritable guardian angel, and the poet expressed her gratitude in a poem she wrote on the back of a new photograph of herself, which would become the dedicatory poem of *Half-voiced:*

> Thank you, my friend,
> for your quiet breathing,
> the tenderness of your sleepy arms
> and whispers of your sleepy lips,
> for your arched eyebrows
> and hollow temples,
> for not possessing the anguish
> of my thick blood,
> for the palm amulet-like
> you lay upon my breast,
> and the fire slows its course
> through my tensed-up veins,
> for my gazing at your face
> with eyes that can see—
> for, my angel, being you,
> and being next to me! (#162)

The general acceleration in Soviet life, which was so alien to Parnok's values, reinforced the poet's sense of separation from the world, yet ironically seemed to leave her no time to die, to escape once and for all. The poet's only female companion in her extreme loneliness and exhaustion was her anguish:

> We sank in a chair at twilight—
> all alone, my anguish and I.
> We'd all have been dead for ages now,
> but there's no time to die.
> And there's no one for complaining to,
> and no one who's to blame,
> that there's no time—
>   to live,
> no time—
>   to rebel,
> and no time—to die,
> that a body's in despair of
> beating the air in vain,
> and the pendulum has wearied
> of swinging night and day. (#186)

That spring Parnok's thoughts kept returning to her poetic fate, which, along with death, increasingly preyed on her mind. Her situation, she wrote in one poem, seemed like a bad dream, as if in half-darkness she had wandered into a "Caucasian mountain inn" and asked the "cat-eyed bartender" for something to eat. But no one heard her voice even when she raised it to a shout, and no one looked at the bench she was seated on as if it were empty. She understood in the dream that she had become "an invisible woman." The dream (and poem) ended with a familiar tableau as the speaker went up to the window and looked out at "the blessed quiet of the dawning day" (#189).

Finally, after what had seemed like a lifetime cooped up inside, in mid-May she recovered sufficiently to emerge from the "half darkness" of her room into the sunlight of a beautiful spring day. She went to sit in the sun in a nearby park, which seemed to represent the whole "sinful paradise" of earthly life for which she had yearned intensely all through the "many years" it seemed she had slept. Next to her on the park bench sat an old woman; a young mother wheeled her baby by in its carriage; a "young komsomol" passed by "with his youthful arrogance"; the sun's catkins played indiscriminately over old and young alike. The poet saw that everyone was happy that it was spring, but she knew that no one "in Moscow, Russia, or the world" was greeting spring that year "with such a song of thanksgiving" as she. In her head, she spoke to "unconquerable life," commanding her "to flourish, have [her] way, and dominate" (#194).

Now Parnok expressed the desire to live a little longer. A poem written on May 25 described a typical moment from her restless nights. A "flourish of lightning" woke her poetic speaker into a half-sleep. As she lay on her side, she sensed her "languid consciousness" glimmer faintly in the utter darkness. A river seemed to be rising, but did not carry her off—it merely "rocked the skiff" she was in. She heard a voice from "melodious paradise" lacerating itself and crying. It was the voice of her soul which she could not respond to because she was still "on the shore." She tried to make her soul understand: precisely because she had already had a glimpse of paradise, she was asking her soul "not to hasten the last moment of bodily life" (#180).

Sales of The Knot's books had unexpectedly been "very good" that spring, and the artel was even showing a profit. Problems had arisen, however, in the completion of the end-of-the-year report. Parnok and Fedorchenko, with whom the poet had become friends over the winter, wanted to make some changes in the operation of the artel. Parnok's dissatisfaction gave some of the other members the mistaken notion that she wanted to quit. She quickly disabused them of that idea. Nevertheless, during the summer she confessed to Fedorchenko that she thought the days of The Knot were numbered. Judging from recent articles in the newspapers, an increasingly hard party line on freedom of expression would "make it impossible to publish poetry."[62]

Parnok, Tsuberbiller, and Erarskaya rented a cottage in Khalepye, Ukraine, for the summer. They arrived there on June 10, and they immediately fell in love with the "beautiful, open, and peaceful" countryside.[63] It seemed incredible to Parnok that not so long ago, Ukraine had been savaged by civil war.[64] That summer proved to be one of the most contented periods in the poet's life. Yet her health continued to be "terrible." "I'm withering by the day," she wrote to Fedorchenko, "coming apart at all the seams, every day brings a new ailment.... I feel like an old woman, forever tired, like mortal sin."[65] Olga and Lyudmila, however, were recovering nicely from the winter. Both of them liked Khalepye very much.

In July, Fedorchenko sent Parnok an essay that she had submitted to the magazine *Ogonyok*. Parnok apparently criticized it rather harshly, to which Fedorchenko replied in a spirit of recantation, blaming herself and her lack of talent. Parnok then responded that she (Parnok) was glad Fedorchenko had taken her "friendly severity" in the right way, but that she should not be so hard on herself, or think she had no talent. "The desire to evoke love for oneself," she wrote, "should not leave a person even in advanced old age: it is a pledge of the eternal youthfulness of one's soul and that's very good, but the desire to please should decline in us in our mature years: it is not a worthy source of motivation."[66]

As soon as August rolled around, Parnok became depressed that her vacation was nearing its end. Anguish about returning to "delirious, nonsensical Moscow" woke her at night, and she compared it to what she imagined people felt who feared death. "I have never experienced a fear of death," she explained to Fedorchenko, "but judging from what people who suffer from that fear have told me, it's a condition that seems to me very similar to what I'm going through now at the thought of Moscow."[67]

Although she was now self-supporting again, she had decided she had to try to find some sort of position that carried a permanent salary in order to supplement and guarantee her income and make her "poor Olyushka's life a little easier." Tsuberbiller was clearly one of those angelic souls who could not refuse to help anyone, and, as a result, she was dangerously overworked. She was supporting two families since her brother was out of work, and her mother was dependent on her too. "I'm going to try to get myself a position at the Academy [of Sciences] or some other place," wrote Parnok, "otherwise, my 'free profession' will lead me to the madhouse."[68] The possibility of sharing Erarskaya's fate always lurked in the poet's consciousness.

Fortunately, the summer had given Olga a good rest, although Parnok thought she was still thin. Lyudmila, on the other hand, had gained weight and become very tanned. Liza had been in Koktebel again, and Sonya was happy that her sister had had a good summer since life was "really very hard for her in Moscow. On the whole," she concluded, "if I knew that all my intimates were healthy and I were surrounded by a normal life rather than this eternal, feverish haste, I would be completely happy."[69]

The women arrived home in Moscow at the beginning of September, and Parnok could not adjust to being back in the city. She was constantly ill and had made up her mind to begin serious treatment for her condition, although what she meant by that is unclear.

That month she worked on several poems concurrently. After a week's effort, she finished another "Excerpt" (#182), this one a nightmare vision of world devastation, which might have been influenced by the horrors described in the books that she was translating at the time, among them the works of Henri Barbusse. A lyric she began the day before finishing "Excerpt" described another very bad night when she again thought death was near. She metaphorized the experience in a traditional way: "I was setting out on a journey,/ only not to the warm countries,/ but a little farther, my friend, a little farther" (#195). The friend and former lover to whom the lyric was addressed remains unidentified. Whoever she was, the poet perceived her as the only "beloved shade" in her dream who was not among the group that "gathered at pierside" before she (the dreamer and poetic speaker) departed into death.

During the two weeks when she was writing this poem about the shades of former lovers, Parnok expressed in another lyric her image of herself as an "old woman." Her persistent sense of being "old" in what was, chronologically, merely her middle age, evidently also stemmed from her Grave's disease, in which the body wears itself out prematurely:

> Old beneath an agèd elm tree,
> old beneath an agèd sky, an
> agèd woman in old anguish,
> I have fallen into thought.
> And the moon drills like a diamond,
> sweeps a coverlet of moon snow,
> spreads a carpet out of moon stream
> over all the midnight fields.
> In an icy sheen enveloped,
> there steps out a shimmering specter,
> in impenetrable silence
> it's impenetrably still—
> And its radiant image sparkles,
> and it floats in pearly vestments,
> passing,
>   passing,
>   passing
> by my outstretched hands. (#191)

At the beginning of October, something caused the exhausted, impoverished, death-obsessed Parnok to recall happier times and to express them in "It was a splendid time!" (#197), a poem in the sharpest possible contrast to others written that fall. In her forty-second year the "old woman" recalled her twentieth, the year she had spent in Europe, in love, abducted away from her "father's threshold" and her revolution-torn homeland. At a time when life could not have weighed more heavily on her shoulders, she exulted in a time when "life did not weigh more than poplar fluff," and she immersed herself in memories of "frightful gaiety." Characteristically, on the same day she began a poem in a different key entirely, the Dostoevskian lyric "Of a certain consumptive little mare." In it she listed all the creatures and causes, both universal and specific, symbolic and actual, that she took trouble for at the expense of her own health.

One such "cause," albeit where her self-interest was involved, was the ill-fated *Almast*. Rumors had been reaching Parnok that Spendiarov might be on his way to finishing the opera, and maybe even thinking of producing it. Going through her papers one day, she came across some old letters from the composer and was moved to write to him:

> Fate brought us together at a very difficult and frightful time and gave us a few years of creative work.... Rereading your letters, I remembered our conversations about *Almast* when you were in the very heat of your creative fire, and as before, I continue to believe that *Almast* is an exceptional and very interesting example of collaboration between musician and poet.... Remember how we dreamed of staging the opera. You intended to have me come to the rehearsals in Tiflis, etc., etc. Write me substantively about how the matter stands, for this is your and my common cause and I want to be fully informed not "by rumors," but from "the horse's mouth."[70]

Sometime before the end of the month, Parnok must have heard from her brother in Paris. Valentin had been maintaining a sporadic correspondence with his sisters after he left the Soviet Union again in 1925. He urged Sonya to consider emigrating, something that she not only did not favor, but felt offended at the very idea of doing. She answered her brother in lyrical form:

> I gaze at the piles of yellow leaves ...
> It's all here, a treasure house of gold!
> Riches do not green my eye with envy—
> Rich is she whom evil does not scare.
> I am playing out my final game,
> I don't know what's dream and what's for real,
> and I'm living life in total freedom
> in a twelve-square-yard paradise.
> Where is there a sunset that's so hopeless?
> Where—a more intoxicating one?

> I am happier, my foreign brother,
> happier than you are, prodigal!
> I do not believe beyond that line the
> air is free, the living—paradise:
> Over there is gaiety, but others',
> here we have misfortune, but our own. (#193)

Defensiveness and reproach characterized Parnok's attitude to her brother in all the poems she wrote to him, and showed how much of a double she, as a reformed prodigal daughter, had found in him. In opposing herself to Valentin, she set what was native to her, Russia (self and mother), against what was foreign, Europe (brother and father). This had been a gendered opposition for her since her first lyrical expression of it in the 1914 poem in which she meditated on her preference for the Byzantine style of church architecture over the Western Gothic. The West was masculine and Russia was feminine; the West symbolized man competing with God, while the East was woman merging with God. In what proved to be her last lyrical communication with her brother, she felt close enough to him to want to tell him she was dying, and to try to explain her condition, that she was slipping so often into dream states that she could no longer discern dream from reality. It was, ironically, her often unreal perceptions and dreams that made it possible for her to transcend the cramped physical and political realities in which she was forced to live, and to attain the liberation that her soul most yearned for.

By early winter she was hurrying herself for a change, trying to complete the poems she wanted for her last book. She was working under the pressure of the end, not only the end of her life, which she had faced so many times that in her own ironic observation she had become a failure at death. She was also working under the end of publishing poetry and the end of The Knot. The pressure of these forthcoming multiple ends could only have been enhanced by her perception of herself as a latecomer to Russian poetry's main stage.

The last poem included in *Half-voiced* was probably written on

November 21—typically, Parnok again was unsure of the date. It was also the last poem that Parnok published. Appropriately, this lyrical end of sorts represented a long-overdue farewell to Adelaida Gertsyk. It expressed the poet's now strong faith in an afterlife and ended with her belief that death signified a final journey to paradise:

> And softly the edge of the vessel is listing,
> as you, like a sleepwalker, pass to the stern,
> and paradise opening out in its glory
> with vacuous eyes do you slowly discern . . .
> Play, Adèle! Play, play . . . (#199)

The collection *Half-voiced* (1928) thus begins with a dedication to Olga Tsuberbiller, whose spirit of calm pervades the book, and ends with a vision of Adelaida Gertsyk eternally at play in paradise. Parnok addressed both Olga and Adelaida as sleepwalkers: in the first poem of her "dream" book (initially she had titled it *Dreams*), she imagined her Olyushka sleepwalking "toward the quiet light" of an "unreal spring" (#162); in the concluding poem (#199) she visualized her Adèle sleepwalking to the stern of her "cradle boat" on its way to the other reality. If Olga Tsuberbiller was the "angel" sent to guard Parnok in her "declining years," as Parnok believed she was, then Adelaida Gertsyk was the "precursoress" friend who had once kept watch over the red-haired, love-troubled poet in her fertile middle years, and then had preceded her charge into the next life.

The thirty-eight poems in *Half-voiced* are divided between the eighteen written in 1926 (mainly contained in the first half of the collection) and the twenty written in 1927. The poems in the book illustrate what Parnok meant by *sotto voce*, an auditory metaphor of a certain way of living, writing, experiencing, and perceiving reality that characterized the lesbian poet's life in these two years. Her *sotto voce* had both major and minor keys, depending on the contents of the song it "whispered." Its major keys and brighter moods predominated in the 1926 poems with their focus on her total oneness and mystical communion with her soul and her "little deer." With one exception, the ten poems addressed and/or dedicated to Tsuberbiller were written in 1926, from the end of January through the end of October, that is, roughly in the period when Tsuberbiller emerged as Parnok's "savior" and became her main emotional (and at times, financial) support.

The second half of the book, however, revealed the minor keys and dark moods (themes) of half-voicedness that expressed the poet's creative aloneness, her isolation from a world that could not hear her (##184, 186, 188–89, 191–92), her nightmares of depravity (#181), universal carnage (#182), whipped and overburdened mares (#183), murderous haste (##184, 186), and her sense of approaching death (##180, 184–86, 195–96, 198–99).

Few rays of light penetrate the gloom in the last half of Parnok's last published book, which begins in a mood of such spiritual wholeness, vigor, and even rapture. Nevertheless, the unexpected modulations into quite distant major keys, if only for moments, make a powerful impression, no doubt because they are so rare. They express the poet's sources of spiritual strength, her "beacons" in the chaotic darkness and night that always threatened to engulf her before death finally asserted possession. Light came from the knowledge that she had realized her soul (#187), had attained freedom in her twelve-square-yard paradise (#193), could affirm life (#194), participate in universal rejoicing (#196), remember the splendid times of her carefree young womanhood (#197), and look forward to the endless play that her female companion poet who had gone before her had, she firmly believed, already found (#199).

6.

"Into the Darkness... the Secret Drawer!"

The New Economic Policy was terminated in 1928, and radical changes in Soviet economic, political, and cultural life followed. By the beginning of the thirties, Stalin had prevailed over his main political opponents and had ascended to absolute power. Stalin's program of "building socialism in one country" led to the forced collectivization of agriculture and the forced industrialization, through five-year plans, of the Soviet Union's still only minimally recovered and backward economy.

From 1927 government and party control of the arts and literature became similarly centralized and dictatorial. All remaining cooperative publishing enterprises were curtailed. A representative of the censor was assigned to the editorial board of all publications. Vicious campaigns of vilification against "nonconformist" writers filled the pages of Communist-controlled literary newspapers and journals. By 1930 only a few large publishing ventures still operated outside of the State publishing house, Gosizdat. They were not independent, however, but controlled by organizations like the Writers' Union, which had become an active espouser and enforcer of the party line on literature.

Russian poetry had entered a new, pre-Gutenburg era, and, like most other lyric poets, Parnok lived with the knowledge, from 1928 until she died, that her poetry could not be published. During this time she wrote either for her "secret drawer," or not at all, and the audience for her poems narrowed to a small circle of trusted friends and intimates.

By the end of 1927 that circle included Vera Zvyagintseva, a former actress and poet with a vast circle of friends and acquaintances in the Moscow intelligentsia and close ties with many artists and writers who had emigrated, including Tsvetaeva. Zvyagintseva had been very close to Tsvetaeva during the latter's last years in Russia, and it is possible that in the twenties she kept Tsvetaeva informed of Parnok's situation. Parnok took Zvyagintseva into her poetic, and later, intimate confidence. She regarded Vera, rightly or wrongly, as a kind of spiritual daughter and friend of her verse.[1] She appreciated Zvyagintseva's positive response to the poems in *Half-voiced,* and in *Music* before it, and came to share with Vera the "sad experiences" with which her life as a poet was increasingly "enriched."[2]

Zvyagintseva was a major source of emotional support to Parnok in her last, stormy love affair. When Vera became ill with acute colitis and dysentery in the summer of 1933, Sonya, who was herself dangerously ill at that time, wrote to her (Sonya's) lover: "I feel very sad not to be taking care of [Vera] when she's so unwell! She was so good and sympathetic to me when I was sick. . . . She always has such awful and prolonged illnesses that I get very frightened for her when she gets sick. If she passed away, it would be a big blow to me—I would lose a poet who is close to me and a devoted friend to whom I have confided my amorous woes. She is our friend, mine and yours. Think of her with love and hope that she lives!"[3]

At the end of 1927, Parnok and Tsuberbiller finally managed to get away for a rest cure at a sanatorium (in the village of Uzkoye). Back in Moscow in January, the poet returned to work on a poem she had begun the previous December. Originally entitled

"Voices," it was a dramatic dialogue that contained the poet's mature poetic self-profile—her own description of what defined a voice like hers, and the reasons why it aroused such anxiety and defensive rejection in her contemporaries. The original version of the poem, which Parnok eventually called "Prologue" (#215), had an epigraph from Dostoevsky, and the world of the poem constitutes, as in Dostoevsky's novels, a world in which characters are identified by their voices.

From the earliest period of her creative life Parnok had valued her artistic independence and nonindebtedness to others. However nonabundant her poems might be, they were her own and owed nothing to anyone. She always took special pride in her muse's idiosyncrasy. As she wrote in a 1926 poem (#203), she and her muse would not "lie for the sake of a rhyme" and did not habitually exaggerate their know-how. They were proud to go their "own, narrow" way and not be the traveling companions of dishonest, self-enhancing, "venerable masters" like the unnamed addressee of that poem.[4]

Parnok always had a healthy suspicion of male poetic and cultural authorities, especially after she learned through her own experience how easy it was for a woman poet to put herself under the tutelage of male "masters." In her youth, she had cooperated in her own oppression by Volkenshtein's intellectual "superiority." But she also had had the courage to wrest off his authority and to forge her own path even when she realized her path led to "peoplelessness"—"And we're all fated to go our separate ways," she wrote in a 1926 poem, "some—to people, others—into peoplelessness, but we'll all be on the same road when we die" (#188). Isolation was the price Parnok paid for her muse's "touchiness."

In "Prologue" the poet cried out the pain caused by her realization that her poetic fate had come about in part because of her refusal to travel the same road as the conformist "we" who did not hear, and did not want to hear her voice. Although she now defined her voice in positive terms and acknowledged its power to bewitch, she made the voices of the "we" turn her poetic powers against her, as if they were, indeed, accusing her of witchcraft:

> You're not traveling our road,
> you confuse us with dreams,
> upset us with talk of heights,
> hobble us with quiet.
> What we hide even from ourselves,
> you dare to say out loud.
> You aspire to parity with your mad century,
> but you are the peer of other days:
> other days—other songs.
> This isn't the time, traveler,
> a time like this, to bewitch us with yearning! (#215)

Parnok's personal political use of her lyrics in a bitter struggle against her self-perceived "judges" had begun in her adolescence as she fought to affirm herself and her "soul's right to existence" against the negative criticism of her father and the "patriarchal virtues" he represented in her eyes. When she entered the prerevolutionary poetic arena, her creative struggle moved from the context of her immediate family out into the larger cultural context of the Russian poetic family. For all its tolerance of diversity, that family basically adhered to the same "patriarchal virtues" in determining aesthetic mores that Parnok's father had upheld in trying to enforce her proper conduct. Then, after the 1917 Revolution, the Communist party became the new espouser and enforcer of the old patriarchal virtues in art and poetry.

"Prologue" and other poems Parnok wrote about her poetic fate make it clear, however, that she felt the isolation enforced on her was qualitatively different from that which befell other poets. She suffered the negative sanctions of Soviet aesthetic "virtues" not because of any external, anti-Soviet tendency in her poems, but because of their subversive personal and political thrust. More tellingly, she felt doubly rejected, not only by the official literary establishment, but, far more painfully, by her poet brethren, who she felt ought to have been sympathetic to her voice. In "Prologue" the poetic speaker appeals for a listener not only to chance passersby, but to a fellow poet and peer. He too refuses to stop and hear her out: "What the hell do I care about your soul?" he hisses and rushes on.

The accusations against the poet in "Prologue" come from voices of the putative "new times" from which she, now an old crone, is alienated, but they are ironically the same voices that she heard in the "other [olden] days," of which, her accusers now tell her, she is "the peer." Her lyrical sins as enunciated by the voices in "Prologue" continue to be nonconformity, enticement to revolt, hubris, and the breaking of a taboo. She insists on traveling her own road to the music of a different drummer. She uses her lyrical powers to lure conformists out of their soul-deadening complacency, and her enticements discomfort—"confuse," "upset," "hobble," and "bewitch"—them.

The voices of the crowd in "Prologue" tell Parnok that she is arrogant and uppity: she refuses to recognize the right of the times to use her songs for the good of its own, antilyrical cause, or to acknowledge that the sound of her "mad century" is greater than her own personal sound, or to concede that her songs about "dreams," "heights," and "quiet" (however disquieting) are irrelevant to contemporary life.

Parnok had once wished for the courage "to dare to shout" what she felt like shouting. She found the courage and with it the full realization that what she dared to shout, or even say out loud, was considered by everyone's "patriarchal virtues" to be unspeakable, "even to oneself." It is hard to imagine what could be thought unspeakable in Parnok's poems if not her poetic speaker's persistent, self-affirming declaration that she is a woman who loves women, she is not ashamed that her private world is as important as the outside world of warriors, and that her soul has a right to existence.

By the beginning of February 1928, the poet's continued physical existence was again threatened by serious illness. As soon as she was well enough to leave her bed, she went to the "hard labor" of speed-translating, eight hours a day or more, for a month. From the financial point of view, her hard labor was "very good," she wrote to Zvyagintseva, and so she accepted it fatalistically as "necessary in the larger plan of [her] fate," adding that "to take life easily, albeit with the equability of a ghost, is evidently unlawful. Nevertheless, dear Vera Klavdyevna," she concluded, "I think that you and I are righteous people, and the fact that it is hard for us is also right."[5]

Her February illness led her to thoughts about "streptococci of evil" that seemed to be ravaging the world, impervious as yet to any cure. Those thoughts, characteristically rooted in the experience of her body, found lyrical expression in the poem "Through the Window" (#216), which she finished by mid-March. It was the last poem she was to write that year. Shortly after she sent it in a letter to Zvyagintseva, she and Olga Nikolaevna exchanged their room in Neopalimovsky Lane for a new one in a communal apartment on Nikitsky Boulevard. Since their new room, in Gornung's description, was "long, narrow, and dark," they appeared to have gotten the worse end of the exchange.

They spent the summer in Novgorod-Seversk. Olga Nikolaevna was totally rundown and "ill all the time." This made Parnok continuously anxious and disenabled her to the point where she could not write. "My soul feels oppressed and dark," she wrote to Zvyagintseva, "Nothing is dear to me, and I also perceive this endless string of illnesses as a sign that I am not loved, and I feel more and more offended."[6]

As the year wore on, her condition worsened. She wrote to Gertsyk that she was in a bad way, life was hard, she was sick— her blood pressure was very high—she had no money and was unemployed. She could not get used to her feebleness; she felt not only useless, but incapable of "indulging anyone, even a little." She had lost all hope of publishing her book and was not in the mood for poetry. "Love is the only thing that binds me to life," she concluded: "the realization that it will be worse for my loved ones without me."[7]

Parnok's physical condition always seemed to deteriorate when something spiritually important to her was lacking or could not distract her from her chronic ill health and poverty. So it was through most of 1928, and with reason. By the end of the previous year, her major creative flow had all but trickled out. The crackdown on autonomous literary organizations sounded the death knell of The Knot as Parnok had feared it would a year before the fact. Although *Half-voiced* was in fact published before The Knot's demise, it was issued in a minuscule number of two hundred author's copies, almost as if it had not been printed at all. Finally, her dear friend and operatic collaborator, Spendiarov, had died (in May 1928) without having completed *Almast,* leaving Parnok with the feeling that she had been creatively widowed and her "brainchild" orphaned.[8]

At the end of the year she made a gift to Gornung of all the editions The Knot had published, packed together in a special green box with the cooperative's trademark emblazoned on the cover. Perhaps this symbolic gesture of farewell helped her to lay this important chapter in her life to rest, absorb its loss, and move ahead.

Her spirits seemed to pick up at the start of the new year. On January 17 she attended a poetry reading at the Union of Writers. There she joked with Gornung about one of the readers, and, upon spotting Volkenshtein in the audience with his second wife (he had by then long since remarried, had children, and become a successful Soviet dramatist), she nudged her young friend and said, with a note of irony in her slightly hoarse, deep voice, "Did you know I was once married to Volkenshtein? But we rather quickly went our separate ways."[9]

In February, after almost a year's silence, she wrote one of her most bitter lyrics, "As a shade with three dimensions, brother,"

(#217), about the bleakness, impersonality, and callousness of Soviet communal existence. Although the "brother" whom Parnok addressed was not, this time, her biological brother, the poem partially contradicted her thoughts about being able to overcome Soviet reality as she had expressed them in her 1927 poem to the "prodigal" Valentin (#193).

In the earlier lyric she had claimed that she could live "at liberty" in her allotted twelve square yards of living space. Now she complained, ironically, not only of the crampedness of communal apartments, but of the spread of overcrowding to spaces that had once provided an escape:

> Moscow's madhouse now is overcrowded,
> and the cemetery has no space
> for your dust in roomy crypts or coffins—
> now you're buried in a metal saucepan.
> Do you wish to die?—Just step behind the
> screen and disincarnate quietly,
> modestly, without disturbing others,
> please, it's not a time for fuss and bother! (#217)

Parnok captured here the admonishing tone that tyrants invariably use to their victims' complaints in order to teach them the invidious lesson that a good citizen submits to suffering, torture, and death without making a fuss. In conditions where the torturers enforce the propriety of going "without hysterics," *refusing* to "disincarnate quietly" becomes an act of courage and moral rebellion. At the end of the poem Parnok revealed the morally deadening complacency that overcomes people who observe the rules and even feel "grateful" for the privilege of dying inconspicuously:

> And you'll die, while hereabouts, unyielding,
> "once again young life will frisk and play":[10]
> belching, drunk, a mother will remember
> as hoarse primuses hiss night and day . . .
> So! Behind the screen a neighbor lived, he lived and left us,
> wasn't killed—and that we count a blessing! (#217)

At the end of March, friends of Gornung's, whom Parnok had known for years, held a poetry reading at their apartment. Parnok attended and read four of her unpublished poems, one of which might have been the most recently written, "A tall wave carries you," a mystical lyric describing the speaker's dream journeys into the fragile, crystalline world of the "blessed, paradisical days of yore," where the air was transparent and rang "with a glass sound" (#218).

Another poem came in April. Entitled "Song" (#219), it concerned the totally alienated poet who had no audience among either her own or the younger generation, but whose great anguish inspired her to sing her song nonetheless. As in her earlier "Song" about her soul's birth (#178), the poetic speaker identified with her peer, the pine tree, while simultaneously emphasizing how much lonelier the world of men was than the forest of pines:

> Great insults make the soul feverish,
> great anguish makes me sing a song.
> Every pine tree can rustle to her forest,
> well, and I'm to tell my news to whom? (#219)

After Spendiarov's death, his colleague, Maximilian Shteinberg, with whom Parnok had worked on an opera before the Revolution, took upon himself the job of completing the orchestration for *Almast*. By spring the opera was nearly finished, and Parnok initiated the long, tortuous process of getting *Almast* approved for production by the Bolshoi Theater. This project consumed most of her energy over the next year.

At the beginning of May, Olga Nikolaevna's brother died at the age of forty-eight, and the support of his five-year-old twin children fell on her and Parnok. Tsuberbiller was already "working like an ox." She had been offered the chance to go to the Caucasus for a rest, but had turned it down because of her "irrational fear of

Caucasian cures—many of her acquaintances happened to die after returning from them." The university also offered to send her to a spa in Sestroretsk, but she refused because it was "too crowded and expensive." As for Parnok, she had been writing poems, but they were so "gloomy" that she did not feel like having anyone read them. "I am a lugubrious poet!" she concluded her letter to Gertsyk.[11]

Her next "lugubrious" poem was not written until the middle of August when she and Olga Nikolaevna were finishing up their vacation in Abramtsevo on the outskirts of Moscow. Dedicated to Zvyagintseva, it expressed Parnok's maternal interest in the younger poet, whose "inexperienced anguish" she was witnessing from the "distance" of "long-sighted old age" (#221). Zvyagintseva had written in one of her poems about her feelings of alienation from her contemporaries on the one hand, and the young generation on the other. But unlike Parnok, her poetic speaker apparently could not comprehend the reasons for her "fate," asking rhetorically, "So what is this, am I neither of these, nor of those?" In her lyrical reply, Parnok gave Zvyagintseva an indirect, maternally supportive answer: "Isn't that because, child, you're one of yourself?" (#221).

Back in Moscow at the beginning of the fall, Parnok plunged into the final stages of work on *Almast*. The management of the Bolshoi theater directed her to write a Communist prologue and epilogue to the opera in order to justify its non-Communist contents. When she had completed this unpleasant chore, she sent the prologue and epilogue to Shteinberg and was somewhat taken aback at the naivete of his response:

> In regard to the text of the prologue and epilogue, about which you delicately noted that two or three expressions are not entirely to your liking—I must tell you that it is not to my liking in its entirety. I thought you yourself would guess that the whole thing was written at the command of the management and on my execution of that

command depended the fate of the whole opera, whose untimely subject required the most vigorous defense.[12]

Parnok began to feel as if she were trying to please two masters, neither of whom understood her point of view as the author of *Almast*. The management kept insisting that a Communist message be forced on the audience. They went so far as to suggest that the epilogue be inserted not after, but before the fourth and final act. They expressed the fear that people would begin to leave and would not hear it if it were sung at the end, to which Parnok quipped, with typical boldness, "So lock the doors."[13] On the other hand, Shteinberg, she felt, did not sufficiently appreciate her efforts to save the opera:

> Now to a sore point: you're right about the prologue and epilogue—I am "not in the grip of authorial zeal"—so much so that if you can suggest to the management your own variant to replace the lines which aren't to your taste and the management accepts it, I won't object. And it's natural that I wasn't seized by authorial zeal.... I was forced to keep tinkering with lines that I hadn't written of my own free will, and I wasted rather a lot of time and energy on them.[14]

At the beginning of October, Parnok asked Shteinberg to send her a copy of the piano score she needed in order to follow what he discussed with her in his letters. More important, she wanted to show the score to a "certain singer," Maria Maksakova, who might be interested in the title role. Despite repeated requests, Parnok did not receive the score until the middle of November, just before the final assignment of parts was made. To her delight, Maksakova found that the role suited her voice and agreed to do it.

Parnok and Shteinberg had various differences of opinion on the libretto and the performance of the opera. Shteinberg hesitated for a long time over whether to have an intermission between acts three and four. Parnok strongly favored an intermission, arguing that "without it, the third and fourth acts will be unbearably tedious."[15] She invoked Spendiarov's desire to have an intermission, but Shteinberg remained studiously quiet on this sore point, forcing Parnok to write him rather archly: "I deeply regret that being myself insufficiently informed about the matter of the intermission between the third and fourth act, I have not yet been able to inform Varvara Leonidovna [Spendiarov's widow] about it in detail."[16]

Negotiations over *Almast* proceeded simultaneously with Parnok's work on a team-translation job that consumed the bulk of her time from mid-October to mid-December. In the middle of the work she wrote to Shteinberg that she was "extremely exhausted."[17]

From that busy fall as well dated the beginning of her correspondence with the elderly French writer Romain Rolland, and the rather burdensome role she assumed, at his urging, in his relationship with his female companion, Maya Kudashova, whom Parnok had known since the days of Adelaida Gertsyk's female poets' circle. In 1923 Kudashova had read Romain Rolland's most celebrated novel, *Jean-Christophe,* and promptly fell in love with the author. She initiated an epistolary relationship with him but stopped writing after a year, apparently because he had reproached her for some incidents in her private life.[18] Four years later, when Kudashova was working as secretary to the head of the foreign language section at Gosizdat, she happened to read the proofs of the Russian translation of *Jean-Christophe.* Her love was rekindled and she wrote to Rolland again. This time their correspondence became more intimate and led to a first meeting in Europe in August 1929.

Kudashova introduced Parnok's poetry to Rolland by giving him a copy of *Half-voiced,* portions of which she translated into French for him. Rolland was particularly impressed by the "proud melancholy, sad visions, and tormenting heaviness of heart" in Parnok's poems. "You have made yourself an isle of dreams amidst reality," he wrote, "that is the island of a proud soul."[19]

After her return to Russia, Kudashova became ill. She consulted a doctor and sent his report to Rolland, who convinced himself that she was suffering from a serious heart ailment. He promptly wrote to Parnok: "I know how good you are for my dear Maya and what solid advice you give her. I am happy to sense your watchful friendship by her side. She needs it now more than ever. Dear Sophie, I entrust my darling to you. We love her. She loves us. My hands bequeath her to your fraternal hands."[20]

Parnok might have viewed Rolland's excessive concern as a tempest in a teapot. Even Rolland noted at the end of his November letter that when he had last seen Kudashova, she appeared "rather robust" to him. Moreover, Parnok had had firsthand experience of Kudashova's penchant for exaggeration, half-truths, and manipulative behavior.[21]

In December Parnok wrote Rolland that Kudashova's "moral state" saddened her more than her physical ailments. Maya apparently manifested a perpetual nervousness so that she "periodically broke into fits of self-torment." Rolland feared that something he had written in one of his letters had suddenly and unwarrantably caused Kudashova to become "hopeless" about the future of their relationship. It seemed to Parnok, however, that Kudashova was upset because she felt Rolland was "testing" her. Rolland denied this, writing, "It was not a question of a test, but of the exigencies of the deed to which my life was subject like the life of every man who has responsibilities and must shoulder them." Again he asked Parnok to intercede for him:

> Try to return Maya's confidence to her when she comes to you, tormented. Lay your calming hands on her—(your hands that perhaps do not hold peace for yourself; but good people have always given more than they have; and it is in this that the promise of the Gospel is proved: it will be returned to them a hundredfold). May Maya not wait until her male friend is no more, to be happy for the portion, large or small, that our fate has allotted us! And don't show any of this letter to her! Who knows how her eyes would read it, what new reasons for pain she could make for herself from it![22]

In the early part of 1930 Kudashova became a frequent visitor to Parnok's apartment. The poet had agreed to store her friend's voluminous correspondence with Rolland, filed in large envelopes, card-catalog fashion, in a twenty-eight-inch plywood box.[23] Gornung recalled one lively and amusing evening in February he spent at Parnok's, listening to her and Kudashova tell anecdotes from their respective flaming youths.

What with Rolland's demands, a recalcitrant Shteinberg, and the pressures of speed translating, Parnok had the energy for only one rendezvous with her muse in the fall of 1929, but it yielded, notably, one of the most earthly (as opposed to seraphic) love lyrics she had written in years. The poem was addressed to two women: its external addressee was a young typist and reader, Marina Baranovich, whom Parnok was attracted to in part because she reminded the poet of Marina Tsvetaeva, the poem's internal addressee.[24] Parnok's memories of Tsvetaeva may have been stimulated the previous spring when she read Tsvetaeva's book *After Russia,* and those memories were rekindled when Parnok attended a reading of Baranovich's, which seems to have been the immediate stimulus for the poem:

> You are young, long-limbed! With such
> a marvelously molded, wingèd body!
> How awkwardly and with such difficulty
> you drag around your spirit, anguish-stunned!
> Oh, I know that spirit's way of moving
> through whirlwinds of the night and ice-floe gaps,
> and that voice that rises indistinctly,
> God alone knows from what living depths.
> I recall the darkness of bright eyes like those.
> As when you read, all voices would grow quiet,
> whenever she, a madman raving verses,
> with her frenzy would ignite our souls.
> How strange that you remind me so of her!
> The same rosiness, goldenness,
> and pearliness of face, and silkiness,
> the same pulsating warmth.

"INTO THE DARKNESS . . . THE SECRET DRAWER!" 255

> And the coldness of serpentine wiles
> and slipperiness. . . . But I've forgiven her,
> and I love you, and through you, Marina,
> the vision of the woman who shares your name. (#220)

Parnok's mediated declaration of forgiveness and love to Tsvetaeva accomplished two important deeds in her emotional and creative life. It laid her relationship with Tsvetaeva to rest and allowed the creative seed Tsvetaeva had once planted in her to bring forth much fruit. In the mid-1920s, after Tsvetaeva had left Russia and Parnok had returned there, one of Parnok's acquaintances had dubbed her the "Sappho" of Tverskaya Yamskaya Street as a way of praising her courage in living her unorthodox personal life at a time of increasing societal and political pressure to conform. Ironically, as Parnok, the "true daughter of Lesbos," realized, her formal Sapphic poems had failed to express her Sapphic creative self. Even the best among them had been mere verbal appropriations rather than real words that spoke directly about her lesbian life.

The inner movement and structure of "You are young, long-limbed!" however, revealed that Parnok had a real Sappho within her. In her expression of desire and love for her two Marina's, she inscribed the feminine gender of the desiring subject and her desired object in a manner strikingly reminiscent of Sappho's procedure in her lyric, "fainetai moi kenos isos theoisin" ("It seems to me that one is equal to the gods").[25]

As Sappho had done, Parnok asserted the feminine gender of the desired object immediately, at the beginning of her poem, in the two feminine adjectives that described the addressee, "young" *(molodàya)* and "long-limbed" *(dlinnonògaya)*. As Sappho also did in "fainetai moi," so Parnok in "You are young" withheld the climactic revelation of the speaker's feminine gender until the end of the poem and inscribed it in a single word (the spiritually most important word in the poem), "forgave," "have forgiven" *(prostila)*. In indicating the poetic speaker's female gender with a past-tense verb form, moreover, Parnok employed one of the unique features of Russian, namely, that in the singular, the past tense of the verb is marked for the gender of the speaker.

But Parnok went Sappho one better, for the end of "You are young" contained a double surprise: not only was the poem's desiring subject female, she desired two women, one from her past and one in her present. Such desire from "premonition and recollection" had repeatedly characterized Parnok's poetic speaker from the time of the poem, "At times premonitions, at times recollections" (1910–11; see chapter 2). The writing of "You are young," therefore, revived a fertile inner thought in Parnok's creative work and prepared her earth for a new seed that would germinate over the next two years, during which time she wrote no lyrics at all.

Almast finally went into rehearsal in the spring of 1930, and Parnok quickly fell into despair over the musical part of the production. Toward the end of April, she wrote to Shteinberg that the situation was "catastrophic" and if the conductor were not replaced, the production would fail. The poet was particularly upset at the sudden decision to remove the prologue and epilogue.

Things had not improved by May. The rehearsals were going terribly. The conductor had made all sorts of changes, and the management agreed with Parnok that they were deleterious. She explained to Shteinberg that "the whole horror of the situation" lay in the fact that the opera had to be put on that season. "The premiere," she wrote, "has been postponed to June twenty-fourth, and the theater closes on the twenty-sixth! There's no point in going on about how the whole thing has upset me on both the human and the artistic level. I am *absolutely sick* about it."[26]

Spendiarov's widow eventually had Shteinberg invited to Moscow to "intercede on behalf of the music of *Almast* and put an end to the conductor's 'sabotage' of the opera."[27] Shteinberg oversaw the final rehearsals, but he did not stay for the first performance. Parnok deeply regretted that, for it was both an astounding success that rightfully belonged in part to him and a personal triumph for her, one of the only moments of public recognition that she enjoyed in her life. She wrote Shteinberg effusively after the premiere in an attempt to share her complex emotions:

> I can't forgive myself for not pleading with you to stay for the first performance. The dress rehearsal gave merely a feeble idea of ... the enthusiasm [the opera] evoked in the audience. After the first act they began calling for the composer. Applause interrupted and accompanied [several] arias.... There were endless curtain calls, and I can say with satisfaction that despite the management's tendency to treat me as if I were already a dead author, I was called back to life by the will of the crowd and rather forcefully announced my rights to existence.
>
> Dear Maximilian Osyevich! It was very lonely for me to go out and take a bow without you.... Only you and I are genuinely, by blood, connected with Alexander Afanasyevich [Spendiarov] in this opera. That's why it especially pained me that you weren't by my side yesterday: there was no one for me to share my grief with that he wasn't with me—at least, in actuality, because I sensed his presence the whole time.... I'm not afraid of appearing sentimental and will tell you that I experience that kind of unity of text and music as a *marriage of the minds,* and I must say that the marriage was exceptionally happy, and after Alexander Afanasyevich's death, his real widow was not Varvara Leonidovna, who bore him six children, but I, who created with Alexander Afanasyevich just one brainchild, and a not-fully-developed one at that....
>
> I am endlessly happy that you and I met each other for real! I don't know how you feel about me, but I remember you with affection. You won the great affection of Olga Nikolaevna—I have not known a better person than she in my life—and she sends you a friendly hello. And I, darling, embrace you with all my heart.[28]

Despite the triumph of the first performance, friction continued over the prologue and epilogue. Ironically, Parnok had come to believe they were necessary to the opera, "not only as a Soviet passport, but artistically as well." Without them it seemed to her that the opera began and ended "unimpressively."[29]

The performance on June 26 was also a success, but less so

in Parnok's opinion than opening night. Despite the enthusiastic response of both audiences, one newspaper had already come out with a review that focused on the political incorrectness of *Almast.* Apparently, all the top Communist party officials, including perhaps even Stalin himself, had attended the performance on the twenty-sixth. "We don't yet know their enlightened opinion," Parnok wrote Shteinberg in her letter three days later.[30]

A director from Tiflis had visited Parnok and told her that he wanted to mount a production of *Almast* in Georgia, but only on the condition that Almast be transformed into a proletarian woman who detested both her husband and her lover and betrayed them both. "I often have reason to regret," Parnok wrote of her response, "that we still have not completely freed ourselves from certain petty bourgeois prejudices and do not consider it acceptable for women, upon hearing such a vile proposal, to send the people who make them straight to where any man would send them."

Joke as she did with Shteinberg, she had been hurt by his response to her letter about the triumph of *Almast:*

> Dear Maximilian Osyevich, your letter upset and angered me. You are wrong not to take my words seriously: I really was lonely (lonely, and not "bored" as you write) on the evening when *Almast* was recognized, and I really do consider that a large part of the success it had belongs by right to you.... Your dry letter in reply to mine, which was so loving, made me so angry that Olga Nikolaevna had to stand your picture in front of me so that I could recall what a dear man you are in actuality.[31]

Shortly after the final performance of *Almast,* Parnok and Tsuberbiller went on a river cruise of the Volga. They traveled to the city of Perm and back, and spent the rest of the summer in the country before returning to Moscow at the end of August. A letter from Shteinberg was waiting for the poet with the news that the Spendiarovs had initiated plans to have *Almast* produced in Ukrainian by the Odessa Opera. Parnok was not enthusiastic. "In general, my ties with that family give me endless grief," she replied.[32]

Although she continued to socialize with Marina Spendiarova, she had neither "the desire nor the energy" for dealing with Varvara Leonidovna.[33]

Almast opened the Bolshoi's fall season and enjoyed very good ticket sales for its six September performances. To Parnok's regret, it was being staged without a prologue and epilogue. In her opinion it also needed "the smallest of overtures," but the Spendiarovs had to be the ones to request Shteinberg to write it. They had not done so, Parnok believed, because, with the exception of Marina, "financial considerations [were] more important to them than artistic ones."[34]

The summer had unfortunately led to no improvement in the poet's health, and, shortly after her return to the city, she caught the flu, which caused her to be bedridden during the first two weeks of October. She heard from Shteinberg that the Odessa Opera had indeed written an official proposal for the right to produce *Almast* in Ukrainian. He had sent her a copy of the proposal for her comments. After thinking the matter over, she decided to have no part in it:

> It will be better for me . . . not to understand what has been done to my poetry and not to have any idea of it from the people involved in this shady business. Therefore, please, please, dear friend, don't put the people in Odessa in contact with me. They've forgotten about me, and that's for the best. If they remember me, I shall have to remind them in the most forceful way that the author isn't dead yet, that they are in danger of breaking a contract and bringing financial loss to Spendiarov's estate. The latter circumstance would necessitate endless explanations with Varvara Leonidovna, for whom I continue to lack the strength.[35]

The poet was already in the process of separating from her brainchild. She had fought her fight and had her moment of triumph. Even in its Moscow version, the opera was no longer the same *Almast* as the one she had conceived and struggled for. Maksakova had left the role and had been replaced by a singer whose "vulgar and unbridled" interpretation had, in Parnok's opinion, eroded the quality of the whole production. She was resigned to the possibility of the opera's further desecration: "All right, so I'll know that somewhere, someone is making a mockery of what is dear to me. I shan't hinder them,—and it's better that I not know what, precisely, they are doing to it."[36]

At the end of the year she and Tsuberbiller again spent several weeks at the Uzkoye sanatorium. After their return to the city, they moved from their room in the courtyard of number 12A Nikitsky Boulevard into another apartment, located in an old, one-story wing at the same address. Their previous room had been on the main hallway of the communal apartment, close to their neighbors. The new room was larger and had two windows that looked out on Nikitsky Boulevard with a view of the tree-lined pedestrian walk running down its center and separating the two lanes of traffic. The pavement outside Parnok's windows had a streetcar line at that time, and she could see the Nikitsky Gates stop to her right when she looked out the window. Best of all, the new room was completely isolated from the other rooms in the apartment. Parnok bought printed cloth to make curtains for the windows. Gornung gave his friends an electric calculator for keeping their accounts with their neighbors. Even more appreciated was his offer of a portable sink:

> Since the kitchen, the only place in the apartment with running water, was far down the hall from their room, washing was awkward and inconvenient. I told them that I had a portable sink, or rather, a reservoir with a cover and a tap at the bottom. It resembled a samovar and could be placed on a low stool with a basin in front of the tap. Sophia Yakovlevna and Olga Nikolaevna were ecstatic and urged me to bring the sink as soon as possible.[37]

Having a larger room allowed the women to entertain more guests at a single time. Tsuberbiller's friends and co-workers, women mathematicians for the most part, came over regularly, and Gornung recalled one of them in particular, "a very nice woman," he noted, who, after happening to hear him admit to the company that he had never liked math, said, "I can teach anyone to like mathematics."[38]

Gornung gave a detailed description of his friends at this time:

> They dressed very simply, and almost alike, always wearing severe, almost masculine attire consisting of jackets and skirts with hems below the knees. Both of them wore shirts and ties. Their shoes were invariably the same style of brown, low-heeled oxford. They were physically quite different from one another, however. Sophia Yakovlevna's poems suggest that she considered herself a redhead, but at this time her hair was more a chestnut-brown color with slightly bronze highlights. Her hair had probably darkened with the years. She had a pale face that was covered with abundant freckles, especially in spring. She was average height, but shorter than Olga Nikolaevna and a little fuller than she. Olga Nikolaevna had dark brown hair and a pale, thin face.[39]

Neither Parnok nor Tsuberbiller wore their "almost masculine" attire when they lived in the country, where it probably would have caused unwanted attention. In the city their dress may have been a way of identifying themselves to other members of the totally closeted lesbian subculture, which was well-represented in the theatrical, artistic, and university communities.

Parnok, though, took a certain pride in her "masculine" accessories. "Once," Gornung recalled, "Sophia Yakovlevna opened wide the door of her linen cabinet, and we noticed how her neckties hung over a string that she had arranged across the back of the door especially for them. Erarskaya exclaimed: 'How cleverly you have hung your ties.' Laughing, Sophia Yakovlevna replied: 'Don't you know this is the only way a proper man hangs his ties.' "[40]

At the end of the year, Parnok completed a translation of an article by Rolland that he had personally commissioned her to do. It was either lost or fell to some other mishap, and another person's translation was published instead. The poet blamed Kudashova for the mix-up, and the two women had words at Parnok's apartment, after which the poet asked Maya to leave. Erarskaya was of the opinion that Kudashova had indeed treated Parnok very shabbily. In February, Rolland wrote to Parnok, begging her not to blame Maya for what had happened and to make up with her for his sake: "Be friends with Maya! It is a joy and comfort for my spirit to know that you are her friend. You are and will remain so, won't you? Even after I am 'gone'? Is that a promise? Thank you."[41]

Parnok's correspondence with the French writer apparently ceased after her reply to his request; at least, no more of his letters to her are extant. She did see Kudashova again to say good-bye when, three months later, Maya was issued a passport and left Russia to join her future husband in Switzerland.

After Maksakova left the role of Almast, her personal relationship with Parnok continued and began to change. Parnok stepped up her suit of the young singer: genuinely smitten with Maksakova's voice and particularly fond of her interpretation of Carmen, she attended almost every one of Maksakova's performances in Bizet's masterpiece. Maksakova could have had no doubts of her new fan's admiration or her ardor and did not discourage her. At the beginning of March she gave Parnok a photo of herself with the inscription: "To my dear Sophia Yakovlevna—thank you for your sincere friendship! I'd like to express my friendship and respect for you more in actuality than in words, but in life we meet only for a few minutes at a time: I would like to be friends with you for the rest of my life!"[42]

For the summer Parnok and Tsuberbiller rented a cottage in Maloyaroslavets. Since they had an extra room, they invited Gornung for a visit. He arrived at the end of the summer and brought his camera with him.[43] His friends met him at the station and took him for a walk around the town, which was full of fruit trees and houses that seemed to sink in the greenery of their surrounding gardens. The women's cottage was located just outside the town and had a large garden where Gornung took pictures of his friends, both alone and with their landlady. He also photographed the surrounding area, its churches and monasteries.

The three friends all enjoyed walking, and on a hot August day at the end of Gornung's stay, they took a walking tour of the entire Maloyaroslavets area. As they walked, Olga Nikolaevna was silent as usual while Parnok began reminiscing about her youth. She recalled her first impression of birch trees when she arrived in the north from Taganrog, how the "beauty of their white trunks" captivated her. This led to memories of all the poets she had met in Petersburg, her evenings at Ivanov's Tower and at the Gertsyks in Moscow where she had also heard Ivanov read his poems.[44] For Gornung, Parnok provided a living link with the poetic culture of the Silver Age that he could never know firsthand and that was increasingly being censored out of Russian literary history.

Suddenly that fall, Parnok began writing poems again. In the first lyric of this autumn renaissance, she assessed her emotional and creative situation:

> My blood and my rhymes have a shortage.
> We're no longer whinnying or snorting,
> we don't frolic, or slant our eyes—
> we're reconciled to this life!
> With age we've become more docile,
> we dream of the warmth of the stable,
> we've forgotten our wild oats,
> in favor of daily groats . . .
> Trudge on, trudge on, my placid gelding!
> Your step is heavy, your step is measured,
> and the fire in your eyes has gone out,
> my Pegasus who has grown stout! (#222)

In acknowledging her reconciliation to mundane reality, Parnok may have realized that she had disregarded her own lyrical advice of five years before and had exchanged her poet's homelessness for a "warm stable" and "daily groats." Previously, she had asserted that no poet would make such an exchange. At the same time, there is an admirable and subversive if unglamorous honesty in her admission that she had given in to unheroic everyday life. It was, after all, the expected outcome of an unsuccessful Bellerophon to whom Parnok had compared herself nine years previously in her antihero revision of his myth (#97). If in that poem her poetic speaker had doubted the reality of heroes who slay Chimeras and poets who invariably overcome their foes, here, in #222, she wondered if a late middle-aged Bellerophon, living under a victorious Chimera, could escape creative stultification. While her Pegasus of 1922 was still winged, by 1931 he had been gelded, shackled, and put out to pasture.

Psychologically, a poet's muse can be understood as her creative self, or the spirit that energizes her creative self. Parnok's 1931 Pegasus thus bespoke a poet in the midst of an age crisis. Having the past summer celebrated her forty-sixth birthday, she suddenly seemed to have realized that she had traded in the "madnesses" of her youth—poetry and passion—for comfort and peace. Her age crisis could well have been brought on by a change in her feelings for Maria Maksakova, which in turn stimulated her long-dormant, "youthful" creativity and challenged her to ungeld her muse.

In the fall she began work on a libretto for an opera Yulia Veisberg was composing, *Gyulnara*. The basis of the libretto was the one Parnok had begun to write for Shteinberg's *Abductress of the Heart* fifteen years earlier and had never finished. Just as she had created Almast in the image of Lyudmila Erarskaya, so she wrote the role of Gyulnara with Maksakova in mind and dedicated the libretto to her. During the final stages of composition her relationship with Maksakova heated up. Her "placid gelding" suddenly quickened its gait, and her own cooled blood began to simmer. The calming power of Olga Nikolaevna's "amulet palm" weakened. Parnok began to move spiritually and creatively, preparing herself for what she would shortly describe as her final "running leap into death, and languor" (#240).

The eight lyrics she wrote in October-November 1931 after

her long creative hibernation expressed the two main emotional-spiritual aspects of her life at that time: her fate as a poet and her infatuation for Maksakova. The revival of her libido in what she considered her old age (her winter) astonished her, as if she were witnessing a natural wonder:

> Does winter really have thunderstorms
> and sky that's bluer than a blueprint?
> I like the fact that you have eyes that slant,
> and also that your soul comes slanted.
> I like the headlong briskness of your gait,
> the chilly feeling of your shoulders,
> your frivolous and none-too-ready talk,
> your tight-drawn thighs, just like a mermaid's.
> I like how when I'm in your chilly breeze,
> as in a raging fire I just melt,
> I like—oh how can I admit to this?!—
> I like that you don't like me yet. (#223)

Parnok's feelings for Maksakova seemed to be that kind of love that feeds on itself, heedless of reciprocity. But the chief attraction, which characteristically Parnok saved for the last line of her poem, had a Dostoevskian, ironic twist expressed in the image of the lover who enjoys even rejection by the object of her desire. Parnok may have felt that evoking a negative response in Maksakova was a more encouraging sign than arousing no response, or Maksakova's "chilliness" may simply have excited her as the diffidence of powerful, passionate women so often had in her life.

By the end of October she was in a more somber frame of mind, which inspired her to write—as "murderous moods" so often did—a metaphoric expression of her creative life in what she felt sure was its last flourishing:

> My unglorious day is waning,
> finally, the end has come . . .
> Oh my ashtree-ice! My poems,
> light-transparent, frigid ones!
> I do not intend to leave my

> useless goods to anyone.
> I am polishing the crystal
> and the silver just for one.
> And my icon lamp is burning,
> getting rosy from inside . . .
> Well, and all of you who spurn it,
> from my feast just hide your eyes . . .
> It's the arctic here. With reason
> I keep warm as daylight wanes
> with this secret heat, emitted
> from my glassy-surfaced blaze. (#224)

Parnok's idiosyncratic and neologistic metaphor of her poetry as "ashtree-ice" may suggest an allusion to Norse mythology's Yggdrasil, the World Ash Tree, which itself is a symbol of the universal mother and the source of all unborn souls.[45] In the poem, however, the definition of the poetic speaker's poetry concerned her less than the expression of what her life was like in complete isolation from other poets and from readers, an isolation such as one would suffer if one inhabited the Arctic circle. The only warmth in her environment came from her "useless goods," and the superfluous emotions of her waning years. She continued her meditations on her poetic fate:

> And truly, one cannot predict
> who in the world will be one's reader:
> a ball can't know what it will hit
> once it's been shot into the distance.
> Well, then, my life-creating verse,
> whom I breathe, in whom I live,
> fly into the darkness, into the void,
> or simply, into the secret drawer!
> Our path was blocked at midpoint by
> a cruel century. But we're not complaining—
> let it be! And yet, and in the main, it's
> a splendid thing, this century!
> Perhaps it has no use for poems,
> or for names and patronymics,

or for separate lonelinesses—
still, it kneads the dough of centuries! (#225)

This poem expressed Parnok's acceptance of the cruel century that had cut her path off at midpoint with revolution, civil war, and violence. Acceptance meant liberation from bitterness and resentment. Yet on the same day she wrote of her acceptance, she also expressed her awareness of the escape offered by suicide:

They've cut a hole through
the dark blue thickness of ice:
an air vent for big fish and little,
water for water hoistings,
a way out for a weary woman traveler,
if, in the end, life turned out
not to be traveling her road,
if she had nowhere to go! (#226)[46]

Despite thoughts of suicide and no-exit situations, Parnok continued writing. She wrote so passionately, that in "Chase verses of the night away" (#227), written in November, the poetic speaker warned herself away from "night chirring," the cicadean music of verses written in the heat of the moment—or, to carry through the implied metaphor of the poem, lyrics written in an orgasmic state. She might also have been warning herself about mistaking "night love" for real love, or for allowing night love alone to inspire her. She had, quite literally, been writing night verses since her adolescence—those gymnasium lyrics she would pen at two in the morning to feed her sexual hunger. Over her long creative maturation the daytime critic in her had come to realize that night verses and orgasmic states produced "preemies of the spirit," because "night assisted at their birth" and "night—is a bad midwife" (#227). Thus, in the first flush of her "belated" creative surge, she reminded herself not to forego her "momentary excitations," but to let them cool down and allow "day which brings all things to light / to spread its cold over the lines" (#227).

Throughout the early winter she remained in a "momentary

excitation" over Maksakova. When she finished her libretto, she dedicated it to the singer in lyric form, asking her to accept it as a "gift of love." Her hope was, she wrote, that Maksakova's feelings would be "enlivened" by the libretto's "brisk, full-blooded story of vindictive love's intrigues," and she concluded the poem with a direct exhortation: "Take a breath—and bloom, Gyulnara,[47] / oh rouse yourself, my *byul-byul*.[48] Sing!" (#228).

Five days later, she again shifted her lyrical attention from her love affair to the sad fate of poets like her in a totalitarian, warrior state. She addressed the "warriors," in whom she saw the "spitting image of [her] century," and wondered "what in the name of God [they were] made of." Nevertheless, she retained her faith that there would still be young people as there had been in the past who

> will dream by the moonlight,
> get shivers from music,
> from hot waves of darkness,
> hang out with the muses,
> and rave the way we raved. (#229)

A passage from Gornung's journal provides a living picture of Parnok at the end of the year in relatively high spirits, which were as native to her as her melancholy, something not easily apparent from her poems. Gornung had come over on the December evening in question to bring Parnok some pictures he had framed for her. He found her enjoying the company of one of her best friends, Faina Ranevskaya,[49] a well-known actress originally from Taganrog, who had dropped by with her latest companion, "a young, very pretty, tall, and elegantly dressed actress from the Chamber Theater."[50] A gifted raconteur, Ranevskaya was almost as famous for her witty and bawdy stories as she was for her superb character acting, and she was in rare form that evening. Gornung decided to stay, and like the others, he fell under Ranevskaya's spell. Parnok herself adored anecdotes and, if she happened to hear ones she liked, recounted them with relish. She too was in her element that evening, laughing and openly delighting in her guests, especially Ranevskaya's companion, Natalya Efron. The young woman stood by Ranevskaya's chair with a continuous smile on her "uncommonly blooming, rosy, dark-eyed face. She spoke little," Gornung recalled, "and only in response to questions from Sophia Yakovlevna, who could not take her eyes off her."

Clearly, Parnok had revived erotically as well as creatively. As if in anticipation of her final act, all stood poised in readiness for the appearance of the woman she would love to her very death and celebrate as her "Music of Musics."

7.

"Hello, My Love! My Grey-Haired Eve!"

The major and often only source of information about the last eighteen months of Parnok's life is the poems she wrote to her last lover, Nina Yevgenyevna Vedeneyeva. Born in Tiflis, Georgia, in 1882, and educated in part abroad, Vedeneyeva was a physicist at Moscow State University and a colleague of Tsuberbiller's. Her brother was a prominent engineer, one of the builders of the Dnieprostroy hydroelectric dam, which meant that she had family connections at the top of the Soviet intelligentsia, a class of people whose lives were ruled by outward conformity, discretion, and meticulous observance of propriety. When she met Parnok, Vedeneyeva was living with her son, Yevgeny (Zhenya). She was either widowed or divorced and had had no previous lesbian relationships, which explains the virginal aura she possesses in some of the poems Parnok wrote to her.

The Vedeneyeva poems are all of a piece, although they are divided into two cycles. The first and shorter cycle of seven poems, or "stars," is called "Ursa Major," and the remaining twenty-three poems comprise the second cycle, "Useless Goods." Together, the Vedeneyeva cycles represent Parnok's lyrical diary of her love affair from her poetic speaker's initial hello over the telephone in

January 1932 to her final, unfinished good-bye on her deathbed in late August 1933.

During her last love affair Parnok continued to live with Tsuberbiller, and on the outside, at least, their relationship remained what it had been in the past. Even if Parnok had wanted to find a room of her own, which apparently she did not, it would have been nearly impossible for her to do so because of her invalid condition and the difficulties of finding another suitable apartment. This meant that she and Vedeneyeva had almost no privacy. Parnok was frequently too ill to go out; Vedeneyeva worked long hours in her laboratory and had no privacy at home because of her son, who seems not to have made Parnok feel particularly welcome.

Vedeneyeva visited Parnok almost daily, especially toward the end of the poet's life, and the lovers created their own world in the room on Nikitsky Boulevard as if the people continually around them did not exist. Their attraction to each other was evidently so powerful that despite their age and upbringing they often disregarded what were considered the most basic social proprieties:[1] "It was as if two people had met who touched at many points. Hence, their mutual adoration and rapture and the intensity of their interaction. When anyone else was present, the two of them would move off into a corner of the room and speak in hushed voices as if they always had something urgent to say to one another and had seemed to forget that there were other people in the room."[2]

Olga Nikolaevna naturally suffered, no doubt in silence, from Vedeneyeva's intrusion into the haven of calm she had created for Parnok. In remembering the past many years after Parnok's death, Tsuberbiller apparently conveyed her belief, without stating it, that Vedeneyeva had not been good for Parnok. The poet herself admitted as much in her poems: in loving Nina Yevgenyevna, she utterly exhausted herself and possibly hastened her already premature death. But the poems also make it clear that that was the way Parnok wanted it. It is a testimony to Olga Nikolaevna's love that she allowed her friend the freedom to love someone else, and, in some sense, to choose her own death.

In addition to the triangular tensions that her "untimely" passion provoked, Parnok suffered from Vedeneyeva's long resistance to physical intimacy. There was a plus side to this suffering, however. As in her adolescence, Parnok's frustration became a potent source of inspiration, but now, in her poetic maturity, it proved the old adage that the greatest love poetry is often written by poets when they are getting the least love.

Vedeneyeva's changeable responses, now warm, now cool, seem to have reminded Parnok, perhaps unconsciously, of her first lover, Nadezhda Polyakova. The Vedeneyeva poems at any rate leave no doubt that the "sixteen-year-old excitement" (#258) that created them made Parnok feel young again. Her behavior in the affair, as impulsive and "mad" as any she had manifested in her life, and the lyrical image she created of her beloved as her "tormentress," her "muse," and her "madcap demon," also recall her first serious love and lover.

Parnok's poems to Vedeneyeva represent a total symbiosis of life, love, and lyric. The poet's whole life had in some sense served as a preparation for this creative act that structurally resembles a giant Mahler symphony of four movements. The first movement, which might be marked *allegro leggiero e appassionato,* moves from January through June (##232–47). Like many of Mahler's first movements, Parnok's is oversized and impressively off-center, just as the poet's mammoth love is "off-target" (#240). Such asymmetry is emblematic of the untimeliness of the poet's love and the unwieldy burden of her passion.

After June 1932 there is a break in the lyrical flow as at the end of a symphonic movement. The second movement, a kind of *scherzo con brio, molto frenetico,* expresses the poet's harsh and despairing "unslakable thirst" during August and September (##249–53). Parnok's *scherzo* could be seen to contain a *Trio* section (#252), in the form of a lyric written for three voices: I,

You, and Death. It contrasts sharply with the rest of the *scherzo* in mood and tempo while reprising the frame *scherzo's* material.

The third movement of the Vedeneyeva poems, *andante molto lyrico* (##254–58), carries the love affair from October through December on an "enormous wave" (#238) of ecstatic nostalgia. It is punctuated by the poet's laments over paradise lost and by one moment of black despair and suicidal resolve "to outstubborn life."

The Vedeneyeva symphony concludes with a farewell *adagio* composed of three lyrical goodbyes (259–61) stretched over a six-month period, and finally Parnok's last poem to her lover, whispered on her deathbed, which someone later copied into the manuscript of the cycles. Like Mahler's symphonic song cycle *Das Lied von der Erde,* Parnok's lyrical symphony of songs begins with a ring, crescendos to a shout, and ends in deathly stillness through the echo of a whispered farewell. There is a striking similarity between the end of "Useless Goods" and "Der Abschied," the last song in *Das Lied von der Erde.*

Despite widely divergent moods, frequent shifts of key from major to minor, and the most far-reaching modulations, Parnok's song cycles are unified by leitmotifs; her familiar themes of anguish, poetry, the elements (wind, water, earth, fire), heat and cold, illness, madness, remembering, and death. The poems are also interconnected through recurrent images of sustenance (eating, drinking) and sound.

Sustenance denotes material and spiritual intake, while sound implies acoustical and creative output. This interrelationship between taking in and putting out is emblematic of the emotional, creative, and amorous interaction between the poetic speaker and her beloved: the poet partakes of her muse/beloved and produces lyrics expressing her love. She brings this "produce," these "useless goods," back to her lover as gifts in a continuous cycle that begins with her inspiration and ends with her expiration.

References to eating and drinking accompany every stage in the narration of the love affair and climax in a highly charged metaphor of sexuality as cannibalism—with a difference. The poetic speaker visualizes herself as a "somewhat toothless" cannibal whose voracious lips have displaced the usual male cannibal's violating teeth.

The consummation of the lovers' passion takes place in an earthly ("sinful") paradise, recalling a real garden in the town of Kashin. Parnok demythologizes and regenders the story of Adam and Eve, employing it subversively to affirm and glorify a love between two middle-aged women that offered "victuals far tastier" than those shared by patriarchy's original, young, heterosexual lovers.

The story of Adam and Eve is only one of the patriarchal stories that Parnok quietly reimagined, and remembered in her magnum opus. If the poetic speaker of "Ursa Major" and "Useless Goods" was "vedeneyevized" by her lover (as she noted in one poem), then the poet of the Vedeneyeva cycles in effect "vedeneyevized" a number of patriarchal must-reads. A partial list of her "regendered" classics includes Dante's *Inferno;* Petrarch's sonnets; Pushkin's *Ruslan and Lyudmila;* Wagner's "Liebestod" from *Tristan und Isolde;* and Mozart's *Don Giovanni.*

The date of Parnok and Vedeneyeva's first meeting cannot be fixed with certainty. They may have met as early as November 1931 or as late as the beginning of 1932. Parnok's first poem to Vedeneyeva, "No enigma is too subtle" (#232), was written in January 1932 and suggests that when Parnok wrote it, she was already strongly attracted to her "stern physicist," strongly enough to be mystified by what the poetic speaker calls "the strange laws of attraction and repulsion" that seemed to be governing "the phone zone" in her communal apartment. Like a young woman in love for the first time, the poetic speaker of the first poem fears rejection and must screw up her courage to call the woman she desires. At the beginning of the last stanza she exhorts herself, "—Should I call? Oh what the heck, I really have to be more daring," and she sounds, for all the world, like the older-friend persona in the adolescent Parnok's gymnasium poem "Correspondence," who urges his younger friend to be bolder with his girlfriend if he wants to make any headway.

The first stages of Parnok's attraction to Vedeneyeva overlapped with her infatuation for Maksakova, which peaked in late January 1932. On January 29 the poet wrote her last love lyric to Maksakova, in which she made the addressee (Maksakova) the speaker who sings a "Gypsy Song" to her lover (Parnok):

> I know who you're mad for, darling!
> And for whom your sighing pleads:
> and it's me who has enflamed you
> with this burning, chilly breeze.
> Don't lie low, don't be persistent—
> either way, you'll come again,
> gypsy love has put its stinger
> in our hearts and done us in.
> I feel frolicsome this evening,
> like a thunderstorm in May . . .
> Oh, you won't forget these shoulders
> and this slant-eyed gaze! (#230)

Vedeneyeva intruded into this gypsy infatuation and inherited the libidinous and creative yearning it had aroused in the poet. She offered an entirely different attraction, however, and a soul-stirring love, one like all great loves that remains opaque to outsiders, and is particularly hermetic in view of the scanty information available about the woman who aroused it. One has little sense of Vedeneyeva apart from Parnok's lyrical perception of her. The one available photograph of Nina Yevgenyevna comes eerily close, however, to confirming Parnok's verbal physical portrait, especially with regard to her lover's youthfulness, "silver-grey head," and "Dantian profile."

By the beginning of February, Parnok was already in love:

> I, like a blind woman, find my way by touch
> to your voice, your warmth, your smell . . .

> In Pluto's garden I shall not get lost:
> where you went in is East, West where you went out.
> All right then, lead me, lead, lead
> even through all the circles of hell
> to that sandstorm blowing up ahead,
> you're the only Virgil that I need! (#233)

The remarkable thing about this and most of the other Vedeneyeva poems is the way Parnok expressed the most poetic thoughts in the simplest, most down-to-earth, colloquial language. She had finally found her own "real words."

In the first stanza of the poem she compared Vedeneyeva to a sun goddess who had come into her sightless (sense-denied) world and had given her a compass to orient herself in "Pluto's garden," the Garden of the Hesperides and mythological space outside the entrance to Hades (Death). Then the poet recast the myth of the sun goddess's trip to the underworld into a classic Christian literary context—Dante and Virgil's trip through the Inferno. She saw herself as Dante and Vedeneyeva as Virgil, a comparison that underscored the equality of the lovers and the homoerotic nature of their passion: they share vocation, creativity, gender.[3] The difference between them at this point is that Vedeneyeva is a pagan "tourguide" (again, shades of the poet's amorous past) and Parnok is a Christian blindwoman. On the verbal level, Vedeneyeva became her poet's leader (Virgil) by virtue of her very name, as Parnok emphasized in her triple repetition of the imperative form of the verb, "to lead," *vedeè*, which plays on the sound of the first two syllables of *Vedeenèyeva*'s surname.[4]

By mid-February the women had become intimate:

> *I dream of you, I dream of pleasure.*
> —Baratynsky
> Your eyes are wide open, your mouth clamped shut.
> And I feel like shouting at you rudely:
> "You senseless woman you! The other way about—
> Shut, shut your eyes, open your lips to me!"
> That's the way, tormentress . . . At long last! . . .

> Let us not make haste in vain.
> Leave rushing to the callow youth,
> in kisses I'm fond of five-year plans! (#234)

Vedeneyeva had already penetrated into Parnok's dream life and had changed it from a private world of spiritual rapture to one of physical excitement and yearning. It seemed to her poetic speaker that the woman she wanted had tormented her for rather a while before opening her lips, and once inside, kissing her, she enthusiastically endorsed a personal political economics of "five-year plans" for kissing. These personal politics represented an ironic play, obviously, on Stalin's five-year plan, for which Parnok had no enthusiasm whatsoever.

The two poems that Parnok wrote on February 24 showed that her patience with Vedeneyeva's reticence was wearing thin, although she could still be good-humored about the slow pace of their "romance" or "novel"(#236). In Russian the word *roman* means both, and the poem "It began with chapter five" (#236) played on this fact. The poet compared her affair to a long, eighteenth-century sentimental novel, the kind of love story in which the lovers seem always about to make love, but never do, and the heroine's virginity remains intact until her marriage at the end. Their novel, Parnok wrote, seemed to have begun in the fifth chapter. No sooner had they met than they "became tongue-tied," aware that they were fated for each other and in love. Their first kiss followed, but then they encountered some obstacle that forced them to spend the night apart. Having come this far, the poetic speaker did not want to start all over again from the beginning and

> Again find out how they drank tea,
> sat decorously side by side,
> exchanged quite accidentally
> a glance that's sort of crazy-eyed . . .

So, she made her lover a proposition:

> Come on, let's read, the two of us,
> "an excellently long, long romance."[5]

Want to make a start together?
But only, please, right in the middle!(#236)

Since the text (romance) they would read represented the body of their love and the love of their bodies, to begin that text "in the middle" acquired implied, but unmistakable, sexual meaning.

For all its lightheartedness and witty word-play, the textual/sexual metaphor of "It began with chapter five" conveyed the serious and frustrating reality of the lovers' situation: they had no place to be alone together in order to "begin in the middle." Considering Vedeneyeva's wariness about a sexual commitment, the obstacle of no room at the inn (or no inn to be had) may have reinforced and provided a rationalization for her reticence. At the same time, it must have driven both women mad with desire to the point where they probably did exchange "crazy-eyed glances" as they "sat decorously side by side, drinking tea" with everpresent friends.

After their first kiss Vedeneyeva apparently retreated behind her previous, clamped-lip defense. Parnok's desire that something magical intercede to break down that defense expressed itself in "Breeze out of Viavocàla" (#235),[6] in which the poet invoked a breeze from a neologistic fantasy island to waft over her beloved, ruffle her "grey locks," make her "heart start to tremble," and "warm up inside." Viavocàla (in Russian, *viogolòsa*) denoted the speaker's dream of an amorous paradise

> where they kiss without palaver,
> where this is the women's creed:
> when you kiss them, you feel happy,
> when you kiss, you won't come smashing
> against a palisade of teeth. (#235)

During March, the most lyrically productive month in the love affair, Parnok wrote seven poems, which completed the first cycle and made the transition to the second. Sometime during the month Olga Nikolaevna went to visit some acquaintances in the Caucasus, and her absence gave the lovers more opportunities to be alone together.

One of Vedeneyeva's visits in March led Parnok to a new, tragic insight into their relationship. She suddenly realized that she had come too late to this love and the creativity it inspired, just as she had recognized as early as 1926 that she had made a tardy appearance in the theater and on the mainstage of Russian poetry. Her desire, as intense as it had been in her adolescence, seemed mockingly inappropriate to her age and "withering" body. As the poet gazed at her beloved, she understood the whole poignancy and pain of still wanting:

> A head of silver grey. And youthful features.
> And Dante's profile. And a wingèd gaze,
> and sorrow runs its fingers over my heart strings:
> ah but the love I feel is out of place!
> But be a little curious, just listen,
> how aging women suddenly go mad . . .
> Yes, I'd like to be a little stronger, drier,
> like old wine—you know, I'm old myself!
> If time could just evaporate this sweetness!
> I've had enough. I do not want to want! . . .
> Happy are those who in their youth can manage
> to get their fill of sparkle, froth, and song . . .
> I've come too late. The curtain has been lowered,
> the hall empties. Not for intermission—it's the end.
> Just in the gallery there one fool's still raving,
> the more despairingly, the more intense. (#237)[7]

Three days later in a very different mood Parnok affectionately reproached Vedeneyeva for her lukewarmness. Such teasing permitted her to relieve some of the tension caused by her frustration. Calling her beloved "not kind, and not malicious, / but dry like standing wood," the speaker of the poem wondered at the mystery of love, at why such a temperate personality had had such an enormous impact on her creative imagination, "soaking [it] like an enormous wave." At the end of the poem she acknowledged the simplest, most irrational explanation: "I love you, so it can't be helped!" (#238).

This is another of the Vedeneyeva poems that recall one of Parnok's earliest love lyrics, to Nadezhda Polyakova, "Why do I love you? Do you know?" (see chapter 1). Such similarities between the poet's earliest and last lyrics—and they are numerous—confirm Parnok's belief that she had known from the beginning *what* she wanted to express, but had had to search long and hard for *how*.

Parnok's mature poetics had begun to emerge in 1922, attained their peak from 1926 on, and reached their "ultimate music" in the Vedeneyeva cycles. Her late poems provide evidence of precisely what she had done in order to realize her gift. Technically, she moved toward life's "ruthlessly monosyllabic" quality: she adopted a shorter line; introduced more rhythmic variation into it; and reduced the number of adjectives in her poems by at least seventy-five percent. In terms of substance, she revised traditional metaphors of love and existence, rejected the hackneyed imagery of nineteenth-century Romantic poetry while retaining its spirit, and ultimately, eschewed "poetic" language altogether in favor of everyday, prosaic speech.[8]

Parnok's tone of affectionate reproach and self-irony continued into the first poem of "Useless Goods," as the poetic speaker accused her "greedy, deaf-mute" lover (and muse) of taking goods she did not need while not accepting them:

> What use to you is all this produce—
> the thundering play of elements,
> the rapid heartbeat of a poet,
> her verse in all its shagginess? (#239)

The combination of Vedeneyeva's avidity and her rejection of the "goods" she was avid for had made Parnok's hunger for her violent. In the last stanza of this poem, the poetic speaker joked to her beloved that poets were "wild women" and "cannibals." Then, quoting lines from a Pushkin poem, which the fairy-tale hero speaks to his nemesis, a monstrous empty head, Parnok's wild woman issued a warning to her beloved: "So just watch out because I'm riding, / 'I ride, I ride—without a peep, / I'll ride you down and it's for keeps'" (#239). The poem is built on an untranslatable pun that is rooted in the chance visual and auditory resemblance between the etymologically dissimilar Russian roots for "eat" *(yed)* and "ride" *(yezd* and *yed)*. The poetic speaker calls herself a cannibal *(lyudoyed,* literally, *eater of people,* but metalinguistically in context, *rider down of people)* who is riding down her prey (her beloved) in order to eat her. The motion verb in the last line, "I'll ride you down" *(nayèdu)* acquires metalinguistic connotations of "I'll eat you down (to my full satisfaction)."[9]

On the same day when she wrote "You're greedy, deaf-mute woman" to Vedeneyeva, Parnok acknowledged in a poem to herself the seriousness of her hunger and the ultimate goal of her furious ride:

> I live, and even from myself I hide
> that I'm exhausted and that I'm
> tormented by you as I am by music!
> I live off-target, out-of-tunely,
> but in a temper, at top speed,
> willfully, defiantly—
> and so, full blast, I'll take a running
> leap into death, as into languor. (#240)

Thus, she vowed to play this "last game" out to its inevitable end, and to play it as rebelliously as she could. The breathtaking enjambment between the penultimate and last lines, "running/ leap," together with the softness of the final feminine rhyme on languor *(nega),* seems truly to convey the extreme drama of a leap into nonbeing from the height of rapture, as if the other side of death really were postorgasmic languor.

In striving for the romantic apogee of love-death, the poet was subconsciously rejecting the mundane, spiritually ungratifying finale that she had once feared she was fated for because of the "unmiraculous" quality of her life in Russian poetry. She was also aspiring to tragic heroinism, choosing the role, which Tsvetaeva had once predicted for her, of the self-willed Shakespearean heroine who could not be saved, no matter what last-minute exertions were made over her grave. Finally, the poem suggested strongly that Parnok's rush into death was an act of will and a victory over both her previous failures to die and the "spiritual dishabille" that had resulted, as she had often thought, from not dying, merely passing the time.

The remaining three March poems had no specific dates. "Oh my love! My madcap demon!" again expressed, both self-ironically, and with a touch of the grotesque, the speaker's hunger for her beloved:

> Oh my love! My madcap demon!
> You're so bony that while eating,
> a cannibal in search of meat
> would very likely break his teeth.
> But I'm above that sort of crudeness
> (and besides, I'm somewhat toothless),
> I won't tear you all to bits,
> since I'll eat you with my lips! (#241)

In the next poem, a musical tour de force constructed on the sound of the four *ye* vowels in V*e*den*ey*eva's name, Parnok inscribed her beloved's sonority (and her own obsession with it) into Russian poetry. All of the rhymes in the poem are on the vowel *ye*, except one masculine rhyme in the last stanza. The other, predominantly feminine, rhymes are almost all made on syllables that constitute inflected forms of the feminine pronoun *ona* (she), e.g. *eyo, yey, yeyu*. (Unfortunately, none of this music can be conveyed in the sound of an English translation, since English lacks inflections.)

> You outsiders see more plainly—
> what am I to do with her,

she, who makes me feel on fire,
she, who ices my desire,
with my . . . *yeyeyèyeva?*
Yeyeyèye, yeyeyèye—
how that *ye*-quartet can hum!
Each and every *ye* I treasure,
each one dizzies me with pleasure,
not mere life, Elysium!
Music haunts me when I'm sleeping:
"*Yeyeyèye*" moans a line.
Water-maiden! *Loreleya!*
Oh how sweetly I am ailing
from the greenness of your eyes! (#242)

The last March poem conveyed a drastically different mood as the poetic speaker fell from exuberance into regret over her beloved's "blind stubbornness." She implied that this stubbornness was deliberate, and exacerbated by her lover's secret fear that if she gave in, the lovemaking would be too good. Thus, at the end of line 2, Parnok deliberately left the adverb "unbearably" without the adjective it modifies, which emphasizes the indescribableness of the togetherness the addressee keeps resisting:

> It seems to me together we'd have been
> so tender, so intense, so unbearably . . .
> Isn't that why, in blind stubbornness,
> you pass by me unresponsively? (#243)

But the poet knew how to play her recalcitrant lover's game. "Fine, have it your way," she seemed to concede in the second stanza, and then went on to indulge in some emotional blackmail of her own:

> So much the better! Let darkness gape,
> and night more bottomlessly yawn—
> or else, I wouldn't be able to die:
> I would drink life from your palms! (#243)

She proceeded to fantasize rhapsodically about the music they *might* have made,

> What dreams we would have dreamed awake,
> what music would have rocked and lulled us—
> like a tiny boat at its mooringplace ...

Here, she broke off, and switching to nonmetaphoric, clipped speech, resumed a posture of indifference:

> But enough. Pass by. I won't call out. (#243)

It would be hard to find a more perfect coordination of the rhythms of lyrical and actual loveplay than are achieved in this poem.

Parnok's strategy of indifference to getting what she most wanted apparently had the desired effect. According to the poem "Ere St. Ròdyon-Icebreaker's" (#245), on or about April 8, thirteen days before the saint's day when the ice on Russian rivers was supposed to break, the ice on the poet's "river" gave signs of cracking:

> Ere St. Ròdyon-Icebreaker's,
> thirteen days ahead of time,
> tremors shook the river's bosom,
> fissures cleaved the stubborn ice.
> I'd not ventured to the river,
> but I caught a certain signal
> and was absolutely sure,
> she was just about to stir:
> water was already streaming,
> coursing warmly through the ice,
> and beneath the crampèd streams a
> mermaid leaned her shapely thighs:
> nature was awake and restless,
> and her wine went to one's head—
> something's on the verge of coming
> that will simply knock 'em dead! (#245)

After the consummation of her love affair, the poet broke out in ghazals to her "utterly beloved" (#244). Parnok combined an archaic, homoerotically encoded poetic form with contemporary urban *realia* (the streetcar that ran down Nikitsky Boulevard outside her window) and colloquial language in order to convey the actuality and timelessness of her love.[10]

> I see: you're getting off the streetcar—utterly belovèd,
> a breeze, and in my heart it breathes you're—utterly belovèd,
> I can't tear my eyes from you because you're—utterly belovèd!
> And however did you come to be so—utterly belovèd?
> You, she-eagle from Caucasian glaciers, where in heat it's cold.
> You, carrier of a very sweet contagion, who never has a cold.
> You, beclouder of your lover's reason with logic clear and cold.
> All five senses reel from your intoxication—utterly belovèd! (#244)

Vedeneyeva apparently had a summer cottage in Kashin, a town not far from Moscow. She was able to get away for a long weekend there at the end of April and invited Parnok and Tsuberbiller to join her. Upon returning to Moscow, Parnok went to Vedeneyeva's apartment to return sixty roubles that she and Olga Nikolaevna had borrowed. Not finding Nina at home, Parnok left the money and a note. The first paragraph of the note was written in the first person plural and explained that she was returning "what we owe you" and asked for suggestions on how to compensate Vedeneyeva's housekeeper for the time and effort she spent "in our behalf."

In the last paragraph of her thank-you note, Parnok shifted to the first person singular and tried to convey—in the Aesopian language she detested, but which was demanded in order to protect Vedeneyeva—what the visit to Kashin had meant to her. As became evident in some of the later Vedeneyeva lyrics, in which Kashin is remembered as an earthly paradise and garden of Eden, she and Nina evidently had the opportunity and the privacy there to be intimate. It was this precious intimacy that Parnok did not want to give back once she was again in Moscow, and that was why, she wrote, that besides compensation due the housekeeper, she was "also not returning the blue cup—let it stay with me a little while longer: it's the only reality that can convince me that my trip was not a dream, and that I really was in Kashin."[11]

After Kashin, Parnok felt herself to be at her lover's feet, both metaphorically and literally (in a later letter to Vedeneyeva she recalled the time in Kashin when she actually found herself "in that position"):

> Exhausted, weary unto death,
> but all—fire, but all—poetry—
> and she's at your feet, here she is,
> the elements' shaggy fosterling!
> You coddle her the way a dove does,
> you pull and tug at her forelock,
> and it seems to you: you love as
> you have never loved before.
> How long and fixèd is your stare!
> But you should not believe your eyes.
> Remember: no zoologist's aware
> what species beasts like her comprise. (#246)

Clearly, the poet had found a special kind of emotional home in Vedeneyeva. The picture this poem gives of the orphan poet's beloved coddling and grooming her "shaggy fosterling" constitutes the only image in Parnok's poetry of her poetic speaker being maternally nurtured by a lover. Yet "Exhausted, weary unto death" expressed a frightening degree of self-irony in the speaker, which came from her dispassionate perception of her own strangeness to her beloved, who was having her first experience of lesbian love. Parnok understood too well that Vedeneyeva was as amazed at "loving as she had never loved before" as she was astonished at the "unknown species" of the "beast" she loved.

Vedeneyeva evidently called Parnok her "lioness" or "lion cub," perhaps because of the poet's astrological sign, or because of her "mane" of chestnut-auburn hair. The poem "Exhausted, weary unto death" emphasized the difference and fundamental alienation (unclassifiability) that Vedeneyeva perceived in her lioness. The ardent, creative, hopelessly middle-aged, woman-loving poet had no place in human science because she *was* wild and elemental.

From this inescapable fact—that there could be no permanent

place for Parnok in Vedeneyeva's cautious and proper life—evolved the whole tragedy of the poet's last love affair. In May Vedeneyeva's brother came to Moscow, and she took him to meet Parnok. Nina Yevgenyevna wanted to include her lover in her family circle, but only, of course, in the "wild beast's" civilized disguise of "friend."

The question of where Parnok and Tsuberbiller would spend the summer that year was obviously complicated. Parnok wanted to be as close to Vedeneyeva as possible, but she also felt she owed Olga Nikolaevna some time together. She tried to coordinate her and Olga's plans with the plans Nina had to visit her brother in Dniepropetrovsk at the end of the summer. At the beginning of May, Olga went to Sokolova Pustyn on the Oka River, not far from the town of Kashira (and Kashin) in order to look at a cottage she and Parnok were interested in renting. She took Gornung with her on this intelligence-gathering foray. The cottage turned out to be ideally located on the high bank of the river near a huge pine forest.

At the end of the month, Parnok took Gornung partially into her poetic confidence and read him a few of her recent poems. She told him that she had poems on intimate themes that she did not always write down, and recited one of them. It is possible that some of her poems to her last love died with her because of the self-censorship she practiced for her lover's sake.

It began to seem to her that the cause of all her sufferings was her "untimely" sexual desire for the woman she loved. The real problem, of course, was the homophobia of the surrounding society. Parnok's own internalized homophobia had expressed itself earlier in her life in her view of passion as the enemy, and she had dealt with the "problem" then by refusing to call sexual passion alone an expression of real love. She took refuge in compartmentalization: this was sex, and that was love, and she should not blaspheme the latter by giving its sacred name to the former.

Like any great love, Parnok's and Vedeneyeva's could not be

compartmentalized and forced both women to accept all their feelings and take responsibility for them. From the moment they became lovers, Parnok began her struggle to shoulder her "passionate burden" and to accept that her passion, for all the suffering it brought, was as viable a part of her love as her compassion. Initially, however, her desire seemed to her an evil that she wanted to run away from.

The two poems she wrote in June revealed how intensely ambivalent she felt about her love and how she wanted to resolve the ambivalence by fleeing the enemy. The poems testified lyrically to the "continual ebbs, armistices, and flows" that characterized her last love affair.[12] During a flow period in June, Parnok wrote one of her most enraptured lyrics:

> Through all that I do, that I think, or remember,
> through all of the voices inside me and out,
> like a moment of stillness more vast than all noises,
> an overtone, aftertaste, ray in the dark—
> like wind which is moved by the stars' exhalation—
> that's just how it was you burst into my life—
> oh darling, my joy! Oh my inspiration!
> Oh bitterly-bitter misfortune of mine! (#247)

Later that month, the bitterness and pain of the poet's unsatisfiable passion found expression in a metaphor of love as a cancer that was metastasizing rapidly:

> How can I root out this awful tumor,
> so it won't grow into my soul, my thoughts, my blood!
> How rid my heart of, cauterize with weeping
> my illness, a creeping cancer—love!
> Run, run, run with my eyes screwed shut!
> Where? God knows where, but just away
> from this fiery subterranean storm
> that at midnight, night lets off its chain! (#248)

Parnok and Tsuberbiller may have spent part of the summer in Kashira as they had planned. At the beginning of August, however, they were in Kashin for a week or more. There, Parnok wrote another self-ironic poem in which she chided herself for her foolishness in falling impossibly in love at her advanced age:

To My Self
When we're on the far side of forty,
it's late to be playing with Muses,
late to moon over music,
gulp down enflaming intoxicants,
take it easy—that's what we oughta do,
oughta fuss over our grandsons,
put our affairs in order,
when we're on the far side of forty.

When we're on the far side of forty,
it's pointless being precipitate;
scribbling love letters? no point in it,
pointless to roam the house nightly,
cursing out dastardly passion,
pointless believing in fantasies,
living in seventh heaven,
when we're on the far side of forty.

When we're on the far side of forty,
when we're on the far side of forty,
we're just the step-kids of Venus,
whether New Yorkers or Moscovites,
we're sent off to live in the boonies . . .
That's how it is, granny Sophie—
that's what they call philo-Sophy,[13]
when we're on the far side of forty! (#249)

"Roaming the house" one sleepless August night, possibly in a real fever as well as a lyrical one, Parnok wrote how it felt to be in the grip of "dastardly passion." She saw herself as "a house where a corpse is laid out," standing in the middle of a forest fire of "burning jungles" (#251). She had been in many such conflagrations of desire in her life, but now she was no longer afraid to scream out her pain: her soul "shouted out loud" and her jungle beast "howled a howl," her heart was "on fire" with yearning:

> Oh, on this night, the last one on earth,
> I want to press my parched mouth, athirst,
> to you, my grey-haired, my fateful passion,
> before the heat has cooled into ashes. (#251)

With characteristic intensity Parnok wanted to drink all of her lover, just as earlier she had wanted to eat all of her with her lips. The enormity of her desire convinced her that Vedeneyeva, like a virulent virus, had overrun her body:

> Don't ask what's laid the poet low
> and why she acts so dreamy:
> she's simply been, from head to toe,
> vedeneyevized completely! (#250) [14]

On or about August 10 Parnok said good-bye to Kashin "begrudgingly"[15] and went off with Olga Nikolaevna on a river cruise they had planned along the Volga to Perm. Vedeneyeva returned to Moscow in preparation for her trip to the Caucasus. She had evidently asked Parnok to join her at her brother's in Dniepropetrovsk, but the poet had refused. She tried to explain why in a letter to her reproachful "Wilhelmina" (one of her pet names for Nina):[16] "Know always that what is yours and gives you happiness is dear to me. And if at those moments when you are with your family, I neither can, nor want to emerge from the shadows, that certainly doesn't mean I'm selfish and egotistical. In a word, despite all my overboilings, in the depth of my being I am transparent, and I am your intimate friend, Wilhelmina."[17]

Parnok and Tsuberbiller's trip got off to a miserable start. Due to a lack of rain that summer, the Volga had become too shallow for large steamships, and the women were forced to disembark at Rybinsk. From the landing there, Parnok wrote to Vedeneyeva that they were hoping to take a small steamer to Nizhny Novgorod and transfer to a "real one" there. She added, "We managed to find a room in a hotel that doesn't have bedbugs. So far that's the only good thing that has happened. But despite the annoyances, I'm enjoying the broad river and the good air."[18]

The lovers both suffered from their separation. Vedeneyeva apparently wrote every other day, but due to Parnok's moving from place to place and to the inefficiency of the postal service, several of her letters never reached Parnok. After twelve days of anxious waiting, the poet finally got two letters in Perm where she and Olga Nikolaevna arrived on August 21, the same day that Nina Yevgenyevna and her son were supposed to arrive in Dniepropetrovsk.

Because the twenty-first was a Sunday, the post office was closed and Parnok had to wait another day for the first news from her lover since leaving Kashin. On that Sunday, hot, dusty, haze-enveloped Perm must have seemed unbearable. Feeling lonely, lovesick, and abandoned, Parnok was suddenly overwhelmed with sadness and wrote one of her most poignant, prosaic, and melancholy lyrics:

> I'd beg from death a
> year or two,
> but it's too little time to breathe in
> all of you.
> And if I lived to be a hundred,
> my misfortune,
> I couldn't finish looking,
> I couldn't kiss my fill.
> So I look and melt away,
> my love,
> clearly, you're too good-looking
> to look at enough! (#252)

Evidently wishing to shield the optimistic Nina from her dark thoughts, Parnok did not show her this poem.

Nina Yevgenyevna was also suffering feelings of abandonment. When she got back to Moscow from Kashin, she too had no mail. To keep in spiritual touch she would read Parnok's poems, but they did not always make her feel secure. She began to wonder if her continually tormented lover did not really think her "unkind," as the poem "Well, you're not kind, and not malicious" seems to say if one reads it literally, despite its declaration of love. She also felt oppressed by her apparent inability to satisfy her lioness. And she began to wonder if the woman she loved would not find a "new deity" to adore. Judging from what Parnok wrote in her letter of August 22 from Perm, Vedeneyeva must have voiced her insecurities in some of her letters:

> There are things one is not grateful for, but it is precisely gratitude that I feel when I reread your letters again and again. They are so affectionate and so "you"! So you wonder whether I know that you are "not unkind." If I didn't know that, none of what has happened would have happened. On the whole, I think that you and I both understand each other, only we have to be together a little more often. I don't like separation, especially when it precedes meetings that are too short, and then, more and more, even if brief, separations. Do you remember Tyutchev's lines? "—Who can murmur goodbye over / the chasm of two or three days?" Yes, Wilhelmina, I'm somehow superstitiously greedy for you, and you should not be angry at me for that, or feel burdened by it. You would like to see me calmer? Don't want that. I'll have plenty of time to be calm! Now, when I know that you're well, that you're thinking of me, and how you think of me, all is right with the world. Even Perm, the worst city I know, has become totally dear. The trip home will be relaxing and happy for me. I know what awaits me, and every day makes sense now.[19]

Resorting to the coded lyrical language of her own poem, "Slowly, slowly evening" (#171), to which Vedeneyeva had apparently made reference, Parnok reassured her of her devotion: "No horned precursors have fallen across my path, nor shall they, and I won't be genuflecting before anyone. Indeed, I am incapable of doing so because I haven't risen from my knees since the moment in Kashin when I found myself in that position."[20]

Vedeneyeva's insecurities must have touched a raw nerve in

Parnok since she returned to them at the end of her letter. She also felt insecure at times about Vedeneyeva's commitment to her and felt jealous of other people in Vedeneyeva's life, but their mutual vulnerability to such doubts and misunderstandings seemed unavoidable in view of the intensity of their love:

> I don't know how you feel about a poet's word, but you evidently consider it less serious than a person's if you expect all sorts of infidelities from me. Understand, then, my human being's word and my leonine word, and believe it utterly. Or are you already losing interest in having to do with lion cubs?
> I know [very well] . . . what kind of woman you are and I know that you are beautiful, but I'm down sick with a bad case of you and that's why I can't always be pleasant and comprehensible to you, just as you can't always be to me, because you are sometimes the source of great pain to me as I am to you. But everything is good between us and everything will be good because we have the most important thing.
> Give my regards to your Zhenya, and remember what I said to you about him. If it isn't silly, give my regards to your brother too.
> I love you tenderly, kiss you tenderly and can't wait to see you. Your S.[21]

Shallow water had plagued Parnok and Tsuberbiller's trip from the beginning. What they had foreseen as a peaceful journey down the river had turned into an adventure as ships unexpectedly ran aground on sandbars. It turned out to be impossible to return to Moscow via the Oka and Moscow rivers as they had planned. Instead, they disembarked at Nizhny Novgorod, and, lacking time for another risky boat trip, took the train back to Moscow.

They arrived home on August 28, which gave Olga Nikolaevna a little time to relax before classes. Parnok worried that Olya had not had a good enough rest, especially during the first part of the trip. She obviously also felt a little guilty about not having been the best company for her friend. Although she had tried hard not to complain and had kept quiet about her troubles, she knew that she had not been her usual ebullient self.

No sooner had Parnok gotten back to Moscow than she suddenly felt she could not endure waiting to see her Wilhelmina until her return later in September. Acting on wild impulse, she up and went to Dniepropetrovsk. From the station there on August 31 she sent the following telegram announcing her unexpected arrival:

GUILTY!
GREETINGS FROM DNIEPROPETROVSK FROM A CANNIBAL AND BARBARIAN FOR WHOM NO NAME EXISTS EVEN IN DAHL.[22]

Vedeneyeva's response to her wild woman's surprise visit is not known, nor is there any information about their relations during September. At the end of the month, however, a lyrical cry of pain issued from Parnok in the poem, "There's no way back for me!" (#253). Feeling trapped and hopeless, the poetic speaker pictured her love affair as a chessboard that she did not control.[23] Restricted in her movements by a lover who, she felt, was giving only half of herself, unable to advance or retreat, she foresaw no chance for victory and almost certain defeat to an implied and unnamed opponent. This is the only poem in the Vedeneyeva cycles for which the autobiographical stimulus remains opaque. In the unidentified opponent Parnok might have been alluding to a rival for Vedeneyeva's affections,[24] perhaps someone she had met in Dniepropetrovsk, but the opponent could equally well have represented the poet's encroaching death, or the negative animus of her resentment over never getting enough of her beloved, or the whole complex of people and circumstances that had been against her from the beginning and whose claims on Vedeneyeva's time and emotions took up half Nina Yevgenyevna's self. The speaker ended her cry of pain with a plea:

> Oh, my ungenerous darling,
> cut me in two parts like you,
> so I could halve my feelings,
> so I'd be half believing,
> so at half-voice I could scream,
> so I could be—not me. (#253)

"HELLO, MY LOVE! MY GREY-HAIRED EVE!" 295

By October, however, the mysterious rival, whoever s/he was, seems to have retreated. Parnok and Vedeneyeva were in one of their flow phases, a flow phase so reminiscent of the previous April after they had become lovers that Parnok chose ghazals again to celebrate it. In this set, the word ghazals itself was the monorhyme word required by the form (the grammatical case it occurs in varies from line to line). The poem suggested that ghazals had entered the lovers' private language and had acquired an intimate meaning, impossible to express in one word, but resonating from it:

> Straight between your lips I whisper to you—ghazals,
> With my breath I want to pour you full of—ghazals.
> Ah, how consonant with my obsession—ghazals.
> You, be careful, don't you dare stop loving—ghazals.
> In midwinter spring is blossoming—in ghazals,
> From his sleep a dead man is waked up—by ghazals,
> When old hops ferment and raise some hell—it's ghazals,
> And I celebrate you, my gazelle—with ghazals! (#254)

Despite this euphoria, on November 2 Parnok wrote one of her harshest, bitterest lyrics, a poem that, for obvious reasons, she did not include in the copy of "Useless Goods" she gave to her lover. The poem had little to do with Vedeneyeva per se, other than perhaps to express a murderous mood that might have been caused in part by another ebb in their relationship. (Parnok's other November poems suggested that things were good between them at this time, however.)

> With no if's, and's, or but's whatever,
> accept your lot right till the end,
> and have the self-possession never
> to interrupt smug, lying men.
> And for your part, to play at something:
> at war, at love, but do it right,
> as long as you still have desire,
> as long as you still have some bite.
> As long as this same gambling fever,
> mad and mischievous, rules the world,

> and death has not mixed up forever
> all the luckless cards you hold.
> No, damn it! I've had it up to here with
> the game—too much of a good thing.
> I've rubbed the corns hard in my heart
> and trashed my spirit, littering—
> that's what life—a stubborn game—has
> left me to remember her by,
> but I will outstubborn her,
> the demoness! It's time! (#256)

The poet's lyrical relationship with her powerful dominatrix, Life, dated back to 1905 and the earliest period of her creativity. Now, after twenty-seven years, the struggle had become too much for her. As a young woman, she had found the game with Life appealing because she understood the rules and had the spirit to play it well. Now, as an "old woman" of forty-seven, she had simply reached the satiation point and no longer wanted to play. But she knew it would not be easy to get out of the game. She would have to marshal all her will to outstubborn Life just as she had once succeeded in outstubborning the saline soil of Sudak in order to make her life-sustaining kitchen garden grow. With hindsight, the poem "With no if's, and's, or but's whatever" suggests that slightly less than a year before she died, Parnok had decided that she lacked the "self-possession to accept [her] lot until the bitter end," and in effect, wanted to die. No wonder she did not want Vedeneyeva to read this poem.

For her lover in November she wrote something else entirely, an anniversary poem and enraptured celebration of their Kashin Eden. Echoing the first words (in the Russian translation) of Don Giovanni's famous duet with Zerlina, "Give me your hand, Zerlina, let's go to our little house,"[25] she began:

> Give me your hand and let's go to our sinful paradise! . . .
> Defying all State Pension Plans of heaven,
> May returned for us in wintertime,[26]
> and flowers blossomed in the greening meadow,

where in full bloom an apple tree inclined
its fragrant fans above the two of us,
and where the earth smelled sweet like you,
and butterflies made love in flight . . .
We're one year older now, but what's the difference—
old wine has also aged another year,
the fruits of ripe knowledge are far more succulent.
Hello, my love! My grey-haired Eve! (#255)

In mid-November the poet was as much in love as ever and enduring sleepless nights because of her "Silver-Grey Rose":

Night. And it's snowing,
Moscow sleeps . . . But I . . .
Oh but I feel sleepless,
my love!
Oh, the night's so stifling,
my blood wants to sing . . .
Listen, listen, listen!
My love:
in your petals glisten
silver streaks of frost.
You're the one my song's for,
my silver rose.
Oh rose of December,
you shine under snow,
giving me sweet comfort
that can't console. (#257)

After she had fallen in love with Vedeneyeva, Parnok's creative life became so intense and single-minded that it seemed to block out her mundane existence or associations with people outside her immediate family circle. The sense of not having a life apart from her lyrics and her love was enhanced when, with the help of Vedeneyeva and Tsuberbiller, she was able to stop working as a translator.

She continued to have visitors and keep up with literary events and gossip. Gornung came over regularly and became the chief "outside" audience for her poems. On December 22, she read him one of her new works and promised to write a few others into his album. She kept in touch with her sister as before, and confessed her love troubles to Ranevskaya and Zvyagintseva who were her main confidantes during her affair with Nina Yevgenyevna. By late August Valya had returned to the Soviet Union, this time for good, and was living in Novy Afon. Whether or not Parnok corresponded with him is unknown.

Grave's disease had increasingly affected her heart. By early winter Parnok had visibly deteriorated, and classic symptoms of heart malfunction showed in her appearance. The last photograph Gornung took of her reveals a body swollen with edema. Her face wears a poignant half-smile and looks grandmotherly and ailing; one would easily give her ten more than her forty-seven years.

At the end of this exhausting year, the last complete one in her life, the poet was again carried away on a wave of rapturous nostalgia for her young Passion and her beloved Nina:

> It still hasn't got any cares, it's still young at heart,
> it still hasn't cut its first teeth, our Passion—
> not vodka, not spirits, yet no longer water,
> it's mischievous, bubbly, melodious Asti.
> You still don't know how to pale when I come up to you,
> your pupil still doesn't become fully widened,
> I know, though, you think that the magic I do
> exceeds what I did in Kashira or affectionate Kashin.
> Oh where is that tiny, forsaken, and gardenfilled town
> (perhaps on the map they don't bother to site it?)
> where my daydream is running as fast as it can
> in some kind of sixteen-year-old excitement?
> Where's the cottage with jasmine and the welcoming night,
> and curlicue arches of hop-plants above us,
> and thirst which could no longer *be* satisfied,
> and sky, and a sky more impassioned than Petrarch's.
> At the end of my last or my next-to-last spring—
> oh how belated it was, our meeting!—
> together the two of us dreamed crazy dreams,
> I burned up my night in a savage, a beautiful fire! (#258)

Things changed rapidly in the space of a month. From the high of this poem, written on December 26, Parnok plummeted into beastlike misery by the end of January. She wrote out some of her anguish in the first of several heartbreaking lyrical farewells to her lover, whom she addressed as her Grey-Haired Muse and her Music of Musics. These lofty epithets punctuated the almost coarse expression of her physical condition:

> and my heart is like a doorbell,
> and someone gave the bell a tug.
> Vibrate, empty jingle-jangler,
> ring the alarm, jingle-jang . . .
> Time for the scrap heap! And I'm leaving
> this life, alive, without a pang.

The poet's most frightening symptom emerged at the end of the poem, however. She had already experienced the indifference to life and inability to feel strong emotions, positive or negative, that characterize the last stages of exhaustion and mortal illness:

> I can't bend over your pillow now,
> I cannot hear your breathing,
> and sin to say it, neither with love
> nor with hatred can I love! (#259)

Ten days later she rallied and was engaged enough in life again to remember one of her and Nina's most intimate and lovely moments in Kashin. The memory of love shared moved her to write her second, this time impassioned, farewell:

> Remember the narrowish corridor
> through the black currant bushes?
> Since then you've been my daydream's music, a
> marvelous motherland.
> You became both life and death for me—
> so very delicate—
> and you evaporated, enervated,
> my belovèd! . . .
> Forgive that I, a guest uninvited,

> don't bring you happiness,
> I too am falling beneath this burden,
> this burden passionate.
> Oh but this grief is unassuageable!
> There is no name for it . . .
> Forgive me for loving you, beloved,
> farewell, forgive me! (#260)

This was the last poem Parnok wrote for six months. During most of the interim she was confined to bed. Vedeneyeva visited her every day. Gornung recalled coming one day and finding Parnok lying on the sofa with Nina Yevgenyevna sitting on its edge, leaning over to catch Parnok's words as they conversed quietly.[27]

By May Parnok was well enough to have more general visitors. One evening Voloshin's widow (Voloshin had died the previous August) came and read her husband's diaries to the assembled company.

In the middle of June Parnok and Vedeneyeva had another tiff that left the poet in a bitter mood. She expressed it in four lines that she later appended to "Silver-Grey Rose" despite the fact that they were in an utterly different key from the rest of that poem:

> Well then, die, die now,
> my soul, my scourge, my beast.
> With you I went to the very edge,
> with you I roamed in paradise.

By the end of the month the women had made up, and Parnok reported to Ranevskaya that they were in another "armistice phase."[28]

When Gornung phoned Parnok on Sunday evening, June 25, he sensed from her voice that she was in a bad way. She asked him to come visit the next day since she would soon be leaving for the summer and did not know if they would see each other again. Gornung interpreted this as meaning that they might not see each other again ever, and exclaimed in his journal, "It's sad! Can it be that she won't survive the summer?"[29]

He arrived the next evening to find his friends' room filled with baskets of flowers. Three days previously there had been a celebration at Moscow State University honoring Olga Nikolaevna for thirty years of service to the academic and teaching profession. Her students had brought all the flowers to her room after the ceremony. Wishing to control his worst fears, Gornung merely noted the facts of Parnok's condition in his notes when he got home: "Sophia Yakovlevna is weak. She speaks softly. Her temperature is 36° C [about 97° F]. She intends to go away for the summer to the Zvenigorod area."[30]

It was Olga Nikolaevna's idea to take Parnok to Karinskoye for the summer, a country town seventy-five kilometers outside of Moscow. Parnok wanted very much to go. Olga Nikolaevna trusted that the medical facilities in the town were adequate in case of an emergency, and that they had all the medicines Parnok needed with them.[31]

The trip to Karinskoye was arduous. About three miles from the village, the car they had hired became stuck in a stream. The driver threatened to put them out of the car and leave them to walk the remaining distance. Fortunately, a cavalry detachment happened along and ten of the soldiers helped pull the car out of the mud.

Karinskoye was a village of about forty houses. The cottage Parnok and Tsuberbiller rented was situated not far from the Moscow River. Parnok refrained from her usual summer habit of long walks. The day she arrived she was exhausted after walking simply from the car to the house. When she had recuperated from the trip and felt strong enough, she would visit friends, walk to the drugstore or the garden of the nearby collective farm, or, via backyards and vegetable gardens, stroll down to the river. There she would lie in a hammock that had been strung between a willow and a birch tree on the steep shore above the river and admire the view of the valley. When she wasn't out walking she often sat on the terrace.

Immediately upon her arrival, she wrote to Vedeneyeva in Moscow, but either that first letter never reached its destination, as Parnok feared—the women were plagued by bad postal service all summer—or it was later lost or destroyed.[32]

The next day Parnok wrote again, and this time sent her letter with the local druggist who was going to Moscow and promised to mail it in the city the following morning. She assured Nina that she and Olga "arrived with difficulty, but safely." Ever since they had arrived, it had been pouring rain, and there was a thunderstorm in progress as Parnok wrote, which "made [her] heart feel even more agitated." Fortunately, she had been sleeping very well; her days passed "in a kind of crazed stupor." She had no idea what the future held as far as her health was concerned and was "afraid to think." She still hadn't heard from Nina and felt "very empty" without her.

Vedeneyeva would be going on vacation in the Crimea in a few days. The distance separating her from Parnok would then be much greater and make Parnok feel, she wrote, "still lonelier." She promised to write several times so as "not to darken [Nina's] vacation with [her] silence."

The tension of the trip and the three days of oppressive rain had made Parnok feel totally apathetic. "Are you bored without me in Moscow," she asked Vedeneyeva, "or are your days so busy with work that you don't have time to notice that I'm not there? I love you very much, Nina! I comfort myself with all sorts of reasonable thoughts that everything is good between us and will be still better. I'm waiting for your visit [at the end of August]. Our room is splendid, the terrace too, and the view is beautiful."[33]

As in the previous summer, lack of news from Vedeneyeva became oppressive. Parnok sent registered letters to Kichkas on the ninth and eleventh of July and, getting no response, sent a telegram on the thirteenth. The telegram took a week to arrive, and Nina's return telegram from July 22, together with a postcard she had sent the day before, did not reach Parnok until July 27.

My dear! I wrote you yesterday morning and sent the letter registered mail, but in view of the exceptional way the post office functions (in Kichkas two of my registered letters and one telegram fell into some inquisitive stranger's hands) I have no faith that the same fate won't befall my letter of yesterday. I have no desire to write to strangers (let them find their own diversions), but I'm an obstinate person and want my letters to reach the people I address them to (even if at second hand!). Therefore, I intend to send this letter with a return receipt requested if that form of negative sanction still exists for insuring the arrival of mail. In your reply telegram you write that you "have written frequently from Dnieprostroy." I have received only one letter and one postcard from there.[34]

Parnok did have some good news to report. After being very ill in the middle of July, she had "come back to life." She was sleeping better and feeling steadier on her feet—apparently, she had been continually falling down or fainting from weakness and had begun to feel as if she were "floating around the room."

Vedeneyeva must have made some veiled allusion to missing and wanting her lover in her letter. At the end of her reply, Parnok indicated that she felt likewise: "Rrrr! Lions are evidently being rated again on the market. I kiss you tenderly, and hard, and in every way possible. Your Lioness."[35]

On the last day of July, Parnok wrote her last complete poem to Vedeneyeva, beginning it with a quotation from one of her beloved's letters:

"Come what may," you wrote, "we shall be happy . . ."
Yes, my darling, happiness has come to me in life!
Now, however, mortal weariness
overcomes my heart and shuts my eyes.
Now, without rebelling or resisting,
I hear how my heart beats its retreat.
I get weaker, and the leash that tightly
bound the two of us is slackening.
Now the wind blows freely higher, higher,
everything's in bloom and all is still—

Till we meet again, my darling! Can't you hear me?
I'm telling you good-bye, my far-off friend! (#261)

The poem was in a far more minor key than Parnok's letter of three days before. Either her relatively high spirits had dissipated rapidly, or she had deliberately kept the truth of her "mortal weariness" from her "far-off friend"—in the poem the addressee's geographical distance from the speaker symbolized her more profound, and inexpressible, existential distance from her dying lover.

Parnok's last poem resonated with literary overtones. It echoed lines from one of her own poems, a memorial lyric she wrote in 1915, "To Karolina Pavlova" (#17), her grandmother by poetic fate (#159), in which the speaker realized that the dead, however adored, still could not see, hear, or remember their living lovers and friends.

"Come what may" also replicated the rhythm and mood of a well-known lyric by Fyodor Tyutchev, "On the Eve of the Anniversary of August 4, 1864." Tyutchev was Parnok's favorite Russian poet and the only poet who had a genuine influence on her early creative development. His verse had often also helped her to communicate important thoughts to Vedeneyeva and other intimates. Tyutchev's poem was a memorial lyric to his dead wife, written on the anniversary of her death, and by choosing it as one subtext to her last good-bye to Vedeneyeva, Parnok seemed to be foreseeing her lover's future anniversary offering to her. This intention, of leaving her Dante some words of her own to remember her with, was indicated by the fact that Parnok's poem came from and began with Vedeneyeva's words to her. Thus, Parnok's last poem was both her own and her other's farewell.

Finally, and perhaps most obviously to a Russian ear, Parnok's poem recalls the bisexual Sergey Yesenin's December 1925 good-bye poem to his friend and lover, "Goodbye, my friend, goodbye," written before he hung himself in the Hotel Angleterre in Leningrad. Parnok had been shaken by Yesenin's death, and this particular literary resonance with him contributed overtones of homoerotic love, suicide, and the poetic speaker's promise of a preordained "future meeting" in the afterlife with her lover/addressee.

It took about three weeks for the multilayered but simply sad truth of Parnok's "Come what may," to reach Vedeneyeva. On the morning of August 20 she arrived back in Moscow and that very afternoon left for Karinskoye. In her letter of July 28, Parnok had taken pleasure in imagining how her lover would alight from the train at Karinskoye station and be met there by a driver with a horse-drawn wagon: "You should get off the train bare-headed," she wrote, "and the driver will be able to spot you in the crowd by your dear white head. And when you get off the train, ask if there isn't someone from Karinskoye there to meet you."

Whatever Vedeneyeva knew or suspected about her lover's condition, she found Parnok in much worse shape than she had hoped. Throughout most of August the poet had been too weak to write and had dictated all her correspondence to Olga Nikolaevna. Shortly after Vedeneyeva arrived, Parnok began falling from weakness again and was forced to stay in bed. At times she did not have the strength to speak.

On her last day, Friday, August 25, she was fully conscious. Lying in bed in the wooden cottage, surrounded by medicine bottles, unfinished plates of food, crumpled bedclothes, and "the oppressive chaos that serious illness brings in its wake,"[36] she realized that her condition was hopeless.

Suddenly, the scene of her father's agonizing death in Taganrog twenty years before must have risen in her mind and would not leave. How horrified she had been then by his sufferings, yet how uncomprehending, unsympathetic, and indifferent she had made herself appear. But now, she seemed to understand both his sufferings and her own merciless lack of empathy. Like a little girl, she must have wanted more than anything her distant father's forgiveness and his comfort in her own agony.

Olga Nikolaevna noticed that her beloved longtime companion, whom she had saved from an emotional breakdown and whose "dreams and secrets" she had shared, suddenly "began to anguish, and to whisper over and over, 'Papa, papa, what is this?! I really am dying. Papa, papa.' "[37]

Toward night she became ill. It began with her stomach; she could not digest some mushrooms she had eaten earlier in the day. Intestinal spasms and retching put a strain on her heart and caused it to malfunction. She began to toss and turn in mortal anguish as she drifted in and out of consciousness and seemed to be staring into the corner to the right of her bed and brushing someone aside. Olga Nikolaevna and Nina Yevgenyevna were both with her the whole time. At some point in the early morning she apparently came to and caught sight of Nina, rigid in a bedside chair, her eyes frightened and doleful, her dear head shining silver-white. The dying poet found the strength to whisper:

> Upon your grey head
> I can't   eyes
> That's   I kiss
> the last time.[38]

At eleven-thirty in the morning, without regaining consciousness, her heart ruptured, and she died.

As soon as Olga Nikolaevna realized that the end was near, she notified Erarskaya in Moscow. "I arrived," Lyudmila wrote to Gertsyk a month later, "at 5 P.M. to find our Sonya already in her coffin.... Her face was amazing. It immediately appeared younger and was smiling with joy. Then, in a few hours, a crease of sadness set in over her brows."[39]

Epilogue

The Karinskoye druggist, who was married to a local acquaintance of Tsuberbiller's and Parnok's, came to Tsuberbiller's aid as soon as he heard that Parnok had died. He contacted all the people whom Olga Nikolaevna needed, obtained the official documents required to transport the poet's body back to Moscow, and made arrangements with a carpenter to make a coffin, a long, wooden box with only a mordant on the exterior for decoration.

At seven in the morning on August 28 the procession of those friends of Parnok's who had managed to gather in Karinskoye began its seventy-five kilometer trek to Moscow. The poet's body was pulled on a horse-drawn cart by the only horse available for hire in the town, poignantly and ironically enough, an old, feeble, overdriven mare. She walked very slowly, covering only two kilometers an hour at first, so that the walkers set out at a brisker pace along the highway in front of her in order to urge her on. Olga Nikolaevna constantly sprinkled Parnok's body with pharmaceuticals "and therefore Sonya did not decompose at all," Erarskaya later recalled.[1]

The procession reached the outskirts of Moscow at one in the morning of the twenty-ninth and began the hardest part of the journey, traversing the streets of the city to Nikitsky Gates. Epidemics were raging in Moscow, and Olga Nikolaevna feared the police would stop and question them and would not accept the official paper she had attesting that Parnok had died of heart failure.

Since horse-drawn vehicles were not allowed on many of Moscow's main streets, the procession was forced to make several unnecessary and time-consuming detours. At every intersection policemen blew their whistles and ordered them to turn off the thoroughfares and proceed via backstreets. It was almost dawn when they finally arrived at 12A Nikitsky Boulevard.

Gornung learned of Parnok's death from an acquaintance who himself had heard the news at the Union of Writers, where Tsuberbiller had immediately telegrammed. He arrived at the apartment on August 29 at eleven in the morning. As he walked into the vestibule, Gornung was greeted by the sight of Nina Vedeneyeva and a woman he did not know nailing flowers to the coffin lid. He entered the room and went up to the coffin. "I looked at [Sophia Yakovlevna] for a long time. She was little changed. Her face was very pale and as usual, covered with freckles. Only around her lips a dark-bluish hue was apparent. Olga Nikolaevna came up to me and I gave her hand a firm shake."[2]

Someone in the room expressed surprise that no announcement of Parnok's death had appeared in *Izvestiia*. Gornung called a friend of his on the paper who promised to look into the matter, but Irina Sergeyevna Yurgenson—the same Irina Sergeyevna who had been close to Parnok in the early 1920s—decided to go to the *Izvestiia* offices herself and make sure that an announcement of the death would appear in the next day's paper. Gornung went with her. On the way they stopped in at the Union of Writers to check if an announcement of the death had been posted there. It had not. Gornung took a sheet of paper, wrote two announcements about the burial, and hung them on the wall.

When he got back to the apartment, he asked Olga Nikolaevna whether she would like him to photograph Parnok in her coffin. At first she hesitated, but then said that she knew she would regret it if she didn't have it done. Gornung drove to some nearby friends and borrowed a large wooden camera. When he returned, it was already 1:30 P.M. With all eyes on him in the silent, stuffy room, he set about taking the pictures. As soon as he was finished, the funeral bureau phoned to say that a horse-drawn hearse was waiting outside to transport the coffin to the cemetery. The final good-byes began.

The vast majority of mourners were women, Gornung noted. As he was waiting his turn to say good-bye to his friend, he spotted among the mourners Volkenshtein and Gurevich. The last person to say a long farewell, just before the coffin lid was lowered, was Olga Nikolaevna. "Her usual reserve began to break down," Gornung later wrote in his journal, "but she quickly got control of herself."[3]

The coffin lid was screwed on noiselessly and then the men began to carry the coffin out of the house. Olga Nikolaevna joined them as a pallbearer in front, on the right-hand side. When they went down the four front steps, the whole weight of the coffin shifted onto the pallbearers in front, but Olga Nikolaevna bore up under its weight.

In the crowd that had gathered around the hearse, Gornung spotted Pasternak and exchanged greetings with him. Then he returned to the empty room for the camera. Vedeneyeva was there, crying. Erarskaya was with her. Gornung had to return the camera, and from there he proceeded directly to the cemetery, arriving before the hearse and procession of mourners.

From the cemetery gates the coffin was carried by Gornung, another man, several women, and Olga Nikolaevna. Among the people at the grave were a woman who had done typing for Parnok, the poet's sister, and several women poets. When the coffin was silently lowered into the grave and the first clumps of earth struck it, Vedeneyeva started to faint and Gornung had to hold her up. Olga Nikolaevna stood by the grave, her cheek pressed against her palm, and stared into space.

A white wooden cross with a rough inscription was brought and mounted, the edges of the grave were evened off, and the women covered it with flowers. They hung a wreathe of carnations on the cross. Then everyone stood in silence for a long time until a monk came and sang the mass for the dead. "We were near Sonya the whole time with such enormous love and affection," Erarskaya later recalled. "We were all so shaken and upset. How much despair surrounded her, how many tears were shed over her grave."[4]

After the other mourners left, Olga Nikolaevna remained alone at the grave with two of her dearest women friends who had helped her to organize the funeral.

In the days immediately following the burial, Gornung visited Olga Nikolaevna and with her permission made copies for himself of his friend's last poems.

On the ninth day after Parnok's death, Nina Yevgenyevna and another woman both went to the woods outside the city to gather conifer branches and red whortleberry greens, which they laid on the grave together with a wreathe of autumn leaves. A mass was sung.

On September 25 Erarskaya wrote to Eugenia Gertsyk: "We so often gather now around Olga Nikolaevna in that huge room with the light-blue lamp. The writing table is covered with a mass of flowers and all the photographs of Sonya that exist. At first it was awful and hopelessly melancholy to be in their room without Sonya. Now it seems that she is alive, that she is with us."

Each of Parnok's friends and lovers gathered there must have sensed that the "eternity promised by love" was real, and that she was the recipient of the poet's promise, as expressed to an unnamed lover and friend in a September 1926 lyric:

> And when upon the earth descends
> the twilight dove-grey-blue,
> an otherworldly female guest,
> I'll come and roam with you . . . (#177)

Appendix

The following errors in the Russian texts of Parnok's poems in *Sobranie sochinenii* (Ardis, 1979) have been corrected in my translation of those poems as they appear in this book.

#69, stanza 2, line 2: "muzhskikh" should be "muzhskoi."

#71, stanza 2, line 2 should read: "nenavistliv serdtsem. A ia toskuiu:"

#114, stanza 1, line 8 should read: "neumolimyi moi!" and stanza 2, lines 5–8 should read: "Snova temnyi krug / somknulsia nado mnoi. / O, moi strastnyi drug, / neutomimyi moi!"

#162, stanza 2, line 2: "vognutye" should be "vygnutye."

#165, stanza 2, line 2: "oklikaia" should be "oklikaiu."

#204, stanza 2, line 4 should read: "a mne èto—rechi slushat'."

Stanza 5, line 4 should read: "sama ty budesh' kaznima."

#220, stanza 2, line 4 should contain the word "zhivykh" in between "kakikh" and "glubin."

#224, stanza 1, line 4 should read: "stikh moi, led-iasenets!"

#247, line 3 should read: "kak mig tishiny, chto vsekh shumov ogromnei,—."

#252, stanza 1, line 2 should read: "godik-drugoi."

#260, stanza 1, line 3 should read: "S tekh por mechte ty stala muzykoi,"

Notes

INTRODUCTION

1. In her "Introduction" to Parnok's *Collected Poems,* Polyakova calls Parnok "a stranger *[inostranka]* in Russian literature" (91). Parnok's lover, Marina Tsvetaeva, hailed her "girlfriend" as "a fair stranger with the brow of Beethoven" (a comparison that alludes to the scope and revolutionary potential of Parnok's as yet, in 1915, unrealized poetic gift) in the ninth poem of "Girlfriend," the cycle of poems she dedicated to Parnok.
2. It is telling that of Polyakova's two ground-breaking works on Parnok, it is the second, *[Ne]Zakatnye ony dni* (Ardis, 1983), in which she revealed Parnok and Tsvetaeva's love affair and discussed its creative progeny, that has became most Slavists' source of knowledge about Parnok and her poetry.
3. Plans are now finally afoot to publish Polyakova's edition of Parnok's poems in Russia. The volume was scheduled to appear at the end of 1993.
4. A. P. Chekhov, Letter to Suvorin of December 6, 1895, *Polnoe sobranie sochinenii i pisem,* t. 6 of *Pis'ma,* Moscow, 1978, 106–7. I am grateful to Katherine T. O'Connor for pointing out this letter to me.
5. See Heilbrun, *Writing a Woman's Life,* and Burgin, "Sophia Parnok and the Writing of a Lesbian Poet's Life."
6. See Laura Engelstein, *The Keys to Happiness: Sex and the Search for Modernity in Fin de Siècle Russia* (Ithaca: Cornell University Press, 1993).
7. Barbara Walker, *The Woman's Dictionary of Symbols and Sacred Objects* (San Francisco: Harper and Row, 1988), 363–64.

8. Parnok referred to herself as a "beast" who had eluded the knowledge of "zoologists" in the 1932 lyric, "Exhausted, weary unto death," #246 in *Collected Poems*.

CHAPTER 1

1. Bodik et al., *Taganrog*, 61. Unless otherwise noted, English translations of all Russian originals, prose and poetry, are my own.
2. Quoted passages describing Taganrog are from Parnakh, *Vospominaniia*, 12–14.
3. Dates from the prerevolutionary period (through 1917) will be given according to the Julian calendar, which the Russians used at that time. In the nineteenth century the Julian calendar was twelve days behind the Gregorian, and in the twentieth century it was/is thirteen days behind. According to our western (Gregorian) calendar, Parnok was born on August 11, 1885.
4. From Parnok's poem, "July Thirtieth," #85, in *Sobranie stikhotvorenii (Collected Poems)*, 1979. Henceforth, all poems quoted from this edition of Parnok's *Collected Poems (CP)* will be referenced by number in parentheses after the quotation, e.g. (#85).
5. R. D. Charques, *A Short History of Russia* (New York: E. P. Dutton, 1956), 208.
6. Ibid., 208.
7. Bodik, *Taganrog*, 67.
8. Parnakh, *Vospominaniia*, 16.
9. Ibid., 16.
10. Bodik, *Taganrog*, 66, 78.
11. Ibid., 65–66.
12. Quoted by Ernest J. Simmons, *Chekhov: A Biography* (Boston: Little, Brown, 1962), 120.
13. Ibid., 324.
14. Parnakh, *Vospominaniia*, 16.
15. Ibid., 100.
16. It is not beyond the realm of possibility that Valentin Parnakh was sexually abused by his father: his obsession with the stepmother whose vagina is too narrow to accommodate a sexually mature man suggests such a possibility.
17. Letter from Parnok to Gurevich of July 22, 1908.
18. Parnok's school records have been lost, and the exact dates of her matriculation and graduation from the gymnasium are not known.

Most likely, she finished the gymnasium in 1903, but 1904 is also possible.
19. Satina, *Education of Women*, 46.
20. The original table of contents of Parnok's 1900 "Notebook of Poems" is in my possession. The originals of her other forty-nine extant juvenile poems are in the possession of her nephew, who lives in Moscow. I have read them and refer to them in the exact copy made for me by Sophia Polyakova. I have numbered them J-2 to J-50 according to the order of their appearance in the notebook and henceforth quotations of these juvenile poems will be referenced by this J-number, given in parentheses after the quotation. None of Parnok's juvenilia have been published.
21. For an in-depth discussion of the invention of literary lesbianism by the late nineteenth century French decadents, see De Jean, *Fictions of Sappho 1546–1937*.
22. The original manuscript in my possession.
23. For a list of German medical works on lesbianism translated into Russian at this time, see Engelstein, "Lesbian Vignettes."
24. Parnakh, *Vospominaniia*, 14.
25. Ibid., 14.
26. This poem is entitled "Excerpt" *(Otryvok)* and is the first of several poems with this title that Parnok wrote during her creative life.
27. Polyakova's "Introduction" (in Russian) to Parnok's *Collected Poems* contains an exhaustive and perceptive discussion of all the Russian poets who played a role in Parnok's creative development. From the nineteenth century, the Romantic poets Yevgeny Baratynsky and Fyodor Tyutchev were closest to her, thematically and lyrically. I have chosen not to discuss Parnok's creative relationship with her Russian forefathers (and foremother, Karolina Pavlova, for that matter) on the grounds that such a discussion will have little meaning for Anglophone readers of this book (regrettably, none of the poets Parnok loved most are generally known outside of Russia), and those who read Russian can refer to Polyakova's excellent discussion.
28. Parnok's teenage preoccupation with sex strikes us today as merely typical of adolescence. In the context of her own time, class, and culture, it seems to me to reflect a certain degree of sexual precocity that was not so typical. It was one thing for a well-brought-up, sixteen-year-old young lady in the late Victorian era to indulge in private, romantic, and even sexual fantasies; it was quite another for her to write about physical lovemaking so explicitly and concretely,

even in the guise of a young man writing a letter to a male friend and mentor. In many of her later poems, Parnok returned to the theme of her passionate nature, and she occasionally connected it with her Jewish origins and, specifically, her father. She also noted in one poem that her mother's emotional make-up was antithetical to hers and, by inference, to her father's. It is not impossible that the "older friend" in the juvenile poetic dialogue, "Correspondence," represented Parnokh's perception of her father's (probably unverbalized) attitudes about sex and love.

29. The image of the black rose is relatively rare in Russian poetry. Outside of Blok, it occurs, as far as I know, only in Baratynsky.
30. The poem contains traditional sexual images, although its meaning in the context of Parnokh's relationship with Polyakova remains elusive. The dewdrops on the roses are a common metaphor for semen, as in the wedding song of the royal bridegroom in the "Song of Solomon" (5:2): "I sleep, but my heart waketh: it is the voice of my beloved that knocketh, saying, Open to me, my sister, my love, my dove, my undefiled: for my head is filled with dew, and my locks with the drops of night." Parnok knew the Old Testament almost by heart and her poetry contains numerous references to it. The lily was once a floral emblem of the goddess Juno in her virgin aspect and symbolized "the female cup holding the divine essence of life" (Walker, *The Woman's Dictionary*, 428).
31. Volkenshtein, Gurevich, Gnesin, Tsvetaeva, Adelaida and Eugenia Gertsyk, and Tsuberbiller all tried in their own ways to "save" Parnok.
32. Parnakh, *Vospominaniia*, 17.
33. As I intend to suggest here, Parnok's perception of her creative spirit seems to contain points in common with the definition of "Muse" given by the American radical lesbian feminist philosopher, Mary Daly, in *Websters First New Intergalactic Wickedary of the English Language* (Boston: Beacon Press, 1987): "*Muse:* the guiding Genius / Demon of a Musing woman; a woman in Touch with her Creative Spirit, her Self."

CHAPTER 2

1. Gornung, *Memoirs* (dated), entry for February 21, 1931, 23.
2. Polyakova, *CP*, 327. Geltser's inscription on the 1926 photo contin-

ued: "The fact that I don't see you doesn't mean that I don't remember you." Geltser was widely rumored to be bisexual.
3. Polyakova, "Introduction," 9–10.
4. Parnok's maternal grandfather was Abram Idel'son. Her maternal uncle, Adolf Abramovich, lived either in Taganrog or in Rostov-on-Don. Idel'son was a rather widespread Russian-Jewish surname, so it is difficult to track down Parnok's relatives on her mother's side. There were Idel'sons living in the Russian colony in Zurich during the last third of the nineteenth century, but whether they were related to Parnok in any way cannot be determined.
5. I have been unable to determine the exact time and place of Parnokh's first acquaintance either with Volkenshtein or Mikhail Gnesin. It is very possible that Volkenshtein had relatives in Taganrog (there was a Jewish family of that name in the city), and Parnok may have met him in her hometown. The other possibilities are that they met in Rostov-on-Don where the Gnesins lived, or even in St. Petersburg where Parnok had an uncle (perhaps on her father's side). The "Impromptu" Sonya dedicated to Vladimir in May 1903 has a tone of familiarity to it, which suggests she and Volkenshtein were by then already friends. Intellectual society in Russian provincial cities was very close-knit, so it is likely that Parnok's relatives in Rostov-on-Don would have known the Gnesins, and if Volkenshtein had relatives in Taganrog, they would have known the Parnokhs.
6. Volkenshtein, "V dni molodosti," 286.
7. Gnesin, "Stranitsy," 138.
8. Zinovyeva-Annibal's novel *Thirty-three Monsters* (1907) was considered the first lesbian novel in Russian literature. See Burgin, "Laid Out in Lavender."
9. Letter from Parnok to Gurevich of February 2, 1909.
10. Ibid.
11. Letter from Parnok to Volkenshtein of August 14, 1905.
12. Letter from Parnok to Volkenshtein of June 23, 1906, quoted by Polyakova, "Introduction," 8.
13. Unless otherwise noted, my translations of Parnok's unpublished early verse from 1905–6 are from exact copies of the Russian originals made by Polyakova and given to me in a notebook in my possession.
14. Letter from Parnok to Volkenshtein of September 10, 1905.
15. Letter from Parnok to Volkenshtein of October 7, 1905.
16. Letter from Parnok to Volkenshtein of December 1905, quoted by Polyakova, "Introduction," 10.

17. Letter from Parnok to Volkenshtein of January 16, 1906.
18. Letter from Parnok to Volkenshtein of May 9, 1906, quoted by Polyakova, "Introduction," 13.
19. Letter from Parnok to Volkenshtein of May 14, 1906, quoted by Polyakova, "Introduction," 13–14.
20. Included with a letter from Parnok to Gnesin of May 31, 1906.
21. The identity of Parnok's companion—her letter is written in the first person plural—is mysterious. If it is Volkenshtein, then he must just have arrived in Moscow (Parnok had written to him in St. Petersburg two weeks previously) and must have just as rapidly changed his plans to accompany Parnok somewhere for the summer (Volkenshtein was back in Petersburg by the end of June). The other possibility is Polyakova, with whom Parnok appears to have been living in Moscow upon her (Parnok's) return from abroad. Parnok's allusion to the generally bad state of affairs might have personal (rather than political) meaning. In her correspondence with Gnesin she was in the habit of alluding to her personal problems (usually love problems) in only the most general terms and dismissing them as "not worth writing about." Gnesin tended to play the serious big brother with Parnok and always insisted that their correspondence be "useful" to the poet.
22. Details of Polyakova's visit to *Golden Fleece* were reported to Volkenshtein in Parnok's letter to him from Taganrog of June 23, 1906. See Polyakova, "Introduction," 12.
23. Letter from Parnok to Volkenshtein of June 23, 1906, quoted by Polyakova, "Introduction," 8.
24. Quoted by Parnok to Volkenshtein in her letter to him of July 26, 1906.
25. Letter from Parnok to Volkenshtein of June 23, 1906, quoted by Polyakova, 12. The Russian *kh* is pronounced similarly to the German *ch*, as in "Ba*ch*."
26. Clarence Brown, in *The Prose of Osip Mandelshtam* (Princeton: Princeton University Press, 1965), surmises that Parnok changed her name in order to hide her Jewish origins, but Polyakova convincingly rebuts him by arguing that a Jewish name was no hindrance to publishing one's work in prerevolutionary Russia, and that Parnok was open about her Jewish origins in several of her lyrics and in her personal life ("Introduction," 309). In my opinion, allegations that Parnok was ashamed of her Jewish origins are likely to be rooted in the homophobic and anti-Semitic attitudes of her detractors. One striking proof of the all-too-common conflation of anti-Semitism and

homophobia is a comment at the end of a letter from Boris Zaitsev to Ivan Bunin and his wife (September 8, 1933). Responding to the news of Parnok's death, Zaitsev has referred to her as "one of us," only to conclude, "Evidently she had a church funeral although she was a Jew by blood (and by certain psychological 'deviations')" (*Novyi zhurnal*, kn. 149 (1982): 129–30).
27. Heilbrun, *Writing a Woman's Life*, 110.
28. Letter from Parnok to Volkenshtein of July 6, 1906, quoted by Polyakova, "Introduction," 11.
29. Letter from Parnok to Volkenshtein of July 26, 1906, quoted by Polyakova, "Introduction," 11.
30. *Narodnaia vest'*, no. 1, 1906 (noiabr'), str. 72.
31. Letter from Parnok to Gurevich of April 27, 1909.
32. The first seven lines of this poem were published as a separate lyric in *Protalina*, vyp. I, vesna 1907.
33. From an unpublished, undated poem, "I do not love love."
34. Parnok's second published poem, which appeared in the almanac *Protalina*, vyp. I, vesna, 1907, deals with the poetic speaker's attempt to free herself from the power that a lover has exercised over her for many years. The addressee of the poem may well be Nadezhda Polyakova.
35. Undated letter from mid-1907 from Parnok to Volkenshtein, quoted by Polyakova, "Introduction," 9.
36. Letter from Parnok to Volkenshtein of May 30, 1907, quoted by Polyakova, "Introduction," 8.
37. Stanley Rabinowitz, unpublished biographical sketch of Lyubov Gurevich, quoted by permission of the author.
38. Letter from Parnok to Gurevich of April 12, 1909.
39. Polyakova, "Introduction," 10.
40. Letter from Parnok to Volkenshtein of January 8, 1909, quoted by Polyakova, "Introduction," 10.
41. Letter from Parnok to Gurevich of February 2, 1909.
42. Letter from Parnok to Gurevich of March 16, 1909.
43. Letter from Parnok to Gurevich of February 2, 1909.
44. *Obrazovanie*, no. 5 (mai) 1908. Here again Parnok's poetic speaker suffers from what I would term a Pechorin complex, that she is fated always to play a destructive role, however unwillingly, in the lives of her lovers.
45. *Obrazovanie*, no. 6 (iiun') 1908, 146.
46. Letter from Parnok to Gurevich of July 22, 1908.

47. Letter from Parnok to Gurevich of July 22, 1908. The translations of Baudelaire's *Poèmes en prose (Stikhotvoreniia v proze)* were published by Posev Press (St. Petersburg, 1909). The names of the translators are not given; Parnok and Gurevich are listed as coeditors.
48. Letter from Parnok to Gurevich of July 22, 1908.
49. Ibid.
50. Letter from Parnok to Gurevich of July 31, 1908.
51. Letter from Parnok to Gurevich of February 2, 1909.
52. Ibid.
53. Letter from Parnok to Volkenshtein of January 25, 1909, quoted by Polyakova, "Introduction," 11–12.
54. Letter from Parnok to Gurevich of February 2, 1909.
55. Information on the symptoms and treatment of Grave's disease at the beginning of the twentieth century is from W. H. Thomson, *Grave's Disease* (New York, 1904), 6–7.
56. Letter from Parnok to Gurevich of February 16, 1909.
57. Ibid.
58. Manuscript included in letter from Parnok to Gurevich of March 16, 1909.
59. Letter from Parnok to Gurevich of March 16, 1909.
60. Letter from Parnok to Volkenshtein of March 25, 1909, quoted by Polyakova, "Introduction," 11.
61. Letter from Parnok to Gurevich of April 12, 1909.
62. Letter from Parnok to Gurevich of April 27, 1909.
63. Adelaida Gertsyk, "Mat' i doch'," *Podval'nye ocherki, Russian Literature Triquarterly*, no. 23, 1990, 373.
64. Letter from Parnok to Gurevich of April 27, 1909.
65. Ibid.
66. "Excerpt," *Messenger of Europe,* April 1910. The poem was probably written in 1909.
67. Letter from Parnok to Gurevich of January 31, 1910.
68. Letter from Parnok to Gnesin of February 6, 1910.
69. Letter from Parnok to Gnesin of April 16, 1910. The translation of the phrase "verses or vice" was suggested to me by Katherine T. O'Connor.
70. Letter from Parnok to Gurevich of May 8, 1910.
71. Letter from Parnok to Gurevich of January 31, 1910.
72. Letter from Parnok to Peter Struve of August 25, 1910.
73. Letter from Parnok to Struve of September 15, 1910 (emphasis in the original).

74. Letter from Parnok to Gurevich of March 10, 1911.
75. Letter from Parnok to Gurevich of March 14, 1911.
76. Ibid.
77. Letter from Chatskina to Gurevich of August 13, 1911.
78. Letter from Parnok to Gurevich of January 4, 1913.
79. Letter from Parnok to Gurevich of October 26, 1911.
80. Undated letter from Parnok to Gnesin from early winter 1911.
81. Letter from Parnok to Gurevich of January 2, 1912.
82. Letter from Parnok to Gurevich of March 21, 1912.

CHAPTER 3

1. Letter from Parnok to Gurevich of January 4, 1913.
2. In her letter of January 16, 1913, to Gurevich, Parnok herself noted the odd combination of serious thoughts on death followed by the most mundane "business" concerns related to *Russian Talk*. Boris Sadovskoy's comment to her that in newspaper writing one appears "in dishabille" obviously made a deep impression on her. She associated appearing in print in dishabille with living (or dying) as merely a way of passing time, an idea that horrified her; "[Sadovskoy] made light of my fear that appearing 'in dishabille' can become a habit. . . . And now I'm thinking that if one looks at life as a way of merely passing the time, one can sink into utter spiritual dishabille."
3. Letter from Parnok to Gurevich of January 4, 1913.
4. Quoted by Parnok in her letter to Gurevich of January 16, 1913.
5. Letter from Parnok to Gurevich of January 16, 1913.
6. Ibid.
7. Letter from Parnok to Gurevich of February 11, 1913.
8. Letter from Parnok to Gurevich of February 24, 1913.
9. Letter from Parnok to Gurevich of March 7, 1913.
10. *Severnye zapiski*, no. 5–6 (mai-iiun') 1913, 95.
11. *Russkaia mysl'*, no. 5 (mai) 1913, 189.
12. Letter from Parnok to Gurevich of September 10, 1913.
13. Ibid.
14. Letter from Parnok to Shteinberg of November 13, 1913.
15. Letter from Parnok to Gurevich of November 3, 1913.
16. Letter from Parnok to Gurevich of December 1, 1913.
17. Postcard from Parnok to Shteinberg of April 3, 1914.
18. *Severnye zapiski*, no. 6 (iiun') 1914, 140.
19. Information on Shanklin and Napier House provided by C. R. Sing,

Assistant Librarian, The John Rylands University Library of Manchester (England).
20. Postcard from Parnok to Lipskerov of July 1, 1914.
21. Letter from Parnok to Gnesin of August 22, 1914.
22. Parnakh, *Vospominaniia*, 44.
23. Letter from Parnok to Gnesin of September 19, 1914.
24. Eugenia Gertsyk, *Vospominaniia*, 21.
25. Ibid., 12, 14.
26. Ibid., 142–43.
27. Ibid., 141.
28. Published in the February 1915 issue of *Severnye zapiski (Northern Annals)*, where Adelaida Gertsyk had become a regular contributor.
29. Gertsyk, *Vospominaniia*, 148.
30. The lesbian love affair behind Tsvetaeva's "Girlfriend" cycle and the identity of the "girlfriend" to whom the poems were addressed was first revealed by Sophia Polyakova in *[Ne]zakatnye ony dni: Tsvetaeva i Parnok* (Ann Arbor: Ardis, 1983). This book shall be referred to henceforth as *NOD*. The Russian texts for my translations of Tsvetaeva's poems to Parnok are those in this book. My description of Parnok and Tsvetaeva's first meeting is a close paraphrase (almost a prose translation) of the tenth poem in "Girlfriend."
31. Tsvetaeva acknowledged her bisexuality in this notation of hers dated June 9, 1921: "To love only women (for a woman) or only men (for a man), consciously excluding the usual opposite—how horrible! But [to love] only women (for a man) or only men (for a woman), consciously excluding the unusual same—how boring!" (quoted by Polyakova, *NOD*, 102). On 123 n. 21, Polyakova provides an overview of the female same-sex theme in Tsvetaeva's creative work as well as noting the frequent comments on lesbian attraction and relationships in her journals and notes.
32. Tsvetaeva's lyrical perception and expression of Parnok's difference bears a striking, if probably chance resemblance to Havelock Ellis's view of lesbians in *Sexual Inversion*, "as both failed women and failed men: failed men because their instincts and physiology are basically female; failed women because they enter masculine professions and seek to adopt a masculine role in relation to other women" (Chris White, " 'She was not really a man at all': The Lesbian Practice and Politics of Edith Ellis," in *What Lesbians Do in Books*, ed. Elaine Hobby and Chris White [London: The Women's Press, 1991], 69).

33. Polyakova, *NOD*, 45.
34. Parnok distinguished two kinds of Salieri, "the great Salieri, who had his Mozart, and Salieri the Wandering Jew, for whom Mozart represents the threat of genius" ("Po povodu poslednikh proizvedenii Valeriia Briusova," *Severnye zapiski*, no. 1 [ianvar'] 1917, 159).
35. Letter from Parnok to Gurevich of February 2, 1909.
36. Parnakh, *Vospominaniia*, 44.
37. Gertsyk, *Vospominaniia*, 143–44.
38. Letter from Voloshina to Obolenskaya of December 30, 1914, *NOD*, 47.
39. My prose narrative of this day essentially translates and slightly augments Tsvetaeva's lyrical account in the seventh poem of "Girlfriend."
40. "Girlfriend" did not become part of the Tsvetaeva canon until the 1970s, and when it was first published, it appeared without the original dedication to Parnok. Some Russian Tsvetaeva scholars continue to deny that Tsvetaeva and Parnok's relationship was sexual or even romantic in nature.
41. Quoted by Losskaya, *Marina Tsvetaeva v zhizni*, 150.
42. Elizaveta Parnokh Tarakhovskaya, *Vospominaniia*. Tarakhovskaya took four years off her age, leading some specialists to list her birthdate mistakenly as 1895.
43. Quoted by Polyakova, *NOD*, 50.
44. Polyakova in *NOD* was the first to argue that Parnok was the probable "internal" addressee of Tsvetaeva's "Lettre à l'Amazone." Tsvetaeva tried to gain acceptance to Barney's Rue Jacob salon, but was apparently snubbed (or simply ignored).
45. Tsvetaeva, "Lettre à l'Amazone," English translation by Edwina Cruise (unpublished typescript, 5).
46. Tsvetaeva, "Lettre à l'Amazone," *passim*.
47. Virginia Woolf wrote *Orlando* as a gift and gesture of revenge against the sexually unfaithful Vita Sackville-West. See Burgin, "Signs of a Response," 225–26 nn. 3, 5.
48. See Burgin, "After the Ball," 426–28, for Blokian overtones to Tsvetaeva's naming Parnok a "fair stranger with the brow of Beethoven."
49. Letter from Voloshina to Obolenskaya of January 21, 1915, *NOD*, 50.
50. On March 13, 1915, Tsvetaeva wrote a poem to Parnok, "The hills outside Moscow are blue," that she originally included in "Girl-

friend" but left out of the final version. It ended with the lines: "I'm already coming down with summer, / Having barely from winter got well" (*NOD*, 97).
51. Tsvetaeva herself acknowledged that this poem was addressed to her in her notation of November 2, 1940: " 'Like a small girl you appeared in my presence ungracefully'—Sappho (by the way, written out by S. Parnok and addressed—to me'" (*NOD*, 122 n. 15).
52. It is interesting that Tsvetaeva ended "Lettre à l'Amazone" with an implied epitaph to Parnok, concluding with the phrase, "When I see the way a willow is weeping, I understand Sappho." In other words, "Sappho" was literally Tsvetaeva's last word on Parnok, and Sappho had been the mediatrix of Parnok's first poem to Tsvetaeva. The reference to a "weeping willow" also conjures up Ophelia and Tsvetaeva's calling Parnok a Shakespearean tragic heroine in the first poem of "Girlfriend." Parnok identified herself with the willow tree in her juvenile love lyrics to Nadezhda Polyakova. It is unlikely that Tsvetaeva knew them, although she may have known from Parnok herself about some of Parnok's former lovers.
53. The text of this poem was discovered and first published by Polyakova in *NOD*, 52–53.
54. Liza Efron, who lived most of her life with a permanent female companion, may have shared Parnok's affectional preference.
55. The addressee of this poem was not indicated by Parnok. I agree with Polyakova's surmise that she was most likely Tsvetaeva.
56. Letter from Voloshina to Obolenskaya of February 5, 1915, *NOD*, 50.
57. Letter from Parnok to Gurevich of February 2, 1909.
58. The von Arnim subtext in this poem was first revealed in Burgin, "After the Ball," 430–33.
59. "Voices with their promising play," written on March 14, 1915, *NOD*, 102.
60. *NOD*, 98.
61. Letter from Voloshina to Vera Efron of May 17, 1915 (copy provided to me by Lena Korkina).
62. *NOD*, 54–55. The laundry list is a delightful piece of mundane testimony to the women's love affair, but I am not entirely in agreement with Polyakova's assumption that Parnok played the "husband" and Tsvetaeva the "wife" in their "conjugal" relationship. To my mind heterosexual sex roles and relationships tell one little or nothing about lesbian sex roles and relationships, and the application

of heterosexual models to lesbian relationships seems merely to reinforce the homophobic stereotypes of lesbians adhered to by many heterosexual readers. Parnok, moreover, played different roles in different relationships.
63. Quoted by Polyakova, NOD, 49. The comment was noted by Tsvetaeva on July 20, 1915.
64. Letter from Voloshina to Liza Efron of June, 1915 (copy provided to me by Lena Korkina).
65. Quoted by Polyakova, CP, 360.
66. "Mandelshtam is a fool: Sophia Yakovlevna is right. Simply stupid, without any particular qualities." Letter from Khodasevich to his wife Anna Ivanovna of June 18, 1916.
67. Anastasia Tsvetaeva, Vospominaniia, 556.
68. Letter from Voloshina to Liza Efron, July 14, 1915 (copy provided to me by Lena Korkina).
69. Letter from Parnok to Shteinberg of June 26, 1915.
70. Parnakh, Vospominaniia, 46.
71. The exact date of Parnok's baptism is not known, but the event occurred after her divorce in 1909 and before the October 1917 Revolution.
72. There is no indication of who the addressee of this poem was.
73. Again, there is no indication of who the addressee of this poem was. The word "brother" could refer to a male associate, friend, or colleague of the speaker's as well as to her biological brother.
74. Letter from Tsvetaeva to Liza Efron of July 30, 1915, quoted by Polyakova, NOD, 57. Tsvetaeva may have chosen Liza Efron to confide in because she knew that Liza was not unsympathetic to Parnok and could thus sympathize with both sides of Tsvetaeva's dilemma.
75. NOD, 38. The poem was written on June 14.
76. The Russian word for "mistress" here (*gospozha*) denotes "lady of the manor" or "missus," not "female lover."
77. Parnok and Tsvetaeva held poetry readings (at Parnok's) on August 19 and September 24, as Maya Kudashova reported to Vyacheslav Ivanov in two letters. Kudashova refers to Marina and Sonya as if they were a couple: "In the early evening I have to go to see Marina and Sonya," Kudashova wrote (quoted by Polyakova, NOD, 124–25 n. 35.)
78. *Severnye zapiski,* no. 7–8 (iiul'-avgust), 1915.
79. Polyakova, NOD, 103.
80. "The gypsy passion of separation" was written in October 1915; the

text is in *NOD*, 104. It reflects, in part, as do two poems on gypsy themes Parnok wrote in September 1915, Tsvetaeva's (and Parnok's) enjoyment of the gypsy singers at the Yar Restaurant in Moscow where they were wined and dined by Saker and Chatskina.
81. Polyakova identified Efron as the intended addressee of this poem (*NOD*, 106–7).
82. Written on November 27, 1915. Text in *NOD*, 105.
83. In Olga Tsuberbiller's copy of *Poems,* Parnok contradicted her own 1915 dating of this poem and wrote in the margin that #24 was written in Moscow, 1916.
84. The "defrocked monk" is an allusion to Grigory Otrepyev, the False Dmitri and husband of Marina Mniszek, who, according to legend, was a runaway monk. In view of Parnok's previous lyrical identification of Tsvetaeva as Marina Mniszek (in "Sonnet," #28), her reference to the "defrocked monk" in "Rondeau" could be read as an allusion to Marina's husband, Sergey Efron.
85. Quoted in Losskaya, *Marina Tsvetaeva,* 150.
86. For a detailed discussion of the critical response to Parnok's first book see Burgin, "Laid Out in Lavender."

CHAPTER 4

1. Tsvetaeva's impressions of Petrograd and all subsequent details about the Kannegisers' party come from her letter to Kuzmin, quoted by Polyakova in *NOD*, 110–14.
2. Simon Karlinsky, *Marina Tsvetaeva,* 56.
3. Polyakova, *NOD*, 126 n. 52.
4. See Burgin, "After the Ball" 431, 434 n. 20.
5. All details of Sonya and Marina's breakup are from Tsvetaeva's letter to Kuzmin, *NOD*, 110–14.
6. Quoted by Polyakova, *NOD*, 125 n. 40. Polyakova rightly cautions against reading the scene of Parnok and Erarskaya talking on Parnok's bed as a sexually intimate scene. She points out that as a semi-invalid Parnok often received visitors at home from her bed. However, surely not all visitors would be invited to sit on her bed, and so Erarskaya's position there was a sign of her intimacy with Parnok, sexual or not. Clearly, Tsvetaeva understood from their posture that they were on intimate terms, or she would not have felt so traumatized by the sight.

NOTES TO CHAPTER 4   327

7. Polyakova gives convincing proof that the unnamed addressee of this poem was Tsvetaeva in *NOD*, 108–9.
8. Tragically, Tsvetaeva was forced to abandon this second daughter, Irina, in a state orphanage during the famine of the Civil War in Moscow, and the two-year-old infant died of starvation. The child's paternity, according to some Tsvetaeva scholars, is in doubt.
9. In her notebook for 1920 Tsvetaeva wrote: "That's the way I suffered at twenty-two from Sonya P——k, but it was different: she antagonized me, embittered me, trampled over me, but—she loved me!" (*NOD*, 51).
10. Noted by Tsvetaeva in her journal for 1915–16 under March 3, 1916. Quoted by Polyakova, *NOD*, 61.
11. The poem is unfortunately untranslatable into English.
12. Mandelshtam's relationship with Parnòk (Parnok stressed the last syllable of her chosen surname) and with her brother (Pàrnakh) played a role in the creation of the autobiographical hero (named Pàrnok) of one of his most abstruse prose works, *Egyptian Stamp*, written in the late twenties and the subject of numerous critical studies. Although some scholars continue to argue that the hero of Mandelshtam's work incorporates traits of Sophia Parnok, the majority (and most recent) believe Mandelshtam's Parnok was based on himself and on Valentin Parnakh, with whom Mandelshtam was friendly in the early twenties. He apparently thought Parnakh's last name was Parnok, like his sister.
13. Letter from Khodasevich to Parnok of July 22, 1916.
14. The addressee was discovered by the present author. Notes for poem in *CP* do not mention the dedication to L.V.E., which was included in the first (1916) publication of the poem.
15. Letter from Erarskaya to Gertsyk of September 25, 1933.
16. Gertsyk, *Vospominaniia*, 161,
17. Letter from Parnok to Gnesin of February 2, 1917.
18. Letter from Parnok to Veisberg of February 9, 1917.
19. Ibid.
20. Letter from Parnok to Veisberg of February 18, 1917.
21. Letter from Parnok to Veisberg of March 29, 1917.
22. Ibid.
23. Letter from Parnok to Voloshin of June 20, 1917, quoted by Polyakova, "Introduction," 20.
24. Letter from Parnok to Voloshin of August 14, 1917, from Moscow.

In her "Introduction," Polyakova gives the impression that Parnok was already in Sudak at this time.
25. Letter from Parnok to Voloshin of August 14, 1917.
26. Letter from Parnok to Voloshin of September 16, 1917, from Sudak. Parnok wrote essentially to send her address, which suggests she and Erarskaya had just arrived in Sudak.
27. From Erarskaya's unpublished *Vospominaniia (Reminiscences),* portions of which are quoted in Marina Spendiarova's chronicle of her father's life, *Letopis' zhizni i tvorchestva A. A. Spendiarova,* 350–51. Erarskaya is a few months off in her dating of Spendiarov's first meeting with her and Parnok.
28. Polyakova, "Introduction," 64.
29. Images of Eugenia Gertsyk as "godmother" and "Sugdalian sibyl" are from poem #77, quoted in full in this chapter.
30. Gertsyk, *Vospominaniia,* 139.
31. Adelaida Gertsyk's poem to Parnok has never been published. My translation was made from a handwritten copy given to me by Polyakova of the autograph in the archive of T. N. Zhukovskaya, Gertsyk's granddaughter. The poem was written in Sudak in 1919.
32. Quoted by Spendiarova, *Letopis',* 355.
33. Letter from Parnok to Spendiarov of October 1926.
34. Quoted in Spendiarova, *Letopis',* 356.
35. Ibid., 358.
36. Letter from Eugenia Gertsyk to Lev Shestov of January 26, 1924, in Gertsyk's *Vospominaniia,* 165–66.
37. Spendiarova, *Letopis',* 360.
38. Polyakova, *NOD,* 126 n. 55.
39. Letter from Parnok et al. to Gorky of March 23, 1921, quoted by Spendiarova, *Letopis',* 361–62.
40. Spendiarova, *Letopis',* 362.
41. Lev Gornung, *Memoirs* (dated), entry for April 15, 1932.
42. Letter from Parnok to Voloshin of May 12, 1921.
43. Quoted by Polyakova, *NOD,* 63.
44. Letter from Spendiarov to Parnok of January 29, 1922.
45. Ibid., quoted by Spendiarova, *Letopis',* 366.
46. Letter from Parnok to Voloshin of April 7, 1922.
47. Ibid.
48. Ibid.
49. Ibid.

50. Ibid.
51. Polyanin [Parnok], "Dni russkoi liriki," *Shipovnik*, No. 1, Moscow, 1922, 157–61.
52. Gornung, in *Memoirs* (dated), notes that a "female companion" or "woman friend" *(podruga)* was living with Parnok in 1923 and 1924. This woman friend might have been Irina Sergeyevna (Yurgenson), whom Parnok refers to in an August 1924 note to Gurevich as someone who lives in her apartment and takes messages for her. The other possibility is that Irina Sergeyevna, also a friend of Olga Tsuberbiller, happened to live in Parnok's communal apartment on Fourth Tverskaya Yamskaya and simply befriended the poet.
53. Letter from Parnok to Voloshin of August 3, 1922.
54. Letter from Parnok to Voloshin of September 4, 1922.
55. Parnakh, *Vospominaniia*, 119.
56. Ibid., 88.
57. Ibid.
58. Note from Volkenshtein to Nikitina at one of the Saturdays, late 1922 (*Nikitina Saturdays* Archive, TsGALI).
59. Letter from Parnok to Gertsyk of January 26, 1923. Polyakova mistakenly read the date on this letter as 1925.
60. Letter from Parnok to Voloshin of November 10, 1922.
61. See De Jean, *Fictions of Sappho*.
62. Vladimir Solovyov, *Stikhotvoreniia. Proza. Pis'ma. Vospominaniia sovremennikov* (Moscow: 1990), 107. It may also be worth noting that Solovyov's sister, Poliksena Solovyova, was a lesbian, albeit a completely closeted one, and a prolific poet. She wrote exclusively with a male persona.
63. An anonymous reviewer of Lokhvitskaya's first volume of poems (1896) said that the young poetess's "sweet songs of love" would insure that "the name of Mme Lokhvitskaya will pass into very distant centuries as the name of the Russian Sappho" (*Russkoe bogatstvo*, 1896, No. 7, 59–60).
64. E. V. Sviiasov, "Safo v vospriiatii russkikh poetov" (1880–1910e gg.), *Na rubezhe XIX i XX vekov. Iz istorii mezhdunarodnykh sviazei russkoi literatury*, (Leningrad: Akademia Nauk 1991), 259.
65. One of the few exceptions was a short poem about Sappho by Sergey Solovyov.
66. See De Jean, *Fictions of Sappho*, on Welcker, 205.
67. P. Mokievskii, review of Otto Weininger, *Pol i kharakter*, in *Russkoe*

bogatstvo, 1908, No. 12, 28. Mokievskii cites from p. 77 of the Russian translation he is reviewing. My thanks to Ira Paperno for pointing this review out to me.

68. Vladislav Khodasevich, "Sof'ia Parnok. *Stikhotvoreniia*," *Utro Rossii*, 1916, No. 274.
69. Parnok did not know classical Greek.
70. Vyacheslav Ivanov, *Alkei i Safo. Sobranie pesen i liricheskikh otryvkov* (Moscow: 1914), 25.
71. Vikenty Veresaev, *Sochineniia* (Moscow: 1948), 3:369.
72. Some Russian male poets such as Derzhavian, Katenin, and Ivanov had important personal and creative relationships (generally of the creative rivalry sort) with Sappho in her hypostasis as Original Woman Poet.
73. First published in *Severnye zapiski*, no. 5–6, 1915.
74. Several things in the poem suggest that the addressee might be Tsvetaeva: (1) the addressee is also a poet, and Parnok's only known lover who was also a poet at the probable time of composition was Tsvetaeva; (2) Parnok discovered "Lesbos, cradle of lyrical song," around the time that she and Tsvetaeva discovered each other and became lovers; (3) the phrase in line 2, "weak from happiness," is often used by Parnok to describe the post-lovemaking state and occurs in her January 1915 poem, "That evening was blazing dimly" (see chapter 3), which was most likely addressed to Tsvetaeva; (4) the addressee's name "attracts the waves," i.e., is associated with the sea; Parnok called her Marina "the namesake of the sea" in her August 1915 poem to her, "Blindly staring eyes" (see chapter 3).
75. Ivanov mistranslated Sappho's fragment as "Sleep on your female companion's breast, sleep on her *voluptuous* breast."
76. Natalie Clifford Barney, *Actes et Entr'actes*, 1910, 66–67.
77. Parnok's self-identification and lyrical self-creation as a latter-day Amazon queen in a poem that was first published in September 1916 in *Severnye zapiski* (which Tsvetaeva must have seen since poems of hers appeared in the same issue) provides more evidence that Tsvetaeva was addressing Parnok in "Lettre à l'Amazone" as much as she was addressing Natalie Barney.
78. Parnok's use of the image "two white doves" to denote a woman's breasts in #73 is a direct quote from one of Pierre Louÿs's *Songs of Bilitis*.
79. M. Vazlinsky's parody was written at the end of 1924 and is in the archive of Maria Shkapskaya, TsGALI.

NOTES TO CHAPTER 5   331

80. Polyakova argues that the Chimera represents Soviet power; I agree and suggest that it also has a more personal symbolism. See Burgin, "Sophia Parnok and the Writing of a Lesbian Poet's Life," 228–29.
81. Parnok's poetic speaker suggests many resemblances to the "hungry femme lesbian" described by Jo Ann Loulan in *The Lesbian Erotic Dance* (San Francisco: Spinsters Book Company, 1990).
82. Nikolai Stavrogin, the morally dead romantic mask and antihero of Dostoevsky's *The Devils*, is described, in the language of the Apocalypse, as being neither hot nor cold, but lukewarm. The spider mentioned in the first line of Parnok's poem also has Dostoevskian overtones—it is a recurrent motif of evil (moral deadness and negation) in all of Dostoevsky's novels. In general, Parnok's poems, letters, and critical articles contain numerous references to Dostoevsky's work.

CHAPTER 5

1. Letter from Parnok to Gertsyk of January 26, 1923. The letter is not from 1925, as cited in *CP*.
2. Ibid.
3. Ibid.
4. I refer to two memoiristic manuscripts of Lev Gornung's: one, which I call *Memoirs* (dated), has already been cited in the notes for chapters 2 and 4; the other is the "Memoirs" Gornung wrote in 1974 for Sophia Polyakova and which she gave me to copy in 1987. I shall refer to these memoirs, which are not specifically dated, as Gornung 1974.
5. Letter from Parnok to Voloshin of June 4, 1923.
6. Gornung 1974.
7. Gornung, *Memoirs* (dated), entry for September 27, 1923, 3–4.
8. Letter from Mandelshtam to his father, [Winter 1923–24], in *Mandelshtam: The Complete Critical Prose and Letters*, edited by Jane Gary Harris (Ann Arbor: Ardis, no date), 490.
9. Gornung 1974.
10. The last four lines of the poem appeared in the autograph version only.
11. Letter from Parnok to Voloshin of June 4, 1923.
12. Sophia Parnok, "B. Pasternak i drugie," *Russkii sovremennik*, no. 2, 1924, 311. For discussion of how this relates to the Parnok and Tsvetaeva love affair, see Burgin, "After the Ball."
13. This anecdote and details of the poetry reading that followed are based on Gornung, *Memoirs* (dated), entry for April 3, 1924, 11–12. Gornung makes a point of noting that the reason Parnok had to cook

the tongue herself was that her female companion was out of town at the time. He fails to name this female companion, however, either out of respect for her privacy or because he did not consider her name worth recording in a literary memoir.
14. Letter from Parnok to Gertsyk of February 5, 1925.
15. Letter from Parnok to Gertsyk of January 11, 1926.
16. Letter from Parnok to Gertsyk of March 13, 1925.
17. Letter from Tsuberbiller to Gertsyk of February 9, 1925. Tsuberbiller signed this letter "Sonya's [intimate] friend" *(Sonin drug)*. Tsuberbiller's letter is in the private archive of Eugenia Gertsyk.
18. Letter from Parnok to Gertsyk of February 5, 1925.
19. Letter from Parnok to Gertsyk of March 13, 1925.
20. Letter from Parnok to Gertsyk of February 5, 1925.
21. Ibid.
22. Letter from Parnok to Gertsyk of May 4, 1925.
23. Letter from Parnok to Gertsyk of July 21, 1925.
24. Ibid.
25. The original of Parnok's complaint is in E. F. Nikitina's archive in TsGALI, and is my source for the history of the poet's experience with this translation.
26. Pavlova herself spoke of the anomaly of being a female poet in Russia in the first half of the nineteenth century through the heroine (Cecily) of her poetic novel, *A Double Life*. The novel has been translated into English by Barbara Heldt and was published by Ardis.
27. A gusla is a lute-like native Russian instrument that the singers of the bylinas (epic songs) strummed in a recitative-like accompaniment to their narrations. Itinerant folk musicians were often blind, which is interesting in view of Parnok's comparison of her poetic speaker to a blind man or woman in several poems. It is also interesting that Parnok's early verse contains a lyric, "Song of the Lake," in which the poetic speaker identifies herself as a lake and rues the fact that she has never "known the seas."
28. Gornung, *Memoirs* (dated), entry for January 3, 1926, 14.
29. Letter from Parnok to Gertsyk of January 11, 1926.
30. Ibid.
31. Letter from Erarskaya to Gertsyk of September 25, 1933. This letter is in the private archive of Eugenia Gertsyk.
32. See Tsvetaeva, "Lettre à l'Amazone," *passim*.
33. Polyakova's phrase is used in her "Introduction" to Parnok's *Collected Poems*.

34. Letter from Parnok to Gertsyk of April 1, 1926.
35. Karlinsky, *Marina Tsvetaeva*, 161.
36. Letter from Parnok to Gertsyk of March 1, 1926.
37. I cannot entirely agree with Polyakova, as she argues in the notes of *Collected Poems*, that the poems in "Dark Wave" are unified by "the image of Carmen and her living double, the gypsy woman and the black angel" (340). Rather, the unifying theme of the cycle's poems is gypsy music and the gypsy mode as exemplified and conjured by Carmen, but also by other real-life women and lovers of the poet who may or may not have been gypsies.
38. Parnok refers or alludes to several goddesses from Greco-Roman mythology that appeared to have had power over her and her creative self in various periods of her life and are suggested in the changing aspects of her poetic speaker. The most dominant goddesses in that speaker's life were Demeter (the mother), Aphrodite/Venus (the lover), Athena (the wise woman), Artemis (the autonomous, celibate, self-actualizing poet), and to a limited degree, Hera (the domesticated poet). For more on the subject of goddesses in women's lives, see Christine Downing, *Goddess: Mythological Images of the Feminine* (New York: 1984).
39. Letter from Parnok to Gertsyk of June 6, 1926.
40. Ibid.
41. Tsvetaeva may also have had news of Parnok from Valentin Parnakh, who was living in Paris at this time.
42. The English editors of Tsvetaeva's correspondence with Rilke and Pasternak omitted Tsvetaeva's letter to Pasternak about Parnok, but quoted Pasternak's reply in full. B. *Pasternak, M. Tsvetaeva, R. M. Rilke, Letters of the Summer 1926*, translated by Margaret Wettlin and Walter Arndt (New York: Harcourt Brace Jovanovich, 1983), 101.
43. Ibid., 103.
44. Ibid., 104.
45. Ibid., 103.
46. Letter from Parnok to Gertsyk of April 1, 1926.
47. The bulk of Adelaida Gertsyk's oeuvre still remains unpublished, but selections of her previously unpublished poems have recently appeared in *Voskresnyi vypusk volkhonko*, Moscow, 16 fevralia, 1992.
48. Letter from Parnok to Gertsyk of May 1, 1926.
49. In today's Russia, anything religious (with respect to Russian Orthodoxy) that was banned during the Soviet period is rushed into print.

Yet, Parnok's most markedly lesbian poems have remained unwelcome. Russian scholars and readers do not recognize the lesbian focus in Parnok's poetry as having a political dimension. The personal emphasis in her verse is counted as a liability that makes her work less important than the work of poets who make more conventional political statements in their verse.

50. Letter from Parnok to Voloshin of May 17, 1926.
51. Letter from Parnok to Kuzmin of April 12, 1926. Archive of M. A. Kuzmin, TsGALI, f. 232.
52. See Walker, *The Woman's Dictionary*, 414–15.
53. Letter from Parnok to Voloshin of June 4, 1926.
54. Parnok appeared to have achieved this precious and precarious integration only in her relationship with Olga Nikolaevna.
55. Parnok's last lover, Nina Vedeneyeva, apparently read #171 as an indication of Parnok's "inconstancy." See Parnok's letter to Vedeneyeva of August 22, 1932, as quoted in chapter 7, note 20.
56. The implicit comparison of the apple tree with a blushing bride as well as this image's eroticism have Sapphic overtones. Parnok may have left the stanza out because of the mention of the word "cupola," a religious reference.
57. Letter of Parnok to Spendiarov of October 1926, quoted by Spendiarova.
58. Letter from Parnok to Gurevich of November 30, 1926.
59. The Proustian text behind the poem: "Momentanement eclipsé mon passé ne projetait plus devant moi cette ombre que nous appelons notre avenir," from *A l'ombre des jeunes filles en fleur* (Paris, 1954), 1:875.
60. The word-play in this poem is untranslatable and derives from the similarity in sound of the phrases, *"ne bit' chelom veku svoemu"* (not to kow-tow [beat one's brow] to one's century) and *"no byt' chelom veka svoego"* (but be the brow of one's century) and the final *"byt' chelovekom"* (to be a human being).
61. The description of how tachycardia feels was written at my request by my colleague and friend, Robin Miller.
62. Letter from Parnok to Fedorchenko of July 12, 1927.
63. Letter from Parnok to Fedorchenko of June 21, 1927.
64. Letter from Parnok to Gertsyk from the summer of 1927.
65. Letter from Parnok to Fedorchenko of July 12, 1927.
66. Letter from Parnok to Fedorchenko of August 8, 1927.
67. Ibid.

68. Ibid.
69. Ibid.
70. Letter from Parnok to Spendiarov of October 8, 1927, quoted in Khudabashian, "Avtor libretto," n. 39.

CHAPTER 6

1. After Parnok's death Zvyagintseva republished *Almast* (Moscow, 1939) in her own, significantly changed and deformed version. See Polyakova, *CP*, 313 n. 69.
2. Postcard from Parnok to Zvyagintseva of December 7, 1927.
3. Letter from Parnok to Vedeneyeva of July 28, 1933.
4. Polyakova argues cautiously that Valery Bryusov is the most likely addressee of this poem, while pointing out that if he is, then Parnok misdated the lyric. The poem is written to a "living" venerable master, Parnok dated the poem to mid-March 1926 and Bryusov had died two years earlier. See Polyakova, *CP*, note to #203, 352. Parnok detested Bryusov and made a point of not attending his funeral.
5. Letter from Parnok to Zvyagintseva of February 22, 1928.
6. Letter from Parnok to Zvyagintseva of July 21, 1928.
7. Letter from Parnok to Gertsyk of 1928.
8. Letter from Parnok to Shteinberg of June 24, 1930.
9. Gornung 1974.
10. Quoted lines are from a poem by Pushkin.
11. Letter from Parnok to Gertsyk of May 4, 1929.
12. Letter from Parnok to Shteinberg of September 22, 1929.
13. Letter from Parnok to Shteinberg of October 5, 1929.
14. Letter from Parnok to Shteinberg of October 10, 1929.
15. Letter from Parnok to Shteinberg of November 15, 1929.
16. Letter from Parnok to Shteinberg of December 6, 1929.
17. Letter from Parnok to Shteinberg of November 12, 1929.
18. Starr, *Romain Rolland* (The Hague: Mouton, 1971), 239.
19. Letter from Rolland to Parnok from Villeneuve, September 30, 1929. English translations of Rolland's French are my own.
20. Letter from Rolland to Parnok of November 20, 1929.
21. Parnok wrote to Voloshin on April 7, 1922:

> Because of Maya [Kudashova] I missed the chance of replying to you via Dr. Nany, who left for Feodosia again after spending three days here. Horribly annoying! For some reason Maya took from Veresaev your last letter to me

despite the fact that Veresaev had wanted to deliver it to me himself. She told him that she sees me "every day" (I haven't seen her once) and then kept the letter for ten days. Why that lie was necessary remains a mystery, but it's all the more annoying since at precisely that time I was combing Moscow for a messenger.

22. Letter from Rolland to Parnok of January 4, 1930.
23. Gornung, *Memoirs* (dated), entry for February 12, 1930, 18.
24. Thus Parnok relived her affair with Tsvetaeva through a namesake, a second Marina, just as Tsvetaeva had tried to relive (and revise) her affair with Parnok through her second Sonya (Sonechka), the actress Sonya Holliday (see Polyakova, *NOD*, 65–66).
25. Excellent readings of this poem are given by De Jean, *Fictions of Sappho*, 317–27, and John Winkler, "Double Consciousness in Sappho's Lyrics," in *The Constraints of Desire: The Anthropology of Sex and Gender in Ancient Greece* (New York: Routledge, 1990).
26. Letter from Parnok to Shteinberg of May 17, 1930, (emphasis in the original).
27. Letter from Parnok to Shteinberg of April 28, 1930.
28. Letter from Parnok to Shteinberg of June 24, 1930, (emphasis in the original).
29. Letter from Parnok to Shteinberg of June 29, 1930.
30. Ibid.
31. Ibid.
32. Letter from Parnok to Shteinberg of June 29, 1930.
33. Letter from Parnok to Shteinberg of September 19, 1930.
34. Ibid.
35. Letter from Parnok to Shteinberg of October 17, 1930.
36. Ibid.
37. Gornung 1974, quoted by Polyakova, *CP*, 325.
38. Gornung 1974, 9.
39. Ibid.
40. Ibid., 15–16.
41. Letter from Rolland to Parnok of February 2, 1931.
42. Photograph in Parnok's personal collection.
43. Account of Gornung's visit to Maloyaroslavets based on his account in *Memoirs* (dated), 24–27.
44. Ivanov had been a close friend of Eugenia Gertsyk's in the years 1906–9 and was fond of calling her "sorella" (sister), as Parnok herself would later call her in several lyrics.

45. Walker, *The Woman's Dictionary*, 460. The ash tree may also be an allusion to Wagner's *Die Walküre*. In this, second, opera of his *Ring* cycle, Wotan, king-of-the-gods, embeds a sword into the ash tree in Hunding and Sieglinde's house during their wedding celebration and declares that only a hero can draw it out. Sieglinde's brother/lover Siegmund turns out to be that hero.
46. Polyakova argues that the "weary woman traveler" in the poem refers to Parnok herself.
47. Yulia Veisberg wrote a humorous ditty to Parnok on how the heroine of her opera, Gyulnara (and, by implication, Maksakova), had stimulated the poet (Parnok) to take up her lyre after a long hiatus. Parnok herself contributed the punch line (in italics here) to Veisberg's epigram, indicating the final four-letter word (that rhymes with *struck*) with four dots:

> Praise, Gyulnara dear, we choir
> to you, who from the poet's lyre
> anew sweet flights of sound has struck,
> though far beyond your grasp, Gyulnara,
> lies lofty poesy's tiara,
> *and though a grey old man you. . . .*

The "grey old man" obviously refers to Gyulnara's lover in the opera, but in the autobiographical context surrounding Parnok's writing of the libretto and her intimate relationship with Maksakova (Gyulnara), the "grey old man" could be read as a typically self-ironic allusion by Parnok to herself as Maksakova's lover. Evidence for such a reading can be found in the age difference between Parnok and Maksakova, who was seventeen years younger than the poet, and in Parnok's lyrical self-image in some of the Vedeneyeva poems as "an old man."
48. *Byul-byul* means "nightingale."
49. Parnok wrote the following ditty to Faina Ranevskaya, who was widely rumored to be a lesbian, rumors she denied vociferously.

> I forgive you almost all your sins
> Only two of them I can't allow:
> Poetry you whisper to yourself,
> And you kiss out loud.
>
> Sin, have fun, and blossom with the years.
> Only heed my motherly advice—

A kiss, my darling, isn't for the ears,
Music, my angel, isn't for the eyes.

50. Gornung, *Memoirs* (dated), entry for December 21, 1931, 27–28.

CHAPTER 7

1. Polyakova, "Introduction," 33.
2. Gornung 1974.
3. Parnok's Dante-Virgil pairing echoes Tsvetaeva's allusion to Orestes and Pylades in the tenth poem of "Girlfriend."
4. Polyakova, "Introduction."
5. Line quoted by Parnok (slightly incorrectly) from Pushkin's narrative poem "Count Nulin."
6. The toponym *Viogolòsa* (which I translate into English as Viavocàla) appears to have been a coinage of Parnok's and possibly a word in her and Vedeneyeva's private language. It has so far eluded the most concerted efforts to find a possible referential context in literature, art, or music that might shed light on its etymology or what Parnok meant by it (if anything). In Russian *Viogolòsa* appears to be composed of two segments: the foreign prefix *vio*, which occurs in borrowed words like *violonchel'* (violoncello), and the native word-root *golos* (voice).
7. The poem contains a subtext to a Mandelshtam poem and through it to Parnok's affair with Tsvetaeva. See Burgin "After the Ball," 441–44.
8. See Polyakova, "Eshche odno zabytoe imia," *Literaturnoe obozrenie,* no. 10, 1989.
9. The verb "to eat" in Russian does not, as in English, have any specifically sexual connotations denoting cunnilingus.
10. The ancient Persian form, *ghazals,* has strong associations with the theme of male homoerotic love both in its native poetic culture and in western European literature where it was introduced by Goethe in the early nineteenth century. Parnok had already used ghazals in *Poems* in a lyric I believe to have been addressed to Tsvetaeva (see Burgin, "Signs of a Response") and for the "Bard's Song" ("Pesnia ashuga") in *Almast,* in which she expressed her love for Erarskaya. As far as I know, Parnok is the only Russian poet to use ghazals for the expression of female homoerotic love.
11. Letter from Parnok to Vedeneyeva of May 2, 1932.

12. Polyakova, "Introduction," 33.
13. In the context of Parnok's triple pun, the word "philo-Sophy" also means "love of Sophia."
14. The quatrain plays on a well-known epigram by Pushkin's brother on the subject of how Pushkin had been "goncharovized" by his beautiful young wife, whose maiden name was Goncharova (Polyakova, "Introduction," 363).
15. Letter from Parnok to Vedeneyeva of August 12, 1932.
16. Like *Viogolòsa* (Viavocàla), the source and possible encoded significance of Parnok's pet name for her lover, Wilhelmina, seem undecipherable. The name Wilhelmina is mainly German, a feminine form of Wilhelm, and it is a royal name in the Netherlands.
17. Letter from Parnok to Vedeneyeva of August 22, 1932. The Russian word *drug* (which I have translated here as "intimate friend") tends to be reserved by Russians for a person of either sex with whom the speaker has a particularly close, deep, serious, and emotionally significant relationship. In appropriate contexts, such as here, *drug* carries connotations of a marital or other permanent love relationship.
18. Letter from Parnok to Vedeneyeva of August 12, 1932.
19. Letter from Parnok to Vedeneyeva of August 22, 1932.
20. Ibid.
21. Ibid.
22. Telegram from Parnok to Vedeneyeva of August 31, 1932. Vladimir Dahl was the nineteenth-century compiler of the authoritative multivolume *Dictionary of Spoken Russian*.
23. Parnok greatly admired the chess poems of Nina Podgorichani in *The Eighth Horizontal*, and one wonders if the imagery in this poem is in any way related to them.
24. This is Sophia Polyakova's interpretation as conveyed to me in a letter. She based it on "unconfirmed gossip" she had heard from one of her informants that Vedeneyeva had another suitor, or romantic interest in her life, probably a man, whom Parnok perceived as a potential rival.
25. My translation of the Russian text of the aria by N. Konchalovskaya, V. A. Mozart, *Don Zhuan* (Moscow: 1983), 84.
26. By wintertime Parnok probably means the winter of her life. "Sinful paradise" in line 1 refers to the "garden-filled town" of Kashin. "Sinful" does not mean "morally wrong," but "earthly" (and sexual) as opposed to "heavenly" (and spiritual).

27. Gornung, *Memoirs* (dated).
28. Letter from Parnok to Ranevskaya of June 29, 1933.
29. Gornung, *Memoirs* (dated), entry for May 25, 1933, 31.
30. Gornung, *Memoirs* (dated), entry for June 26, 1933, 31–32.
31. Gornung, *Memoirs* (dated), "Rasskaz Ol'gi Nikolaevny," 33.
32. It seems likely that Vedeneyeva destroyed some of Parnok's letters. After Parnok's death, Vedeneyeva ceased relations with the other women in the poet's intimate family circle, and she never reestablished contact with them.
33. Letter from Parnok to Vedeneyeva of July 7, 1933.
34. Letter from Parnok to Vedeneyeva of July 28, 1933.
35. Ibid.
36. Polyakova, "Introduction," 35.
37. Reported by Olga Tsuberbiller in her "Account" (told to Gornung) of Parnok's last days.
38. Quoted by Polyakova, "Introduction," 35.
39. Letter from Erarskaya to Gertsyk of September 25, 1933.

EPILOGUE

1. Letter from Erarskaya to Gertsyk of September 25, 1933.
2. Gornung, *Memoirs* (dated), entry for August 29, 1933, 35.
3. Ibid., 36.
4. Letter from Erarskaya to Gertsyk of September 25, 1933.

Bibliography

PUBLISHED SOURCES

Batashev, Aleksei. "Egipetskii povorot. Zametki o Valentine Parnakhe." *Teatr*, 1991, no. 10: 114–29.

Bodik, L. A., et al. *Taganrog. Istoriko-kraevedcheskii ocherk.* Rostov: Rostovskoe knizhnoe izdatel'stvo, 1971.

Burgin, Diana Lewis. "After the Ball Is Over: Sophia Parnok's Creative Relationship with Marina Tsvetaeva." *The Russian Review* 47 (1988): 425–44.

———. "Laid Out in Lavender. Perceptions of Lesbian Love in Russian Literature and Criticism of the Silver Age, 1893–1917." In *Sexuality and the Body in Russian Culture*, eds. Jane Costlow, Stephanie Sandler, Judith Vowles, 177–203. Stanford: Stanford University Press, 1993.

———. "Signs of a Response: Two Possible Parnok Replies to Her *Podruga*." *Slavic and East European Journal* 35 no. 2 (1991): 214–27.

———. "Sophia Parnok and the Writing of a Lesbian Poet's Life." *Slavic Review* 51 no. 2 (Summer 1992): 214–31.

De Jean, Joan. *Fictions of Sappho, 1546–1937*. Chicago: University of Chicago Press, 1989.

Engelstein, Laura. "Lesbian Vignettes: A Russian Triptych from the 1890s." *Signs: Journal of Women in Culture and Society* 15, no. 4 (Summer 1990) 813–32.

Gertsyk, Eugenia, *Vospominaniia*. Paris: YMCA Press, 1973.

Gnesin, Mikhail F. "Stranitsy iz vospominanii." In *M. F. Gnesin. Stat'i, vospominaniia, materialy*, 122–61. Moscow: Sovetskii kompozitor, 1961.

Gorchakov, G. N. "Sophia Parnok: ... *Beschudesnyi podvig moi!*" *Nashe nasledie*, 1989, no. 2: 87–89.
Heilbrun, Carolyn G. *Writing a Woman's Life*. New York: W. W. Norton, 1988.
Ivanov, Viacheslav. *Alkei i Safo. Sobranie pesen i liricheskikh otryvkov*. Moscow, 1914.
Karlinsky, Simon. *Marina Tsvetaeva: The Woman, Her World, and Her Poetry*. Cambridge: Cambridge University Press, 1985.
———. "Russia's Gay Literature and History" [eleventh-twentieth centuries]. *Gay Sunshine*, no. 29/30 (1976): 1–7.
Khudabashian, K. "Avtor libretto opery 'Almast' A. Spendiarova—Sophia Parnok" *Aleksandr Spendiarov. Stat'i i issledovaniia*, 187–210. Yerevan: Izdatel'stvo Akademii nauk Armianskoi SSR, 1973.
Losskaia, Veronika. *Marina Tsvetaeva v zhizni*. Tenafly, N.J.: Ermitazh, 1989.
Parnok, Sophia. "B. Pasternak i drugie." *Russkii sovremennik*, 1924, no. 2: 307–11.
———. *Sobranie stikhotvorenii* [Collected Poems]. Ann Arbor: Ardis, 1979.
Poliakova, Sophia. "Eshche odno zabytoe imia. O poezii Sofii Parnok." *Literaturnoe obozrenie*, 1989, no. 10: 107–9.
———. *[Ne]zakatnye ony dni: Tsvetaeva i Parnok*. Ann Arbor: Ardis, 1983.
———. "Vstupitel'naia stat'ia" [Introduction]. In *Sobranie stikhotvorenii S. Ya. Parnok*, 7–106. Ann Arbor: Ardis, 1979.
Polianin, Andrei [Sophia Parnok]. "Dni russkoi liriki," *Shipovnik. Sborniki literatury i iskusstva*, no. 1. Moscow: Izdatel'stvo "Shipovnik," 1922: 157–61.
———. Reviews and review articles in *Severnye zapiski*. 1913 ("Otmechennyia imena," no. 4: 111–15; "V poiskakh puti iskusstva," no. 5–6: 227–32); 1914 (no. 2: 180–84; no. 4: 184–85; "Petersburg" no. 6: 134–42); 1915 (no. 1: 250–51; no. 2: 220–21; no. 3: 178–79; no. 7–8: 261–64 [on Remizov]; no. 10: 231–34); 1916 (no. 4–5: 240–43; no. 6: 218–20; no. 7–8: 238); 1917 ("Po povodu poslednikh proizvedenii Valeriia Briusova," no. 1: 157–61).
Satina, Sophie. *Education of Women in Pre-revolutionary Russia*. New York, 1966.
Spendiarova, Marina. *Letopis' zhizni i tvorchestva A. A. Spendiarova*. Yerevan: Izdatel'stvo Akademii nauk Armianskoi SSR, 1975.
Sviiasov, E. V. "Safo v vospriiatii russkikh poetov" (1880–1910e gg.). *Na*

rubezhe XIX i XX vekov. Iz istorii mezhdunarodnykh sviazei russkoi literatury. Leningrad: Akademia nauk, 1991.
Taubman, Jane A. *A Life through Poetry: Marina Tsvetaeva's Lyric Diary.* Columbus, Ohio: Slavica Publishers, 1988.
Tsvetaeva, Anastasia. *Vospominaniia.* Moscow: Sovetskii pisatel', 1984.
Tsvetaeva, Marina. *Mon frère feminin [Lettre à l'Amazone].* Paris: Mercure de France, 1979.
———. "Podruga." In *Zakatnye ony dni: Tsvetaeva i Parnok*, 21–38. Ann Arbor: Ardis, 1983.
Volkenshtein, Vladimir M. "V dni molodosti." In *M. F. Gnesin. Stat'i, vospominaniia, materialy*, 284–87. Moscow: Sovetskii kompozitor, 1961.
Walker, Barbara. *The Woman's Dictionary of Symbols and Sacred Objects.* San Francisco: Harper and Row, 1988.

UNPUBLISHED SOURCES

Chatskina, Sophia
  Letter to Lyubov Gurevich. Archive of L. Ya. Gurevich, TsGALI, f. 131.
Gornung, Lev
  Memoirs (dated). Typescript. Partially published in *Nashe nasledie*, 1989, no. 2. Cited in English translation by permission of the author.
  Vospominaniia. 1974. Typescript in the possession of S. V. Poliakova. St. Petersburg.
Khodasevich, Vladislav
  Letters to Anna Ivanovna Khodasevich. Archive of V. F. Khodasevich, TsGALI, f. 537 (op. 1, ed. khr.45).
  Letters to Sophia Parnok. Archive of V. F. Khodasevich, TsGALI, f. 537.
Parnakh, Valentin
  Pansion Mober. Vospominaniia Parnakha. Mashinopis' s pravkoi avtora. TsGALI, f. 2251 (op. 1, ed. khr. 44).
Parnok, Sophia
  "Gymnasium Notebooks." The poem "Our fine musical ear" and the table of contents of the nonextant notebook are in my possession [DLB]. The original of the other notebook is in the private archive of Parnok's nephew in Moscow; poems J2–J50 [my numbering system] are cited from an exact copy of the notebook that was made for me by Sophia Poliakova.)

Letter to Anna Akhmatova. Archive of A. A. Akhmatova, TsGALI, f. 13 (op. 1, ed. khr. 148).
Letters to Sophia Fedorchenko. Archive of S. Z. Fedorchenko, TsGALI, f. 1611 (ed. khr. 95).
Letters to Eugenia Gertsyk, 1925–29. Private archive of E. K. Gertsyk in the possession of T. N. Zhukovskaya, Moscow.
Letters to Mikhail Gnesin. Archive of M. F. Gnesin, TsGALI, f. 2954 (op. 1, no 614).
Letters to Lyubov Gurevich. Archive of L. Ya. Gurevich, TsGALI, f. 131.
Letters to Konstantin Lipskerov. Archive of K. A. Lipskerov, TsGALI, f. 1737.
Letters to Maximilian Shteinberg. Archive of M. O. Shteinberg. Manuscript collections of the Leningrad Institute of Theater, Music, and Cinematography, f. 28, G. 617.
Letters to Pyotr Struve. Archive of P. B. Struve, Saltykov-Shchedrin Library, St. Petersburg.
Letters to Nina Vedeneyeva. Private archive of N. E. Vedeneyeva, in the possession of her son in Moscow.
Letters to Yulia Veisberg-Rimskaya-Korsakova. Archive of Yu. L. Veisberg. Saltykov-Shchedrin Library, St. Petersburg, f. 639 (ed. khr. 274).
Letters to Maximilian Voloshin. Archives of the Institute of Russian Literature and Art, St. Petersburg, f. 562 (op. 3, No 931). (Portions of these letters were recently published in 1992).
Letters to Vera Zvyagintseva. Archive of V. K. Zvyagintseva, TsGALI, f. 1720.
"Written Complaint to the Arbitration Commission of the All-Russian Union of Writers against Nikitina Saturdays Publishers Cooperative." Archive of E. F. Nikitina, TsGALI, f. 341.
Rolland, Romain
Letters to Sophia Parnok. Archive of S. Ya. Parnok, TsGALI, f. 1276, ed. 15.
Tarakhovskaya, Elizaveta
Vospominaniia o starom Koktebele. Typescript (unpaginated), 1964.
Tsvetaeva, Marina
"Lettre à l'Amazone," trans. Edwina Cruise. Typescript.
Voloshina, Elena
Letter to Liza Efron. Copy in the possession of E. B. Korkina, Moscow.
Letter to Vera Efron. Copy in the possession of E. B. Korkina, Moscow.

Index of First Lines of Poems by Parnok Cited in This Book (in the order of their appearance)

An asterisk indicates that the poem appears in its entirety.

CHAPTER I

As cold is bitter, heat can be intense (#85) 16
Without a staff and pilgrim's wallet (#157) 20
You seem to have resurrected, spring (#2) 21
Our fine musical ear (J-1) 25
The smell of magnolias (J-10) 27
Her voice was enchanting (J-8) 27
The rustle of green cypress leaves (J-23) 27
So strong, like death, seductively-superbly (J-11)* 28–29
And he was submissive. (J-12) 29
A pedagogue of splendid wisdom (J-14) 29
How I envy you (J-16) 30
Spring . . . a new force is born. (J-21) 30
When just now I recognized (J-22) 30
Leave here as soon as possible! Oh, faster! (J-24)* 31
Believe me, my friend, they're not worth despising (J-18) 31

345

There stands before you passion's victim (J-26) 32
I've finally known the power of feeling (J-25) 33–34
"What is life if it lacks enchantment?" (J-27) 34–35
Sweet sounds quiver again (J-28) 35
Love is gone . . . the tuberoses have faded (J-31) 35
There can't exist a person who (J-34) 36
Your moral lectures interest me, they really do! (J-32) 36
Fate's as carefree as a child (J-35) 36
My poems breathe (J-36) 37
I'm in pain. I lack the strength to speak . . . (J-37)* 38–39
Perhaps your beauty is deceptive (J-41) 39
The colder the letters you write (J-42) 39
Why do I love you, do you know? (J-43) 39
The force and passion of your kiss (J-46) 40
Our Russia is enormous (J-44) 40, 40–41
A sleeping beauty, yes. (J-47) 40
Israel, long-suffering people! (J-45) 41–42
Twilight time autumnal. Greyish all around . . . (J-48)* 42
Farewell, my information bureau! (J-50) 42

CHAPTER 2

Why oh why from my paternal threshold (#95) 45, 46
In blank indifference there is 49
Life is a woman. Merely by her own seductions* 50
Perhaps because I wished to fall in love with being* 50
Just listen, how amidst inspired dreaming* 51
Suddenly you stood still 51–52
I am still, for I fear I will fall out of love 54
In mournful luxury of trees that have been gilded* 56–57
How can one write about the quiet fading* 57–58
I know profoundly well—you've shown me everything* 58
Soon the leaves of the green poplar trees 58–59
I don't love love because my thought 59
In a romance I like (#39) 64, 65
I'm afraid of my heart as never before 66
Look, the moon, a weaveress of wiles 67
Oh mistress Anguish! You, the muse of incantations* 73–74
As if in a small box imported from the East 77–78
In words, in their cold interlacing* 78
What was that song about and had it any words? 81
Whose strange and savage will had cast a spell on us* 82–83
Amid the crowd's collective breath 83

At times our premonitions, at times our recollections* 83–84
Beauty casts a spell upon my life 87

CHAPTER 3

A light profound, a light endearing* 94
We hadn't noticed what the dusk was up to* 95
I don't like churches where the architect (#7) 99
You wrote your sister, "What a pity!" (#16)* 117–18
"Like a small girl you appeared in my presence ungracefully (#59)* 118–19
Embroidery has covered up (#56)* 119–20
That evening was blazing dimly 120–21
Again we have the signal to depart! (#60)* 122
You watched the little boys at all their games (#28)* 124
What do I care for the scorn on those cruel lips! (#46)* 128
Again I gaze at your steepbrowed profile (#45) 129
All ablaze, the clouds fly by (#13)* 130
The cranes have flown southward (#43) 131
Blindly staring eyes of the (#9)* 131
Probably my voice is heartless (#37) 133
You really are good-looking, shapely youth (#53) 133
I am the queen of hearts. The others, all three (#36) 134
How light the light is today! (#11) 135
I love you in your expanse (#24) 135
I'll remember everything. In one boundless moment (#42)* 135–36

CHAPTER 4

I.
A seed can't bloom in infertile soil (#52) 141
To blush for poems that you wrote (#82)* 142–43
Oh my God, I am unworthy of this! (#151) 144
Can a lynx ever really be tamed (#138)* 146
Again, just like a bird who's wounded (#140) 147
They won't come and it's really no matter (#147)* 149
On its delicate stalk droops a flower . . . (#142)* 150–51
Shade from the windmill (#114)* 153
Thus, on other shores, by another melodious sea (#68)* 154
Into the most savage sun (#115) 154–55
How spicy the air (#124) 155
Clearly, here, not all of us are sinners (#113) 155
So softly and so wonderfully (#106)* 155–56
No, today I do not want you (#104)* 156

Jutting sharp-edged points, the moon (#123) 157
Can such a midnight really be from God? (#144) 157
Every evening now I pray (#122)* 158
If you should cry out in your sleep (#146)* 160
Unsated, saline soil had eaten into everything (#110) 161
The Lord has not heeded my yearning (#94)* 168
In those days the first words (#107) 168–69
For long I lived in love with liberty (#120)* 169
The Lord has made note of me too (#96)* 169
Oh, the unconquerable heaviness (#108)* 170

2.

Hue of inspiration! Roses of Pieria! (#61) 178
The first lyre, poet, was made by a god's first whimsy (#62) 178
Once I hear the song of the Aeolian lyre (#38)* 179
The whole of me was drunk on recollections (#64) 179
I dreamed, I'm calling to my dear companion-lovers (#65) 179–80
"Believe me, someone in the future will remember us" (#66) 180
You sleep, my companion-lover, just like (#67)* 180–81
I am not tuning my heart for the voluptuous mode (#69) 182
A bold challenge deserves but one reply, the spear! (#70) 182
I went into battle armed with a deathless rose (#71)* 182–83
My homeland is the place where my spirit rose (#77)* 185
I remember, remember the service (#78)* 186
You were in nature's unconscious (#80) 187
Your stormy day is drawing to a close (#83) 187
Yes, he once flew up on high (#97) 188
Not spirit yet, but hardly flesh (#91)* 188
You came in just as thousands have entered (#81)* 189
To suddenly glimpse in your other's heart (#86) 190
"What time is it?" "The mad hour. Come take a look" (#87)* 190
A spider wove my dark hinged-icon (#99) 190–91
My heart will burn to ashes (#100)* 191

CHAPTER 5

Like music I love your sadness (#109)* 194
It's not passion's bed that is sacred (#145)* 195
I haven't died yet (#155)* 197
Nobody ever has anything to do with anyone (#148) 198
My life! My unleavened chunk! (#149) 198
And suddenly it will happen (#159) 206
You overstrain yourself, my brother (#200) 207
What did I give our days? (#160) 207–8

I'm walking somewhere (#154) 208
A cloud lit up from inside. (#156)* 208
People treasure-hunt at midnight (#173)* 210
Drowsily an agèd pine (#178)* 210
Each person has a wingèd hour (#158) 210
I sing about the kind of spring (#163)* 211–12
A mare snorts beneath her covering (#164)* 212
Like the ratcatcher's pipe (#165) 212–13
Doubly beautiful the flower on its stalk (#133) 216
Whosoever falls out of love with the flesh, cools to incarnation (#161) 216
"I loved you," "I love you," "I'll always love." (#204)* 220
And here we've parted at the gates . . . (#167) 221
Cigarette after cigarette. (#168)* 223
I'm like a patient, from hospital (#174) 225
Mumbling behind the wall (#179) 225
Always more distant, always quieter (#177) 226
Your widened pupil (#175) 226
Slowly-slowly evening (#171) 226–27
A kind of barely perceptible sign (#176) 227
Is it mutiny again? Well, hardly (#196) 228
My earthly day is finishing (#198)* 229
And here's a dream I have (#181) 229–30
From ultimate loneliness (#192) 230
Don't seduce me with comfort (#208) 230
Softly do I weep and sing (#185)* 230–31
Thank you, my friend (#162)* 231
We sank in a chair at twilight (#186)* 232
I dreamed: I'm wandering in darkness (#189) 232
I think: Lord, how many years I've slept through (#194) 232–33
. . . And suddenly, at mid-sky, flourish of lightning (#180) 233
On autumnal St. Arina's, when the cranes fly (#195) 235
Old beneath an agèd elm tree (#191)* 236
It was a splendid time! (#197) 236
I gaze at the piles of yellow leaves . . . (#193)* 237–38
And a voice called to you in the deep of the night (#199) 239

CHAPTER 6

I won't lie for the sake of a rhyme (#203) 243
And we'll all go our separate ways (#188) 243
A huge city. Wind. Evening. (#215) 244
As a shade with three dimensions, brother (#217) 247–48
Great insults make the soul feverish (#219) 249
I follow from afar—forgive me my distance (#221) 250

You are young, long-limbed! With such (#220)* 254–55
My blood and my rhymes have a shortage. (#222)* 263
Does winter really have thunderstorms (#223)* 265
My unglorious day is waning (#224)* 265–66
And truly, one cannot predict (#225)* 266–67
They've cut a hole through (#226)* 267
Chase verses of the night away (#227) 267
You're coming in, and I'm departing (#228) 268

CHAPTER 7

No enigma is too subtle (#232) 274
I know who you're mad for, darling! (#230)* 275
I, like a blind woman, find my way by touch (#233)* 275–76
Your eyes are wide open, your mouth clamped shut. (#234)* 276–77
It starts right in with chapter five (#236) 277–78
Breeze out of Viavocàla! (#235) 278
A head of silver grey. And youthful features. (#237)* 279
Well, you're not kind, you're not malicious (#238) 279–80
Yes, you're greedy, deaf-mute woman (#239) 280
I live, and even from myself I hide (#240)* 281
Oh my love! My madcap demon! (#241)* 282
You outsiders see more plainly (#242)* 282–83
It seems to me together we'd have been (#243)* 283–84
Ere St. Ròdyon-Icebreaker's (#245)* 284
I see: you're getting off the streetcar—utterly belovèd (#244)* 284–85
Exhausted, weary unto death (#246)* 286
Through all that I do, that I think, or remember (#247)* 288
How can I root out this awful tumor (#248)* 288
When we're on the far side of forty (#249)* 289
Sun rises in smoke and sets dimly in smoke (#251) 289–90
Don't ask what's laid the poet low (#250)* 290
I'd beg from death a (#252)* 291
There's no way back for me (#253) 294
Straight between your lips I whisper to you—ghazals (#254)* 295
With no if's, and's, or but's whatever (#256)* 295–96
Give me your hand and let's go to our sinful paradise! . . . (#255)* 296–97
Night. And it's snowing (#257)* 297
It still hasn't got any cares, it's still young at heart (#258)* 298
I'm miserable, the way beasts are (#259) 299
Remember the narrowish corridor (#260)* 299–300
"Come what may," you wrote, "we shall be happy . . ." (#261)* 303–4
Upon your grey head* 306

Index

Akhmatova, Anna, 63, 93, 139, 167, 192, 195
Albrecht, Iraida, 95–96, 98–99, 106, 108, 110, 122, 137
Alexander III, 16–18
Amazons, 102, 114, 123, 154, 170; "Penthesilea," 177, 182–83, 330 n. 77
Andersen, Hans Christian, 68
Annensky, Innokenty, 5, 199
Arnim, Bettina Brentano, 102, 106, 122–24

Baranovich, Marina, 254
Baratynsky, Eugene, 32, 276
Barbusse, Henri, 235
Barney, Natalie Clifford, 94, 114, 174, 179
Baudelaire, Charles, 24, 67–68, 114, 177
Bely, Andrey, 73, 98–99
Blok, Alexander, 23, 63, 67, 73
Bryusov, Valery, 82, 150, 167, 323 n. 34, 335 n. 4
Butkova, Eugenia, 162, 166

Chatskina, Sophia, 63, 67, 86, 97, 112, 139, 150
Chekhov, Anton, 4, 8, 19

Dostoevsky, Fyodor, 2, 85, 129, 145, 172, 236, 243, 265, 331 n. 82

Efron, Ariadne, 104, 113, 125–26, 144
Efron, Liza, 110, 120–21, 126–27, 324 n. 54, 325 n. 74
Efron, Natalya, 268–69
Efron, Sergey, 104, 125, 129, 132–34, 180
Efros, Abram, 192
Erarskaya, Lyudmila, 11, 141–42; health, 151, 164, 193; mental breakdown, 200–204, 209, 213; and Parnok, 147, 152–53, 158–59, 160, 162, 233, 235, 261, 306–7, 309–10; personality, 146; and Tsuberbiller, 209

False Dmitri, 124, 326 n. 84
Fedorchenko, Sophia, 208, 233–34

Gautier, Théophile, 87
Geltser, Yekaterina, 44–45
Gertsyk, Adelaida, 101–3, 137, 155, 157, 162, 204, 221, 239, 252, 333 n. 47
Gertsyk, Eugenia, 11, 101, 110, 147–48, 152, 171–72, 192–94, 200–201,

351

Gertsyk, Eugenia (*Continued*)
203, 209, 217, 221, 225, 246, 250, 310; creative meaning for Parnok, 173, 185, 189; faith, 154; love for sister, 102; Sudak years, 161, 185
Giraudoux, Jean, 200
Gnesin, Mikhail, 46–48, 51, 53–54, 61–62, 70, 79–80, 87, 96, 100, 148
Gogol, Nikolai, 67, 159
Gorky, Maxim, 162
Gornung, Lev, 193; friendship with Parnok, 195–96, 199, 246–47, 254, 260–63, 268, 287, 298, 300, 308–10, 331–32 n. 13
Guenderode, Karoline, 102, 122
Gumilyov, Nikolai, 195
Gurevich, Lyubov, 11, 62; friendship with Parnok, 67–69, 71–73, 75, 81, 84–89, 91–94, 96–97, 122, 200, 229, 309

Hall, Radclyffe, 94
Holliday, Sophia, 143, 336 n. 24

Ivanov, Vyacheslav, 47, 63, 73, 101, 176, 263, 325 n. 77, 336 n. 44

Kerensky, Alexander, 149
Khodasevich, Vladislav, 5, 137, 145–46, 167, 176, 193
Klyuev, Nikolai, 93
Kudashova, Maya, 102, 252–54, 261–62, 325 n. 77, 335–36 n. 21
Kuzmin, Mikhail, 63, 139–40, 223

Lenin, Vladimir, 160, 162–63
Lermontov, Mikhail, 34, 319 n. 44
Lipskerov, Konstantin, 99, 134, 137, 147, 152
Lokhvitskaya, Mirra, 174, 329 n. 63
Louÿs, Pierre, 177, 183, 330 n. 78

Mahler, Gustav, 272–73
Maksakova, Maria, 251, 259, 262, 264, 268, 275, 337 n. 47
Mandelshtam, Alexander, 126–27, 196
Mandelshtam, Osip, 126, 140, 142, 144–45, 151, 196–97, 327 n. 12
Mayakovsky, Vladimir, 165
Mirolyubov, Viktor, 55–56
Mniszek, Marina, 124–25, 326 n. 84

Nicholas II, 17–18, 53
Nikitina, Eudoxia, 165, 172, 193, 200, 204–5

Obolenskaya, Yulia, 110, 116, 121

Parnakh, Valentin, 18, 62, 74–75, 237, 298; childhood of, 18, 20, 314 n. 16; experience of anti-Semitism, 18, 41, 100, 171; falling-out with sister, 128–29, 220; musical tastes, 171–72; Russophobia, 21–22, 41, 100, 109, 127; *Simoom*, 172; trip to Palestine, 100, 109
Parnok, Sophia, 1–3; adolescent love affairs, 27, 33–36, 39, 40, 45; allegory in verse of, 35–37, 49–50, 52, 59, 66, 284; *Almast*, 152–53, 158–60, 164, 228, 237, 247, 249–52, 256–60; arrest and imprisonment, 162; attitudes to death, 74, 77–78, 81, 89–92, 131–32, 135–37, 149, 163, 190–91, 204–5, 213, 228–29, 230–31, 234–36, 238–39, 264, 267, 281–82, 291, 294, 296, 299, 321 n. 2; attitudes to Jews, 41–42, 68, 168–69, 318 n. 26; birth of, 16; Bratovshchina poems, 225–27; and brother (Valentin), 41, 67, 100, 109, 128–29, 172, 196, 207, 220, 237–38, 248; censorship of, 170, 192–93, 197, 204, 217–18, 221–23, 233, 241–42, 245; childhood of, 20–22; creative struggle of, 4–9, 11, 24, 43, 53–54, 57–58, 68–69, 72, 76, 78,

INDEX 353

84–85, 148–49, 170, 177, 184, 206, 210, 243–44, 255–56, 263–64, 267, 280; critical writings by, 92–94, 98–99, 192–93, 197–98, see also Polyanin, Andrey (Parnok's pseudonym); death and funeral of, 305–10; divorce, 70, 74–76, 80; dreams in the work of, 52, 84–86, 94, 179–80, 185, 187, 208–9, 211–12, 217–18, 223–25, 227, 229–30, 232, 235, 238–39, 249, 252, 277; early verse (1905–12) of, 49–52, 54, 56–59, 66–67, 73, 78, 82–84, 87, 94–95; education, 22–23, 29, 42, 63, 68, 72; and Sergey Efron, 116, 125, 133–34, 326 n. 84; emotional breakdown, 192, 200–202, 302–3; and Erarskaya, 141, 143–44, 148, 150, 152–53, 157–60, 164, 193, 201–3, 209, 235; and father (Yakov Parnokh), 20, 32, 37–38, 45, 54–56, 60, 89–90, 92, 113, 155, 186–87, 244, 305, 315–16 n. 28; and E. Gertsyk, 148, 154–56, 185, 192; goddesses in the life and work of, 10, 143, 177–78, 183–84, 211, 217, 223, 226, 333 n. 38; Grave's disease, 57, 67, 84, 135, 140, 231, 236, 298; and Gurevich, 62, 68–69, 72, 75, 79, 81, 84–86, 88, 91, 94, 96, 98, 229; gypsy poems, 147, 162, 214, 216–17, 275, 325–26 n. 80, 333 n. 37; *Half-voiced*, 207, 212, 224–25, 231, 238–40, 242, 247, 252; homecoming of, 54, 154, 172, 185, 208, 223–25; internalized homophobia of, 9, 222, 287; invalidism of, 57, 67, 72, 76–77, 80, 92, 148, 156, 163, 166, 188–90, 192, 198–99, 213, 223, 228–29, 234–35, 246–47, 259, 271, 298–301; juvenilia of, 23–33, 35–43, 48, 50, 58, 66; and Khodasevich, 145; and The Knot, 209, 213–14, 219, 221, 223,
229, 233, 238, 247; lack of ambition, 37, 40, 61, 66, 69, 136; and lesbianism, 5–6, 8–9, 24–26, 32, 34, 38, 43, 49, 58–60, 64, 66, 78, 80, 95, 99, 112, 118, 120, 137, 170, 177–78, 180, 183–84, 198, 222, 245, 255, 331 n. 81, 333–34 n. 49; life and fate as a poet, 9, 96, 136–37, 170–71, 184, 186–88, 198–99, 206–8, 215–16, 230–32, 243–44, 249, 263–68, 279, 297; marriage of, 37, 61–62, 64–65, 70–71, 73, 106, 247; and mother (Alexandra Parnokh), 20, 117–18, 317 n. 4; music in life and work of, 28–29, 42, 45, 52, 74, 132, 172, 186, 189, 191–92, 198–99, 208–10, 212, 214–17, 262, 268–69, 272–73, 282–83, 332 n. 27; and *Music*, 214–18; nature lyrics of, 57, 67, 77, 223–25, 227; novella by, 73, 96–97; opera libretti by, 96, 98, 127, 148, 153, 264, see also Parnok, Sophia, *Almast*; participation in poetry circles, 193, 195–96, 198–99, 218; poems to Erarskaya, 144, 146, 150–51, 153, 157–58, 160, 190, 214, 225; poems to Maksakova, 265, 268, 275, 337 n. 47; poems to Polyakova, 35–36, 39, 58, 316 n. 30, 319 n. 34; poems to Tsuberbiller, 194, 211–12, 226, 231, 239–40; poems to Tsvetaeva, 112, 118–21, 123–24, 129–32, 137, 141–43, 254–55, 330 n. 74; *Poems*, 134, 136–38, 151; pseudonyms of, 55–56, 92; religious poetry of, 31, 99, 113, 135, 168–69, 191, 221–22; and revolution(s), 51, 149–50, 167–68, 236, 244; and Romain Rolland, 252–54, 261–62; *Roses of Pieria*, 172–73, 177–84; and Russia/Russophilism, 40–41, 46, 51, 91, 93, 109, 132, 135, 149–50, 163, 167, 208–9; and *Russian Talk*, 86–

Parnok, Sophia, (*Continued*)
87, 90–93, 97; and self-censorship, 92, 148, 222, 287; "seraphic eros" in poetry of, 211, 213, 226–27; sexual love in life and poems of, 38–40, 43, 45, 52, 58–59, 64–65, 71, 78, 80, 82–85, 95, 156, 189, 195, 219–20, 265, 267, 274, 287–89, 315–16 n. 28; spiritual searchings of, 90, 99, 103, 113, 128, 148, 154–56, 167, 169, 191, 210–11, 223–24, 236, 239–40; Sudak in life and poetry of, 154–55, 159, 161, 173, 184–85, 187, 204; suicidal thoughts of, 34, 267, 273, 282, 296, 304–5; translating activity of, 54, 67, 196, 200, 204–5, 229, 235, 246, 252, 261, 320 n. 47; travels abroad of, 45, 51, 52, 98–99; and Tsuberbiller, 194–95, 203, 205, 209, 214, 231, 242, 257–58, 260–62, 271, 287–88, 290–91; and Tsvetaeva, 103–4, 106–8, 110–12, 116, 119, 122, 125, 129, 132–34, 139, 143–44, 213, 254–55, 336 n. 24; "Ursa Major," 10–11, 270, 274; "Useless Goods," 270, 274, 280, 295; and Vedeneyeva, 272, 274–75, 277, 279, 281, 284–86, 291–95, 300, 302–3, 305–6; Vedeneyeva poems (cycles), 270, 272–74, 276–91, 294–99, 303–4, 306; and views on creativity, 47, 52, 75, 84–85, 148, 167, 193–94, 198, 205–7, 210–11, 243, 250, 263–64, 266, 280; *The Vine,* 167–68, 171, 173, 184–92; and Volkenshtein, 47–49, 61, 65–66, 70, 74, 76
Parnokh, Alexandra, 16, 20–21
Parnokh, Sophia. *See* Parnok, Sophia
Parnokh, Yakov, 16, 18, 21, 37, 55, 60, 89–90, 92
Parnokh, Yelizaveta. *See* Tarakhovskaya, Yelizaveta Parnokh

Pasternak, Boris, 197–98, 213, 218–19, 309
Pavlova, Karolina, 5, 206, 304, 332 n. 26
Plekhanov, Georgy, 51–52
Polyakova, Nadezhda, 11, 35; and Parnok, 36, 53–54, 58, 60–61, 70, 74, 87; role as muse-lover, 43, 59–60; and Vedeneyeva poems, 272, 280
Polyakova, Sophia, 2, 6
Polyanin, Andrey (Parnok's pseudonym), 92–93, 98–99, 132, 144–45, 150, 167, 170
Proust, Marcel, 229
Pushkin, Alexander, 32, 45, 139, 274, 281, 339 n. 14

Ranevskaya, Faina, 268–69, 298, 300, 337–38 n. 49
Remizov, Alexey, 132
Rimsky-Korsakov, Andrey, 112, 136
Rolland, Romain, 252–54, 261–62

Sackville-West, Vita, 116
Sadovskoy, Boris, 86–87, 91–92, 321 n. 2
Saker, Yakov, 63, 97, 112, 139, 150
Sappho of Lesbos, 118; and Parnok, 119, 138, 154, 173, 177–78, 180, 255–56, 324 n. 52; in *Roses of Pieria,* 178–81; in Russian poetry, 118–19, 173–77, 330 n. 72
Seluc-Rasnatowskaya, 28–29
Severyanin, Igor, 93
Shteinberg, Maximilian, 96–98; *Abductress of the Heart,* 127, 148; *Almast,* 249–52, 254, 256–59
Silver Age, 5; and anti-Semitism, 18, 41; and attitudes to lesbianism, 8, 24, 26, 138, 175–77; decadence and symbolism, 7, 23, 25, 47, 53, 174; emergence of women poets, 5, 174–77; Parnok's memories of, 263; perception of Sappho, 138, 174–77

Sologub, Fyodor, 63, 167
Solovyov, Vladimir, 174
Solovyova, Polixena, 329 n. 62
Spendiarov, Alexander, 152, 162, 165; and *Almast,* 152–53, 158–60, 164, 228, 237, 247, 252, 257; arrest and imprisonment, 163; death, 247
Spendiarova, Marina, 162, 164, 259
Spendiarova, Varvara, 252, 257, 259
Stalin, Yosef, 241, 258, 277
Struve, Peter, 81–82, 93, 136

Taganrog, 15; cultural life in, 19; economy of, 17; Jews in, 18; and Parnakh, 171; and Parnok, 31, 55, 61
Tarakhovskaya, Yelizaveta Parnokh, 21, 62, 74–75, 100, 112–13, 125–27, 172, 224, 235, 323 n. 42
Tarnovsky, Dr. Ippolit, 26
Tolstoy, Lev, 67
Tsuberbiller, Olga, 194; life with Parnok, 201–2, 213, 231, 233–34, 246, 249–50, 257, 263, 271, 278, 285, 287, 293, 297, 301, 305–10; sicknesses, 204, 246, 260
Tsvetaeva, Anastasia, 102, 125–27
Tsvetaeva, Marina, 3, 11, 102, 119–20, 124–26, 131–32, 137, 139–40, 142, 242, 282; bisexuality and lesbianism of, 105, 112, 115, 322 nn. 31, 32; break-up with Parnok, 142–44; desire for child from Parnok, 114–15, 211; efforts for Crimean writers, 164; feelings for Parnok, 107–8, 110, 117, 129–30, 133–34, 136, 164, 218, 322 n. 32; "Lettre á l'Amazone," 114–15, 324 n. 52; "Girlfriend" poems, 103–9, 111, 113–14, 116–17, 122–23, 142, 219–20, 323 n. 40

Tumanian, Hovaness, 152
Tyutchev, Fyodor, 32, 292, 304

Vazlinsky, Mikhail, 183–84
Vedeneyeva, Nina, 11, 270–72, 275, 280, 285, 287, 290, 297, 302, 306, 308–10; love affair with Parnok, 271, 274, 278–79, 286, 291–92, 294–95, 300, 303, 305
Veisberg, Yulia, 51, 90, 96, 112, 148–49, 230, 264, 337 n. 47
Veresayev, Vikenty, 176–77
Verlaine, Paul, 24, 177
Vivien, Renée, 174, 179
Volkenshtein, Vladimir, 46–49, 51–56, 60–61, 63, 67, 70–72, 74, 76, 106, 147, 172, 243, 247, 309
Voloshin, Maximilian, 63, 125, 137, 150–51, 163–67, 171, 173, 193, 218, 224, 300
Voloshina, Yelena (Pra), 110, 116, 121, 125–27, 193

Weininger, Otto, 175–76
Welcker, Johann G., 175–77
Wilamowitz-Moellendorff, Ulrich, 175–76
Woolf, Virginia, 116

Yesenin, Sergey, 304–5
Yurgenson, Irina, 199, 308, 329 n. 52

Zaitsev, Pyotr, 195
Zhukovsky, Dmitri, 102
Zinovyeva-Annibal, Lydia, 47, 317 n. 8
Zvyagintseva, Vera, 242, 246, 250, 298, 335 n. 1